ISBN 978-0-282-65452-8
PIBN 10860621

THE KNIGHTS HOSPITALLERS IN THE HOLY LAND

BY

COLONEL E. J. KING, C.M.G., M.A., F.S.A.

KNIGHT OF JUSTICE AND LIBRARIAN OF THE BRITISH ORDER OF ST. JOHN OF JERUSALEM

WITH 23 ILLUSTRATIONS AND 13 MAPS AND PLANS

METHUEN & CO. LTD.
36 ESSEX STREET W.C.
LONDON

First Published in 1931

PRINTED IN GREAT BRITAIN

TO

MY DEAR WIFE

WHOSE CONSTANT INTEREST AND ENCOURAGEMENT
HAVE SO GREATLY ASSISTED ME IN THIS WORK

PREFACE

THE two centuries during which the Knights Hospitallers were fighting for the Christian Faith in the Holy Land constitute the heroic period in the history of the Order of the Hospital of St. John of Jerusalem. It is a great and noble story, which has long been waiting to be told, and the writing of it has only been rendered possible by the lifelong labours of that learned and devoted student of the history of the Order, the late Joseph Delaville Le Roulx. To his first essay *De prima origine*, to his monumental *Cartulaire-Général*, and to the conclusions that he has drawn from it in his *Hospitaliers en Terre Sainte*, the present writer is deeply indebted. Delaville Le Roulx has provided with lavish hand the materials upon which every historian of the early centuries of the Hospitallers must always base his work. For the general historic background to the deeds of the Knights of the Hospital the author has relied mainly upon Stevenson's *Crusaders in the East*, and Lane-Poole's *Life of Saladin* and *Egypt in the Middle Ages*, and for the military history of the period upon Oman's *History of the Art of War*. He has been greatly assisted in his work by two of his confrères in the Order of St. John, Mr. H. Pirie-Gordon, D.S.C., F.S.A., Knight of Justice, who has read through and corrected the whole of the manuscript, and made many most helpful suggestions, and by Mr. H. W. Fincham, F.S.A., Knight of Grace and Assistant-Librarian to that Order, who has arranged the whole of the illustrations, to them both he desires to tender his most grateful thanks. He must also thank Miss Ethel Stokes for her valuable assistance in the translation of many of the original documents, Sir Charles Oman for his courtesy in permitting him to use some of the maps in his *History of the Art of War*, Mr. Lane-Poole for permission to use one of the maps in his *Life of Saladin*, and *The Times* newspaper for the photograph of the Castle of Le Crac. The history of the Knights Hospitallers in the Holy Land is but a part of the long and dramatic story of the venerable Order of St. John of Jerusalem. Should this book meet with the approval of the public, it will be the ambition of its author to complete that story in two subsequent volumes describing the career of the Knights Hospitallers in Rhodes and Malta down to the present day.

E. J. K.

CONTENTS

APPENDICES

LIST OF ILLUSTRATIONS AND MAPS

BIBLIOGRAPHY

Boisgelin: *Malta, Ancient and Modern,* 1805.

Boissat de Lixieux: *Histoire de l'Ordre de St. Jean.* 1612.

Bosio: *Istoria della Sacra Religione ed Illustre milizia di San Giovanni Gerosolimitano.* Rome. 1594.

Les Vies des Saints de l'Ordre de St. Jean de Jerusalem. Edition Baudoin. 1631.

Delaville Le Roulx: *De prima origine Hospitalariorum Hierosolymitanorum.*

Cartulaire-Général des Hospitaliers. 4 volumes.

Les Hospitaliers en Terre Sainte.

Mélange sur l'Ordre de St. Jean de Jerusalem.

Dickie: *On the Church of Mar Hanna.* Palestine Exploration Fund. Quarterly Statement. January, 1899.

Edwards: 'Historical Notes on the Knights Hospitallers in Scotland.' *Scottish Ecclesiological Society's Transactions.* 1909.

Falkiner: 'The Hospital of St. John of Jerusalem in Ireland.' *Proceedings of the Royal Irish Academy.* 1907.

Fincham: *The Order of the Hospital of St. John of Jerusalem.* 1915.

Giraud: *Le Bienheureux Gerard.* Aix. 1919.

Harot: *Essai d'Armorial des Grands Maitres de l'Ordre de St. Jean de Jerusalem.* Rome. 1911.

Hellwald: *Bibliographie Methodique de l'Ordre de St. Jean de Jerusalem* 1885, *with the Appendix by Rossi published in Rome.* 1924.

King: *The Knights of St. John in England.*

Larking and Kemble: *The Knights Hospitallers in England.* Camden Society. 1857.

Mifsud: *The English Knights Hospitallers in Malta.* 1916.

Phillips, Alison: 'Knights of St. John of Jerusalem.' *Encyc. Brit.* 11th Edition.

Poli, The Viscount Oscar de: *Les Onze Premiers Grand-Maitres, &c., Annuaire du Conseil Héraldique de France.* 1892.

Porter: *History of the Knights of Malta.* 1858.

Rey: *L'Architecture Militaire des Croisés en Syrie.* 1871.

Round: *The Foundation of the Priories of St. Mary and St. John, Clerkenwell,* 1899. Communicated to the Society of Antiquaries.

Garnier de Nablus. *Archaeologia.* Vol. LVIII.

Schick: *The Muristan.* Palestine Exploration Fund. Quarterly Statement. January, 1902.

Taaffe: *Order of St. John of Jerusalem.* 1852.

Vertot: *Histoire des Chevaliers de Malthe.* 1726.

BIBLIOGRAPHY

THE MASTERS OF THE HOSPITAL

Blessed Gerard. 1100–20.
Blessed Raymond du Puy. 1120–60.
Fr. Auger de Balben. 1160–2.
Fr. Arnold de Comps, Prior of St. Gilles. 1162.
Fr. Gilbert d'Assailly, Commander of Tyre. 1162–70.
Fr. Caste de Murols, Treasurer of the Hospital. 1170–2.
Fr. Jobert. 1172–7.
Fr. Roger des Moulins. 1177–87.
(Fr. William Borrell, Lieut.-Master. 1187–8.)
Fr. Armengaud d'Aspe, Prior of St. Gilles. 1188–90.
Fr. Garnier de Nablus, Prior of England. 1190–2.
Fr. Geoffrey de Donjon, Treasurer of the Hospital. 1193–1202.
Fr. Alfonso of Portugal. 1203–6.
Fr. Geoffrey le Rat, Castellan of Le Crac. 1206–7.
Fr. Garin de Montaigu, Marshal of the Hospital. 1207–28.
Fr. Bertrand de Thessy, Castellan of Selefkeh. 1228–30.
. Guerin, Prior of France. 1230–6.
Fr. Bertrand de Comps, Prior of St. Gilles. 1236–9.
Peter de Villebride, Commander of the Hospital. 1239–42.
(Fr. William de Senlis, Lieut.-Master. 1239–41.)
William de Chateauneuf, Marshal of the Hospital. 1242–58.
(Fr. John de Ronay, Lieut.-Master. 1244–50.)
Fr. Hugh Revel, Commander of the Hospital. 1258–77.
Fr. Nicholas le Lorgne, Commander of Tripolis. 1277–85.
Fr. John de Villiers, Prior of France. 1285–93.

THE KNIGHTS HOSPITALLERS IN THE HOLY LAND

CHAPTER I

THE ORIGINS OF THE HOSPITAL

THE history of the Order of the Hospital of St. John of Jerusalem, more generally known to later times as the Sovereign Order of Malta, from its occupation of that island, is the history of a brotherhood, which was first formed by the Crusaders after the capture of the Holy City in 1099, and which has now existed for over eight hundred years. Throughout that period this venerable Order has displayed so remarkable a capacity for adapting its ideals and policy to the changing requirements of time and circumstance, that unlike so many other ancient institutions it has never outlived its usefulness.

The original object of this brotherhood at its foundation was the maintenance of a hospice in Jerusalem for the use of those on a pilgrimage to the holy places. Within less than a generation they added to their charitable duties, the defence of those holy places against the Moslems, and became a military as well as a charitable brotherhood. Their organization rapidly increased in wealth and power, until the Knights of the Hospital with their comrades and rivals, the Knights of the Temple, had become the chief defenders of the Holy Land. When after two hundred years of heroic fighting against hopeless odds, abandoned by Europe, they were driven out of Syria, their broad lands and immense wealth presented a serious temptation to the governments of the day. The Knights of the Temple, unpopular owing to their arrogance, were the first to be selected for plunder and destruction, and to justify one of the most revolting legal crimes that the world has ever witnessed, their memories were blasted and defiled by their enemies with such vile and shameful accusations that decency shrinks from recording them.

The Knights of the Hospital, taking warning from the fate of the Templars, realized that if they were to survive they must continue to justify their existence. They seized the derelict island of Rhodes, and making of it one of the strongest fortresses in the East, for more than two centuries held in check the expanding naval power of the Ottoman Turks. Driven at length from Rhodes, they occupied Malta and there played a similar rôle as the chief protectors of the Mediterranean coastlands against the raids of the Barbary Corsairs. From the wars of the French Revolution a new Europe arose that had no further need for the military services of the Knights of St. John, and for a time it seemed as if their venerable Order would be unable to justify its further existence. But even when their military power was at its zenith, they had never forgotten their original charitable duties, and had always maintained magnificent hospitals at Rhodes and Malta. Now that their military rôle was ended probably for ever, they remembered once more that ancient rule of their Order that they should 'adorn their Knighthood with a true charity, the mother and solid foundation of all virtues'.[1] Turning therefore to what was the original object of its foundation, the Sovereign Order of Malta has devoted its entire energies in recent years to the support of Hospitals, and more particularly to the relief of the suffering and misery caused by war, a policy in which it has been equally followed by its offspring the Prussian Johanniterorden and the Russian and British Orders of St. John.

During the Middle Ages many military religious orders were founded, as is naturally to be expected, when we consider the ideals and the conditions that then prevailed. The Christian religion was still fighting for its very existence against the followers of Mahomet throughout all the Mediterranean lands. Religion was then a living force in man's every thought and word and deed, to an extent that is difficult now even to realize. The very ritual of knighthood had become clothed in such mystic and symbolic ceremonies that to the true knight even his sword seemed consecrated to the service of God. Sinful men felt that however steeped in iniquity their lives might have been, nevertheless if they died in battle for the Christian faith, the everlasting joys of Paradise were assured to them. To all thinking men alike the ideal life seemed to be that of the monk, who renounced entirely the things of this world to devote himself to the service of God.

But there were many different religious orders serving God in many different ways. There were monks who never left their convents, devoting their entire lives to prayer and religious contemplation. There were other orders in which they led more active lives, teaching and preaching, nursing the sick, helping the poor and suffering in hospitals and other institutions. There were monks who devoted themselves to the missions to the heathen, only too frequently to meet their end in death by torture in its most hideous forms. Nothing

[1] See Statutes of the Order, Title 1, Para. 2.

could be more natural to the age than the foundation of yet other religious orders, in which the monks renouncing the things of this world and taking the same three solemn vows of chastity, obedience and poverty, should devote their lives to fighting against the heathen and the infidel in defence of the Christian faith. Religious orders of such a nature would appeal irresistibly to the noblest spirits of that hard-fighting military aristocracy then supreme throughout Europe. Gallant young gentlemen, filled with the spirit of adventure and burning with religious zeal, were ready enough to take the vows and renounce the things of this world, if it was to be accompanied by the congenial military life that they loved, and possibly by the most glorious of all ends, sword in hand, with their faces to the foe, fighting the battles of Christ. The foundation of the military religious orders was the natural outcome of the spirit of the age.

With one exception, the Templars, all the most famous of these orders survive to the present day, though greatly changed in outward form, and even the Templars still live in the Orders of Christ, and of Our Lady of Monteza, instituted for the express purpose of receiving them on their suppression.[1] There were three theatres of war in which the battles for the Christian faith were fought out to the bitter end, and each of them saw the creation of special religious orders, whose warrior monks were pledged to devote their lives to the pursuit of the Holy War. In the East were the four great orders of the Hospital, the Temple, St. Lazarus and the Teutonic Knights, as well as the little English Order of St. Thomas Acon, composed of English knights with St. Thomas à Becket as their patron saint, an order which died out in the fourteenth century. In the Spanish Peninsula conditions were very similar to those prevailing in the Holy Land, owing to the constant wars against the Moors, who still owned more than half the country, and here too four famous orders were instituted, the Knights of Aviz, Calatrava, Santiago and Alcantara.[2] The third theatre of war was in the far north, where the Germans were engaged in imposing the Christian faith at the point of the sword on the heathen Lithuanians. Here were founded the Order of Dobrzin on the Vistula, and the Knights of the Sword in Livonia, but neither existed for many years and both were absorbed by the Teutonic Knights, when they transferred their energies from the Holy Land to the shores of the Baltic.

The origins of that famous hospital from which the venerable Order of St. John derives its name were very humble, as we know from the gusto with which the greatest of mediaeval historians William

[1] For an account of the Military Religious Orders, see Appendix A at the end of this book.

[2] The two minor Orders of St. Marie de Montjoye (later the Order of Montfrac), and St. George of Alfama, were absorbed by the greater Orders, the former by the Knights of Calatrava, and the latter by the Order of Our Lady of Monteza.

Archbishop of Tyre[1] remarks, 'How petty was the beginning of the Hospitallers.' For the learned Archbishop cordially disliked the Knights of the Hospital upon whom the Pope had conferred privileges so detrimental to the authority and revenue of the bishops. But these origins were so old and so obscure that when the Latin conquest of Jerusalem enabled the Hospitallers to incorporate in their possessions the adjacent Greek monastery of St. John Baptist, it was possible for them to adopt also without incongruity the group of legends[2] that already clustered round that ancient foundation. These legends made an irresistible appeal to devout minds in that credulous age, and were well calculated to enhance the glory and honour of their Order, as well as to attract the contributions of the faithful.

The story runs that King Antiochus was the founder of their hospital in the days of Judas Maccabaeus. They related how the king had come to Jerusalem to punish the high-priest Melchior for sacrilegiously plundering the tomb of David. But Our Lord appeared to him in a vision on Calvary, and ordered him to pardon the high-priest, and to build and endow near that spot a hospital for the care of the sick and the poor. In accordance with the divine command the king endowed the hospital with 12,000 drachmas, and appointed as its first governor Melchior, now repenting of his sacrilege.[3] And when Melchior departed this life, Our Lord came in a vision to Zacharias, the father of St. John Baptist, and ordered him to go to Jerusalem and take his place until Julian the Roman should come. In course of time Julian the Roman was sent by the Emperor to the Holy Land to collect the tribute. He was shipwrecked off Rhodes, and only saved by the miraculous intervention of Christ Himself, who revealed to him that he should succeed Zacharias as governor of the hospital,

[1] William of Tyre was of French extraction, and probably born in the Holy Land about 1130. He was appointed Archdeacon of Tyre in 1167, tutor to the young Prince Baldwin in 1170, Chancellor of the Kingdom of Jerusalem in 1174, Bishop of Bethlehem in the same year, and Archbishop of Tyre in 1175, probably dying in 1187. His *Historia Hierosolymitana* is the chief authority for the Latin Kingdom of Jerusalem between 1127–84.

[2] The text of these legends is published in Delaville Le Roulx, *De prima origine Hospitalariorum Hierosolymitanorum*, pp. 97–118. But they obviously belong to that class of legend so dear to the hearts of the early Greek ecclesiastics, and must almost certainly have originated in the Greek monastery of St. John Baptist in the south-west quarter of the Muristan. That monastery to judge from its church dates from the fifth century, but Delaville Le Roulx does not seem to have been aware of its antiquity.

[3] The story of Antiochus and Melchior is apparently based on certain incidents in the second book of Maccabees. Melchior is the name of one of the three Magi; no high-priest of this name is known, but a certain Heliodorus did plunder the temple treasure, not the tomb of David, with disastrous results to himself, see 2 Macc. iii., and Judas Maccabaeus (not Antiochus) certainly gave the sum of 2,000 drachmas for prayers for the dead, though not for a hospital, see 2 Macc. xii. 43.

which during his rule should be sanctified by the bodily presence of his Saviour. And whilst Julian still governed the hospital, Our Lord lodged there with his apostles on several occasions, and there gave utterance to many of the sayings recorded in the Gospels. The legend went on to relate that during the period of the Crucifixion, the Virgin Mary and St. John the Evangelist lodged in the hospital, and that it was there that Our Lord appeared to his disciples eight days after the Resurrection, and again a week later to St. Thomas. It was there too that Ananias and Sapphira met their tragic end, and it was only natural that in the hospital, St. Stephen and his brother deacons should be elected to administer the charities of the early Christian Church. Such was the mediaeval legend, which endeavoured to make of it one of the most sacred sites in Jerusalem. Gradually the earlier part of the legend assumed a more historical form, and the Vice-Chancellor Caoursin,[1] writing at the end of the fifteenth century, boldly claims Judas Maccabaeus and John Hyrcanus as the founders of the hospital, which they had instituted for the benefit of pilgrims on a visit to the Temple of Solomon.

The real origin is probably to be found in the hospice for pilgrims established by Pope Gregory the Great. Of this hospice however we know absolutely nothing except that about the year 600 the Pope sent the Abbot Probus to the Holy Land with instructions to found a hospice in Jerusalem for the use of pilgrims, and apparently placed large sums of money at his disposal for this purpose.[2] Fourteen years later there fell upon the Holy City a disaster so complete that it can only be compared to the destruction wrought by the Romans under Titus. The eastern defences of the Roman Empire had collapsed before the armies of the Shah Chosroes the Victorious,[3] and in 613 the Persians occupied Damascus. The following year they invaded Palestine, and on 15 April laid siege to Jerusalem. As the Persian armies advanced they were joined by the submerged Jewish population, who wreaked their vengeance to the full on the Christians, in one of those outbursts of fanatical hatred to which their race was prone. After a siege lasting three weeks the northern wall was breached, and on 6 May the city was carried by assault. There followed scenes of indescribable horror and destruction, due not so much to the wild Persian soldiery, as to the implacable fury of the Jews. No Christian was safe, their churches and houses were sacked

[1] William Caoursin, Vice-Chancellor of the Order under the Grand Master Peter d'Aubusson, in *Stabilimenta Rhodiorum militum*, Ulm, 1496. The text is published in *De prima origine*, pp. 129–31.

[2] The text of the authorities is printed in full in *De prima origine*, p. 133.

[3] Chosroes Parviz, Shah of Persia, 590–628. The word Parviz apparently means 'victorious'; see Bury's *Note to Gibbon's 'Decline and Fall'*, 1911, Vol. V, p. 56.

and burnt, and the monk Antiochus who was present,[1] tells us that the number of dead bodies actually counted and buried was 62,445. So maddened were the Jews by their lust for blood, that they actually purchased their prisoners from the Persian soldiers for the pleasure of cutting their throats, and 24,518 Christian men, women and children[2] were collected together and slaughtered in cold blood at the pool of Mamilla, not far from the Jaffa Gate. The skilled artisans and their families were spared, and carried off into captivity in Persia, and with them the venerable Patriarch Zacharias, and that most sacred of all Christian relics the True Cross. All the Christian churches and convents appear to have been destroyed by the infuriated Jews, and amongst them doubtless the hospice so recently established by St. Gregory, as well as the Greek Monastery of St. John Baptist, where, according to the monk Antiochus, no fewer than 4,219 dead bodies were found.

The Persian occupation lasted over fourteen years, and once the country had settled down under its new rulers, there were no very serious complaints to make against the government, except that it necessarily regarded the Jews as its main support, and tended to favour them against the Christians. A year after the capture of the city, the work of reconstruction began under the direction of Modestus Abbot of St. Theodosius,[3] the vicar and successor of the captive Patriarch Zacharias. He was assisted in this work in the most liberal manner by that famous Patriarch of Alexandria, known to future generations as St. John Eleemon, or St. John the Almoner. Together they had provided the means for the rebuilding of the Churches of the Resurrection and of Calvary. But the saintly Patriarch, whose charity towards the Christian refugees from Palestine had known no limits, was himself doomed like his brother of Jerusalem to end his life in exile. The Persian occupation of Egypt began in 616, Alexandria was captured two years later, and the Patriarch fled to his birthplace, the city of Amathus in Cyprus, and died there shortly after.[4]

[1] Antiochus Strategos, a monk of the Monastery of St. Saba, was present and was carried off into captivity with the Patriarch, but afterwards escaped. He wrote an account of these events, of which a Georgian version exists. A translation by F. C. Conybeare was published in the *English Historical Review*, July 1910.

[2] After the massacres were over, burial parties were organized by a saintly Christian man named Thomas, and he afterwards gave the monk Antiochus a detailed return showing the number of bodies collected, and where they had been found.

[3] The Abbey of St. Theodosius in Jerusalem is referred to at different periods, and perhaps for the last time in a bull of Pope Honorius III in 1216. Jeffrey, *The Holy Sepulchre*, p. 13.

[4] See *Life of St. John the Almsgiver*, by Duckworth, Oxford, 1901. But the Patriarch must have died in 618 not 616, since Alexandria cannot have been captured by the Persians before the end of July 618. See Bury's Edition of Gibbon's *Decline and Fall*, Vol. V, p. 76.

He has left behind him such a reputation for lovingkindness and gentle sympathy, for generous self-sacrifice and all true charity, as can never perish.[1]

The Romans only recovered Jerusalem, after the peace which followed the death of the Shah, who was deposed and murdered in 628. In a suicidal war that had lasted twenty-five years, the two great empires of Rome and Persia had torn each other to pieces. Utterly exhausted by their efforts, they had only cleared the stage for the entry of the ragged followers of the great prophet of Arabia. The Persian viceroy Shahrbaraz did not evacuate Syria and Egypt until 629, and on 14 September in that year the victorious Emperor Heraclius made his state entry into Jerusalem, and restored the True Cross to its ancient habitation. The sacred relic had been carefully preserved in Persia by its Christian queen the beautiful Shirin, the favourite wife of Chosroes, whose romantic love for her has been celebrated by Firdousi, the greatest of Persian poets. The Emperor on the recovery of Palestine had promised an amnesty to the Jews, but public opinion was too strong for him, and a terrible vengeance was exacted in Jerusalem and Galilee. During the few years that were left of Christian rule in the Holy City, the restoration was completed of the more sacred and necessary of the buildings destroyed in the sack of 614, and amongst these we can safely include the hospice established for pilgrims by St. Gregory. It is true that we are nowhere expressly told that the hospice was so restored, but there can be no reasonable doubt of the restoration of a building, which had been long found to be so necessary.

During the protracted war between Rome and Persia, there had arisen in Arabia a great religious teacher, destined to change the entire course of history. In 610 Mahomet began to preach the unity of God to his idolatrous countrymen. Driven from Mecca in 622, he fled to Medina and appealed to the sword. By a mixture of persuasive eloquence and ruthless war, reinforced by unlimited promises of plunder in this world and paradise in the next, he succeeded in welding the shifting populations of the desert into a united nation, inspired by fanatical devotion to the new religion. When the prophet died in 632, such a storm was ready to burst forth from the deserts of Arabia, as would bring down in ruins the exhausted empires of the East. Within ten years the followers of Mahomet had wrested the provinces of Syria and Egypt from the power of the Roman Emperor, and had shattered into fragments the mighty realm of his rival the Shah. The

[1] The body of the saint was afterwards translated to Constantinople, from there to Buda in Hungary in 1458, and on the conquest of that country by the Turks, found its last resting-place in the Cathedral of Pressburg on 23 January 1532, and that date is kept by the Roman Church as the saint's anniversary. See Duckworth's *Life of St. John the Almsgiver*.

Arab hordes under Abu Obeidah, one of the companions of the Prophet, laid siege to Jerusalem in July 637.[1] By the end of the year it had become obvious that no possibility of relief existed, and the Patriarch Sophronius offered to capitulate, on condition that the Caliph Omar should be present to ratify in person the terms of surrender. For the Moslems also Jerusalem is a sacred city,[2] second only to Mecca for holiness, and the Commander of the Faithful consented to make the long journey from Medina. There was as yet none of that bitter religious hatred between Christian and Moslem that was to arise in the future, and early in 638 the Arabs entered the Holy City in peace. The Christians were promised security of life and property, with complete freedom of worship. The churches and other religious buildings were treated with respect, and there can be but little doubt that St. Gregory's hospice for pilgrims continued to serve the purpose for which it was originally founded.

The early centuries of Moslem domination do not appear to have inflicted any very grave hardship upon the Christian communities. It is true that they were necessarily in a position of inferiority towards the conquering faith, but as a rule their position was in no way intolerable, and the agreement made between the Caliph and the Patriarch at the capitulation was on the whole honourably observed. In the event of serious injustice or oppression the Christians looked to the Emperor at Constantinople as their natural protector, and except when he was actually at war with the Caliph, his representations were not likely to be ignored. But in 797 the Empress Irene scandalized all Christendom by deposing and blinding her son the Emperor Constantine VI, and proclaiming herself Empress in her own right. That a woman should be the head of the Roman Empire was utterly contrary to the spirit of the age, and men began to turn their eyes towards the West, where reigned the mightiest monarch of the day, Charles, King of the Franks and Patrician of Rome, more generally known to history as Charlemagne.

The Spanish Christians were the first to place themselves under his protection,[3] and then in 799 there arrived an envoy from George Patriarch of Jerusalem, bearing relics of the True Cross, and suggesting that he should assume the protection of the Christians in the Holy Land. Charlemagne received the suggestion with keen approval, and at once sent one of his domestic chaplains, Zacharias, on a confidential mission to the Holy City. He returned the following year with the Patriarch's representatives, two monks, one from the Monastery on

[1] For the chronology of the Arab conquest of Syria and Palestine, see Bury's Edition of Gibbon's *Decline and Fall*, Vol. V, Appendix 20.

[2] Jerusalem is sacred to the Moslems as the scene of Mahomet's miraculous ascent into heaven, and as the place where the Moslems will assemble at the Last Day.

[3] In 798 Alphonso, King of the Asturias, sent Charlemagne part of the spoils taken in a raid against the Moslems of Lisbon, and recognized him as his overlord.

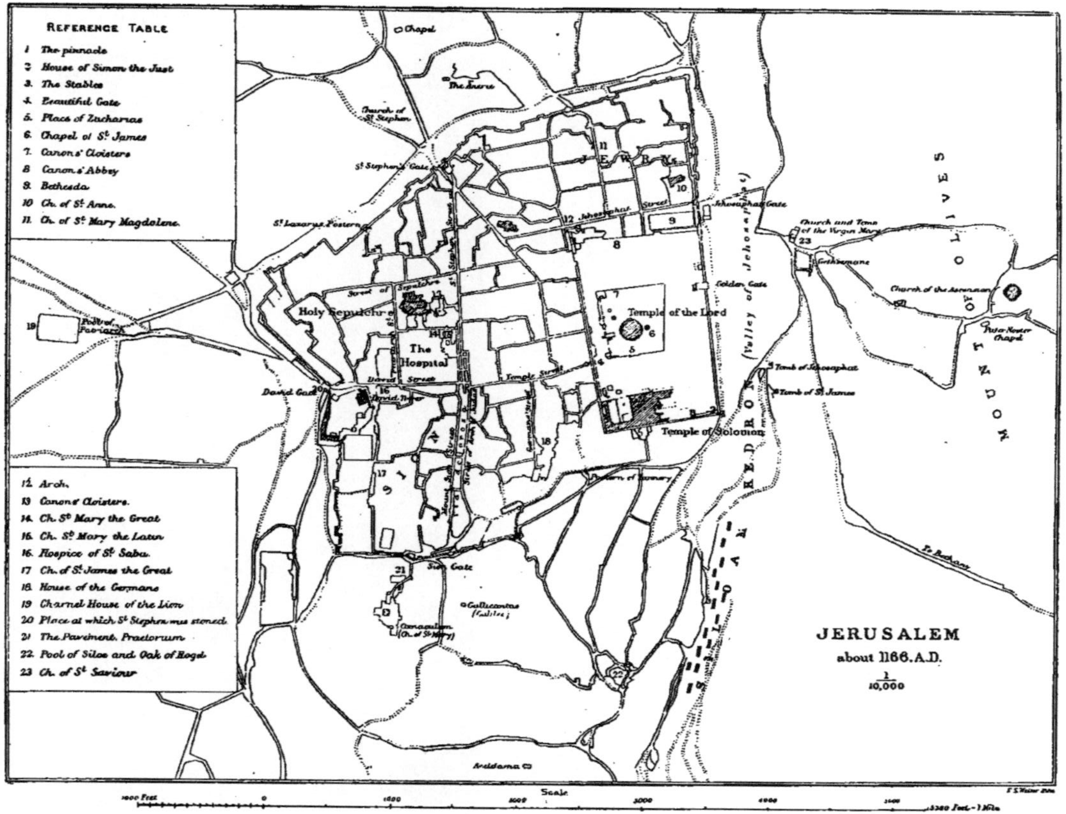

MAP OF MEDIAEVAL JERUSALEM

the Mount of Olives, and the other from the Monastery of Saint Saba, bearing the keys of the Churches of the Resurrection and of Calvary, and a consecrated banner. The significance of these gifts becomes obvious when we consider that the Popes had presented the keys of the shrine of St. Peter and a banner to the Kings of the Franks, on recognizing them as Patricians of Rome. At the end of that year on Christmas Day Charlemagne was proclaimed Emperor in Rome, and in 801 an embassy arrived from the Caliph Haroun er-Raschid in reply to the embassy sent by him four years earlier. Amongst the magnificent presents was an elephant, which long excited the greatest wonder and amazement in the land of the Franks. Whilst the Caliph was on the worst possible terms with the Emperors at Constantinople, his relations with the rival Emperor of the West were always of the most cordial nature, and in 807 his ambassador Abdallah formally recognized the protection of Charlemagne over the Christians of the East.[1] The powers exercised by the Emperor in the Holy Land appear to have closely resembled those exercised by the Kings of France in the eighteenth century. Politically the Caliph remained supreme, but the Emperor acting through the Patriarch controlled the administration of the Holy Places and other Christian establishments, and had a general supervision over justice so far as the Christian population was concerned.[2] With the ever-increasing feebleness of the descendants of Charlemagne, these powers gradually drifted back again into the hands of the Emperors of the East.

The great Emperor took his duties and responsibilities very seriously as protector of the Christians in the Holy Land, and from time to time large sums of money were sent out to Jerusalem for the maintenance of the Holy Places, and the other Churches and Convents. But above all he was interested in the welfare of the Latin pilgrims, for whose benefit he erected certain buildings, known collectively in the early Middle Ages as 'Latinie' to distinguish them from the Greek foundations.[3] Amongst his other works he restored the hospice or hospital for Latin pilgrims, founded by St. Gregory two hundred years before, and for their use he built a church close by dedicated to St. Mary, where the services should be conducted in the Latin tongue. Both hospital and church were placed in charge of a community of Benedictines (until then) residing on the Mount of Olives.[4] From Bernard

[1] The chief authority for the negotiations with the Patriarch and the Caliph is Einhard, the friend and biographer of Charlemagne, and one of his principal ministers. The texts relating to these incidents are printed in *De prima origine*, pp. 134–9.

[2] See Delaville Le Roulx, *Les Hospitaliers en Terre Sainte*, pp. 6, 7.

[3] See *De prima origine*, p. 77.

[4] These Benedictines referred a question of dogma to Pope Leo III for solution in 809, and described themselves as residing on the Mount of Olives. See *Les Hospitaliers en Terre Sainte*, p. 8.

the Monk, who visited Jerusalem in the year 870 and wrote an account of his pilgrimage, we learn that the Benedictines were by then residing near the Church of the Holy Sepulchre. He tells us that a fine library was attached to the Church of St. Mary, which was endowed with property in the Valley of Jehoshaphat, and that in front of the hospital there was a market-place, in which the rent of a shop was two gold pieces a year.[1] That the hospital restored by Charlemagne and his church of St. Mary stood just south of the Holy Sepulchre on the famous site, where the Convent of the Knights of St. John afterwards stood, there can be no reasonable doubt.

Under the rule of the Caliphs of Bagdad, the descendants of Abbas, the uncle of the Prophet, the Christians had no serious cause for complaint, but in 969 the Holy Land was torn from them by their rivals the Fatimite Caliphs of Egypt, who claimed descent from the Prophet's daughter Fatima by Ali his cousin, and in 996 the notorious el-Hakim succeeded to the throne of his fathers. He was then an eccentric lad 11 years of age, but he quickly developed into a cruel and bloodthirsty fanatic. There can be little doubt but that he was a madman in the ordinary sense of the word, suffering from homicidal and religious mania. His insanity culminated in 1016 in the claim that he was himself the Incarnation of the Godhead, and men were ordered to worship his name. One night early in 1021 the mad Caliph rode out into the desert to pray according to his custom, and was never heard of again, but his ass was discovered badly maimed, and his robe was afterwards found pierced by the thrust of daggers. To the present day the Druses of Syria worship the name of el-Hakim, and look for his second coming.

In the year 1005 the Caliph began a systematic attempt to crush out the Christian religion. All Christians in Egypt and Palestine were ordered to become Moslems, or to wear a heavy cross at all times, even in the baths, to distinguish them from their fellows, or else to leave the country. The edict resulted in conversions on an enormous scale, especially amongst the peasantry. Then followed a decree for the destruction of all churches throughout his realms, and the confiscation of their endowments. In the Holy Land the first fury of persecution seems to have fallen upon the Latin churches, but all Christian buildings were systematically destroyed, except only the Church of the Nativity at Bethlehem.[2] The most sacred of all shrines, the Church of the Resurrection was pulled down in 1009, and an unsuccessful attempt was even made to hack out the rock-cut tomb of Our Saviour. So complete was the destruction that the Arab historian el-Makrizi[3]

[1] Quoted in *De prima origine*, p. 77, note 3.

[2] Chronicle of St. Martial de Limoges, quoted in *De prima origine*, p. 145.

[3] Taki ed-Din Ahmed ibn Ali, called el-Makrizi from Makriz near Baalbek, the original home of his family. He was born in Cairo in 1364, and died there in 1442. He wrote a history of the Fatimites, and many other works, mostly dealing with Egypt.

tells us that at the end of 1012 no fewer than 3,000 churches had been demolished in Egypt and Syria. It must have been at this time that the restored hospital of St. Gregory and Charlemagne's church of St. Maria Latina were destroyed, because we know that they were still in existence in 993, when Hugh Marquis of Tuscany and Julitta his wife endowed them with considerable property in Italy.[1]

With the death of el-Hakim the persecution of the Christians ceased, and the question of restoring the sacred shrines began to be considered at Constantinople. The protectorate of the Holy Places had long passed out of the hands of the Emperors of the West, and was now in 1021 [2] officially recognized as being vested in the Emperor Basil II. In the year 1027 a treaty was concluded between his successor Constantine IX and the Caliph ez-Zahir, by which the Emperor agreed to allow the restoration of the Mosque in Constantinople, on condition that he was permitted to restore the Church of the Resurrection in Jerusalem. The work was begun by Romanus III, and on the death of the Caliph the treaty was renewed by the Emperor Michael IV in 1037, with his successor el-Mustansir, a boy of 7. The restoration was completed by Constantine X Monomachus in 1048.

The Latins were no less eager than the Greeks to restore their ruined buildings, and the Caliph appears to have authorized their return to Jerusalem in 1023.[3] The lead was naturally taken by the Republic of Amalfi, a powerful maritime state, which at that time almost monopolized the Egyptian and Syrian trade. Amalfi had risen to importance in the ninth century, her fleets had assisted to save Rome from the Saracens in 849, and a century later her merchants at Constantinople were as numerous and important as those of Venice. During the eleventh century she was at the height of her glory, until the Norman Conquest of southern Italy brought about her downfall. In 1073 she was forced to acknowledge the suzerainty of Robert Guiscard, and in 1131 was conquered by King Roger of Sicily, only to be sacked by the Pisans four years later, a blow from which she never recovered.

If the Latin Christians returned to Jerusalem in 1023, then the restoration of their ruined buildings is not likely to have been delayed much beyond that date. In fact Ekkehard, Abbot of Aura, who made the pilgrimage to the Holy Land in 1101, tells us that the hospital had always existed,[4] which suggests that it can hardly have stood in ruins

[1] The document is printed in full in *De prima origine*, pp. 142–5.

[2] See *Les Hospitaliers en Terre Sainte*, p. 9.

[3] The value of the evidence for this date has been questioned, but it is not probable that the consent would have been long delayed. See *Les Hospitaliers en Terre Sainte*, p. 11, note 2.

[4] See *De prima origine*, p. 80.

long after the persecution had ended. The work of restoration was carried out by the republic of Amalfi, and William of Tyre gives us considerable details as to what was actually done.[1] From his account it is clear that not only were the old buildings restored, but considerable additions were made to them, and he tells us definitely that they were to the south of the Holy Sepulchre, within a stone's throw of it. In other words there is not only no reason for doubting the continuity of the hospital from the days of St. Gregory through its restorations by Charlemagne and Amalfi down to its occupation by the Knights Hospitallers, but rather every reason to the contrary.

The Amalfitans rebuilt Charlemagne's church of St. Maria Latina, with the monastery attached to it for the Benedictines, who served its needs and those of the hospital. This church stood in the middle of the square enclosure, known at the present day as the Muristan and disappeared [2] between 1130 and 1140, when the Knights Hospitallers erected their new buildings. Close by stood the restored hospital, with its chapel dedicated to St. John the Almoner, the gentle Patriarch of Alexandria, whose devoted charity during the horrors of the Persian invasion had never been forgotten by the Christians of the Holy Land. To the east of this old hospital, and separated from it by a lane, a new hospital for the women pilgrims was built by the Amalfitans, with its chapel dedicated to St. Mary Magdalene, where the German church of the Redeemer now stands. Important additions were made to these buildings by Mauro of Amalfi, one of the merchant princes of that city, about 1050, and he also built a similar institution at Antioch.[3] Both these hospitals in Jerusalem were under the control of the Benedictine Abbot of St. Maria Latina, who appointed the lay staff necessary for their administration, and the hospital for women always remained under Benedictine control, even after the hospital for men had become transformed into the Military and Religious Order so famous in history.[4] The monks for the church of St. Maria Latina are thought to have been drawn from the famous monastery of La Cava near Amalfi.[5] It was always distasteful to the Knights of St. John to think that their hospital in its early days had been under the Benedictines, and they flatly denied that it had ever had so humble a saint as St. John the Almoner for its patron. The Italian knight William de St. Estène,

[1] William of Tyre's account is printed in full in *Les Hospitaliers en Terre Sainte*, pp. 20–2.

[2] Dr. Conrad Schick identified this church as St. Mary Major, but there can be little doubt that the church of St. Mary Major stood where the German church of the Redeemer now stands, see Jeffery, *The Holy Sepulchre*, p. 151, and *Les Hospitaliers en Terre Sainte*, pp. 29, 30.

[3] Chronicle of Amatus of Monte Cassino printed in *De prima origine*, p. 35. See also Curtis' *Roger of Sicily*, pp. 387, 388.

[4] See *Les Hospitaliers en Terre Sainte*, p. 31, note 3.

[5] Ibid., p. 12, note 4.

Commander of Cyprus,[1] writing at the end of the thirteenth century states plainly that St. John Baptist had always been their patron, and that the contrary opinion was due only to a confusion of names. But on this subject the statement of so careful a historian as William of Tyre, writing over a century earlier, would seem to be conclusive.

For four hundred years the once mighty empire of Persia had now lain in ruins, shattered to pieces by the Arab Conquest. Its revival in the eleventh century under a vigorous dynasty of Turkish princes of the House of Seljuk, was one of the chief causes of the First Crusade, and therefore indirectly of the foundation of the Order of the Hospital of St. John of Jerusalem. The first of the dynasty was a certain Toghrul Beg, whose victory in 1040 over the son of the great Mahomet of Ghuznee, raised him to the throne of the Shahs. In 1055 he entered Bagdad, and made it the capital of the new Persian Empire. His nephew and successor Alp Arslan, 'the valiant lion', in 1071 defeated the Emperor Romanus IV in the decisive battle of Manzikert, and began the Turkish conquest of Asia Minor. But already a few months earlier his armies under the Emir Atsiz ibn Auk had overrun Palestine up to the Egyptian frontier, and driven the Fatimites out of Jerusalem. The Egyptians made repeated attempts to recover their lost possessions in Syria, but the Turkish troops under the Emir Ortok ibn Eksek, who succeeded Atsiz in 1079, had no difficulty in retaining the Holy City, and when Ortok died he was succeeded there by his sons el-Ghazi and Sukman.

The occupation of Jerusalem by a Turkish garrison constituted a veritable revolution. The arrival of the Turks had been accompanied by the usual massacres and abominations for which their race has always been so notorious, and we are told that Atsiz invited the principal officials of the city to his camp, and then executed them, following it up by the slaughter of three thousand of the citizens. The continued presence of the Turks meant the end of all law and order, and in the words of Jeremiah the prophet[2] concerning another race of similar type, it was no longer safe to go forth into the field, nor walk by the way, for the sword of the enemy and fear was on every side. The Saracens were a highly civilized people, and so long as they ruled in the Holy City, the lot of the Christian had never been intolerable, except during the persecution of el-Hakim, and the agreement made by the Caliph Omar had generally been honestly maintained. But with the arrival of the Turks everything was changed, and to those barbaric

[1] William de St. Estène, or more probably San Stefano, was a Knight of the Priory of Lombardy, and Commander of Cyprus 1282–1303. He wrote the first known compilation of the Statutes of the Order about 1287, to which he added in a second edition in 1302 a dissertation on the origins of the Order generally known as the Exordium Hospitalis. See Delaville Le Roulx, *Les Statuts de l'Hôpital*, 1888.

[2] Jeremiah vi. 25.

soldiers of fortune the Christian pilgrims merely represented so much additional plunder. It was not long before the changed conditions in Jerusalem began to be known in Europe, and as the returning pilgrims related the story of the cruelties and insults and injuries to which they were now subjected, the anger and indignation of Christendom grew deeper and deeper, until men began to feel that the Holy City of their Saviour must be freed once and for all from the profanation of the infidel. At last in the year 1094, so the story goes, there came on a pilgrimage to Jerusalem that prophet, whose inspired preaching was to rouse all Europe to arms. Peter the Hermit was a native of Amiens, of knightly birth, and was now 44 years of age. He was a small insignificant man, with a long brown beard, and had been a soldier in his youth, but was now filled with the spirit of earnest religious devotion. From the Patriarch Simeon he learned with fierce indignation of the abominable profanities of the Turks in the Holy Places, and it was afterwards related that as he knelt absorbed in prayer in front of the Holy Sepulchre, Our Saviour appeared to him in a vision, and said to him: 'Arise, Peter, the time is come. Go forth and tell the tribulations of My people. The time is come that My servants should be succoured and that My Holy Places should be free.' And so Peter the Hermit left the Holy Sepulchre, a man inspired, believing himself to be specially chosen by God to preach throughout Europe the Holy War.

We know practically nothing of what happened to the Hospital during the twenty-five years of the Turkish occupation, but it goes without saying that it must have suffered, just as all Christian institutions suffered, from the prevailing tyranny and oppression. Almost the only record of this period that we possess [1] is that John Archbishop of Amalfi made the pilgrimage to Jerusalem in 1082, that he was received by the Amalfitan colony there with the greatest honour, and that he visited the Hospital. From William of Tyre we learn that towards the end of the Turkish occupation, the Hospital for women was under the care of a Roman lady of noble birth, named Agnes, and that over the Hospital for male pilgrims the Rector was a certain very saintly man, destined to become famous in history as the Blessed Gerard, the founder of the Order of St. John, and one whose name has always been held in deepest reverence down to the present day. Both had seen the abomination of desolation in the Holy Places, and both were to live to see the infidel driven out, and the Holy City once more in Christian hands.

[1] See the Anonymous Chronicle of Amalfi, the extract is printed in *De prima origine*, p. 36.

CHAPTER II

BLESSED GERARD AND THE FOUNDATION OF THE ORDER

THE great invasion of Asia by the nations of Western Europe, since known as the First Crusade, might well be regarded in many of its aspects as the last of those great national migrations, which accompanied and followed the collapse of the Roman Empire in the West. Like all the great events of history, it was the result of many different causes. But two of these were of supreme importance. Firstly, the grave political situation in the Near East, where the Turkish advance in Asia Minor was beginning to threaten Constantinople. None realized more clearly than the Popes, that that great city had now become the frontier fortress of Christendom, and that something must be done to relieve the Mohammedan pressure in that quarter before it was too late. Secondly, public opinion, so far as it then existed, had been deeply stirred by the sufferings of the pilgrims in the Holy Land, and by their stories of the horrible sacrileges committed by the infidels in the most sacred of all shrines, the Churches of the Resurrection and of Calvary. There were also many other causes at work, the desire of the great maritime states, Genoa, Pisa and Venice, to establish trading settlements on the Syrian coast, the ambition of adventurous princes to carve out new realms at the point of the sword, the land hunger of the younger sons of noble families, and the misery, poverty and consequent restlessness of the lower classes. But behind all this the real driving force of the Crusade was religious fanaticism, fanned to fever heat by the revivalist preaching of men like Peter the Hermit. All classes alike felt that a pilgrimage in arms to save the Holy Places from the intolerable profanation of the infidel was a Holy War, in which those who completed the pilgrimage would have their sins forgiven to them however vile, and those who fell by the way would inherit the everlasting joys of Paradise.

In March 1095, Pope Urban II presided over a synod at Piacenza, at which a fresh appeal for help against the Turks was received from the Emperor Alexius. The required assistance was promised, and a further council was held at Clermont in November. Here the Pope addressed an immense gathering, and in eloquent phrases appealed for the deliverance of Jerusalem from the infidel. Deeply moved by his words, a great cry went up from the assembly, 'It is the will of God', and amidst scenes of the wildest enthusiasm, men cut up their mantles in the form of crosses and fixed them to their garments and those of their neighbours, as the outward sign that they were pledged to serve in the Holy War. From Clermont the preachers went forth to rouse the people to arms, and none was more successful than Peter the Hermit. Everywhere he was received as one divinely inspired, and the very ass that he rode was regarded as sanctified by the service of the man of God. As the firstfruits of their labours, five tumultuous hordes of fanatics started in the following spring to march across Europe to Jerusalem. As the outward sign of their religious zeal they murdered the Jews, wherever they could find them, whilst they satisfied the needs of their bodies by plundering the countryside. Three of these hordes were massacred by the indignant peoples of the territories through which they passed. Two of them, marvellous to relate, actually reached Constantinople, one led by a disreputable military adventurer known as Walter the Penniless,[1] and the other by Peter the Hermit. The Emperor hastily transported these undesirable allies across the Bosporus. Ignoring the advice of the Imperial generals they at once advanced against the nearest Turkish garrison, and as was naturally to be expected were cut to pieces, their leaders alone escaping.

Meanwhile the soldiers had been busy for nearly a year in raising, organizing and equipping the forces necessary for the great expedition, and in the autumn of 1096 they began to concentrate at Constantinople. The army was very large, so large that the wildest statements became current regarding its numbers. Probably its strength was about 150,000,[2] including a mixed multitude of camp followers and women. The real force of the army lay in the knights, all heavy cavalry armed with lance and sword, and perhaps composing as much as one-fourth of its total strength. The infantry were regarded as useful for garrison duty and siege operations, but as having little value on the battlefield. A Burgundian and German contingent was led by Godfrey de Bouillon, Duke of Lower Lorraine, accompanied by his brothers Eustace and Baldwin, and by Baldwin du Bourg, a son of the Count of Rethel. The Anglo-Normans, French and Flemings were led by Robert Duke of Normandy,[3] William the Conqueror's eldest son, and with him was his brother-in-law Stephen, Count of Blois,

[1] Walter the Penniless, senzaver, sine conta, sine censu, sine habere. It is interesting to note that a certain Hugh Senzaver was constable of Tripolis from 1161 to 1163.

[2] Godfrey's contingent consisted of 10,000 knights and 30,000 foot. Bohemond had 7,000 knights. See Ernest Barker's article on the 'Crusades' in the *Encyclopaedia Britannica*.

[3] During the siege of Antioch, the Duke of Normandy was reinforced by a small English contingent under Edgar the Atheling, the rightful King of England.

THE HOLY SEPULCHRE OF OUR SAVIOUR

whose son was afterwards King of England, together with the Count of Flanders, and Hugh the Tall, Count of Vermandois, the French King's brother. Raymond de St. Gilles, Count of Toulouse and Marquis of Provence, led a powerful Provençal contingent, and the Normans of Italy were under Robert Guiscard's eldest son Bohemond, Prince of Tarento, with his nephew Tancred, the most romantic figure of the Crusade. There was no commander-in-chief, and the only co-ordinating authority was the Papal legate, Adhémar, Bishop of Puy.

The advance through Asia Minor, which formed the Turkish Sultanate of Roum, began in the spring of 1097, the Imperial army and fleet co-operating. Nicaea, the Turkish capital, was taken after a month's siege, and at Dorylaeum on 1 July an overwhelming defeat was inflicted upon the Sultan Kilij-Arslan. The march continued almost unopposed through Iconium, Heraclea, Caesarea and Marash. In the autumn Tancred overran Cilicia in the name of his uncle Bohemond, whilst Godfrey's brother Baldwin occupied Turbessel (Tell-bashir), and laid the foundations of what was to become five months later the County of Edessa. By 21 October the Crusaders had concentrated at Antioch, and on that date began the famous siege of the ancient metropolis of Syria.

Politically the situation could not possibly have been more favourable for the Crusaders. The greatest of the Turkish princes of the House of Seljuk, Malek Shah, son of Alp Arslan, Lord of Persia and Mesopotamia, of Syria and Asia Minor, had died in 1092 and his mighty empire had relapsed into a state of anarchy. In Syria the Emirs of Aleppo and Antioch, of Damascus and Jerusalem, had become practically independent rulers, and bitterly jealous of each other, whilst in the south the Fatimite Caliph of Egypt was only watching for an opportunity to recover his lost province. The siege of Antioch dragged on for seven weary months, and the city only fell on 3 June owing to the treachery of a senior Turkish officer. A relieving force from Mosul was defeated on 28 June, and then after prolonged friction with Raymond of Toulouse, Bohemond, the ablest and most ambitious of the leaders, was proclaimed Prince of Antioch. Meanwhile El-Afdal, the capable vizir of the Caliph of Egypt, hearing of the fall of Antioch, advanced into Palestine in August, and drove the Turks out of Jerusalem.[1]

During the summer of 1098 the papal legate died, and there was none left capable of exercising control over the princes, whose constant quarrelling and jealous rivalries now began to jeopardize the success of the Crusade. Gradually Godfrey de Bouillon, by far the finest character of them all, began to assume the leadership. A tall red-bearded man, still under 40 years of age, he was one of the hardest-

[1] The date is sometimes given as 1096, but see Stevenson, *The Crusaders in the East*, p. 20.

fighting knights in the host. But unlike the others, he was devoid of earthly ambition, and fought only for the love of Christ. Gentle and kindly to the very humblest of the pilgrims, he was a man of pure life, when few were pure, and of him alone amongst the princes no scandalous stories were whispered in the camp. A devout man of deep religious feeling, his followers told how in churches he became so wrapt in prayer that he would forget the very hours for meals. Such was Duke Godfrey, who in May 1099 prevailed upon Raymond of Toulouse to postpone his ambitious designs on Tripolis, and to join in the march southwards. The crusaders took the coast road to Jaffa, and then turning inland, on the morning of 7 June reached Jerusalem. We are told that as they first caught sight of the Holy City, that army of Christian soldiers flung themselves in the dust, and lifted up their voices and wept. At last the end of their long pilgrimage was in view, for which they had sacrificed everything, and suffered all that it is possible for men to suffer and still live. Of all that mighty host that had started on the great Crusade, according to Raymond of Agiles,[1] when the siege of Jerusalem began, there were but 12,000 fighting men left, of whom only 1,300 were knights.

The Egyptian garrison of Jerusalem was small, only 400 horse and 500 Soudanese foot.[2] The civilian population of military age, in so cosmopolitan a city, can scarcely have had much fighting value, and the capture of the city therefore was not a very serious operation. The crusaders endeavoured to carry it by escalade on 13 June but were beaten back. They then settled down to the construction of the machines necessary for a regular siege. By the middle of July they were ready, and two belfrys, large wooden towers on wheels, were moved up to the walls. One was burnt by the besieged; with the help of the other Duke Godfrey on the afternoon of 15 July stormed the city at its north-east corner. Men afterwards remarked with awe how the Holy City had fallen into Christian hands on a Friday at three o'clock, the very day and hour on which their Saviour had died. The Egyptian governor Iftikhar-ed-Daula, seeing that all was lost, surrendered the citadel known as the Tower of David to Raymond of Toulouse, who escorted him and his garrison in safety to Ascalon. His action caused great indignation amongst those, who had thus been deprived of the pleasant duty of slaughtering the enemies of God.

The capture of Jerusalem was followed by the worst massacre that the Holy City had ever known. The Egyptian garrison had escaped them, but the helpless civilian population was entirely at their mercy.

[1] Raymond of Agiles was a cleric, and one of the followers of Count Raymond of Toulouse. He wrote the *Historia Francorum qui ceperunt Jerusalem*; his account is honest and straightforward, and one of the best authorities for the First Crusade.

[2] See Stevenson, *The Crusaders in the East*, p. 33, note 2.

Mad with fanaticism and the lust for blood the troops broke loose from the control of their leaders, and spared neither man, woman nor child, whilst the Jews were burnt alive in their synagogues. So horrible was the slaughter that we are told that the narrow streets were ankle-deep in human blood, and that the knights were splashed in it as they rode into the Temple area. At last when even was come, these pious pilgrims, red from the wine-press of the Lord, flocked to the Holy Sepulchre, to join their blood-stained hands in prayer before the tomb of the gentle Saviour, whose holy cause they had so utterly disgraced. Tancred spared 300 unhappy people in the Mosque of El-Aksa, but even his banner was unable to protect them, and a body of exultant pilgrims murdered them all. Raymond of Toulouse also gave protection in the Tower of David to such as could succeed in reaching that place of refuge, and sent them in safety to Ascalon. But the massacres lasted for several days, and in the words of Raymond of Agiles, who was present, 'Such a slaughter of pagan folk had never been seen or heard of before, none knows their number save God alone.'

Meanwhile Duke Godfrey, as soon as he had seen that victory was assured, had passed with three attendants to the Church of the Holy Sepulchre, to humble himself in prayer at the tomb of Our Lord. Eight days after he was elected the first Christian King of Jerusalem. But he would take no kingly title in the city, where his Lord had suffered, nor wear a crown of gold where his Saviour had worn a crown of thorns. Content with the humble title of Defender and Baron of the Holy Sepulchre, he devoted the few months of life still left to him to consolidating the new Christian kingdom. On 12 August an Egyptian army commanded by El-Afdal in person, was surprised and almost annihilated at Ascalon, and then Tancred was sent to Tiberias as Prince of Galilee, to organize the northern districts on the side of Damascus. Three days after the first anniversary of the capture of Jerusalem, Godfrey died of a fever and was buried in the Church of the Holy Sepulchre at the entrance to the Chapel of Adam, and his sword was hung over his tomb.[1]

The capture of Jerusalem by the Crusaders in 1099 is the true natal day of the Order of St. John. Until then it had been but a local charity of the Benedictines for the assistance of pilgrims; within a few years of the Christian occupation it had become a great international religious order with ramifications in every country of Europe. When the Crusading army marched south to the siege of Jerusalem, it would scarcely be safe for the European population to remain at the

[1] The monument was never restored after the fire of 1808, owing to the jealousy of the Greeks, but the stone ledge on which it stood can still be seen. His sword, spurs and cross are preserved in the Latin sacristy to the north of the north aisle. A replica of the monument of Godfrey de Bouillon can be seen in the Cathedral of Boulogne.

mercy of any sudden outburst of Moslem fanaticism, and they appear to have withdrawn, as we should naturally expect. But the Blessed Gerard, the guardian and administrator of the Hospital, preferred to remain at the post of duty. It was no empty danger that he had to face, and no sooner was the siege begun than a charge was brought against him of concealing treasure and maintaining communications with the enemy. The Egyptian governor Iftikhar-ed-Daula ordered his arrest, and according to William of Tyre he was thrown into prison, and examined under torture.[1] Probably he would have forfeited his life, had not the siege terminated so quickly. Concerning this episode a story had become current fifty years later that he was only saved by a miracle. As is well known, the besieging army suffered great hardships, especially from the scarcity of provisions. According to the story, Gerard, knowing this, made a practice of visiting the walls three or four times a day with a basket of bread. Joining the men detailed to hurl stones upon the enemy troops engaged in sapping the walls, he hurled not stones but loaves of bread. In due course he was observed and taken before the governor, still carrying his basket of bread. But when the basket was examined, the loaves of bread were found to have been miraculously turned into stones, and the governor, believing the story to be false, at once ordered the holy man to be released, and to be allowed to visit the walls whenever he thought fit.[2]

We know little concerning the early life of the Blessed Gerard, famous though he afterwards became, and the very country of his origin is by no means absolutely certain. Even his name was at one time in doubt, and certain writers have conferred upon him the surname of Tunc, varying the spelling to suit their differing theories. For if the family to which Gerard belonged ever possessed a surname, it certainly was not Tunc. That name is due simply to the error of some copyist of a Latin text, who seeing the words 'Gerardus tunc' mistook the adverb for a surname.[3] According to the generally accepted tradition, Gerard was a Provençal born about the year 1040 at Martigues, formerly known as the Isle of St. Genès, at the entrance to the Etang de Berre. Proud of their saintly and illustrious countryman, the people of Martigues in 1869 erected a statue [4] to his memory in front of one of their churches, one of the squares of the town has

[1] See *Les Hospitaliers en Terre Sainte*, p. 34, note 1.

[2] This story is included amongst the mediaeval legends concerning the origins of the Order. The text is published in *De prima origine*, pp. 112, 113.

[3] See Boisgelin, *Ancient and Modern Malta*, Vol. II, p. xii, and *Les Hospitaliers en Terre Sainte*, p. 36. The word Tunc has been made to read Tum, Teuc, Turc, Tenque, Tenches, etc., as convenient.

[4] The statue bears the inscription, 'Le Bienheureux Gerard Tenque, la gloire de la cité', and is the work of Nazaire Bernard, a native of Martigues.

been called after him, and in 1891 the Societies of the Cigale and of the Félibres placed a commemorative inscription[1] on the Hôtel de Ville. But the claim of Martigues to be the birthplace of the Blessed Gerard is not unchallenged. Scala, near Amalfi, also claims that honour, in the seventeenth century his portrait stood in their public square,[2] and the noble family of Sasso places the name of Gerard amongst its illustrious ancestry. Neither claim is capable of exact proof, we can only say that the Provençal tradition seems to be older, more persistent, and altogether more convincing. On the other hand, there is this to be said for the claim of Scala, that we should expect to see an Italian rather than a Provençal at the head of a hospital controlled by the citizens of Amalfi. Perhaps there is truth in both stories, and Gerard may have been a native of Martigues, who settled at Scala and then in the course of time was thought to have been born there. In that case he would have embarked at Amalfi, on his departure about the year 1080, for the pilgrimage to Jerusalem, which was destined to change his entire life. He appears never to have left the Holy City, but to have entered the service of the Hospital, of which he was appointed Rector by the Abbot of St. Maria Latina some time before the First Crusade.[3]

When Gerard was released from prison by the Crusaders, he at once resumed his duties as Rector of the Hospital. But his position was now very different to what it had been under Moslem rule. Probably he had been able to render some sort of assistance to the Crusaders before the capture of the Holy City, and certainly as a European resident in Jerusalem for many years his services must have been of the greatest value to them after its capture. Besides all this, his Hospital had now from time immemorial been the centre for the Latin pilgrims visiting Jerusalem, and would naturally have received within its walls as many of the wounded Christian soldiers as it could accommodate. The historians[4] of the Order assure us that Godfrey de Bouillon personally visited the Hospital, as we should expect, and his

[1] The inscription, which is in Provençale, is as follows: 'In the year of Our Lord Jesus Christ 1040, in our town of Martigues, was born the Blessed Gerard Tenque, founder of the Order of the Hospitallers of St. John of Jerusalem, and on 11 August 1891 the Societies of the Cigale and the Félibres erected this tablet in honour of the memory of this illustrious and charitable Provençal.'

[2] See *Les Hospitaliers en Terre Sainte*, p. 37.

[3] See *Le Bienheureux Gerard*, pp. 5–7, by Canon F. Giraud, published at Aix, 1919.

[4] The first great historian of the Order of St. John was James Bosio, and upon his work all the later histories are based. He was born at Chivasso in Piedmont, and was for some years Agent-General of the Order in Rome. In 1577 he was sent by the Pope on a mission to Malta, and there conceived the idea of writing his great work, to which he devoted the remainder of his life.

interest in it is shown by the gift of the Casal Hessilia (Es-Silsileh) and two bakeries.[1]

It is undoubtedly at this time that the great transformation of the Hospital must have taken place. It had now become far more important than the Abbey of St. Maria Latina, upon which it had so far depended. We hear nothing of the Benedictines, who had presumably withdrawn from Jerusalem before the siege, and Gerard was able to secure the independence of his Hospital, and to form a new Order of Hospitallers, although the Benedictines retained their control over the establishment for women.[2] The Hospitallers are said to have taken the three solemn vows of poverty, chastity and obedience in the Church of the Holy Sepulchre before the Patriarch Dagobert of Pisa, who confirmed the formation of the new Order,[3] and like the Order of the Holy Sepulchre also founded under Godfrey de Bouillon, they adopted the Augustinian rule,[4] as a further sign of their complete separation from their former patrons. Their habit was originally the black *cappa clausa*, that is the long monastic bell-like cloak with a slit on each side for the arms, with a white eight-pointed cross on the breast,[5] and it is not uninteresting to note that the arms of Amalfi include this eight-pointed cross.[6] It can also only have been at the time of the Latin Conquest of Jerusalem that the Hospitallers secured possession of the ancient Greek monastery of St. John Baptist. Until then the Latin buildings had occupied only the northern portion of that great enclosure known since the days of Saladin as the Muristan; the southern part had been occupied from early Christian times by the buildings of the Greek monastery. From this the Greek monks must at some time have been expelled in order to transfer it to the Hospitallers, and there is no time at which this can have been possible except at the Latin conquest, accompanied as it was by a veritable

[1] See Delaville Le Roulx, *Cartulaire-Général des Hospitaliers,* Vol. I, p. 1. It is often stated that Godfrey de Bouillon presented to the Hospital the manor of Montboise in Brabant, but this gift was in reality made by Godfrey III, Duke of Lower Lorraine, in 1183. *Cartulaire-Général,* Vol. I, No. 649.

[2] See *Les Hospitaliers en Terre Sainte,* p. 31, note 3.

[3] Father Louis Beurrier in his *Sommaire des vies des fondateurs et reformateurs des Ordres Religieux,* 1635, states that Gerard and his brethren only took the vows in 1106, but gives no authority for the statement, which is in direct conflict with the charters.

[4] The Augustinian rule was only composed towards the end of the eleventh century, and was adopted by a large number of the clergy of Collegiate churches living in community. It was based on the writings of St. Augustine.

[5] See Alison Phillips, 'Knights of St. John of Jerusalem', *Encyc. Brit.,* 11th Edition, p. 13, but I know not his authority for stating that the eight-pointed cross was adopted at so early a date. Canon Giraud in his *Life of the Blessed Gerard* states that in his day the Hospitallers used an ordinary Latin cross, and that Raymond du Puy introduced the eight-pointed cross, but gives no authority for this statement.

[6] See *Les Hospitaliers en Terre Sainte,* p. 37.

revolution in the condition and ownership of property. With the addition of the Greek monastery to their former buildings, its patron St. John Baptist naturally became the patron saint of the Order, taking the place of the original patron saint of the Hospital, St. John the Almoner.

When the Crusaders returned to Europe from the Holy War, many of them must have been filled with gratitude for the care and attention they had received in the Hospital when sick or wounded. The new Order speedily became famous in every Christian land, and the twenty years of life that lay before the Blessed Gerard were years of steady progress and increasing usefulness. From the great Cartulary of the Order, which we owe to the researches of that distinguished student Delaville Le Roulx, every step in its advancement can be clearly traced. Gifts of lands and houses followed in rapid succession in all the Mediterranean countries, and when its founder died in 1120, the Order of Hospitallers was firmly established in Italy, Southern France, Spain and Portugal. In the Kingdom of Jerusalem and the other states of Syria its progress was equally rapid, and in 1110 it was granted a charter by King Baldwin I confirming to it all its possessions, a charter which was repeated two years later, and again confirmed by his successor Baldwin II in the year of Gerard's death.[1] In 1112 the Patriarch of Jerusalem and the Archbishop of Caesarea exempted the Hospitallers from the payment of tithes,[2] and then in the following year the formation of the Order was finally confirmed by the Bull of Pope Paschal II.

The Papal Bull dated 15 February 1113 [3] is the real foundation charter of the Hospitallers, placing them in the same position as the other great religious orders. Under its terms they were taken under the protection and guardianship of the Popes for all time, and have so remained to the present day.[4] Their possessions were confirmed to them, both in Syria and in Europe, they were exempted from the payment of tithes, and were granted the privilege of electing their own superior, whenever a vacancy should occur. In this bull the Blessed Gerard is called the Founder and Provost of the Hospital in Jerusalem, but he appears to have been more generally known as the Rector or Governor, though the Charters refer to him under a variety of titles.[5] The more important possessions of the Order in Europe are mentioned by name; they are called Hospitals of Jerusalem or Poor-

[1] See *Cartulaire-Général*, Vol. I, Nos. 20, 28, 53.

[2] Ibid., Nos. 25, 29.

[3] See Appendix to this chapter.

[4] This remark naturally does not apply to the independent offshoots of the Sovereign Order in Germany, Sweden, Russia and England.

[5] The various titles in the Charters are Hospitalarius, Servus Ospitalis Sancte Jerusalem, Pater ipsius domus, Prior, Servus et Minister Hospitalis, Institutor ac Prepositus Hierosolymitani Xenodochii, Fidelis Elemosinarius qui preest

houses, and were apparently resthouses for pilgrims on their way to the Holy Land, they were at this time seven in number:

St. Gilles. Bari.
Asti. Otranto.
Pisa. Tarento.
Messina.

Of these St. Gilles, Messina and Pisa were at a later date the seats of Priors, and the two former were for long the most important possessions of the Order in Europe, since it was here the pilgrims assembled to embark for the Holy Land. The superior of the Hospital at St. Gilles was at this time a certain Prior Pons, who may be the same as the Pons who was afterwards Hospitaller of the Order in the Convent at Jerusalem.[1] The bull of Pope Paschal was confirmed by a bull of Pope Calixtus II in 1119, and subsequently by other popes.

The work of the Blessed Gerard was now completed; he had successfully laid the foundations of what was ultimately to become the greatest and most powerful order of chivalry the world has ever known. During the seven years of life that remained to him, his Order continued to increase and prosper, more especially in France and Spain, whilst its Syrian possessions in the County of Tripolis and the Principality of Antioch were confirmed to it by their rulers.[2] He died at about 80 years of age on 3 September 1120, and his epitaph in Latin has been handed down to us by Fulcher of Chartres,[3] a chaplain of King Baldwin I. Its translation is as follows:

'Here lies Gerard the humblest man in the East, the servant of the poor, hospitable to strangers, meek in aspect but noble in heart, one sees in these walls how good he was: provident and active, exerting himself to provide all things, he extended his arms far and wide to obtain the wherewithal to nourish his own: on the 17th day of the passage of the Sun under the sign of the Virgin (i.e. Sept. 3rd) he was transported to heaven in the arms of the Angels.'

From the little we know of him, Gerard appears to have been a gentle kindly charitable man, with no thoughts beyond the work to which he had devoted his life. But that he was also a sound and

Jerosolimitano Hospicio, Dei Servus et Procurator pauperum Christi. *Les Hospitaliers en Terre Sainte*, p. 39.

[1] See the list of dignitaries of the Order given in *Les Hospitaliers en Terre Sainte*, Appendix, pp. 411, 415.

[2] See *Cartulaire-Général*, Vol. I, Nos. 43, 45.

[3] Fulcher of Chartres was a priest, who served in the contingent of Robert Duke of Normandy during the First Crusade. He afterwards became chaplain to King Baldwin I, and wrote the *Gesta Francorum Jerusalem Peregrinantium*, one of the most trustworthy sources for the history of this period. He died at Jerusalem in 1127. The date of Gerard's death has been given by some historians as 1118, but Fulcher's statement, reinforced as it is by the charters, is conclusive. See *Recueil des Historiens des Croisades*, Vol. III, p. 446, footnote.

HOTEL DE VILLE, MANOSQUE

EGLISE DE JONQUIÈRES, MARTIGUES

EGLISE DE FERRIÈRES, MARTIGUES

EGLISE DE L'ILE, MARTIGUES

RELICS OF THE BLESSED GERARD

capable administrator is clearly proved by the progress made by the Hospital under his rule. He was evidently regarded by his contemporaries as a man of very saintly life, and was canonized after his death by the Patriarch of Jerusalem,[1] receiving the title of Blessed, which in the twelfth century was the equivalent of Saint. The influence of his personality has never ceased to be felt in the Order, which he founded, and changed though its character afterwards became, that influence has ever inspired its works of charity throughout its history.

The body of Gerard was not destined to rest in peace in the Conventual Church in Jerusalem, where it was no doubt originally interred, but after the loss of the Holy City was translated to Acre and thence to Rhodes, as is evident from its subsequent history. As early as 1283 important relics described as the body of the Blessed Gerard were preserved at Manosque in Provence, afterwards a Bailiwick of the Order. These relics were contained in a silver-gilt reliquary, studded with precious stones, and in 1400 we learn that there was also an arm of the saint encased in silver.[2] As to when and why these relics were taken to Manosque, where they were kept in the chapel of the castle, we have no knowledge, but probably they were in reality relics of St. Gerard d'Aurillac and there was confusion between him and the Blessed Gerard, to whom the cult and the festival day of the former appear to have been transferred.[3] The body of the Saint on the surrender of Rhodes was taken with them on their wanderings by the Knights of St. John. In 1528 it was at Nice, and in that year during the absence of the Grand Master in England, John Boniface Bailiff of Manosque, his Lieutenant, appears to have translated it to Manosque, and to have placed it with the other relics there. Nine years later he completely restored the chapel of the castle, placed the whole of the relics of Gerard in a new reliquary of gilded wood, and decorated the altar containing it with a reredos representing Our Lady of Philermo, St. John Baptist and the Blessed Gerard.[4] The reliquary bore the inscription:

HIC JACENT OMNIA OSSA BEATI GHERARDI.

It was the custom on the feast-day of the saint (13 October) after Mass, to carry his relics in solemn procession, and whenever the country-side had need of rain the relics were always thus carried, for it was the confident opinion of the people that the Almighty would never remain deaf to the prayers of the Blessed Gerard.[5] In 1630 the Provincial Chapter of the Grand Priory of St. Gilles decided that for greater convenience in the procession, a silver bust of Gerard should

[1] See Canon F. Giraud, *Le Bienheureux Gerard*, p. 26, note 1.
[2] See *Le Bienheureux Gerard*, pp. 33–5.
[3] Ibid., pp. 67, 68. [4] Ibid., pp. 37–41. [5] Ibid., p. 65.

be made to contain some of the relics, and the work was entrusted to Pierre Puget, the famous sculptor of Marseilles. Apparently the original silver reliquary of the thirteenth century was now broken up to supply the material for the new reliquary, as it is never heard of again.[1] The relics remained in this condition until the French Revolution, when the castle of Manosque was destroyed, the reliquary of gilded wood burnt, and the remains of Gerard thrown to the winds. Some fragments were preserved in the Church of St. Saviour until 1841, when they disappeared, and there is a certified relic in the Church of Notre Dame.[2] The silver bust by Puget is preserved in the council chamber of the Hôtel de Ville.

The most important relics of the Blessed Gerard still existing are at Martigues, his birthplace. In 1727 the citizens petitioned the Grand Master, Manoel de Vilhena, for some part of the relics of the saint preserved at Manosque. As a result in the following year they received the upper part of his right arm, which was placed in a reliquary in the Eglise de l'Isle. Then the other two parishes of Martigues, Jonquières and Ferrières, petitioned the Grand Master to grant them the same favour. Before the year 1728 was ended, each parish received three of the vertebrae of the saint, which were placed in reliquaries in their respective churches. The reliquary in the church of Jonquières is the most interesting of the three, and has on its base the inscription 'Reversus est in patriam suam'. Unlike Manosque, Martigues was spared the more violent manifestations of the French Revolution, and there in his native town there still rest in peace the last remains of the Blessed Gerard.[3]

APPENDIX

BULL OF POPE PASCHAL II

CONFIRMING THE FOUNDATION OF THE ORDER

Dated 15 *February* 1113

Paschal, Bishop, Servant of the Servants of God, to his venerable son Gerard, founder and Provost of the Hospital in Jerusalem, and to his lawful successors in perpetuity. The request of a devout desire ought to meet with a corresponding fulfilment. In as much as of thine affection thou hast requested, with regard to the Hospital which thou hast founded in the city of Jerusalem, near to the church of the Blessed John Baptist, that it should be supported by the Apostolic See, and fostered by the patronage of the Blessed Apostle Peter. We therefore much pleased

[1] See *Le Bienheureux Gerard,* pp. 48–50. [2] Ibid., p. 50.
[3] Ibid., pp. 60–3.

with the pious earnestness of thine hospitaller work do receive thy petition with our paternal kindness, and do ordain and establish by the authority of the present decree, that that house of God the Hospital, shall now be placed and shall forever remain under the protection of the Apostolic See and the guardianship of the Blessed Peter. All things whatsoever therefore which by thy persevering care and solicitude have been collected for the benefit of the said Hospital, for the support of pilgrims and for the necessities of the poor, whether in the church in Jerusalem, or in the parishes within the limits of other cities, or whatsoever things may have been offered already by faithful men, or for the future may through the grace of God be so offered, or collected by other lawful means, and whatsoever have been or shall be granted to thee or to thy successors, and to the brethren engaged there in the care of pilgrims, by the venerable brethren the Bishops of the churches in Jerusalem, we hereby decree shall be retained by you in peace and undiminished. Moreover as to the tithes of your revenues, which ye collect everywhere at your charge and by your toil, we do hereby ordain and establish that they shall be held and possessed by your Hospital, all opposition on the part of the Bishops or the officials of the Bishops notwithstanding. We also decree as valid all donations, which pious princes have made to the said Hospital from their tribute moneys or other revenues. We ordain furthermore that at thy death no man shall there be appointed by any underhand subtlety or violence to be overseer and Provost of the said institution, but only he whom the professed brethren there have duly elected. Moreover all dignities and possessions which the said Hospital at present holds either beyond or on this side the sea, that is to say in Asia or in Europe, or those which hereafter by God's bounty it shall obtain, we confirm them to thee and to thy successors, who shall be devoting themselves with pious zeal to hospitaller duties, and through you to the said Hospital in perpetuity. We further decree that it shall be lawful for no man whatsoever rashly to disturb the said Hospital, or to carry off its possessions, or to retain those so carried off, or to lessen them, or to harass it with vexatious annoyances. But let all its possessions be preserved intact for the sole use and enjoyment of those for whose maintenance and support they have been granted. As for the Hospitals or Poor Houses in the western parts at Bourg St. Gilles, Asti, Pisa, Bari, Otranto, Tarento and Messina, which are known by the name of Hospitals of Jerusalem, we decree that they shall remain in perpetuity under the rule and disposition of thee and thy successors, as they are at the present day. If therefore in the future any person, whether ecclesiastic or secular, knowing this section of our constitution shall attempt to oppose its provisions, and if after having received a second or third warning he shall not make a suitable satisfaction and restitution, let him be deprived of all his dignities and honours, and let him know that he stands exposed to the judgement of God for the iniquity he has perpetrated, and let him be deprived of the most sacred Body and Blood of our God and Saviour our Lord Jesus Christ, and at the Last Judgement let him undergo the severest punishment. But to all who deal justly towards the said institution, on them be the peace of our Lord Jesus Christ, that they may receive here the rewards of a good action, and before the Judge of all mankind may enjoy the blessings of everlasting peace. Amen. Amen.

(Signed) Paschal, Bishop of the Catholic Church
Richard, Bishop of Albano
Landulf, Archbishop of Benevento
Conan, Bishop of the Church of Praeneste
Anastasius, Cardinal Priest of San Clemente
Gregory, Bishop of Terracina
John, Bishop of Malta
Romoald, Cardinal Deacon of the Roman Church
Gregory, Cardinal Priest of San Crisogono

Given at Benevento by the hand of John, Cardinal of the Holy Roman Church and Librarian, on the 15th day before the Calends of March, in the 6th Indiction, in the year 1113 of the Incarnation of Our Lord, and in the fourteenth year of the Pontificate of our Lord Pope Paschal II.

CHAPTER III

THE MILITARY CHANGES OF RAYMOND DU PUY

THE successor of the Blessed Gerard was a man of a very different type, a true representative of the Church militant in its most aggressive form. Under the recent Bull of Paschal II the Hospitallers now enjoyed the privilege of electing their own superior, and their choice fell upon the famous Raymond du Puy, who in his long and glorious reign of forty years was to change completely the whole character of their Order. The old historians inserted between Gerard and his successor a certain Roger or Broyant Roger, quoting certain charters as their authority. But we know this to be an error from a letter [1] of Raymond du Puy to the Bishops of Christendom thanking them for the alms they had sent to him, in which he speaks of himself as 'Raymond by the grace of God after the death of the Lord Gerard elected servant of Christ's poor', etc. It has been suggested as a possible explanation of the mistake that the name read Broyant Roger, was in reality Raymond Roger, and that this was the full name of Raymond du Puy.[2] According to the usual tradition of the Order, Raymond du Puy was a Burgundian from Dauphiné and belonged to the noble family known at a later date as Du Puy-Montbrun, but there is much to be said for the suggestion that in reality he belonged to the family of Du Puy-Montgueil of Languedoc [3] and Bosio says that he was a near relative of the papal legate Adhémar, Bishop of Puy.[4] However that may be, if he was really 80 years of age at his death he was born about 1080, and may very likely have come out to the Holy Land with the First Crusade. The official Chronicle of the Masters,[5] compiled in the fourteenth century, states

[1] See *Cartulaire-Général,* Vol. I, No. 46.

[2] See *Les Onze Premiers Grand Maîtres, etc.,* of the Viscount Oscar de Poli, in the Annuaire du Conseil Héraldique de France, 1892, p. 64.

[3] Ibid., pp. 59–64. A claim that he belonged to the family of Poggio di Porçari of Lucca cannot be taken seriously, see *Les Hospitaliers en Terre Sainte,* pp. 44, 45.

[4] See Bosio, *Les Vies des Saints de L'Ordre de St. Jean de Jerusalem,* Edition Baudoin, 1631.

[5] The official *Chronicle of the deceased Masters* is printed in Appendix B, at the end of this work.

that he was the first brother of the Order, which presumably means that he was Preceptor of the Hospital, and Gerard's second-in-command.

One of the earliest works of the new Master, as the superior was now beginning to be known, must have been the publication of the first rule of the Order, the simple foundation on which the voluminous statutes and ordinances of later times are built up. For the Blessed Gerard appears never to have drawn up any special rule for his Order, and to have been content for it to live according to that of the Augustinians.[1] But the time had now come when regulations specially applicable to their Order had become necessary, and not long after his entry into office the new Master issued that code of rules, which has been ever since known as the Rule of Raymond du Puy.[2] We do not know the date of publication it is true, but that it must have been published in the early years of his reign is clear from the fact that it does not contain the slightest allusion to the military duties, which the Order was now so soon to assume. The official chronicle states that the Rule and Statutes were confirmed by Eugenius III, who was Pope between 1145 and 1153. The Rule consisted originally of fifteen clauses to which four further clauses were subsequently added, and as we should expect they are based on the Augustinian rule, from which clauses 4, 8, 13 and 17 have been taken in their entirety. The whole code deals only with the simple problems of the primitive monastic institution, the vows and conduct of the brethren, their food, clothing and morality, the collection of alms, and the care of the sick. Its subordinate establishments, the existence of which the Papal Bull of 1113 has already revealed to us, are referred to as houses or obediences, and their superiors as Master Procurator or Prior, whilst the superior of the entire Order is spoken of as the Master, and describes himself as 'Servant of Christ's poor and Warden of the Hospital of Jerusalem', but Master of the Hospital appears to have been the title in ordinary use from now onwards.[3] The Rule shows the brethren of the Order to have been divided into the two classes of monks and serving brothers, as in other religious orders.

Now Raymond du Puy had succeeded the Blessed Gerard at a moment when new ideas concerning the objects permissible to religious orders were coming into vogue in the Holy Land. The conquest of the country had never been quite complete, the occupation of Jerusalem and Tiberias carried with them only the submission of the hill-country and the Jordan Valley with their unprotected towns and villages, and

[1] See *Les Hospitaliers en Terre Sainte*, p. 32.

[2] See Appendix E, at the end of this work.

[3] Certain of the early chroniclers sometimes use the term Grand Master, but that is only in order to distinguish him from the Masters of the subordinate establishments, and is in no sense a formal title such as it afterwards became in the fifteenth century.

THE INSTITUTION OF THE HOSPITALLERS AS A MILITARY ORDER
From the Painting in the Gallery of the Crusades at Versailles

the heavily fortified cities of the sea-coast presented a grave problem to the Crusaders. They only fell gradually one by one with the help of the fleets of the Italian maritime republics, and it was not until the capture of Beyrout and Sidon in 1110 that the sea-coast could be regarded as an integral part of the Latin kingdom. Even then Tyre in the north remained in Moslem hands until 1124, whilst the Egyptian garrison of Ascalon, the gateway into Palestine, was a constant menace to the southern frontier for more than half a century. That historic fortress lay on the flank of the pilgrim route from Jaffa to Jerusalem less than thirty miles away, and the great road along which practically the whole of the pilgrims from Europe had to pass was continually exposed to their raiding parties. How to police that route efficiently so long as Ascalon remained in Egyptian hands was a problem that can never have been entirely absent from the minds of the Kings of Jerusalem.

In 1118 King Baldwin I died on a raid into Egypt, and was buried by the side of his brother Godfrey in the Church of the Holy Sepulchre. He was succeeded by Baldwin du Bourg Count of Edessa. A year after the accession of the new king the problem of how to afford protection to the pilgrims on the road from Jaffa to Jerusalem found a solution that was to have the most far-reaching results upon the future history of the Latin kingdom. In that year a devout Burgundian knight Hugh de Payns [1] and his friend Godfrey de St. Omer a Flemish knight, resolved to devote their lives to the duty of protecting the pilgrims on the Jaffa road. They were soon after joined by six other knights, and this little band of comrades decided to forsake worldly chivalry 'of which human favour and not Jesus Christ was the cause', and to form themselves into a religious community living under the Benedictine rule. The new Order was approved by the Patriarch Germond of Amiens, before whom in the Church of the Holy Sepulchre they took the three solemn vows of chastity, obedience and poverty in order to 'fight with a pure mind for the supreme and true King'. Baldwin II granted to these knightly monks, who now called themselves the 'Poor Fellow Soldiers of Jesus Christ', quarters in a part of the royal palace next to the former Mosque of El-Aksa, generally known as the Temple of Solomon, from which comes their more usual name of Knights of the Temple. By 1127 it had become desirable that the formation of the Order should receive the papal confirmation, and Hugh de Payns proceeded to Europe, where he gained the enthusiastic support of St. Bernard, Abbot of Clairvaux, then at the height of his fame. In the following year the Rule of the Temple drawn up under the inspiration of St. Bernard was approved by the Council of Troyes, and the order was formally taken under the protection of the popes by Honorius II. Such was the origin of the famous Order of

[1] Payns is a fief in Champagne near Troyes.

the Temple of Solomon, the first of the military religious orders and the model on which the other similar orders were based.[1]

It has never been possible to state exactly when the Hospitallers became a military order, and the reason for this is perfectly clear that like so many great historic changes it was a gradual process. Had there been any particular moment at which they ceased to be merely charitable and became military also, an event of such importance could never have been forgotten in the Order. The first definite indication that the Hospitallers had begun to support a military establishment is in the beginning of the year 1126, when a certain Durando is recorded as being the Constable of the Order.[2] Now Constable in the twelfth century is the title of a high military official, whose duties would be the same as those performed in the next and subsequent generations by the Marshal of the Order, one of its great dignitaries. If then in 1126 it was necessary for the Hospitallers to have a Constable, they must already have been supporting a military force, and the process of their conversion into a military order had therefore begun. But the fact that a Constable existed in 1126 does not mean that the office was only created in that year, and from the history of the Holy Land it is possible to reconstruct what was the probable course of events.

The object of the Hospitallers, as we know, was the care of pilgrims, and when Hugh de Payns and Godfrey de St. Omer formed their little society of ' Poor Fellow Soldiers of Jesus Christ ' to protect the pilgrims along the Jaffa road, there must naturally and inevitably have been co-operation between the two fraternities. Whilst the Hospitallers continued to carry out their charitable duties, the Templars undertook the corresponding military duties, and were apparently at first supported by the older Order, and were regarded as its daughter society.[3] But in 1123 the Latin kingdom was suddenly confronted with the gravest danger that it had had to face since the conquest. Joscelin Count of Edessa had been taken prisoner the previous autumn by Balak the Victorious, Emir of Mardin and Aleppo. King Baldwin anxious for the safety of Edessa, the northern bulwark of the Latin States, crossed the Euphrates in the spring of 1123, but in April was himself taken prisoner by Balak at Karkar. Meanwhile the Caliph of Egypt [4] was being strongly urged by Toktagin of Damascus and

[1] For the Knights Templars see the article by Alison Phillips in the *Encyclopaedia Britannica*, 11th Edition, and Addison, *The Knights Templars*, 1851.

[2] See *Cartulaire-Général*, Vol. I, No. 74.

[3] See Porter's *History of the Knights of Malta*, Vol. I, p. 58, also Vertot's *Histoire des Chevaliers de Malthe*, 1726, English Edition, Vol. I, p. 30.

[4] The Caliph was El-Amir, who had ascended the throne as a child of five in 1101. He had recently assassinated his capable Vizier the famous El-Afdal, and replaced him by El-Mamun, a man of very inferior calibre, whom he crucified in 1125; he was himself murdered by the Assassins in 1130.

El-Burski of Mosul to take advantage of the king's absence in the north to invade the Holy Land. Faced with the knowledge that the naval and military preparations of the Egyptians were nearing completion, the sudden news of the disaster to their king far away on the Euphrates spread dismay in Jerusalem. The veteran Constable of the Kingdom, Eustace Garnier,[1] called out the whole available force of the realm to meet the impending danger, and would naturally be supported by the religious orders to the full extent of their power. When therefore we find the Hospitallers maintaining a military establishment only two and a half years later, it is no idle conjecture to assume that they probably began to do so in this crisis of 1123, and that the first step towards militarizing their Order took place in that very year. And moreover it seems equally probable that the Order of St. Lazarus entered upon its military career at the same time by the institution of a class of military brethren, but its military duties were never to assume the same importance as in the Order of St. John, and it always remained primarily a charitable Order. The Egyptians advanced into the Holy Land in May and laid siege to Jaffa by land and sea, but five days later Eustace Garnier fell upon them and drove them in utter rout to Ascalon, whilst their fleet was annihilated by the unexpected arrival of a Venetian squadron. The great crisis was over, but it marks an epoch in the history of the Hospitallers, who had now entered upon their military career, and probably they furnished a contingent the following year for the long and successful siege of Tyre.

The older historians loved to dwell on the story of how Raymond du Puy, the first of the great heroes of their Order, deeply moved by the constant dangers to body and soul in which the Christian population passed their lives, formed the design to add to the duties of his Order the defence of the Christian faith.[2] How it long formed the subject of his earnest meditations and prayers, until at last the divine call came to him, and he summoned his monks together, and proposed that they should take up in defence of their fellow Christians those swords, which they had flung aside when they entered the service of the Hospital. The brethren accepted with alacrity the proposals of their revered Master and it was agreed that whilst they must in no way relinquish their original vows, or relax their care of the sick and the poor, a part of the monks should always be in readiness to take up arms against the attacks of the infidels. The new proposals were placed before the Patriarch of Jerusalem and received his blessing, and

[1] Eustace Garnier, a Flemish knight from Thérouanne, served in the First Crusade under Godfrey de Bouillon. Baldwin I gave him the fiefs of Caesarea in 1101 and Sidon in 1110, thus making him the most powerful baron in the Holy Land. He died on 15 June 1123, a little more than a fortnight after his great victory over the Egyptians.

[2] See Vertot, *Histoire des Chevaliers de Malthe*, Book I.

Raymond du Puy at the head of his monks, all armed and mounted, placed their services at the disposal of King Baldwin II. Such is the story of the great change as it has been handed down to us, but it seems far more probable that it was to the king's representative Eustace Garnier in the year of the Egyptian invasion that the Hospitallers offered their services, rather than to the king himself, who did not return to Jerusalem from northern Syria until two years later.

King Baldwin II died in the year 1131 and was succeeded by his son-in-law Fulk, Count of Anjou, who had married his eldest daughter and heiress the Princess Melisende, and was the grandfather by a first wife of the future King Henry II of England. It is under the new king that we next hear of the military activities of the Hospitallers,[1] and it becomes evident that the Order was now definitely assuming that form, which it was to retain for the next seven hundred years. Fulk of Anjou was a great castle-builder like all his race, and two years after his accession built the castle of Bêtenoble (Beit Nuba), midway between Jaffa and Jerusalem, to protect the pilgrim route from the Egyptian raiders. Then evidently regarding the fortress of Ascalon as too powerful for capture, he decided to control the activities of its garrison by surrounding it with a circle of castles.[2] Already Hugh of St. Abraham, as Hebron was called by the crusaders, had granted to the Hospitallers the village of Beit Jibrin on the main road from Ascalon to Hebron, and he can only have made a grant of this exposed outpost because the Hospitallers were already a military Order, and could be relied upon to defend it. King Fulk decided to build the first of his new castles at Beit Jibrin, which the crusaders wrongly identified with the biblical Beersheba, and confirming the grant of the village to the Hospitallers in 1136,[3] handed over to their safe custody his castle of Jibelin, as it was usually called, a fortress which they held successfully against all comers until Saladin re-conquered Jerusalem. It was a moment of the utmost importance in the history of the Order of St. John, for it marks the beginning of their great and noble career as the defenders of the outposts of Christendom against Islam, a career that terminated only in 1798 when Napoleon Bonaparte deprived them of Malta.

There is a legendary story relating to the garrison of Jibelin, dear to the old historians of the Order, but sternly rejected by the Abbé Vertot as a fable, and likely to excite the mockery of licentious persons,

[1] The Bull of Pope Innocent II dated 1131 used to be quoted as the first clear indication that the Hospitallers were already a military Order, but that bull is now known to be false. See *Les Hospitaliers en Terre Sainte*, p. 45, note 2.

[2] There were three of these castles, Jibelin on the road to Hebron, Ibelin (Yabna) on the road to Jaffa, built in 1141, and Blanche Garde (Tell es-Safiyah), nearly half-way between the two, built in 1142. See Stevenson, *The Crusaders in the East*, pp. 136, 146.

[3] See *Cartulaire-Général*, Vol. I, No. 116.

rather than to conduce to the edification of the serious-minded.[1] There were stationed at Jibelin three knights from Laon in Picardy, all brothers, who were wounded and taken prisoners in a skirmish with the garrison of Ascalon. On recovering from their wounds they were sent to Cairo, where the Caliph of Egypt, presumably El-Hafiz,[2] endeavoured to convert them to the faith of Mahomet. Finding all his efforts in vain, he at last entrusted the task to his daughter the Princess Ismeria, a young lady as learned as she was charming. But far from converting the three knights, their eloquent stories of the beautiful life of the Blessed Virgin Mary, so enchanted the princess that she begged them to let her see an image of Our Lady. Deeply distressed at their inability to do so, the three brothers spent the night in earnest prayer, and suddenly there came to them the sound of angelic voices praising God, and the sweet perfumes of Paradise, and their prison cell was filled with a great light, and in the midst of it the image of Our Lady. And when the princess heard of the miracle, she confessed her belief in Our Lord Jesus Christ, and took away the sacred image. That night the Blessed Virgin Mary appeared to her in a vision, and commanded her to deliver the knights from their captivity, and promised that her name should be changed to Mary, and should be held in high honour for evermore for that deed's sake. And so when day was come she released the knights from their prison, and conducted them on their way, and as they slept by the roadside overcome by fatigue, all four were miraculously transported into Picardy near to the home of the three brothers. As they rose up to go on their way, the princess forgot for a moment her precious image by the side of a spring, and from that day the waters of that spring developed healing properties, and are said to have been a certain cure for all kinds of fevers. And Ismeria was received into her house by the mother of the brethren, and was baptized by the Bishop in the name of Mary, and there she spent the remainder of her life in works of devotion and charity. The three knights built a church close by, at a spot where the holy image had miraculously grown too heavy for the princess, and had slipped from her hands. There the chronicler tells us it was still remaining in the seventeenth century, where it was held in the deepest reverence under the name of Notre Dame de Liesse, and was reputed to have been the cause of many miracles.[3]

[1] See Vertot, *Les Chevaliers de Malthe*, Preface.

[2] El-Hafiz succeeded his cousin El-Amin as Caliph in 1130, and strange to say died a natural death in 1149 at the age of 75. He was the owner of the magic drum that so astonished one of Saladin's soldiers. See Lane-Poole's *Egypt in the Middle Ages*, p. 169.

[3] This legend is related at great length by Boissat de Lixieux, *L'Histoire de l'Ordre de St. Jean de Jerusalem*, Edition Baudoin, 1643, Book I, Chapter II. He even tells us the names of two of the brothers; one was the Seigneur d'Aipe, the second was the Seigneur de Marchois, and the third was landless.

A further example of the new policy of utilizing the military religious orders for the defence of the frontiers was seen a few years later in 1140, when the Templars built their great castle of Safed north of the Sea of Galilee for the defence of the Holy Land on the side of Damascus. Then in 1142 Raymond I, Count of Tripolis,[1] alarmed at the increasing power of Zanki, the great Emir of Mosul and Aleppo, decided to entrust to the Hospitallers the guardianship of his exposed frontier the valley of El-Bukaia, the Eleutherus of classical writers. Zanki, Imad-ed-din, 'the Pillar of the Faith', always known to the Latins by a play upon his name as the Sanguinary, was the most dangerous enemy that they had yet encountered, and the beginner of that Moslem reaction which was to culminate under Saladin in the conquest of Jerusalem. Lord of Mosul he had extended his sway over Aleppo, had carried fire and sword through the Principality of Antioch, and was now attempting to bring Damascus under his rule. In 1138 he had occupied the city of Homs (Emesa),[2] and the previous year had captured from Count Raymond the border castle of Mont Ferrand (Barin) whose garrison had long maintained a reign of terror over the fertile plain of Homs and Hama. The County of Tripolis lay along the sea-coast, separated from the Moslems of Central Syria by the mountain range of Lebanon, through which the main gateway was the valley of the Eleutherus. That gateway was now in 1142 placed in the hands of the Hospitallers, and Count Raymond ceded to them a group of border fortresses Raphanée (Rafaniyah), Mont Ferrand (Barin), Mardabech, Le Crac (Hisn-el-Akrad) and La Bochée (el-Bukaia), with all the lands dependent upon them.[3] Of these castles the most famous is Hisn-el-Akrad, 'the castle of the Kurds', now more usually known as Crac-des-Chevaliers from its long association with the Knights of the Hospital, or by its modern Arabic name Kalat-el-Husn. It speedily became one of their most important possessions in the East, and was successfully held by them until almost the last days of Latin rule in Syria. The Hospitallers had now become the Wardens of the marches of Tripolis, and the importance of their new position is clearly revealed by the treaty that Count Raymond made with them, that he would never make peace with the Moslems without their consent.[4]

Raymond du Puy had now ruled over the Hospital for more than twenty years, and during that period had completely revolutionized

[1] Raymond I succeeded his father Pons, Count of Tripolis, who was killed by the Saracens in 1136, and was himself killed by the Assassins in 1152.

[2] Homs, the classical Emesa, was known to the crusaders as La Chamelle: the Count of Tripolis had fishing rights in the Lake of Homs, which he ceded to the Hospitallers. See *Cartulaire-Général*, Vol. I, No. 144.

[3] Le Crac and La Bochée were ceded to the Hospitallers with the consent of their lord, a certain William du Crac. See *Cartulaire-Général*, Vol. I, No. 144.

[4] See Stevenson, *The Crusaders in the East*, p. 147.

THE CASTLE OF LE CRAC

its character. He had found it an Order of monks, devoted to works of charity, whose principal object was the care of the pilgrims visiting Jerusalem. A capable and far-sighted administrator, inspired by the soldierly ideals of the hard-fighting aristocracy to which he belonged, he had so impressed his own forceful personality upon his monks, had so utilized the course of events and moulded and guided the policy of the Hospitallers, that at the end of twenty years their military and political importance was beginning to outweigh their charitable duties, as it was to do throughout the remainder of their history until recent times. In founding and developing the military side of his Order, Raymond du Puy doubtless influenced by the example of the Templars, adopted a policy that could only result in completely militarizing the Hospitallers. He might have raised and maintained a military force at the cost of the Hospital, as other religious Orders have done from time to time, keeping it distinct from the Order itself. Instead he decided to make his soldiers actual monks of the Order, taking the same three solemn vows, just as the Knights of the Temple were doing, and to meet the changed circumstances an addition was subsequently made to the object for which the Order existed, causing the first clause of the Rule to read : 'Firstly I ordain that all the brethren engaging in the service of the poor *and the defence of the Catholic Faith* shall keep with God's help the three promises that they have made', etc. But he took care at the same time to lay down the guiding principle that his knights must never draw the sword, except when the Standard of the Cross was displayed, either for the defence of the kingdom of Jerusalem, or in the siege of some pagan city.[1] Raymond du Puy is always rightly credited by the historians of the Order with the organization of its three historic classes of knights, chaplains, and serving brothers.[2] But it was no new organization that he gave to his Order, but merely a natural adaptation of the existing organization to meet the new situation. The Hospitallers like other religious orders consisted originally of monks and serving brothers, to these were now added a body of knights, whose esquires were incorporated amongst the latter. And so we have the historic organization of Knights Chaplains and Serving Brothers, the latter sub-divided into the two classes of Serving Brothers-of-Arms, generally known during the twelfth and thirteenth centuries as Serjeants, and Serving Brothers-of-Office.[3]

The Knights of the Hospital and the Temple in the early days of

[1] See *Cartulaire-Général,* Vol. I, No. 527.

[2] See Vertot, *Les Chevaliers de Malthe,* Book I.

[3] See Statutes of the Order, Title II, Para. 2. These distinctions have been retained to the present day, what were formerly known as Serving Brothers-of-Arms, being now known in the Sovereign Order as Donats of Justice, and in the British Order as Commanders or Officers, and the Serving Brothers-of-Office, being known in the Sovereign Order as Donats of Devotion and in the British Order as Serving Brothers.

primitive faith and enthusiasm led a life of the simplest nature. They were for the most part rough unlettered soldiers of noble (i.e. knightly) birth, drawn from all the nations of Europe, but with a large preponderance of Frenchmen. The only object of their existence was the prosecution of the Holy War against the infidels, the enemies of Christ, and they resented a period of peace as an unnatural almost a sacrilegious interference with their sacred duties. They were inspired by a spirit of the fiercest and most merciless fanaticism, the more infidels they could send to hell, the greater their own chances of salvation, death on the battle-field was the certain pledge of Paradise, and they rarely gave or received quarter. The bitter hatred with which they were not unnaturally regarded by the Saracens is exemplified in the attitude of the usually merciful Saladin after the Battle of Hattin, when he ordered the execution of all the Hospitallers and Templars amongst his prisoners. St. Bernard has drawn for us a somewhat idealized contemporary picture of these soldier monks.[1]

'They live together without separate property in one house under one rule, careful to preserve the unity of the spirit in the bond of peace. Never is an idle word or useless deed or immoderate laughter, or a murmur, if it be but whispered, allowed to go unpunished. Draughts and dice they detest. Hunting they hold in abomination, and take no pleasure in the frivolous pastime of hawking. Soothsayers, jesters and story-tellers, ribald songs and stage plays, they eschew as insane follies. They cut close their hair, knowing as the apostle says that "it is a shame for a man to have long hair". They never dress gaily and wash but seldom. Shaggy by reason of their uncombed hair, they are also begrimed with dust, and swarthy from the weight of their armour and the heat of the sun. They strive earnestly to possess strong and swift horses, but not garnished with ornaments or decked with trappings, thinking of battle and victory, not of pomp and show. Such hath God chosen for his own, who vigilantly and faithfully guard the Holy Sepulchre, all armed with the sword, and most learned in the art of war.'

The formation of the military Orders was so thoroughly in keeping with the spirit of the age, that they sprang into immediate and universal popularity. Donations and legacies were showered upon Hospitallers and Templars alike in every country of Europe, and their wealth and importance annually revealed an almost incredible increase in these early years of their existence. Their rapid progress may be said to have culminated in the startling legacy of Alfonso the Fighter, King of Aragon and Navarre, who was so convinced that the hope of Christendom rested upon the valour of these military monks, that dying childless in 1134 he left his two kingdoms to be equally divided between the Hospitallers, the Templars and the Canons of the Holy Sepulchre.[2] It was an impossible legacy, and it was never very likely that his subjects would submit to being partitioned in this manner. The first result was that the two kingdoms separated, after having been united

[1] See Archer and Kingsford, *The Crusades*, p. 174.
[2] See *Cartulaire-Général*, Vol. I, Nos. 95, 106.

THE BLESSED RAYMOND DU PUY

for half a century, Navarre choosing for its king Sancho-Ramirez of its old royal line, whilst Aragon chose Ramiro II, brother of its late King Alfonso, and at that time a monk in the monastery of St. Pons-de-Thomières in Languedoc. For the moment it looked as if the military orders would gain nothing from their strange legacy. However, King Ramiro II, who had married Agnes of Aquitaine under a special papal dispensation, had a daughter Petronilla born to him in 1137. Having lost his wife and feeling that he had done his duty to his country in providing an heiress to the throne, he at once betrothed the infant princess to Raymond-Berenger IV, Count of Barcelona, abdicated and returned to his beloved monastery. The Count of Barcelona, who had made an agreement with the king to marry the Princess Petronilla as soon as she should reach a suitable age, thereupon took possession of her kingdom under the title of Prince of Aragon. But it was clear that his legal claim to the kingdom was a little shaky, since it depended upon the life of the infant princess, who might never live to be his bride. The military orders, which had already abandoned all hope of obtaining anything in Navarre,[1] realized the opportunity that the situation in Aragon presented, and determined to press the Count of Barcelona for the best terms possible in return for recognizing his claim to the throne. Accordingly in 1140 Raymond du Puy decided to make the journey to Spain, in order that he might conduct in person the somewhat delicate negotiations, and the Templars and the Canons of the Holy Sepulchre agreed to place their interests also in his hands.[2]

The personal intervention of Raymond du Puy was crowned with complete success, and Count Raymond-Berenger granted to the revered Master of the Hospitallers concessions of the utmost value, which must have far exceeded the expectations of the three Orders. In a document dated 16 September 1140,[3] Raymond du Puy formally abandoned to the Count of Barcelona the claims of his Order to one-third of the Kingdom of Aragon, a course followed by the other two Orders, on the understanding that if the Count of Barcelona and the young Queen Petronilla died without children, then the original legacy of King Alfonso the Fighter should hold good. In return the Count of Barcelona granted to the three Orders wide privileges in six of the most important towns in Aragon, a tenth part of all the taxes raised throughout the kingdom, and one-fifth part of the plunder to be obtained in the Moorish wars. Moreover, in all places to be recovered from the Moors in the future, the three Orders were to be granted a certain number of military fiefs, whose holders should serve under their standards in all warfare against the infidels. Lastly it was agreed that the King of

[1] See *Les Hospitaliers en Terre Sainte*, p. 48.
[2] Ibid., pp. 48, 49, note 1.
[3] See *Cartulaire-Général*, Vol. I, No. 136.

Aragon should never make peace with the Moors without consulting the Masters of the Hospital and the Temple, and the Patriarch of Jerusalem, as the superior of the Canons of the Holy Sepulchre.[1]

It was probably during his visit to Europe in connection with the legacy of Alfonso of Aragon, that Raymond du Puy took the opportunity of settling with the Holy See the irritating question of the continual disputes and quarrels with the German Hospital in Jerusalem, which had become the cause of considerable scandal.[2] The Hospital of the Virgin Mary had been established in Jerusalem by a rich German pilgrim and his wife in 1127 for the benefit of poor pilgrims from their native land, and had apparently been placed in some way under the general supervision of the Master of the Hospitallers. These German brethren also followed the Augustinian rule, and wore a white mantle with a black cross. They were doubtless already aspiring to complete independence, and were destined in less than a century to develop into the famous Order of Teutonic Knights, the third of the great military religious orders. We have no knowledge of the nature of the dissension that had arisen between the Hospitallers and the German Hospital, beyond the fact that the latter was evidently chafing at its position of subordination. But whatever the particular disputes may have been, the representations of Raymond du Puy were entirely successful, and by two Bulls of Pope Celestine II in 1143 the German Hospital was made directly dependent upon the Master of the Hospitallers, subject to the condition that its Prior and brethren must always be chosen from amongst those able to speak the German tongue.[3] When Raymond du Puy returned to Jerusalem from his visit to Europe he had the satisfaction of knowing that he had settled definitely the two burning questions of the day, the legacy of Alfonso of Aragon and the disputes with the German Hospital, whilst he had had the additional advantage of inspecting personally the administration and organization of the Order in the countries of Southern Europe.

[1] For the story of these negotiations, see Vertot, *Les Chevaliers de Malthe*, Book I, and *Les Hospitaliers en Terre Sainte*, pp. 47, 48. The six towns in Aragon were Saragossa, Huesca, Jaca, Barbastro, and south of the Ebro, Calatayud and Daroca.

[2] See Delaville Le Roulx, *Les Anciens Teutoniques*, 1889, in his *Mélanges sur l'Ordre de St. Jean de Jerusalem*, and also *Les Hospitaliers en Terre Sainte*, p. 49.

[3] See *Cartulaire-Général*, Vol. I, Nos. 154, 155.

CHAPTER IV

EARLY CAMPAIGNS AND THE QUARREL WITH THE BISHOPS

IN the autumn of 1143 the sudden death of Fulk of Anjou, King of Jerusalem, caused consternation throughout the Latin states of Syria. He had ridden out of Acre on the morning of 10 November and whilst chasing a hare, his horse put its foot in a hole and fell to the ground with its rider. Struck on the head by the heavy saddle, the king was carried back to Acre a dying man, and expired three days later. He was buried with his predecessors in the Church of the Holy Sepulchre on the right-hand side near the entrance. The new king Baldwin III was only 13 years of age, and his mother Queen Melisende assumed the regency, appointing her cousin, Manasses de Hiérges, to be Constable of the Kingdom. Fulk of Anjou could scarcely have died at a more unfortunate moment, for the doom of one of the four Latin states was close at hand, and when the blow fell only a child reigned in Jerusalem.

Zanki, the Turkish lord of Northern Mesopotamia, the Sanguinary as the Christians called him, had grown ever stronger and stronger with the passing of the years, and in 1144 realized that at last his hour had come. Raymond of Poitou, Prince of Antioch,[1] had left for Constantinople to do homage to the Roman Emperor. Joscelin II, Count of Edessa,[2] a gallant but luxurious and pleasure-loving prince, lay at his favourite castle of Turbessel (Tell Bashir), south of the Euphrates, and the strong city of Edessa beyond the river, the northern outpost of the Latin states was held by but a slender garrison. Suddenly on 28 November, without the slightest warning Zanki appeared before the doomed city with a powerful force, and pressed the attack with the utmost vigour. Count Joscelin appealed to Queen Melisende for assistance, but on 23 December, long before help could arrive,

[1] Raymond of Poitou was the younger brother of William X, Duke of Aquitaine. He became Prince of Antioch in 1136 by his marriage with its heiress, the young Princess Constance. A man of prodigious strength, he was always known as the Hercules of Antioch.

[2] Joscelin II, Count of Edessa, often called 'the Young' to distinguish him from his father, Count Joscelin the Old, succeeded to the county on the death of his father in 1131. He was taken prisoner in 1150 by the troops of Nur-ed-din. His eyes were put out, and he died in prison in Aleppo nine years later.

Edessa was carried by assault, and two days later the citadel surrendered. Zanki lived up to his name and reputation by massacring the garrison, although he had pledged his honour to spare their lives.

The news of the fall of Edessa created a veritable sensation in Europe, its true significance was fully understood, and men suddenly realized that all they had fought for in the First Crusade was once more endangered. Unless Edessa could be retaken and the old frontier re-established, the security of the Latin states was at an end. The reigning pope, Eugenius III, decided that a fresh crusade had become imperative, and entrusted to the fervid eloquence of St. Bernard the task of once more rousing the nations to arms for the Holy War. The two greatest of the monarchs of Europe responded to the sacred call, Louis VII of France and the Emperor Conrad III. By the summer of 1147 their armies were on the march for Constantinople, following in the footsteps of Godfrey de Bouillon, and the Second Crusade had begun.

The German army crossed the Bosporus in October 1147, some weeks before the arrival of the French, and took the same route across Asia Minor as the First Crusade, with a detached force 15,000 strong under the Emperor's brother Otto, Bishop of Freisingen, moving along the western road through Smyrna and Ephesus. Both forces met with grave disaster. The main army was large, how large we cannot tell from the fantastic stories of the day, but its supply train broke down after passing Dorylaeum, and it found itself quite unable to live upon the country. The Emperor was forced to fall back upon Nicaea, closely pressed by the Turkish light horse, and in a series of disastrous rearguard actions is said to have lost 30,000 men. Meanwhile the Bishop of Freisingen, after successfully crossing the Meander, suffered an overwhelming defeat near Mount Cadmus, south of Laodicea. At Nicaea the Germans found their French allies beginning to arrive, and both sovereigns taking the road followed by the Bishop, advanced to Ephesus, where they spent Christmas. Here the Emperor's health completely broke down, and he returned to Constantinople. The King of France pursuing his march through Laodicea and Cibyra, after narrowly escaping disaster in the passes of Mount Cadmus, on 2 February 1148 reached the port of Attalia, where he embarked with his mounted troops for Antioch, arriving there early in March, after being long delayed by contrary winds. There were no ships for the unfortunate infantry; after waiting some months 8,000 attempted to march by the coast-road to Tarsus, but were cut to pieces by the Turks at the passage of the Eurymedon, and the remainder gradually dispersed. The Emperor Conrad embarked with what was left of his army at Constantinople on 10 March, and sailed for Acre, where he arrived early in April.[1]

[1] For the march of the armies of the Second Crusade, see Oman's *History of the Art of War in the Middle Ages*, Vol. I, pp. 243–8.

Meanwhile in Syria the political situation had entirely changed. Zanki 'the Pillar of the Faith' had been murdered by one of his slaves in September 1146, and his dominions had been divided between his sons. Saif-ed-din Gazi[1] now ruled in Mosul, and in Aleppo his younger brother Nur-ed-din Mahmud, destined before many years far to surpass his father's fame. As soon as Zanki's death was known Count Joscelin attempted to recover Edessa; in November he occupied the city, but failing to take the citadel, was eventually driven off with heavy losses by the arrival of a relieving force under Nur-ed-din. In the south the old understanding between Jerusalem and Damascus for common action against their mutual enemy Zanki was ended by his death, and in 1147 King Baldwin III began hostilities by a raid into the Hauran, thus forcing Anar,[2] the all-powerful vizier of Damascus, to enter into an alliance with the new lord of Aleppo. The real objective of the Second Crusade was the recovery of Edessa and the re-constitution of the northern frontier; on that the whole future of the Latin kingdom depended, as the result was ultimately to show. But now that the fear of Zanki was removed, a second and more attractive objective presented itself in the rich city of Damascus, and the king and barons of Jerusalem brought all the weight of their influence to bear upon the Crusaders to concentrate their forces in the south. In vain the Prince of Antioch and the Count of Edessa impressed upon them that the real strength of the Mohammedan world lay in Mesopotamia. The Emperor at Acre apparently came to the conclusion that the south had no real need for the help of the Crusaders, but allowed himself to be overpersuaded, whilst the King of France at Antioch seems to have been swayed between the two opinions. He remained there until June, when he was forced to come to a decision by the scandalous indiscretions of his gay young Queen Eleanor of Aquitaine, who after the annulment of her marriage was to become the wife of King Henry II of England. Her name was now being coupled in a most unfortunate manner with that of her uncle the Prince of Antioch, and King Louis suddenly left the city by night for Jerusalem carrying off his Queen with him. The die was now cast, the needs of the north were forgotten, and Damascus was to be the objective of the Second Crusade.[3]

A great council of war met at Acre on 24 June, and there were present the Emperor Conrad, the Kings of France and Jerusalem, with the chief feudatories of their crowns, and amongst the latter the

[1] Saif-ed-din Gazi died in 1149, and was succeeded at Mosul by another brother, Kutb-ed-din Maudud, who reigned until 1170.

[2] Muin-ed-din Anar was a mameluke of Toktagin of Damascus; he defended that city against Zanki in 1135, and held Homs against him from 1137 to 1138. After the murder of Mahmud of Damascus in 1139, Anar was all powerful, and as vizier the real ruler of the city until his death in 1149.

[3] The rival policies that confronted the leaders of the Second Crusade are very fully presented in Stevenson, *The Crusaders in the East*, Chapter IV.

Masters of the Hospital and the Temple. Conspicuous by their absence were the great magnates of northern Syria, the Prince of Antioch and the Counts of Edessa and Tripolis; to the Mohammedan world was revealed the fatal weakness that the Latin princes were unable to act in unity, even when the armies of Europe were behind them. Amongst those present at that council of war, there can have been no soldier of greater experience in Oriental warfare than Raymond du Puy, Master of the Hospital; he was now 68 years of age, and had lived half a century in the East. His colleague, Everard des Barres, Master of the Temple, must have been a soldier of little less experience, and during the latter stages of the march through Asia Minor, had acted as chief of the staff to the King of France.[1] For the first time in history we see the Masters of the two great military Orders taking their place amongst the military chiefs of the realm. The strength of the contingents furnished by their respective Orders for this their first great campaign is not on record. But if twenty years later the Hospitallers were able to put in the field a force of 500 knights and 500 Turcopoles[2] they were probably able to furnish at this period between 200 and 300 knights and as many Turcopoles, whilst the Templars would probably have furnished nearly double the number, since we know from James de Vitry that in his day they normally had about 300 knights in their Convent.

The Christian armies concentrated at Tiberias early in July, and towards the latter half of the month advanced to the frontier town of Bélinas (Banias), the junction of the roads from Tyre and Sidon to Damascus. This fortress, which had changed hands four times in eleven years,[3] was now held for the King of Jerusalem by Renier Bruce, an Englishman, upon whom it had been originally conferred in 1129. From Bélinas the army took the main road to Damascus, and crossing the spurs of Ante-Lebanon descended into the plain of Marj Suffar between the Abana and Pharpar, and went into camp at Dariya. It was organized in three divisions: the van consisted of the barons of the Holy Land with the Hospitallers and Templars, under the command of their young King Baldwin III, now 18 years of age, and with him went the Patriarch Fulcher bearing the True Cross; the French

[1] See Oman's *History of the Art of War in the Middle Ages*, Vol. I, p. 247.

[2] This was the strength of their contingent for the expedition to Egypt in 1168. Turcopoles, from the Greek Τυρκοπουλοι, meaning 'Sons of Turks', a name given in Syria to the children of Christian fathers and native mothers. The term is used with a technical military meaning for the native light cavalry, armed and equipped as horse-bowmen like their Turkish opponents.

[3] Bélinas was captured from Buri of Damascus by King Baldwin II in 1129; it was recovered by Ismail of Damascus in 1132, when King Fulk was engaged in hostilities with the Count of Jaffa; it was taken by Zanki from Ismail's brother and successor Mahmud in 1137 and was recaptured by King Fulk in 1140 with the assistance of Damascus, then his ally.

Crusaders formed the centre under their King Louis VII, and the rear-guard was composed of the Germans under the Emperor Conrad. It was by far the most powerful Christian army that had yet been seen in the Holy Land, and properly led should have had no difficulty in conquering Damascus and its dependencies. But unfortunately the army was like a kingdom divided against itself, and friction, jealousy and conflicting ambitions were rampant amongst its leaders. There were the national antagonisms inevitable in so mixed a force, there was an attitude of superiority on the part of the European Crusaders towards their Syrian colleagues that was deeply resented, and there were violent differences of opinion as to how the spoils were to be divided. The barons of the Holy Land considered that any extension of the frontiers should be for the benefit of those who, like themselves, had been bearing the heat and burden of the day, and not for newcomers from Europe. On the other hand the armies of the Second Crusade, like those of the First, included princes anxious to carve out new realms in the East, and the rumour that Theodoric Count of Flanders had already been selected to be the first Christian Prince of Damascus caused the bitterest indignation. There were also some amongst the wiser of the Syrian barons, who doubted the soundness of the new policy in attacking a city, until so recently a valued ally against the Moslems of Mesopotamia and northern Syria. These men knew Anar the all-powerful vizier personally, and to them it must have been clear that he would prefer to surrender his city to Nur-ed-din of Aleppo, rather than to allow it to fall to the Christian, and in that case all Mohammedan Syria would then be united in the hands of Zanki's capable son. The morale of the Christian army was in such a condition, that the slightest reverse or disappointment would almost certainly be sufficient to bring the expedition to failure.[1]

On Saturday, 24 July, the siege of Damascus began, and the Crusaders advancing from Dariya found before them a mass of orchards, gardens and enclosures covering the city on its south-west side. These natural obstacles were vigorously defended by the Saracens foot by foot, but by the evening the Crusaders had fought their way through to the city wall, the young King Baldwin with whom were the Hospitallers and Templars performing prodigies of valour. And then the whole operations came to a standstill, there seemed to be no real driving force behind them, and for the next two days, the 25th and 26th, the Crusaders stood on the defensive behind felled trees. Already reinforcements were pouring into Damascus, and it was reported that a relieving force under Nur-ed-din was on the march. And now all the latent distrust and jealousy, and ambitious rivalry and greed, that animated the Christian host came to a head, whilst Anar the vizier,

[1] For a sound description of the causes of the failure of the Second Crusade, see Stevenson, *The Crusaders in the East*, pp. 160–3.

opening communications with the Syrian barons, warned them that if the siege were pressed he would certainly hand over the city to the Lord of Aleppo. During the 27th the Saracens began to take the offensive, the following night the Christians broke up their camps, and by the morning of the 28th were in full retreat, closely followed by the enemies' light horse. The causes that led to the retreat have never been made clear and can only be inferred from the circumstances; to the people of Damascus it seemed nothing less than a miracle from heaven, and due to the direct intervention of the Almighty. The whole operations were utterly discreditable, a single Mohammedan city had successfully defied the two greatest monarchs of Europe, the Emperor and the King of France, and their prestige was hopelessly compromised in the East. An attempt was made to organize an expedition against Ascalon, but the Syrian barons appear to have refused to co-operate with the Crusaders from Europe, and nothing was done. The Emperor returned to his own land in September, and the King of France after the following Easter. The Second Crusade, which might have accomplished so much, had been nothing but a ghastly failure,[1] and from now onwards the Latin kingdom of Jerusalem began to decline. Everybody appears to have tried to explain the failure by accusing everybody else of treason and treachery, and there were some sufficiently ridiculous to accuse even the Hospitallers and Templars of having sold the Christian cause to the infidel, in spite of the absurdity of bringing such a charge against men who had sacrificed everything in order to devote their lives to the prosecution of the Holy War.

The years that followed the Second Crusade were fraught with disaster for the Latin states of northern Syria. On 29 June 1149 the Prince of Antioch was defeated and slain by the forces of Nur-ed-din in an attempt to raise the siege of the castle of Anab, and it is said that the prince was killed by the hand of Shirkoh, the uncle of Saladin. King Baldwin hurried north to the help of Antioch, and arranged terms of peace with the Lord of Aleppo. On his return to Jerusalem the king determined to complete the plans of his father Fulk of Anjou for encircling Ascalon with a ring of castles. During the winter he erected a strong fortress at Gaza astride its line of communications with Egypt, and following what had become the usual frontier policy handed it over to the Templars to hold. The following summer saw fresh trouble in the north, and in May 1150 the Count of Edessa was defeated and taken prisoner by the troops of Nur-ed-din. It was now obvious that what was left of the unfortunate northern county could no longer be held, and it was decided to evacuate the Latin population,

[1] The one real lasting success of the Second Crusade was the capture of Lisbon from the Moors by a party of English crusaders on their way to the Holy Land.

and to hand over the fortresses to the Roman Emperor of the East. King Baldwin went north in August to superintend the evacuation, accompanied by the Count of Tripolis and a strong detachment of the Hospitallers and Templars. There was heavy fighting with Nur-ed-din on the road from Duluk to Ain Tab and even farther south, but the operation was carried out successfully, and the garrisons and civil population conducted safely to Antioch.

Although the young King Baldwin III had now reached manhood, his mother Queen Melisende remained reluctant to lay down the power that she had wielded as regent during his minority. In this course she was supported by her cousin Manasses d' Hiérges the Constable. An attempt at compromise was made by a partition of the royal domain, the king taking Acre and Tyre, and the queen-mother keeping Jerusalem and Nablus. But at Easter 1152 there was an open breach, and the king determined to put an end to a situation that had become intolerable. He first shut up Manasses d' Hiérges in his castle of Mirabel (Ras el Ain) north-east of Jaffa, forced him to surrender and expelled him from the kingdom. He then seized Nablus and marched on Jerusalem. The queen-mother attempted to hold the capital against her son, but the citizens threw open the gates to their king, and the queen withdrew into the Tower of David, as the citadel of Jerusalem was called. After a short siege Queen Melisende capitulated to her son, who allotted Nablus as her place of residence, and there she lived in retirement until her death ten years later. The troubles in the kingdom of Jerusalem did not escape the notice of the Mohammedan princes. Damascus was fortunately once more an ally, and Nur-ed-din, fully occupied in seizing the remnants of the county of Edessa, but a Turkoman chieftain, Ṭimurtash of Mardin,[1] determined to strike a blow for the city that had once belonged to his grandfather Ortok ibn-Eksek. In a wild cavalry raid he traversed the entire length of Syria, and to the consternation of the citizens suddenly appeared before Jerusalem one evening and camped on the Mount of Olives. But he must have forgotten that the Holy City contained the Convents of the Hospitallers and Templars, and was the headquarters of the most formidable warriors in the East. That night the military monks made a sortie from St. Stephen's Gate, and entering the camp of the raiders, cut the tent ropes, set fire to the tents and drove their occupants in panic-stricken flight along the road to Jericho. There the unhappy Turkomans met a strong force of knights under King Baldwin coming to the assistance of Jerusalem. After suffering heavy losses, what was left of them turned northwards, and galloped wildly away in the direction of Nablus. Here they fell into the hands of the feudal levy,

[1] See Stevenson, *The Crusaders in the East*, p. 171. William of Tyre calls him Hieroquin, and Boissat de Lixieux and the Abbé Vertot speak of two princes called the Jaroquins, no doubt a corruption for Ortokins.

which was concentrating in that area, and the few that escaped were for the most part drowned in crossing the fords of the Jordan.

The increasing weakness of the Egyptian Government, which had long been in a state of hopeless decadence, now once more drew the attention of King Baldwin to the possibilities of capturing Ascalon 'the bride of Syria', from the days of the First Crusade such a thorn in the side of the Latin kingdom. The young Caliph Ez-Zafir cared for nothing but amusement and pleasure, his vizier Ibn-es-Salâr a Kurd was universally detested, and the government showed signs of sinking into chaos.[1] The time seemed ripe for a serious attempt against Ascalon, and in the winter the district was plundered and harried up to the walls of the city. After Christmas King Baldwin called out the feudal levy of his realm, and on 25 January 1153 the long siege of Ascalon began. The advanced base of the besiegers was Jibelin, the castle of the Hospitallers, and by far the largest and most important contingents in the Christian army were the Hospitallers and Templars, the former under their veteran Master Raymond du Puy, now 73 years of age, and the latter commanded by a new Master, Bernard de Tremelaye, who had succeeded Everard des Barres[2] in 1151. A blockading squadron of fifteen galleys held the sea under Gerard of Sidon, the eldest son of old Eustace Garnier the Constable.

Ascalon was what we should now call a first-class fortress, and was always held by a powerful garrison, which was relieved every six months owing to its exposed situation. The governor at this time was the Emir Abbas, a stepson of the vizier Ibn-es-Salâr. The city was shaped somewhat like a crescent; William of Tyre compares it to a bow with the sea-shore as its string. It was situated upon low cliffs overlooking a reef, which constituted a landing-stage, for there was no harbour, and it was surrounded by sand-dunes, with a fertile district of gardens and orchards to the north. Since the occupation of Gaza by the Templars the city had depended for its communications entirely upon the sea, of which the Egyptians had complete command, when they chose to exercise it.[3]

Month after month the siege dragged on, King Baldwin maintaining a close blockade by land and sea. At Easter the army and fleet were heavily reinforced by the pilgrims, who always arrived at that season. The king purchased the pilgrim ships in order to use their timbers for the construction of siege engines, and operations were able to be pressed more vigorously. In April the Emir Abbas left

[1] For the condition of Egypt at this period, see Lane-Poole, *A History of Egypt in the Middle Ages*, pp. 171, 172.

[2] Everard des Barres abdicated his position as Master of the Temple in 1151, and entered the monastery of Clairvaux, where he gave up the remainder of his life to the most rigorous penance and mortification.

[3] For a description of Ascalon, see Conder, *The Latin Kingdom of Jerusalem*, p. 114.

Ascalon for Egypt in order to assume the duties of Vizier, having successfully instigated his son Nasir[1] to murder his predecessor and stepfather Ibn-es-Salâr. The city was now beginning to feel the pressure, and at the end of May Nur-ed-din of Aleppo and Abak of Damascus[2] attempted to create a diversion by attacking Bélinas, doubtless at the request of the Egyptian Government. But the two princes were unable to act in harmony and in consequence withdrew their troops. In June however a relieving force arrived by sea from Egypt, escorted by no less than seventy galleys, and in the face of so powerful a fleet, Gerard of Sidon was compelled to raise the blockade, and the Egyptians landed their troops and stores practically unopposed.

For a moment despair descended upon the Christian camp; it seemed as if all their efforts had been in vain, and that nothing was left but to abandon the siege. Even King Baldwin, gallant young soldier though he was, despaired of success. But old Raymond du Puy, by far the most experienced officer in the army, brought all the weight of his great influence to bear upon the king, and vigorously supported by the Patriarch Fulcher, at last prevailed upon him to continue the siege at all costs. For a time the reinforced garrison of Ascalon assumed the offensive but their continual sallies were beaten back with heavy losses, and in August the Templars were able to push one of the wooden siege towers up to the eastern gate. During the night the Saracens succeeded in setting fire to the tower, but the wind suddenly changed, blowing the flames back upon the city, and the intense heat caused the collapse of a part of the walls, opening a considerable breach. Bernard de Tremelaye, the Master of the Temple, at once led his knights to the assault, without apparently notifying King Baldwin of what had occurred, being doubtless anxious to obtain for his Order the honour of capturing Ascalon. He succeeded in fighting his way to the centre of the city, but was there cut down with forty of his Templars, and the Saracens, driving back the remainder, barricaded the breach. William of Tyre, who like his brother bishops always detested the military orders, is naturally delighted to record the scandalous story that the Master of the Temple actually prevented the entry of reinforcements, lest he should have to share with them the plunder of the fortress, a story too ridiculous to be taken seriously.

[1] Abbas and his son Nasir murdered the Caliph Ez-Zafir in 1154, and fled to the Holy Land. Abbas was slain by the garrison of Montreal (Shaubak) near Petra, on his way to Damascus, and his son was captured by the Templars of Gaza, who sold him to the murdered Caliph's women for 60,000 dinars, and they had him tortured to death. This unsavoury episode was exaggerated to the still further discredit of the Templars by the voice of scandal, which alleged that the miserable Nasir was already a half-convert to Christianity. Lane-Poole's *Egypt in the Middle Ages*, p. 172.

[2] Mujir-ed-din Abak was a grandson of Toktagin of Damascus, and became its nominal ruler in 1139 with the great Anar as his vizier.

The Saracens, encouraged by their success in beating back the assault, made a determined counter-attack upon the Christian camp, only to be heavily repulsed in their turn, and then decided upon obtaining the best terms possible. Conditions of surrender were agreed upon on 19 August and on the 22nd [1] the Christian army entered Ascalon, escorting the garrison and inhabitants with their personal possessions in safety to El Arish, in accordance with the terms. The chief mosque of the captured city was cleansed and consecrated as a Christian cathedral dedicated to St. Paul, and the king conferred the city upon his brother Amaury, Count of Jaffa. So ended the long siege of Ascalon, the greatest Christian success in the Holy Land since the taking of Tyre in 1124. If the capture of Ascalon was due to any one man, it was due to the resolution and determination of Raymond du Puy, the Master of the Hospital, and its capture might well be called the crowning glory of his illustrious old age.

In the year following the fall of Ascalon, the long-pent-up indignation of the bishops against the ever-increasing privileges of the Hospitallers was brought to a head by a new bull of Pope Anastasius IV, confirming all their old privileges and conferring upon them several new ones. Ever since Pope Paschal II had taken the Order under his protection in 1113, and granted it exemption from the payment of tithes, there had been a steady flow of privileges and exemptions from Rome, which had withdrawn the Hospitallers almost entirely from the spiritual control of the bishops. Not only did that constitute a serious blow to their dignity and prestige, but it also affected them financially in a multitude of ways and had gravely diminished the revenues of their sees. For the loss of tithes was a far more important matter than in the countries of Europe, since tithes in the Holy Land had been extended to include a share of the plunder gained in warfare against the infidel, a highly lucrative source of revenue. In 1135 Pope Innocent II had forbidden the bishops to place the churches of the Hospitallers under the Interdict,[2] and in cases of a General

[1] For the dates, see Stevenson, *The Crusaders in the East*, p. 171, note 3.

[2] *Note on the Interdict.*—'Of all the ecclesiastical penalties inflicted by Popes and Bishops upon sinners, that of a General Excommunication or Interdict, though scarce so much as known in the primitive church, was at that time the most frequent. They made use of it against Princes that were refractory to the Church, the thunderbolt was levelled at their dominions; all their subjects were involved in the sentence, and a multitude of innocent persons suffered on account of a single offender. The form and manner of executing this sentence had nothing in it but what was dismal and even terrible. The altars were entirely stripped; the crosses, the shrines for relics, the images and statues of the saints were laid flat upon the ground, and covered all over to signify that it was a time of grief and mourning; the bells ceased to be rung, and were even taken down from the belfreys. No sacrament was administered but baptism to children newly born, and confession and the communion as a viaticum to dying persons. No mass was said in churches but with the doors shut; flesh

Interdict gave them the right to celebrate divine service for themselves.[1] Two years later the same pope gave them the right in time of interdict to be buried with full religious ceremonies, and granted them the privilege of opening the churches once a year, celebrating divine service and making a collection.[2] That constituted a still further blow to the revenues of the Church, for the privilege of celebrating divine service under such conditions meant the receipt by the Order of gifts and offerings, which the secular clergy regarded as properly belonging to themselves, and therefore little better than robbery. Then in 1139 the Pope decreed that those contributing to the funds of the Hospitallers should have one-seventh part of their penitence remitted,[3] and that too very frequently had a definite pecuniary value. Very naturally relations began to be intensely strained between the Bishops and the Hospitallers, and the new buildings now being erected by the latter excited the bitter indignation of the Patriarch Fulcher, because they seemed to him more imposing and magnificent than his own church and palace just opposite. And he alleged moreover that when he preached, the knights made a point of sounding their bells in order to drown his voice. In their anger his clergy did not hesitate to bring the wildest accusations against the Hospitallers, and even went so far as to hang up a bundle of arrows before the shrine of Calvary, declaring that they had been shot at them by the knights [4] when in the performance of their sacred duties. In 1150 Pope Eugenius III began to extend the privileges of the Order to its confratres,[5] who were societies of laymen affiliated to the Order, and sharing in the spiritual benefits derived from its prayers, alms, sufferings and good works. When his successor Pope Anastasius IV by his Bull of 21 October 1154 [6] not only confirmed all the existing privileges of the Hospitallers, but even granted to them the right to have clergy of their own, who should be entirely free from the juris-

was prohibited during the Interdict as much as in Lent; and to such a height was this rigour carried, that people were forbidden to greet one another or be shaved, nor was it permitted to give the tonsure, or cut the hair of the priests and clergy.'—Vertot, *Les Chevaliers de Malthe*, Book I.

[1] See *Cartulaire-Général*, Vol. I, No. 113.

[2] Ibid., Vol. I, No. 122.

[3] Ibid., Vol. I, No. 130.

[4] These arrows are probably those referred to by the Armenian writer, Matthew of Edessa, whose chronicle covers the period 963–1136, and who flourished in the first quarter of the twelfth century. He tells us that there were three arrows shot into the roof of the Holy Sepulchre by the Turkoman chieftain Sukman ibn-Ortok in the days before the First Crusade, and that they had been seen hanging there for a long time afterwards. A later story alleged that the arrows were shot by Saladin at a dove bearing fire from heaven, and became fixed in the roof of the Holy Sepulchre. See *Les Hospitaliers en Terre Sainte*, p. 54, note 2.

[5] See *Cartulaire-Général*, Vol. I, No. 193.

[6] See Appendix to this Chapter.

diction of the bishops, the latter felt that they could stand no more, and that the limits of their endurance had been reached. They determined that one last effort must be made to put an end to this continual encroachment upon their powers and privileges, and decided to proceed in a body to Rome with the Patriarch himself at their head, and to place their views in person before the new Pope Adrian IV, the only Englishman who has ever sat upon the throne of St. Peter.[1]

In the spring of 1155 the Patriarch, in spite of his great age, for he was now nearly one hundred years old, embarked for Italy accompanied by the Archbishops of Tyre and Caesarea and the Bishops of Acre, Sidon, Lydda, Sebaste and Tiberias.[2] Disembarking at Otranto, the Bishops proceeded to Brindisi, but all southern Italy had been in a state of uproar ever since the death of King Roger of Sicily the previous year, and the overland journey to Rome was impossible. Accordingly they re-embarked for Ancona, and thence reached Rome in safety, only to find to their disappointment that the Pope had departed for Ferentino. No doubt the political situation and the siege of Benevento by the forces of the King of Sicily had called him south, but some of the bishops professed to think that his absence was due to the intrigues of the Hospitallers, and that owing to heavy bribery he desired to avoid meeting the Patriarch. Their reception at Ferentino was cold to an extreme degree, and ominous for the mission on which they were engaged. William of Tyre says that they were received like 'adulterine brethren', and as persons unworthy to approach the Pope. Their case against the Hospitallers was duly presented by their advocates, and argued before the papal court. But in reality it was simply a despairing protest against the policy deliberately adopted by the papacy towards the military orders, and had from the first not the slightest chance of success. From the strictly legal standpoint they really had no case at all. To complain that the Hospitallers declined to pay tithes, when they were legally exempt from doing so, was ridiculous. The worst that they could allege was that they had sometimes abused their privileges. That they had occasionally admitted excommunicated persons to divine service, and had administered to them the Last Sacrament, and buried them in their cemeteries. That they had reduced an Interdict to

[1] Nicholas Breakspear was born at Langley near St. Albans sometime before 1100, his father was a priest, a certain Robert of Bath. Educated in Paris he entered the monastery of St. Rufus near Arles, rose to be Abbot, was created Cardinal Bishop of Albano, and elected Pope in 1154, taking the title of Adrian IV.

[2] Under the jurisdiction of the Latin Patriarchs of Jerusalem there were eventually four Archbishops, Tyre, Caesarea, Nazareth and Petra, and nine Bishops: under the Patriarchs of Antioch four Archbishops and seven Bishops. Pope Paschal II in 1113 fixed the River Eleutherus as the boundary between the two Patriarchates. See Conder, *The Latin Kingdom of Jerusalem*, pp. 117, 192, 193.

contempt by ringing their church bells, which was strictly forbidden, that they received alms that should have gone to the parishes, and that they presented their chaplains to livings without first obtaining the consent of the bishops. Out of all the college of cardinals only two could be found to support them, Octavian, Cardinal of St. Cecilia, and John de Morson, Cardinal of St. Sylvester and St. Martin, of whom the latter had been Archdeacon of Tyre when the Patriarch Fulcher was its Archbishop. After numerous interminable discussions it became obvious that it was perfectly useless to press the case further, and in the autumn the Patriarch and his bishops returned to the Holy Land, their mission a complete and utter failure. William of Tyre, as we should expect, in the bitterness of his annoyance does not hesitate to accuse the Pope and the whole college of cardinals of having been bribed by the Hospitallers, stating that only the Cardinals Octavian and John were faithful to their duty.[1] If bribery and corruption really did play any part in this affair, it certainly seems far more probable that two cardinals were bribed by the bishops, rather than that the Pope and practically the entire college were bribed by their rivals.

Two years later the Hospitallers suffered their first military disaster. In 1154 Nur-ed-din of Aleppo suddenly seized Damascus, before the King of Jerusalem could come to its rescue, and the most important step towards the complete union of all Mohammedan Syria had been taken. However, Nur-ed-din desired to avoid any complications in the south, in order that he might have a free hand against the Turkish Sultan of Roum, and concluded a treaty with King Baldwin for two years, undertaking to pay him the same subsidy as his predecessor Abak had paid, namely 8,000 dinars a year.[2] The treaty was renewed at the end of 1156, but when in the following February King Baldwin heard that large droves of horses and herds of camels, cattle and sheep, in reliance upon the recent treaty, were being pastured close to the frontier in the neighbourhood of Bélinas (Banias), the temptation was too much for him. He was very short of money at the time, and the iniquitous doctrine that it was unnecessary to keep faith with an infidel provided sufficient excuse for breaking his pledged word, and so the king at the head of his knights suddenly fell upon

[1] William of Tyre is the chief authority for the quarrel between the Bishops and the Hospitallers, and the mission to Rome. The story is given in full by Vertot, *Les Chevaliers de Malthe*, and in *Les Hospitaliers en Terre Sainte*.

[2] See Stevenson, *The Crusaders in the East*, p. 174. The Saracen dinar, generally known to the Christians as the besant, was the standard coin of the East, in which all large payments were made. It was a gold piece weighing 52–4 grains, and was therefore worth about eight shillings. In the fourteenth century it was largely superseded by the Venitian sequin or ducat, a somewhat heavier coin weighing 54–8 grains. Schlumberger, *Numismatique de l'Orient Latin*.

the unsuspecting herdsmen, killed some, drove away the others and carried off the rich booty to Jerusalem. It was unhappily rarely possible for a Mohammedan to accept the word of a Christian with any certainty that it would be kept, and the Latin states of Syria were always insupportable as neighbours owing to their habits of brigandage in the name of religion.

Humphrey of Toron,[1] Constable of the Kingdom, and now lord of Bélinas by his marriage with the daughter of Renier Bruce the Englishman, realized that Nur-ed-din was not likely to be long in taking his revenge for this abominable act of treachery. He therefore decided to hand over that exposed fortress to the Hospitallers for safe-keeping, agreeing to divide with them the revenues of the town and the villages dependent upon it. In the absence of Raymond du Puy in Europe, his representative Gerard Fitz Hugh, Preceptor of the Hospital, accepted the charge, and sent forward a strong body of knights with a convoy of stores to take over the fortress. But on 24 April as they drew near to Bélinas the Hospitallers were surprised at Ras-el-Ain [2] by Nur-ed-din's brother the Emir Nasir-ed-din, and suffered very heavy losses. Possibly Gerard Fitz Hugh was himself killed in this action, as we do not hear of him again, and a few months later we find Garin de Maulne holding the office of Preceptor.[3] It was the first severe check the Hospitallers had experienced.

His brother's victory determined Nur-ed-din to lay siege to Bélinas, and on 11 May he left Damascus. The town was captured on the 19th, but the castle defended by Humphrey of Toron and such Hospitallers as had escaped from the recent action, offered a vigorous resistance. It was not long before a relieving force under King Baldwin arrived, whereupon Nur-ed-din burnt the town and raised the siege of the castle, but remained in close observation of the Christian army. The king after restoring the defences of Bélinas and reinforcing and revictualling the garrison, started on his return march to Jerusalem, having already sent away his infantry. Nur-ed-din thereupon making a wide detour east of Lake Huleh crossed the Jordan by Jacob's Ford, and striking the road to Tiberias in advance of the Christians laid an ambuscade for them. On 19 June King Baldwin marching carelessly, never thinking that the Saracens might be in front of him, walked into the trap, and suffered an overwhelming defeat, only escaping with extreme difficulty to the Templar castle of

[1] This is Humphrey II, sometimes known as Humphrey the Young to distinguish him from his father, Humphrey the Old, to whom King Baldwin I granted the fief of Toron in 1107, on the death of the original holder, Hugh de St. Omer.

[2] Ras-el-Ain not Ras-el-Ma, see *Les Hospitaliers en Terre Sainte*, p. 53, note 1.

[3] Gerard Fitz Hugh is recorded as holding the office of Preceptor of the Hospital in 1155 and 1157, and Garin de Maulne as holding the same office on 25 January 1158. See *Cartulaire-Général*, Vol. I, Nos. 237, 249 and 263.

Safed. The Order of the Temple was almost annihilated in this disastrous affair, no less than 300 of its knights were slain and 85 of them taken prisoners, including Bertrand de Blanquefort,[1] Master of the Temple, and Odo de St. Amand, one of the most important of his brethren, and Marshal of the Kingdom. Nur-ed-din was now able once more to resume the siege of Bélinas, and again captured the town. But the castle with its garrison of Hospitallers proved far too strong to be taken, and eventually he was compelled to abandon the siege owing to the threatening attitude of the Sultan of Roum on his northern frontier. In October 1157 King Baldwin confirmed to the Hospitallers Humphrey of Toron's grant of half the castles of Bélinas and Chateauneuf (Hunin), on the opposite side of the valley.[2]

In the spring of 1158 Nur-ed-din returned to Damascus and resumed the offensive. Whilst his trusted lieutenant, Shirkoh the Kurd, 'the Lion of the Faith', carried out a raid into the territory of Sidon, he himself conducted operations in the Suwad, the district beyond Jordan known to classical writers as Gaulonitis extending from the Yarmuk to Bélinas, and laid siege to the castle of La Grotte (Hippos). King Baldwin marched north to its relief, and Nur-ed-din advancing to meet him the two armies joined battle on 15 July at the bridge of Sennabra, the wooden bridge across the Jordan just below the Sea of Galilee. The contingents of Hospitallers and Templars present must have been very much weaker than usual after their heavy losses of the previous year, and that of the former in the continued absence of Raymond du Puy was presumably under the command of Garin de Maulne, the new Preceptor. In this battle King Baldwin took an ample revenge for the disasters of the previous year; it was claimed that 6,000 Saracens were left dead on the field of battle, and Nur-ed-din himself only escaped capture owing to the devoted loyalty of his bodyguard. In the following year a truce for two years was concluded.

During the war with Nur-ed-din, Raymond du Puy had been absent from the Holy Land on a long tour of inspection and re-organization in Europe. It was now seventeen years since he had crossed the Mediterranean, and during that period of time there had been an immense extension of the possessions of the Order, especially in France, Spain and England, and some modification in the rudimentary organization of the early years had become imperative. Of the first establishments of the Order in Europe, by far the most important were the Hospitals of Jerusalem at St. Gilles and Messina, where the

[1] Bertrand de Blanquefort was a Frenchman from Guienne, and succeeded Bernard de Tremelaye as Master of the Temple, when the latter was slain in the siege of Ascalon. He was eventually released by Nur-ed-din owing to the intervention of the Emperor Manuel Comnenus.

[2] See *Cartulaire-Général,* Vol. I, No. 258. Conder in his *Latin Kingdom of Jerusalem,* p. 139, identified Chateauneuf with Castle Jacob, built in 1178 to cover Jacob's Ford, but see Lane-Poole's *Saladin,* p. 207, footnote.

pilgrims were assembled for embarkation on the voyage to the Holy Land. The Masters of these establishments, or Priors as they soon began to be called, appear to have been the chief agents of the Order in the administration of its widespread properties beyond the sea, the former for the Western countries, the latter for Southern and Central Europe.[1] When Raymond du Puy visited the Spanish Peninsula in 1140, on the affair of the legacy of Alfonso of Aragon, he appears to have found the administration by the Prior of St. Gilles already unwieldy, and to have introduced a certain limited measure of decentralization. From this period we find separate Priors for conducting the affairs of the Order in Portugal, Navarre and England, apparently however not entirely independent, but still subordinate to the authority of the Prior of St. Gilles.[2] With the rapid expansion of the Order that had since taken place in the West, more especially in the Spanish Peninsula, it was no longer desirable or even possible to keep everything in the hands of the Prior of St. Gilles, and the Venerable Master of the Hospital, advanced though he was in years, determined to visit personally the chief centres of administration, before deciding on what changes to make.

Raymond du Puy must have left the Holy Land for his second visit to Europe early in 1157,[3] and appears to have been accompanied throughout his tour by his future successor, Auger de Balben. Affairs in the Holy Land were left in the hands of Gerard Fitz Hugh, the Preceptor of the Hospital. The Master first visited the establishments of the Order in the Spanish Peninsula, where the conditions so closely resembled those prevailing in the Holy Land, owing to the constant wars against the Moors. In April 1157 he was in Portugal, where King Affonso Henriques, the founder of the kingdom and one of the most valiant heroes of the Moorish wars, confirmed to the Order all its possessions in his realm.[4] There is no record of the presence of Raymond du Puy in Castile, and in the following year the first of the Spanish military orders was founded in that country, the Knights of Calatrava, who followed the Cistercian rule and wore the white mantle with a red cross. We next hear of him in Aragon in the autumn of 1157, when Queen Petronilla and her husband Count Raymond-Berenger of Barcelona conferred upon the Hospitallers many new possessions, including Sigena, soon to be the seat of the most famous

[1] See *Les Hospitaliers en Terre Sainte*, pp. 362, 374, 378.

[2] The Priors of Portugal begin with Arias in 1140, those of Navarre with William de Belmes in 1142, and those of England with a certain Walter in 1143. We know that the Prior of England was at first subordinate to the Prior of St. Gilles, and it is only reasonable to assume that the Priors of Portugal and Navarre were in the same position. See *Cartulaire-Général*, Vol. I, No. 149.

[3] At the beginning of 1157 he was still in the Holy Land, see *Cartulaire-Général*, Vol. I, No. 250.

[4] See *Cartulaire-Général*, Vol. I, No. 255.

of all the houses for the sisters of their Order.[1] The Bishop of Lerida was scarcely less generous in his gifts than his sovereigns.[2] From Aragon the Master of the Hospital proceeded to St. Gilles,[3] the headquarters of the Order in Europe, and there no doubt spent the winter with Guichard Aimery, the Prior, and in consultation with him decided what changes were now desirable in the administration of their Order.

We know nothing of what took place during this visit, but we do find that in this year there was a re-organization of the Order in Spain, and that about this time the Prior of England ceased to be dependent upon the Prior of St. Gilles. It would be scarcely reasonable to suppose that these changes were entirely unconnected with the visit of Raymond du Puy to his chief representative in Europe. In Spain the rôle of the Hospitallers owing to the Moorish wars, was practically identical with their rôle in the Holy Land, and it was not convenient that they should be any longer subordinate to a purely administrative official like the Prior of St. Gilles. So far there had been a Prior of Portugal, who doubtless also conducted the affairs of the Order in Castile, for Portugal and Castile were always closely united in the Order's administrative history, and a Prior of Navarre. It was now decided to withdraw Aragon and Catalonia from the direct control of the Prior of St. Gilles, and to place them under the Castellan of Amposta,[4] who whilst performing the functions of a Prior always retained the title of Castellan, and the first holder of the new dignity was a certain Geoffrey de Brésil.[5] As for England, we hear no more of its being subordinate to the Prior of St. Gilles, and we can only assume that Raymond du Puy decided that it was far too distant to remain any longer under his supervision.

During the first six months of 1158 we know nothing of the movements of the Master of the Hospital, but on 16 July he was at Forez, where a conference was taking place between the Archbishop of Lyons and Count Guy II of Forez, and the latter granted to the Hospitallers freedom from all tolls both by land and by water.[6] From Provence he passed into Italy, where after a delay of no less than eighteen years the reigning Pope Adrian IV had at last consented to confirm the arrangement made in 1140 between the Count of Barcelona and the three Orders concerning the legacy of Alfonso of Aragon.[7] In October

[1] See *Cartulaire-Général*, Vol. I, No. 251.

[2] Ibid., Vol. I, No. 252.

[3] Ibid., Vol. I, No. 253.

[4] Amposta was an important frontier fortress of Aragon, south of the Ebro, near the mouth of that river. It was conferred upon the Order by Count Raymond-Berenger in 1149, subject to certain rights possessed by the Templars, which they renounced in 1153. See *Cartulaire-Général*, Vol. I, Nos. 181, 220.

[5] See *Cartulaire-Général*, Vol. I, Nos. 251, 257.

[6] Ibid., Vol. I, No. 270.

[7] Ibid., Vol. I, No. 267.

1158 we find him at Verona, where he had an interview with the Emperor Frederick Barbarossa, who took the Hospitallers formally under his protection and confirmed to them all their rights and privileges in his dominions.[1] His visit to Europe was now at an end. It had been one long triumphal progress in which Pope and Emperor kings and princes had vied with one another in showing honour to the revered Master of the Hospital, and when Raymond du Puy returned to the Holy Land he could feel that his life's work was at last complete.

The old hero had only a few more months to live and according to the tradition of the Order he died in 1160, over 80 years of age. For forty years he had ruled over the Hospital, and during that period it had grown and prospered to a degree almost inconceivable. From a local charitable society it had developed into one of the greatest and most powerful institutions in Christendom. In the East its influence and wealth were wellnigh incalculable, and in the West from England to Hungary, from Scandinavia to Sicily, all Europe had combined to shower gifts and grants of lands and privileges upon a society which represented so completely the spirit of the age. If the Blessed Gerard was the founder of the Order of St. John, Raymond du Puy was its real maker, and the first and greatest of the military Masters of the Hospital. He was doubtless buried in the Conventual Church in Jerusalem, and shortly after his death was canonized by the Patriarch receiving the title of Blessed like Gerard his predecessor.[2] The greatest of all the heroes of the Order, his end is best described in the eloquent words of the Abbé Vertot,[3] which represent the tradition handed down from the past.

> 'The venerable old man, covered with wounds and worn out with years, had withdrawn himself to the House of the Hospitallers of St. John at Jerusalem. There in a profound retirement, amidst serious reflections, and in continual exercises of piety, this genuine soldier of Jesus Christ prepared himself for the great day that is so terrible, even to the holiest monks. He saw at last that dreadful moment arrive, which decides the fate of an eternity; but if he saw its approaches with a wholesome fear, it was also with the filial confidence of a true Christian, who had exposed his life a thousand times in defence of the Holy Places, where the Author of life Himself vouchsafed to die for the salvation of man. Thus Raymond du Puy ended his days in the arms of his brethren, the first of the military great Masters, much greater by his solid piety and rare valour, than by his dignity, and such as we may compare at the same time to the holiest founders of regular orders, and the greatest generals of that age. The Hospitallers and indeed all the Latin Christians of the East, who had been witnesses of his virtues, anticipating his canonization, revered him as of the number of the Blessed; a title which posterity confirmed to him.'

---

[1] See *Cartulaire-Général*, Vol. I, No. 270.

[2] He never became the object of any popular cult like the Blessed Gerard, but early in the seventeenth century his image could be seen in the Chapel of St. John Baptist in Valetta. See Bosio, *Les Vies des Saints de L'ordre de St. Jean de Jerusalem*, Edition Baudoin, 1631.

[3] See *Les Chevaliers de Malthe*, Book I.

APPENDIX

BULL OF POPE ANASTASIUS IV GRANTING WIDE PRIVILEGES TO THE ORDER

Dated 21st October 1154 [1]

ANASTASIUS, Bishop, Servant of the Servants of God, to his well-beloved son Raymond, Master of the Hospital of the Holy City of Jerusalem, and to his brethren both present and future to be maintained in their order for ever.

It is the pious belief of the Christian religion and faithfully confessed that our Lord and Saviour Jesus Christ, when the richest of all, for our sakes became poor, and to those who thus follow in His Footsteps, His words of consolation promise a certain reward: 'Blessed,' He says, 'are ye poor, for yours is the kingdom of Heaven.' And He who was the father of the fatherless and the refuge of the poor exhorts us in the Gospel to charity and good works, saying: 'Inasmuch as ye have done it unto one of the least of mine, ye have done it unto Me.' Again His approval of such true loving-kindness is plain to us when He says that even a cup of cold water shall receive its reward. We therefore, whose office lays upon us the duty of providing with fatherly care, both for those who are far away and for those who are close at hand, thankfully fold to our heart your devotion, and following the example of our predecessors of blessed memory, Innocent Celestine Lucius Eugenius, Roman pontiffs, take the Hospital and House of the Holy City of Jerusalem under the protection of the Blessed Peter, and strengthen the persons and things thereto belonging within the privilege of the Apostolic See, decreeing that by our command all possessions of whatsoever kind, and all goods for the support of pilgrims and the necessities of the poor, and of the church of Jerusalem or of other churches in parishes and in the territories of cities, reasonably acquired for the said Hospital by your watchful foresight, or given to you by others, or which may hereafter be, by God's grace, granted you by kings or princes, or which by any other just means you shall happen to acquire, and also all things that have been lawfully granted you by our venerable brothers the Patriarchs of the See of Jerusalem, shall always be kept undisturbed and intact in your hands, and the hands of your successors, and of the brethren in charge of the pilgrims.

And if any lands be given to your venerable House by persons of piety and devotion, you shall be at liberty to erect buildings thereon, and to construct churches and cemeteries for the use of all men dwelling there, provided always that there be not in the neighbourhood any abbey or college of religious men, who might be disturbed thereby. But whenever any just title to any land is given you, you shall have power and permission to construct oratories thereon and to make cemeteries for the

[1] The Latin Text of this bull is printed in *Migne. Patr. Lat.*, CLXXXVIII, Col. 1078.

use of the pilgrims only, and of such brethren as shall be of the household there. And for the same reasons we decree that the receivers of your brotherhoods or communities, saving the rights of their lords, shall be under the protection of the Blessed Peter and of ourselves, and shall have peace in all the lands in which they may be. In like manner we ordain that whosoever shall be received into your brotherhood, if it shall happen that the church to which he belongs be prohibited from the celebration of the divine offices, and he chance to die, ecclesiastical burial shall not be denied to him, unless he be excommunicate, or interdicted by name. Moreover if any of your brethren be sent out by you as receivers to such brotherhoods and communities, and come to any city, castle or village, if it chance that place be interdicted from the divine offices, out of reverence for Almighty God, at their auspicious coming the churches shall be opened once in the year, and the excommunicate being excluded, the divine offices shall be celebrated there.

But your resources must be devoted before all things else to the support of the pilgrims and the poor, and should be reserved strictly for these objects: therefore we decree that no man, be he clerk or layman, shall presume to exact from you tithes from the undertakings carried on at your charge. And we command that no bishop shall promulgate sentence of interdict suspension or excommunication in the churches subject to you. And moreover if a general interdict be pronounced in those places, the divine offices shall be celebrated there in their entirety, behind closed doors and without the ringing of bells, excommunicates and persons interdicted by name not being suffered to enter.

And in order that nothing may be wanting to you for the perfect salvation and care of your souls, and that you may the more conveniently provide for the celebration of the sacraments of the church and the divine offices for yourselves and for the poor of Christ, we ordain that you shall have liberty to receive clerks and priests coming to you from all parts, taking care however that you first have such proof of their honesty and of their having been ordained, so far as you can obtain it by means of authentic written or oral testimony, and to retain them with you, both in your chief house and also in your subordinate establishments, provided that if they come from the neighbourhood, you shall make request for them from their own bishops, and that they shall not be answerable to any other profession or order. But if such bishops should refuse to give them up to you, you shall none the less by the authority of the Holy Roman Church have permission to receive and to retain them. And these same clerks shall be subject to no person outside your Chapter, except to the Roman Pontiff. Moreover we give you power to receive free laymen in intercourse, and for the service of the poor of Christ, without contradiction from any man. But once your brethren have taken the vows, and been received in your sacred college, after the making of such profession and the assumption of the religious habit, we forbid any return to secular life. Nor shall any of them after such profession, be at liberty to cast off the cross of our Lord and the habit of your Order, after having once assumed the same, or to transfer himself to any other place, not even to a monastery under pretext of sterner or lighter religious vows, without the knowledge and consent of the brethren, and the permission of the Master for the time being. Nor shall any person, ecclesiastic or secular, have leave to receive or retain them. But consecrations of altars or churches, ordinations of clerks to be promoted to holy orders, and other sacraments of the church shall be carried out by the bishop of the diocese, if he be Catholic, and in favour and communion with the Apostolic See, and will willingly do you such service without any perverseness. Otherwise you shall be at liberty to approach any Catholic priest you shall choose, and he shall have our authority to carry out what you require of him. But if the spiritual head of the place oppose you, no one shall be set up by craft or violence, but only such a man as the brethren, with the fear of God in their hearts, shall elect.

Further we confirm to the said Hospital all the honours or possessions, which it now has or hereafter by God's grace may by reasonable means acquire, on this side of the sea or beyond the sea, in Asia or in Europe, ratifying them to and through you, who are zealously carrying out the work of the Hospital. Therefore let no one, etc., etc.

Given at the Lateran, by the hand of Roland, Cardinal Priest of the Holy Roman Church and Chancellor, on the 12th day before the Calends of November, in the 4th Indiction, in the year 1154 of the Incarnation of Our Lord; and in the 2nd year of the Pontificate of our Lord Pope Anastasius IV.

CHAPTER V

THE CONVENT AND ORGANIZATION OF THE ORDER

WITH the death of the Blessed Raymond du Puy in 1160 the time has arrived when it is necessary to investigate the internal condition and organization of the Hospitallers, if their subsequent history and development are to be fully understood. The death of the first military Master of the Hospital marks a real epoch in the history of the Order of St. John, because it is the end of its formative period, the foundations have been firmly established and a definite organization constructed, out of which the more elaborate system of later days gradually and naturally evolved. The only real revolution that has ever taken place in the Order of St. John came from outside, and was occasioned by the loss of Malta in 1798 when for the first time since the days of the Blessed Raymond du Puy, it ceased to exercise territorial authority. Any inquiry into the condition and organization of the Hospitallers must naturally fall under the following four heads:

A. The Convent and its buildings.
B. The personnel of the Order.
C. Its central organization.
D. The provincial organization.

A. THE CONVENT

The term Convent was used throughout the history of the Order of St. John with a special technical meaning as the Headquarters of the Order, and is clearly defined in the later Statutes[1] in the following words: 'The Convent is the place where the Master, or his Lieutenant, the Church, the Hospital and the Inns or eight Languages are together.' The Convent of the Hospitallers in Jerusalem occupied that area of ground immediately to the south of the Church of the Holy Sepulchre, known since the re-occupation of the city by the Saracens, as the Muristan.[2] It is nearly square, being 160 yards from east to west and

[1] See Statutes of the Order, Title XIX, Para. 2.

[2] Muristan is a word of Persian origin meaning mad-house. There is a tradition that Saladin established a mad-house in the Convent, but it may be only a term of derision, like the name 'rubbish-heap' applied to the Church of the Holy Sepulchre. See Jeffery, *The Holy Sepulchre*, p. 150.

143 yards from north to south, and stands almost in the centre of Jerusalem, being bounded in the Middle Ages on the north by the street of the Palmers, on the south by David Street, on the west by the street of the Patriarch, now Christian Street, and on the east by a line of bazaars and cook-shops for the pilgrims, known as Malcuisinat. When the new Order of Hospitallers obtained possession of this area at the Latin conquest its south-western quarter was occupied by the Greek monastery of St. John Baptist, whose church, now known as

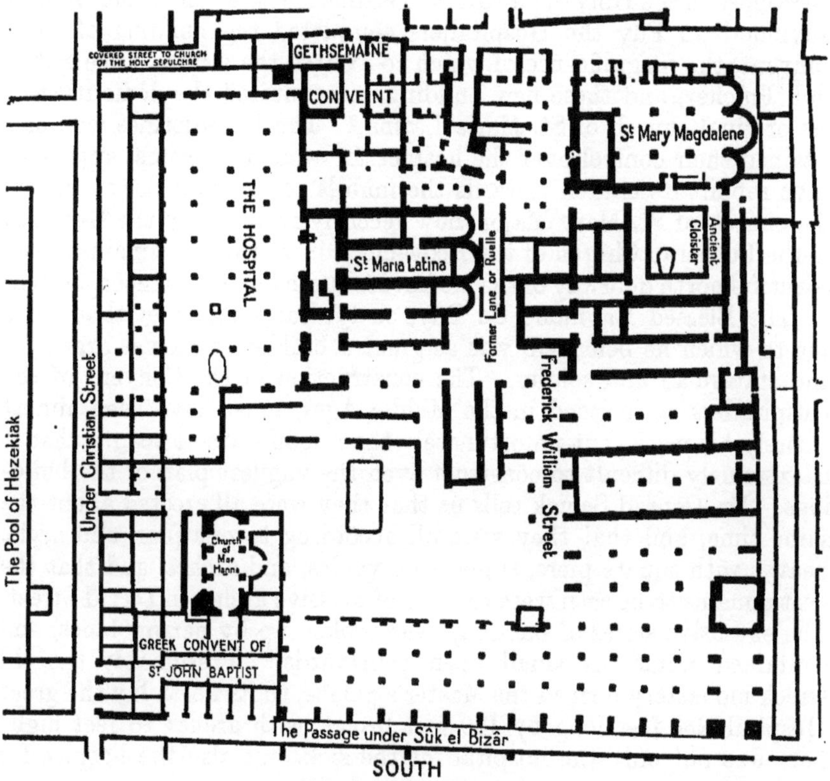

PLAN OF THE MURISTAN

Mar Hanna, was one of the oldest in the Holy City.[1] In the centre and north-western quarter was the Benedictine Abbey of St. Maria Latina with its hospice for male pilgrims, and to the north-east,

[1] Jeffery in *The Holy Sepulchre*, p. 154, speaks of this church as comparatively modern, but see Dr. Conrad Schick, *The Muristan*, p. 48, published in the Palestine Exploration Fund Quarterly Statement, January 1902, whilst a full description of it by Archibald Dickie appeared in the Quarterly Statement, January 1899. The Greek Monastery existed in 614, when the Persians captured Jerusalem, and Antiochus Strategos tells us that after the massacres 4,219 dead bodies were found in it. Bishop Arculf, who visited Jerusalem in 680, also speaks of the Church of St. John Baptist.

separated by a narrow lane, known as the Ruelle, now Prince Frederick William Street, was the Benedictine hospice for women pilgrims, with its church dedicated to St. Mary Magdalene.[1]

The early history of the Convent of the Hospitallers is very obscure, and difficult to unravel. The Greek monks completely disappear, their ancient church becoming the conventual church of the new order, whilst the Benedictines apparently withdrew to the opposite side of the street of the Palmers, and erected a new church and monastery there close to the Holy Sepulchre.[2] During the long rule of the Blessed Raymond du Puy the Hospitallers completed the building of their Convent, the magnificence of which so excited the wrath of the Patriarch Fulcher, and these new buildings necessitated the demolition of the original church of St. Maria Latina.[3] The Benedictines who had retained their control over the hospice for women pilgrims, appear to have rebuilt its church towards the middle of the twelfth century as the church of St. Mary Major, now recently restored by the Germans as the Lutheran Church of the Redeemer,[4] in which the remains of the beautiful north doorway of the medieval church have been incorporated.

The Blessed Raymond du Puy, so typical a figure of that virile age to which he belonged, was as great a builder as he was organizer and statesman and soldier. The construction of the Convent of the Hospitallers as it stood in the Middle Ages, must have been almost entirely his work, but unfortunately the remains are so scanty that it is extremely difficult to construct even the vaguest plan of the buildings. Dr. Conrad Schick tells us that they were all erected about the same time, and that they were all according to one plan and style, heavy, with square piers, supporting vaults, and arches, and that the best remains to be seen were the row of massive arches in David Street. The extensive series of buildings was broken up by narrow lanes, and contained numerous small open courtyards.[5] Presumably the old Greek monastery formed the Master's palace, to its north lay the great Hospital, 230 feet long by 120 feet broad, with arches 18 feet high; here was not only the hospital for the sick, but also the hospice for

[1] The church here identified as the original St. Maria Latina was called by Dr. Conrad Schick St. Mary Major, whilst Jeffery states that the original St. Maria Latina was in the present parvis of the Holy Sepulchre, see page 75 of his work. But see Delaville Le Roulx, *Les Hospitaliers en Terre Sainte*, p. 30.

[2] See *Les Hospitaliers en Terre Sainte*, p. 29.

[3] Ibid., p. 30, but they built no new church as Delaville Le Roulx suggests, apparently unaware of the age of the Byzantine church of Mar Hanna.

[4] Dr. Conrad Schick regarded this church as St. Mary Minor, see *The Muristan*, p. 47. Jeffery regarded this church as replacing his original St. Maria Latina in the twelfth century, and identifies St. Mary Magdalene as St. Mary Minor, placing it to the west of the present Prince Frederick William Street, possibly on the site of the present Gethsemane Convent. See *The Holy Sepulchre*, pp. 120, 121, 152, 154. But see *Les Hospitaliers en Terre Sainte*, pp. 30, 31.

[5] See Dr. Conrad Schick, *The Muristan*, p. 49.

pilgrims visiting the Holy City. The quarters of the knights were in the south-east of the Convent, and the stables for their horses are generally considered to have lain along the line of David Street.[1] Probably the last of the buildings to be erected by the Blessed Raymond du Puy was the great bell-tower of the conventual church, with the pealing of whose bells the Patriarch was so infuriated. In the south-west corner of Mar Hanna there is a triangular-shaped mass of masonry thought to be the base of this bell-tower.[2]

There are in existence several contemporary descriptions of the famous Hospital, written by pilgrims who had visited it, from which a definite idea can be gained of its size and accommodation. A German pilgrim John of Wurzburg, who was in Jerusalem about 1160, the year of Raymond du Puy's death, writes as follows:

> 'Over against the Church of the Holy Sepulchre on the opposite side of the way towards the south is a beautiful church built in honour of John the Baptist, annexed to which is a Hospital, wherein in various rooms is collected together an enormous multitude of sick people, both men and women, who are tended and restored to health daily at very great expense. When I was there I learned that the whole number of these sick people amounted to two thousand, of whom sometimes in the course of one day and night more than fifty are carried out dead, while many other fresh ones keep continually arriving.'[3]

A few years after John of Wurzburg, a certain Theodoric made the pilgrimage to Jerusalem, and in his account of it states:

> 'Here on the south side of the church of the Holy Sepulchre stands the Church and Hospital of John the Baptist, no one can credibly tell another how beautiful its buildings are, how abundantly it is supplied with rooms and beds and other material for the use of the poor and sick people, how rich it is in the means of refreshing the poor, and how devotedly it labours to maintain the needy, unless he has had the opportunity of seeing it with his own eyes. Indeed, we passed through this palace and were unable to discover the number of sick people lying there, but saw that the beds numbered more than one thousand.'[4]

The Hospital was still standing in 1322, when Sir John Mandeville made the pilgrimage to Jerusalem, and he tells us:

> 'Before the Church of the Holy Sepulchre, two hundred paces to the south, is the great Hospital of St. John. In it are 124 pillars of stone, and in the walls of the house, besides the number aforesaid, there are 54 pillars that support the house. From that hospital going towards the east is a very fair church, which is called Our Lady the Great, and after it is another church very near, called Our Lady the Latin.'[5]

But at the present day there is little left to be seen of the once great Convent of the Hospitallers, except the Church of Mar Hanna,

[1] See Dr. Conrad Schick, *The Muristan*, p. 50. [2] Ibid., pp. 48, 51.
[3] See Palestine Pilgrims' Text Society, Vol. V, p. 44.
[4] Ibid., p. 22.
[5] See *Early Travels in Palestine*, Bohn, 1848, p. 168. Dr. Conrad Schick counted the remains of 116 of these pillars: *The Muristan*, p. 50.

the arches in David Street, and the remains of the north door of St. Mary Major in the modern Church of the Redeemer.

B. THE PERSONNEL OF THE ORDER

At its formation the Order of Hospitallers consisted as we know of monks and serving brothers like other religious orders. Its militarization by the Blessed Raymond du Puy brought with it the addition of the military classes of knights and their esquires or attendants, and as the result of this addition, the organization of the brethren, the Religious, finally crystallized in three distinct classes, Knights to do the fighting, Priests or Chaplains to conduct the religious services, and Serving Brothers partly military in attendance on the Knights and generally known at this period as Serjeants, and partly civil for the service of the Hospital and Convent. What was the total number of Religious is not easy to estimate. There were we know 500 knights for the expedition to Egypt in 1168, but here the term probably means heavy cavalry as contrasted with Turcopoles, and would therefore include Serjeants, and many would be lay tenants of the Order, or hired soldiers. To put this number in the field we also know that the Order had to strain its resources to the utmost, and therefore must have stripped its garrisons to the lowest possible figure. Probably the number of Knights and Serjeants in the Convent never exceeded 200, with about 20 Chaplains, but for the Serving Brothers of Office there is nothing to guide us, and most of them were doubtless hired servants rather than Religious, or professed brethren of the Order. Besides the brethren in the Convent there must have been at least as many, probably at one time rather more, serving in the East in the various garrisons and on other duties. As regards the number of Religious in Europe engaged in administrative duties, or novices on probation, or veterans in retirement, we can only say that most probably they largely exceeded the total numbers stationed in the East.

In theory it was a part of the Master's prerogative to sanction the admission of new brethren to the Order, but in practice he necessarily had to delegate authority from time to time to his representatives in European countries, since men could not as a rule be expected to make the journey to the Holy Land without the certainty of being admitted on arrival.[1] But in Spain where the Hospitallers were constantly fighting the Moors, they appear to have had a general authority owing to these special conditions, to receive such new brethren as might be found necessary.[2] The ceremony of reception was the same for all classes of the Order, and took place on a Sunday before the assembled brethren. On the conclusion of the ceremony the superior invested the newly received brother with the mantle of the Order, and

[1] See *Les Hospitaliers en Terre Sainte*, p. 289.
[2] Ibid., p. 291.

he and all the brethren present then embraced him, and gave him the kiss of peace. When not on military service, the life of the brethren in the convent or its establishments in Europe during the early days of the Order, was much the same as monastic life elsewhere under the Augustinian rule, and discipline was maintained by similar penalties. For minor breaches the Septaine or Quarantaine, the former seven days' fasting with bread and water only on Wednesday and Friday, accompanied on those two days by flagellation during the recitation of the psalm 'Deus misereatur nostri'. The Quarantaine was the same as the Septaine, except that it lasted forty days, during which period they took their meals seated on the ground, and received the discipline as flagellation was called, on the bare back.[1] For very trivial offences a brother might be deprived of his wine or beer for a period, and be condemned to drink water only. For serious offences the brother was deprived of his habit, that is expelled from the Order, for a period, but after seeking and obtaining pardon, was restored to the Order and after undergoing Quarantaine received back his habit. For very grave offences such as heresy, false witness, desertion, abominable vice, and cowardice in action, he was deprived of his habit for ever without hope of pardon.[2] A brother who considered himself treated contrary to the statutes could demand in chapter an inquiry by his brethren,[3] from which custom there ultimately developed a special court and procedure known in later history as the Court of Egard.

To understand the three classes of brethren it is necessary to examine them in detail.

The Knights

The knights were the most important and numerous class, almost the whole of the power was in their hands, practically the whole of the great executive and administrative offices were reserved for them, and they so entirely overshadowed the other two classes, that the Order of St. John is generally spoken of in history as if it consisted of knights only, in the Holy Land as Knights Hospitallers, later as Knights of Rhodes, and later still as Knights of Malta, its general name to the present day, even though Malta has been lost for over a century. When the Order became military naturally only knights, or men suitable for knighthood, were admitted in the class of knights, that is to say men belonging to the military aristocracy of Europe, to the class holding land on condition of rendering military service. The ancient custom of the Order as embodied in the later Statutes lays down regarding the qualification :

[1] See *Les Hospitaliers en Terre Sainte*, pp. 320, 321; and Mifsud, *The English Knights Hospitallers in Malta*, p. 171, note 3.

[2] See *Les Hospitaliers en Terre Sainte*, p. 322.

[3] Ibid., pp. 290, 322.

'He must have received the Order of Knighthood from a Catholic Prince qualified to give it, before he can receive the habit, and make his profession; but if he has not, he must receive it from the person that takes his profession, or from some other Knight of the Order; and after this is done, he may be admitted to make his vows, etc.'[1]

A century later when hereditary armorial bearings had come into universal use as the outward sign of membership of the military aristocracy of Christendom, the qualification was defined more closely: 'Such as desire to be admitted Knights, must prove by authentic evidence that they are born of parents noble both by name and arms.'[2] It was the custom amongst many noble families to place their sons, whilst still children, in the houses of the Hospitallers to be brought up by them, and these boys were naturally admitted as knights on reaching full age.[3] Every knight had the right to three horses.

The Chaplains

The Chaplains of the Order were of two classes, those doing duty in the Convent and therefore known as Conventual Chaplains, and those acting as chaplains to provincial establishments, whilst retaining their ordinary benefices, and known at a slightly later date as Priests of Obedience. The former were received into the Order in the same manner as the other brethren, but the latter were enrolled by the Priors and Commanders according to their requirements.[4] At the head of all the chaplains was the Conventual Prior, or Prior of the Church, and in the provincial establishments where there were sufficient chaplains to render it necessary, their head was also styled Prior in the early history of the Order. These ecclesiastical Priors, comparatively humble officials, are very easily confused with the administrative Priors,[5] who are amongst the highest dignitaries in the Order, but they fortunately disappear for the most part in later history.

The Serving-Brothers-of-Arms, or Serjeants [6]

The Serving-Brothers-of-Arms, generally spoken of as Serjeants during the twelfth and thirteenth centuries, were in the early days of the Order far more numerous than in its later history, when they had dwindled to a very small proportion of the whole. It is difficult

[1] See Statutes of the Order, Title II, Para. 2. [2] Ibid., Para. 17.

[3] See *Les Hospitaliers en Terre Sainte*, p. 190.

[4] See Statutes of the Order, Title II, Paras. 29, 31.

[5] See *Les Hospitaliers en Terre Sainte*, p. 294.

[6] Originally in the Middle Ages the heavy cavalry were known collectively as Milites or Knights. Towards the end of the twelfth century a definite distinction had begun to be made between those of noble birth and those not of noble birth, the former only continuing to be styled Milites or Knights, and the latter being styled Servientes or Serjeants. Later still, in the thirteenth century, when the term Knight was applied only to the comparatively small number

during this period to tell what proportion of the Serjeants were professed brethren, and what proportion were merely hired soldiers. In their origin they were probably the esquires of the knights, and could at one time rise into the knightly class, until this was definitely forbidden by statute [1] in the fourteenth century. But long before that they had ceased to be esquires to the knights, as in 1303 we know that each knight was entitled to two esquires, and each Serving-Brother-of-Arms to one esquire,[2] and these esquires were almost certainly not members of the Order. In the days when the class had become very unimportant, the Abbé Vertot still speaks of them as 'Demi-chevaliers',[3] which is perhaps the best definition of them. The only qualifications required of this class were that they should be of respectable parentage, and never have been engaged in any menial or servile employment. In the Holy Land they appear to have served side by side with the knights as heavy cavalry, and each of them was entitled to two horses.[4] Two high offices in the Order were originally reserved for the Serving-Brothers-of-Arms, both of them under the Marshal [5]:

1. The Turcopolier, who commanded the native light cavalry in the pay of the Order.[6]
2. The Master Esquire, who was the remount officer of the Order.

The Serving Brothers of Office

The Serving Brothers of Office were employed in the ordinary domestic duties of the Convent and Hospital, and must always have occupied the same position in the Order as they did in the days of the Abbé Vertot, who speaks of them as, 'employed in the meanest offices of the Convent and Hospital, details of so little consequence, that I do not think it proper to trouble the reader with them'.[7] The statutes describe them simply as 'Servants of Office for common drudgery',[8] the Priors and Commanders had the right to engage such as they needed for their service or business,[9] and they can scarcely be regarded

of distinguished persons solemnly invested with that dignity, those who had not attained to knighthood tended to amalgamate with the class of Serjeants, who were thus raised in status and ultimately regarded as belonging to the class of the lesser nobility, or gentry. See Oman's *Art of War in the Middle Ages*, Vol. I, pp. 371–4.

[1] See Statutes of the Order, Title II, Para. 33.

[2] See Mifsud, *The English Knights Hospitallers in Malta*, p. 81.

[3] See *Les Chevaliers de Malthe*, Book XV, *Traité du Gouvernement*, Article I.

[4] See *Les Hospitaliers en Terre Sainte*, p. 292.

[5] Ibid., pp. 292, 345, 346, 350.

[6] The Turcopolier was placed upon the same footing as the other great dignitaries of the Order in 1304, and the office was after that date reserved for the knights.

[7] See Vertot, *Traité du Gouvernement*, Article I.

[8] See Statutes of the Order, Title II, Para. 2.

[9] Ibid., Title II, Paras. 29, 31.

as properly speaking members of the Order. The great majority can only have been hired servants liable to discharge, and only a very small proportion, doubtless employed in positions of trust, can have been professed brethren of the Order.

The Confratres and Donats [1]

The Confratres were societies of laymen affiliated to the Order, they enjoyed all its spiritual privileges, and had the right of burial in its cemeteries. In return they undertook to do their utmost to protect the interests of the Order, and to make a certain fixed donation on St. John Baptist's Day. They were enrolled by the heads of the houses to which they were affiliated, with the authority of the Master of the Order.

The Donats had to be of knightly birth, they enjoyed the same advantages, and undertook the same liabilities as the Confratres, and in addition were eligible for reception in the Order. They seem to be identical with the holders of corrodies, who in return for a suitable donation, had the right to free lodging in the various establishments of the Order. When they were received, their reception was made the occasion of manifestations of joy on the part of their new brethren, so noisy and turbulent in nature as to amount to a scandal, and in 1270 had to be checked by a special statute. Probably in origin the Donats were knights on crusade, who during their crusade served under the banner of the Hospital, and fought side by side with its brethren, making a donation to the Order in return for the privilege. By 1357 conditions had so entirely changed that it was laid down that the Donats need not be of noble birth, and in the later history of the Order the Confratres and Donats become so confused as to be indistinguishable.[2]

C. THE CENTRAL ORGANIZATION [3]

The Master, and the Conventual Bailiffs

At the head of the Order of Hospitallers was the Master of the Hospital, who did not take the formal title of Grand Master until 1489, when the Order of the Holy Sepulchre was amalgamated with the Order of St. John by Pope Innocent VIII,[4] but he is none the less often spoken of as Grand Master. He had to be a knight, the son of a knight and born of a legitimate marriage, and was elected by a some-

[1] For the Confratres and Donats, see *Les Hospitaliers en Terre Sainte*, p. 297, and Mifsud, *The English Knights Hospitallers in Malta*, pp. 84, 86.

[2] See Statutes of the Order, Title II, Paras. 34, 37.

[3] The central organization of the Order has been very thoroughly investigated by Delaville Le Roulx in *Les Hospitaliers en Terre Sainte*, Book III.

[4] See Eugene Harot, *Essai d'Armorial des Grands Maîtres, etc.* (Rome, 1911), p. 8.

what curious procedure, closely resembling that followed by the Templars. A Chapter-General specially summoned for the purpose elected a Commander of the Chapter, charged with the duty of securing the election of the new Master. He selected three brethren, one from each class, a knight, a priest and a serving-brother-of-arms. These three selected a fourth, the four electors selected a fifth, and so on until the number thirteen had been reached, representing in number Christ and His twelve apostles. These thirteen electors chose the new Master. The system was apparently devised to prevent a multiplicity of candidates, and to render intrigues and canvassing impossible.

The Master was the supreme chief of the Order, he was elected for life, and subject to the statutes and customs of the Order his power was almost absolute. The sole real check upon his power was the Chapter-General, which could only be summoned by his direction. He had the right to nominate a Lieutenant, exercising his powers in his absence, policy, command, discipline and the reception of new brethren were part of his prerogative, and he could nominate the Bailiffs or great officers of the Order, subject to confirmation by the next Chapter-General. His private household was large, suited to the dignity of his high office, and enabling him to take his place amongst the sovereign princes with whom he was continually brought into contact. He was assisted in the performance of his onerous duties by the Convent, and used in this manner the term has in reality the meaning of Council, a word by which it was superseded in later history. In the phrase the Master and Convent, the latter means the Conventual Bailiffs, the great administrative officials at headquarters, who constitute the Master's ordinary chapter,[1] and by whose advice he was necessarily greatly influenced. For such questions as the purchase or sale of property their concurrence would be absolutely essential.[2] These Conventual Bailiffs were originally five in number, to which a sixth, the Drapier, was added in 1221, they were:

1. *The Prior.* Sometimes described as Prior of the Clergy of the Hospital, sometimes as Master of the Clergy and Warden of the Church, sometimes as Conventual Prior, and in later history simply as Prior of the Church. He was head of the Chaplains of the Order, exercising over them the same powers as a Bishop.

2. *The Preceptor.* The senior lay official after the Master, taking his place when absent or sick, and generally acting as his lieutenant. Originally known as the Preceptor of the Hospital, after the loss of Jerusalem he becomes the Grand Preceptor, to distinguish him from the other Preceptors, and soon after begins to be known as the Grand Commander. He exercises a general supervision over the estates and properties of the Order, and is responsible for all consumable supplies.

3. *The Marshal.* Probably known originally as the Constable.

[1] See *Les Hospitaliers en Terre Sainte*, p. 314. [2] Ibid., p. 329.

Responsible for the military administration, and for the supply of arms, remounts, and military equipment and stores.

4. *The Hospitaller.* Sometimes called the Infirmarian. Responsible for the Hospital and its stores, he had a seal of his own, and under him were the doctors and attendants. He appears also to have had an almoner under him, and to have been responsible for the distribution of alms, which were important in Jerusalem.

5. *The Drapier.* Responsible for all clothing, linen, etc., a department which previous to his creation must have come under the Preceptor. In the later history of the Order he became known as the Grand Conservator.

6. *The Treasurer.* Responsible for the money and accounts of the Order.

The Bailiffs of Syria

The Master of the Hospital was assisted in the administration of the estates of the Order in the East by a body of high officials known collectively as the Bailiffs of Syria,[1] and ranking with the Conventual Bailiffs and the Bailiffs d'Outremer, those high administrative officials in Europe, known in later history as Grand Priors. The Bailiffs of Syria consisted of the Preceptors, or Commanders[2] of Acre, Antioch, Armenia, Cyprus, Jaffa, Tripolis and Tyre, and the Castellans of the two great fortresses of Le Crac and Margat, but the Commander of Armenia was originally the Castellan of Selefkeh. For a few years during the thirteenth century there was also a Castellan of Mount Tabor, and prior to the conquests of Saladin there were Preceptors of Bethany, Emmaus, La Liche (Latakieh), Spina and Tiberias, with Castellans of Belvoir (Kaukab-el-Hawa) and Jibelin.

The Chapter-General[3]

Whilst the Master of the Hospital was the supreme executive officer of the Order, wielding almost absolute power, his actions were ultimately subject to the control of the Chapter-General, the supreme legislative authority of the Order. It was summoned at the discretion of the Master, and was composed of the Conventual Bailiffs, the Bailiffs of Syria and the Bailiffs d'Outremer or their representatives, with any other brethren of experience, whose presence the Master might desire, and it sat for ten days. The Chapter-General opened with a religious service, after which the Master indicated briefly the work that lay

[1] See the thirteenth-century 'Judgements and Customs of the Order', Para. 109, published in the *Cartulaire-Général,* Vol. II, No. 2213.

[2] At a later period they were known by the title of Bailiff, but in Cyprus the Bailiff was always known as the Grand Commander of Cyprus.

[3] For details concerning the Chapter-General, see 'Statutes of Alfonso of Portugal', 1205, published in the *Cartulaire-Général,* Vol. II, No. 1193, and the 'Judgements and Customs of the Order', No. 2213.

before it, and one of the senior brethren recalled the good rules and customs of the Order. Then each of the Bailiffs rendered his report and delivered up his insignia of office, first the Conventual Bailiffs, then the Bailiffs of Syria and lastly the Bailiffs from beyond the seas. After this complaints were heard and judgement given, and any proposed new statutes were discussed by a special committee in consultation with the Master, and adopted. The election or re-election of the Bailiffs followed, but only after asking the advice of the Master, and finally the report of the proceedings was read over. Questions were asked and answered, petitions were heard for pardon and restoration to the Order by brethren who had left it, the Master delivered a closing address, the Prior of the Church read the usual prayers and the Chapter-General was at an end.

D. THE PROVINCIAL ORGANIZATION [1]

The Priors, or Bailiffs d'Outremer

The provincial organization of the Hospitallers was built up slowly and gradually to meet the ever-changing requirements necessitated by their continual expansion, which for two centuries never ceased, and it only finally crystallized after the downfall of the Templars and the absorption of their estates in the fourteenth century. As we know,[2] the first agents of the Order in Europe were the Masters of the Hospitals of Jerusalem at St. Gilles and Messina. They were originally known by a variety of names, Masters, Hospitallers, Procurators, Priors, etc., but eventually quite early the title of Prior became general, and extended to all fresh appointments of a similar nature. These Priors, ranking with the other great officers of the Order, are frequently referred to in early days as the Bailiffs d'Outremer, and their position is clearly defined in the later Statutes,[3] where it is laid down, ' Under the name of Bailiff are comprehended the Conventual Bailiffs, the Capitular Bailiffs, the Priors and the Castellan of Amposta '. The term Prior unfortunately presents a certain difficulty owing to its vagueness, and the looseness with which it is used until quite a late period, for it is not only the specific name for these great officials, and sometimes also used in early history to denote the senior ecclesiastic in a Priory, but it is also occasionally used as an alternative to Commander in certain cases, notably in Torphichen in Scotland and Eskilstuna in Sweden, because their Commanders were the senior knights of the Order in their respective countries, and every house of the sisters of the Order was a Priory and its superior a Prioress. It was no doubt owing to the confusion liable to be caused by such loose

[1] The provincial organization of the Order has been very thoroughly investigated by Delaville Le Roulx in *Les Hospitaliers en Terre Sainte*, Book III, Chapter IV, and Book IV.

[2] See page 57. [3] See Statutes of the Order, Title XIX, Para. 6.

terminology that the Priors who were Bailiffs eventually became known as Grand Priors. But officially they were always styled simply 'the Priors of the Order', and whenever that term is used by the historians and statutes and ordinances of the Order, it means those great administrative officials, who were included amongst the Bailiffs and in later times wore the Grand Cross, and does not include those lesser officials whose style varies between Commander and Prior in so distracting and deceptive a manner.

The first Priors of whose existence we have any knowledge were Pons of St. Gilles between 1118 and 1126, and Hubald of Messina in 1136. Their primary duties were naturally the administration of the local Hospitals of Jerusalem in their charge, but when the Order began to accumulate property in Europe, it is evident from subsequent administrative developments that they also became responsible for the collection of the revenue, known from early times as Responsions,[1] and its transmission to the Convent in Jerusalem. With the militarizing of the Order, the Priors became responsible for sending out drafts to the Convent, and from time to time received authority from the Master to receive new brethren into the Order. In the performance of their duties they were assisted by a provincial chapter, which met normally on St. John Baptist's Day. The position of the Prior within his priory resembled that of the Master within the Convent, and he had the same right to name a Lieutenant to act for him in his absence. At his death the Preceptor of the house where he died summoned a meeting of the twelve nearest Preceptors, and they elected a Prior *ad interim*, pending a new appointment by the Master of the Order. But if the Prior died outside the priory, then his Lieutenant nominated the Prior *ad interim*.

The Priories

The original Priory of St. Gilles, comprising practically all Western Europe, suffered a series of dismemberments to meet the changing requirements of the Order. First subordinate Priors were established in Portugal, Navarre and England, perhaps as the result of the Blessed Raymond du Puy's first visit to Europe in 1140, then following on his second visit in 1157 these Priors were made absolutely independent and placed on the same footing as the Prior of St. Gilles, whilst Aragon and Catalonia were detached and formed into a new Priory under the Castellan of Amposta. In Spain there was a further change in 1190, when Castile and Leon were detached from Portugal to form a new priory, and in Ireland a priory was formed in 1202, as the result of the English conquest of that island. St. Gilles was still further dismembered in 1179 when the Priory of France was created, comprising roughly the territory north of the Loire, and again about 1230 when

[1] See *Les Hospitaliers en Terre Sainte*, p. 306.

the Priory of Auvergne came into existence, covering the central massif of the Cevennes and Jura, but corresponding to no geographical or political boundary.[1] There were no further alterations in France until after the loss of the Holy Land, and the sweeping changes caused by the suppression of the Templars, and the absorption of their estates. But there were three subordinate administrative districts that need consideration, because their chiefs are sometimes spoken of as Priors, although not Bailiffs and only comparatively minor officials. In Toulouse the Prior of St. Gilles had from the end of the twelfth century an agent, frequently termed the Prior of Toulouse, and in Burgundy he had an agent termed indifferently the Master Prior or Preceptor of Burgundy; both were destined ultimately to become true Priors, the latter under the title not of Burgundy, but of Champagne. Again in Normandy there was an official from the end of the twelfth century also termed Master Prior or Preceptor, under the Prior of England until Normandy was annexed to France, and then under the Prior of that country, disappearing towards the end of the thirteenth century.[2] The priories formed out of the original Priory of St. Gilles during the occupation of the Holy Land, with the dates of the first known priors, were as follows:

St. Gilles, 1118	Aragon, 1157
Portugal, 1140	France, 1179
Navarre, 1142	Castile, 1190
England, 1145	Ireland, 1202

Auvergne, 1230

When the Hospitallers first established themselves in England is not certainly known; Shingay in Cambridge is said to have been granted to a certain Prior Walter in 1140, but the date is not entirely satisfactory.[3] We reach firmer ground when we come to the charters [4] of Jordan of Bricett, a younger son of Ralph Fitz Brian of Breton origin. Jordan of Bricett gave the Hospitallers an acre of land at Clerkenwell at some unknown date, and then about 1148 granted them five acres of land on which their Priory of Clerkenwell was built, the headquarters of the Order in England. At this time Walter was still Prior, and the complete list of his successors is known to the present day. From England the Hospitallers spread into Scotland, and in 1153 King Malcolm IV confirmed by charter [5] the foundation of their house at Torphichen, whose Preceptor or Commander, often spoken of

[1] See *Les Hospitaliers en Terre Sainte*, p. 371.

[2] Ibid., pp. 365, 366, 370.

[3] Ibid., p. 425, note 2.

[4] See Appendix to this Chapter.

[5] It is generally stated that the Preceptory of Torphichen was founded by King David I, but there is no evidence to that effect. When the rights and privileges of the Order were confirmed in Scotland in 1488, the earliest charter

as the Prior of Scotland, was always under the rule of the Prior of England. In Ireland the Hospitallers first appeared in 1174, when Richard Strongbow, Earl of Pembroke, granted them Kilmainham, where they built their Priory.[1] Their possessions in Ireland increased so rapidly that by 1212 they possessed no less than 142 different properties, and in 1202 they were formed into a separate Priory with a certain Maurice de Prendergast as their Prior.

The early development of the Order in Italy and Central Europe is far more obscure than its development in the West. It is assumed that originally the Prior of Messina held an analogous position to the Prior of St. Gilles,[2] and that the course of events was probably somewhat similar. Apparently about 1169 Italy was detached from the control of the Prior of Messina, and divided up between two new priories: Barletta, at first known as Apulia, in the south, and Lombardy in the north. From the latter three other priories were formed a generation or two later, Venice, Rome and Pisa, whilst a new Priory of Capua was carved out of Barletta. In Central Europe about 1180 we find Priories of Bohemia and Germany; from the former the new Priories of Hungary and Poland were evolved, whilst out of the latter was taken the Priory of Denmark or Dacia, as it is more generally known, a corruption of the Latin form Dania, and comprising the kingdoms of Denmark, Norway and Sweden. Finally at the end of the thirteenth century the Priory of Germany was divided into the two priories of Upper (South) Germany and Lower (North) Germany. It is interesting to notice that the Priory of Bohemia and the Priories of Italy still survive, the latter now reorganized into three, Lombardo-Venetia in the north, Rome in central Italy, and the two Sicilies in the south. The Priories of Italy and Central Europe, during the occupation of the Holy Land, with the dates of the first known Priors, were as follows:

Messina, 1136	Rome, 1215
Barletta, 1169	Hungary, 1217
Lombardy, 1176	Pisa, 1231
Bohemia, 1182	Dacia, 1231
Germany, 1187	Poland, 1252
Venice, 1198	Capua, 1255

The Preceptors or Commanders

The Priors being responsible for the collection of Responsions, naturally had the right to appoint the necessary agents. According

mentioned was that of King Malcolm IV about 1153. See Edward's 'Historical Notes on the Knights Hospitallers in Scotland' in the Scottish Ecclesiological Society's *Transactions*, Aberdeen, 1909.

[1] See Falkiner, 'The Hospital of St. John of Jerusalem in Ireland' in the *Proceedings* of the Royal Irish Academy, Dublin, 1907.

[2] See *Les Hospitaliers en Terre Sainte*, p. 374.

to the Abbé Vertot,[1] the collection of revenue was at first farmed out to laymen, a procedure that proved extravagant owing to their lack of honesty. Then apparently the Priors replaced them by brethren of the Order in whom they had confidence, establishing houses in each district where there was sufficient property to render it necessary. The heads of these houses were at first known by varying names such as Hospitaller, Master, Rector, or even Prior, but very soon received the definite title of Preceptor, a title which gradually changed during the thirteenth century to the well-known form of Commander. As early as 1195 we find Preceptor and Commendator both used in the same charter,[2] and it is difficult to say when the former term had been finally superseded by the latter. For purposes of convenience in this work we use Preceptor down to the time of the Third Crusade, and after that date Commander. But generally speaking, Preceptor is the name of this official in Latin, and Commander is the corresponding title in French and English.[3]

The house of the Preceptor was naturally termed the Preceptory, or later Commandery, and contained the staff necessary for the administration of the properties in his charge. Some of the staff were professed brethren, but the majority were probably laymen. In addition no doubt there might be brethren billeted on the house by the Prior, after a tour of duty in the East. The Preceptors were drawn from all three classes of the Order, but the greater number were generally knights.[4] To be eligible for appointment they had to be of at least three years' standing. Their primary duty was to forward the largest sums of money possible to the Priors, after providing for the cost of their own establishments. They were appointed by the Priors with the assistance of the provincial chapters, and were in theory removable by the same authority, but gradually Priors and Preceptors alike obtained a vested interest in their appointments, which were usually made by seniority, and in practice they eventually became immovable except for definite misconduct.

The Grand Preceptors, or Grand Commanders

When the Blessed Raymond du Puy died in 1160 there were six Priories already in existence, five in the West and Messina, and it

[1] See Vertot, *Traité du Gouvernement*, Article III.

[2] See *Cartulaire-Général*, Vol. I, No. 972. According to Vertot, *Les Chevaliers de Malthe*, Book III, the term Commander was substituted for Preceptor at a Chapter-General held at Caesarea in 1270, as a result of an alteration in the wording of the commission to read 'Commendamus, etc.', an opinion contradicted by Boisgelin, *Ancient and Modern Malta*, Vol. I, p. xxii.

[3] See Delaville Le Roulx, *Les Hospitaliers en Terre Sainte*, p. 303.

[4] But not necessarily so. In 1336 there were 36 Commanderies in England, of these 13 were held by Knights, 7 by Chaplains, and 16 by Serving-Brothers-of-Arms. See Prior Thame's Report in Kemble and Larking, *The Knights Hospitallers in England* (Camden Society).

was evidently thought in the Convent that the multiplicity of Priors tended to weaken the authority of the Master, and that some central authority in Europe was necessary. Accordingly in 1164 it was decided to establish a special Preceptor beyond the seas, corresponding to the Preceptor of the Hospital in the Convent, and like him exercising a general supervision over the estates and properties of the Order. This official was a Bailiff acting as the Lieutenant of the Master in Europe, and by virtue of that fact the superior of the Priors, and known in the Convent as the Grand Preceptor d'Outremer, or to those in Europe as the Grand Preceptor deçà mer.[1] His usual place of residence was in Provence, as we should naturally expect.

But just as it had been found impossible to keep the establishments of the Order in Spain under the control of the Prior of St. Gilles, owing to the Moorish wars, and separate Priories had been created, so it was found impossible to keep the Spanish Priories under a Grand Preceptor residing out of the Peninsula. In 1170 therefore a Grand Preceptor of Spain was created, who appears to have resided in Castile,[2] but the Castellan of Amposta remained under the control of the Grand Preceptor d'Outremer down to 1208. By 1230 the representative of the Master in Spain is known by the title of the 'Grand Preceptor in the five kingdoms of Spain'.

The policy adopted in Spain was tentatively extended to Italy and Germany in 1186, when Grand Preceptors were created for each of these countries. As a result we occasionally find the Grand Preceptor d'Outremer spoken of simply as the Grand Preceptor of France, the two titles being apparently regarded as interchangeable.[3] But the appointment of separate Grand Preceptors for Italy and Germany seems to have been found unnecessary, and from 1200 to 1249 none were appointed. But in the latter year a continuous line of Grand Commanders of Germany begins, exercising control at first only over the Priors of Bohemia, Germany, Dacia and Poland, though the Priors of Dacia declined to recognize their authority for some years. The Priory of Hungary down to 1266 followed the fate of Italy, and until that year remained under the Grand Commander d'Outremer, who was by virtue of his appointment also Grand Commander of Italy.[4]

[1] See *Les Hospitaliers en Terre Sainte*, p. 358.

[2] It was probably due to their residence in Castile that the creation of a Prior of Castile and Leon was not found necessary until 1190, forty years after the institution of Priors in the other kingdoms of the Peninsula. See *Les Hospitaliers en Terre Sainte*, p. 382.

[3] There was never a Grand Preceptor d'Outremer and a Grand Preceptor of France at the same time, and no other inference seems possible.

[4] Raimbaud de Voczon is described as Grand Commander d'Outremer in 1247 and 1248, and Grand Commander of Italy in 1250, 1252 and 1254; it is presumed that he combined the two offices, since there is no record of anyone else holding the appointment of Grand Commander d'Outremer until 1259.

But when the Priory of Germany split at the end of the thirteenth century into the two Priories of Upper and Lower Germany, the Grand Commander of Germany began to be regarded simply as the Grand Prior of the two German priories, and the Priors of Bohemia, Hungary, Dacia and Poland gradually asserted their independence and declined to recognize his authority.

The system of exercising control over the Priors through Grand Commanders was changed with that complete reorganization of the constitution, rendered necessary by the absorption of the Templar estates, and which transferred what had been in theory a cosmopolitan Order into a federation of national societies.

APPENDIX

DOCUMENTS RELATING TO THE FOUNDATION OF THE PRIORY AT CLERKENWELL

1. Date about 1144–8

Jordan of Bricett's grant of land to Robert the Chaplain

Be it known to all the faithful of Holy Church, as well present as to come, that I Jordan son of Ralph son of Brian, have given to God and to St. Mary and to all the saints and to Robert the Chaplain, in alms for me and my wife, and for the souls of my father and mother and of my brother and of all my relatives and friends, living and deceased, fourteen acres of land in the field lying next Clerken-well, free and quit of all things, so to wit that the people of the Hospital cannot claim anything in the said acres, nor make any challenge thereupon, but they shall be entirely separate from the acre which I have given to the said Hospitallers in the same field for the thirteen pence, which I had promised I would give the Hospital of Jerusalem in alms every year. I have also given to the same Robert the place and site to make a mill, saving and reserving to myself my own multure, and the first place of the mill. These things I have granted to Robert to enable him to erect upon the said acres a house of prayer, and therein to arrange for such religious services as he pleases, for praise and prayer to God. These are witnesses :—Alan, Bernard and Hugh, Canons.

2. Date about 1148

Settlement of the dispute with the Nuns of Clerkenwell

To all the Sons of God's Holy Church, as well prelates as its humblest members, present and to come, Walter servant of the Hospital of Jerusalem and Prior of the Brethren who are in England, sendeth greeting. Know ye that we have utterly disclaimed and renounced the dispute and controversy in which we engaged with respect to the ten acres between our house and the monastery of the Nuns of Clerkenwell. And therefore we have determined and do will, and by witness of this present writing do establish, that the aforenamed monastery shall for ever have and possess the aforesaid acres, free and quit of all manner of claim and disturbance from the house of us and our successors. And for the stopping of this strife Jordan, lord of the soil of both houses, has given to our house five acres to hold for ever. And this composition has been made in the presence of Ralph the Dean; William, Richard and Richard the Archdeacons; Master Aubrey; Hugh; Robert de Auco, and the other Canons, and of the whole Chapter of the Church of St. Paul, London. Witness also Jordan, the lord of the said soil.

Endorsement: Deed of Walter, Prior of the Hospital of Jerusalem, concerning ten acres at Clerkenwell.

3. Date about 1148

Confirmation of the above settlement by the Prior of St. Gilles

To all the Sons of God's Holy Church, as well prelates as its humblest members, present and to come, Arnold servant of the Hospital of Jerusalem and Prior of St. Gilles, sendeth greeting in the Lord. We have been informed that there has been a dispute and controversy with regard to ten acres of land between our house and the monastery of the Nuns of Clerkenwell. And to put an end to the dispute, Jordan lord of the soil of both houses, has given to our London house five acres to hold for ever. And accordingly Walter, Prior of the Brethren who are in England, guided by true religion and devotion, with the advice of religious men and of the brethren and sisters, utterly renounced and disclaimed this controversy. Now we ratify and approve this composition and concord, and by witness of this present writing do confirm it, to wit, that the aforenamed monastery, and the nuns there serving God shall for ever have and possess the aforenamed ten acres, free and quit from all manner of claim annoyance and disturbance from the house of us and our successors of the Hospital of Jerusalem. These are witnesses etc.

Endorsement: Grant of Arnold: Clerkenwell.

NOTE

The above three documents are published in Latin in the *Cartulaire-Général*, Vol. I, Nos. 2, 148, 149. According to an entry in Dugdale's *Monasticon*, Jordan of Bricett founded the Hospital of Jerusalem at Clerkenwell in 1100, on ten acres of land purchased from the nuns there. The date is an error since the Nunnery of St. Mary at Clerkenwell was only founded in 1144, and the Hospital was apparently founded on five acres granted to it by Jordan to terminate a dispute concerning ten acres belonging to the nuns. The first document refers to a previous grant of one acre to the Hospitallers, and probably should be dated between 1144 and 1148, since the Hospital was founded after the Nunnery. The other two documents can be dated approximately 1148, since six out of the seven witnesses to the first of them are found signing a St. Paul's Charter of that year.

Jordan of Bricett was the younger son of Ralph Fitz Brian, belonging to a Breton family which had settled in England after the Norman Conquest, and received a grant of lands in Essex, as well as Bricett in Suffolk. He married an heiress Muriel de Munteni, by whom he had four daughters, and died some time after 1160, his widow afterwards marrying Maurice of Great Totham in Essex. See Round, *The Foundation of the Priories of St. Mary and St. John, Clerkenwell*, 1899, communicated to the Society of Antiquaries.

CHAPTER VI

GILBERT D'ASSAILLY AND THE STRUGGLE FOR EGYPT

THE Blessed Raymond du Puy was succeeded in the Mastership of the Hospital by Auger de Balben, who was evidently high in his confidence since he had been selected by his venerable chief to accompany him on his recent tour of inspection of the houses of the Order in Southern Europe. Singularly little is known, however, concerning the new Master, and all that the official chronicle can tell us is that he was a man overflowing with piety and strictly upright. The older historians call him Balben, and state that he came from Dauphiné and was born at Risoul, and there really is not the slightest reason for throwing any doubt on this statement. Everything indicates that he probably belonged to the family of De Balbins of Dauphiné, whose arms were attributed to him at a later date.[1]

Auger de Balben entered upon office during one of those rare periods of comparative peace in the Holy Land, for a truce still reigned between Jerusalem and Damascus. But it was a period of bitter strife within the Catholic Church, which was once more compelled to endure the scandal of two rival popes. Adrian IV the Englishman had died in 1159, and Alexander III had been duly and canonically elected to fill the vacant throne of St. Peter by an immense majority of cardinals. But the election was not congenial to the Emperor Frederick Barbarossa, and encouraged by his attitude Cardinal Octavian, who had supported the Bishops of the Holy Land against the Hospitallers in 1155, was proclaimed pope by two of his colleagues under the title of Victor IV. The arrival of a papal legate in the Holy Land, made it necessary for the Patriarch and his bishops to decide which of the two popes they should recognize. They met in the Synod of Nazareth, where opinions were found to be divided, for many of the bishops remembered with gratitude how the anti-pope had supported them against the Hospitallers only five years before. King Baldwin suggested as a compromise that they should refuse to recognize either

[1] See *Les Onze Premiers Grand Maîtres, etc.*, pp. 67, 68. Delaville Le Roulx was apparently not aware of the existence of this family, when he wrote p. 62 of *Les Hospitaliers en Terre Sainte.*

pope until a general council of the Church should have adjudicated upon their respective claims. The compromise would probably have been accepted had it not been for the vigorous attitude adopted by the Archbishop of Tyre, supported by the Master Auger de Balben. They represented that there was no question as to whether Alexander III had been canonically elected, and that his so-called rival was simply an unscrupulous and ambitious cardinal, using the political situation for his own selfish purposes. As a result Alexander III was accepted as the rightful pope, and the anti-pope with the two cardinals supporting him were solemnly excommunicated by the Patriarch. There can be little doubt but that the Hospitallers played a prominent part in obtaining this decision against their old enemy the Cardinal Octavian, a decision in which the interests of their Order were deeply involved.[1]

In spite of the truce between King Baldwin and Nur-ed-din in the south, the usual border warfare never ceased between Prince Reginald of Antioch [2] and the governor of Aleppo, and the year 1160 ended in a serious Christian reverse. In July the governor of the frontier fortress of Harenc (Harim), Joscelin III, titular Count of Edessa, was taken prisoner, and flung into the very same dungeon in which his unhappy father had lingered so many years. Then in November the Prince of Antioch himself was captured, as he was returning from a raid on Marash, gorged with plunder. King Baldwin at once hurried north to the assistance of the Princess Constance, and succeeded in arranging there also a truce for two years with Nur-ed-din, who desired to be free to make the pilgrimage to Mecca. The king remained in Antioch throughout 1161, being engaged in negotiations for the marriage of the young Princess Maria with the Emperor Manuel, and towards the end of the year was taken ill. Early in 1162 he moved south, and died at Beyrout on 10 February only 32 years of age. He was a gallant young prince, and a worthy representative of the great house of Anjou. The esteem in which he was held is best exemplified by the chivalrous remark of his enemy Nur-ed-din, when urged to take advantage of his death and to break the truce, 'We ought to pity this people's righteous sorrow, for they have lost a prince whose like is not now left in the world.' [3]

King Baldwin was childless, and his natural heir was his younger brother Amaury, Count of Jaffa and Ascalon, now 26 years of age:

[1] The story is told at some length by Vertot, *Les Chevaliers de Malthe*, Book II.

[2] Reginald de Chatillon was a French knight, who came out to the Holy Land with the Second Crusade, and entered the service of King Baldwin III. In 1153 he married the widowed Princess Constance, and so became Prince of Antioch. He remained in prison in Aleppo for no less than fifteen years, and never returned to Antioch, since his wife the Princess Constance was dead, and his stepson Bohemond III had succeeded to the principality.

[3] See Archer and Kingsford, *The Crusades*, p. 231.

He had already proved his fitness for the throne, and had shown that he was likely to make a strong and capable king. No doubt for that very reason a powerful party amongst the great barons, by nature resentful of all authority, began to talk of the crown being elective and not hereditary. There was a moment when the situation seemed drifting inevitably towards civil war, and we are told that it was largely due to the personal influence of Auger de Balben that this calamity was avoided. He pointed out that their choice lay between accepting the rule of Prince Amaury, or ultimate conquest by Nur-ed-din, and gradually brought the opposing barons into a more reasonable frame of mind.[1] The Master of the Hospital died within a short time of the coronation of the new king. During his

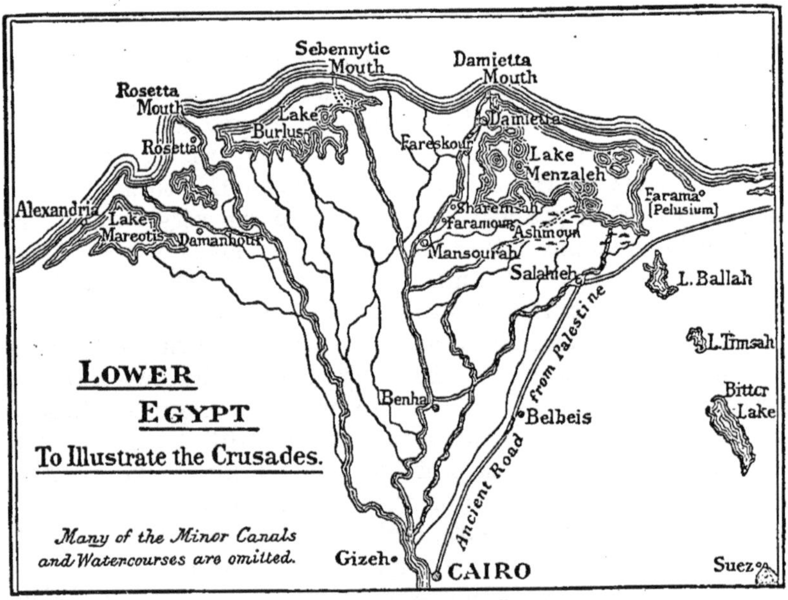

MAP OF LOWER EGYPT

two years of office he had worthily maintained the prestige of his Order, and had twice been able to make his influence felt for good upon the government of the Holy Land.

The new Master of the Hospital, Arnold de Comps, was an elderly man, and ruled only a few months, dying before the year was out. He is said to have been a Frenchman from Dauphiné, and is generally assumed to have belonged to the same family as the later Master of his name. Probably he is identical with the Arnold Messager who was Prior of St. Gilles from 1143 to 1150, but beyond that we really know nothing about him. The official chronicle only states that he was very aged and that during the short time that he lived, he pro-

[1] See Vertot, *Les Chevaliers de Malthe*, Book II.

cured many advantages for the Religion, and served the sick with great kindness.[1] He was succeeded by one who was destined to play a great part for a few years in the history of his Order, and of the Holy Land.

Gilbert d'Assailly is one of the few Masters of the Hospital who can be claimed as English. But in reality as little is known of his origin, as in the case of most of the early Masters. The claim that he was English, or rather Anglo-Norman, is merely based on a conjecture of the Abbé Vertot, due to the fact that England was the country to which he turned in his retirement. He most probably originated from the family of Assalit, a name well known in Languedoc.[2] At the time of his election towards the end of 1162, he had been one of the Bailiffs of Syria for at least sixteen years, having been appointed Preceptor of Tyre in 1146.[3]

With the accession of King Amaury to the throne of Jerusalem, the state policy of the Latin kingdom underwent a complete change, partly no doubt owing to the force of circumstances, but largely influenced by the new king's previous career as Count of Jaffa and Ascalon, and guardian of the southern frontier. From the earliest days of the Latin conquest the eyes of the Kings of Jerusalem had always been turned anxiously northward. They fully realized that the now decadent Caliphs of Egypt could be treated with contempt, and that the strength of the Moslem world lay in Mesopotamia. Nearly all their more important campaigns had been undertaken, not for the extension of their kingdom, but in support of the Counts of Edessa and the Princes of Antioch. But for the nine years preceding his accession to the throne King Amaury's entire attention had been riveted upon Egypt. Twice he had conducted raids into that country,[4] and he must have been well acquainted with the weakness and corruption of its government, which had at last consented to pay an annual subsidy of 33,000 dinars to the Kings of Jerusalem.[5] Its Caliphs for more than a century had been mere puppets in the hands of their viziers, who were accustomed to rise to power by the assassination of their rivals. The ruling classes, mostly of foreign extraction and differing in their religious views from the bulk of the population, who followed the Sunnite creed, were rotten to the core, whilst the people themselves were amongst the most unwarlike races known to history. In the words of Nur-ed-din's famous general, Asad-ed-din Shirkoh, 'Egypt was a country without men, and with a precarious and contemptible

[1] The chronicle of the deceased Masters confuses the personalities of Arnold de Comps and Gilbert d'Assailly but the necessary correction is obvious. See Appendix B at the end.

[2] See *Les Onze Premiers Grand Maîtres, etc.*, p. 69.

[3] See *Cartulaire-Général*, Vol. I, No. 166.

[4] See Stevenson, *The Crusaders in the East*, p. 186, note 1.

[5] See Lane-Poole's *Egypt in the Middle Ages*, p. 177, note 1.

government'.[1] It was obvious to King Amaury that the country was ripe for conquest, and its immense wealth famous throughout the East constituted an almost irresistible temptation. In the new policy that he adopted the king was enthusiastically seconded by the Hospitallers, who from their fortress of Jibelin had so long shared in the guardianship of the southern frontier, and Gilbert d'Assailly was amongst his warmest supporters. But neither the king nor the Master of the Hospital appear to have sufficiently appreciated the fact, that if they massed their forces against Egypt, their resources would be insufficient to hold Nur-ed-din in check in the north, and the Lord of Mesopotamia and Moslem Syria was scarcely likely to remain a disinterested spectator of events.

In 1163 the condition of Egypt showed signs of passing from bad to worse. Two years earlier the vizier, Talai-ibn-Ruzzik, who had ruled the land with a rod of iron since the flight of his predecessor Abbas, was murdered at the instigation of the women of the Caliph's harem. His son and successor in his turn was slain by Shawar, the Arab governor of Upper Egypt, who succeeded to his blood-stained office. Seven months later there was a fresh *coup d'état*, and the Emir Dirgham seized the reins of government, but failed to secure the person of his rival and Shawar fled to the court of Nur-ed-din. Failing to realize that there might be serious danger in the direction of Damascus, and that the kingdom of Jerusalem was a buffer state, whose friendship was essential to his security, Dirgham deliberately provoked King Amaury by declining to pay the subsidy, and war inevitably followed. At the end of August 1163 the king of Jerusalem at the head of his feudal levy, which must have included the usual contingents of Hospitallers and Templars, crossed the Egyptian frontier. Moving by the coast-road through El-Arish and Farama, the ancient Pelusium, and then marching south along the eastern bank of the Nile, the first fortress to block his route was Belbeis at the head of the Wadi Tumilat to the south of the Bubastis of classical writers. The town was held by Dirgham's brother Nasir-el-Muslemin,[2] but on 1 September he suffered a severe defeat at the hands of the Christians, and was driven within the walls. King Amaury thereupon laid siege to Belbeis, but the Nile was now in flood, and Dirgham cutting the dikes inundated the country-side, and so forced the king to raise the siege and to retire to his own land, after offering him some sort of compromise on the question of the subsidy.

No sooner had the Christian army withdrawn and disbanded than it became clear that grave danger was threatening to Egypt from the direction of Damascus. Shawar had reached that city in October, and there found that the all-powerful Kurdish general Shirkoh was

[1] See Lane-Poole's *Saladin*, p. 84.

[2] See *Les Hospitaliers en Terre Sainte*, p. 66.

disposed to support his requests for aid. In his anxiety to return to power the exiled vizier was prepared to offer the most extravagant promises for the assistance of a Syrian army, and undertook not only to meet the entire cost of armed intervention, but also in addition to pay to Nur-ed-din as annual tribute one-third of the revenues of Egypt.[1] But that sovereign was cautious by nature, and up to now his policy had been concentrated upon expansion in the north. It required all his favourite general's influence to induce his master to sanction an expedition to Egypt for the purpose of restoring Shawar. Meanwhile Dirgham, terrified at the progress of his rival's negotiations, resolved to throw himself into the arms of King Amaury, to whom his envoys offered a largely increased subsidy in return for a firm alliance, and thereupon Nur-ed-din, realizing that Egypt must inevitably become the prey either of Jerusalem or Damascus, decided definitely upon intervention.

In April 1164 the Syrian army led by Shirkoh, the 'Lion of the Faith', was on the march for Egypt to restore the worthless Shawar, and with Shirkoh went his gallant young nephew Saladin, soon to be so famous. To cover the dangerous flank march through the desert along the borders of the Christian realm, Nur-ed-din made a fierce raid across the northern frontier of the Latin kingdom.[2] Shirkoh reached Egypt unmolested, defeated Dirgham at Belbeis and occupied Fostat. Dirgham, who had fallen back upon Cairo, was abandoned by his army and murdered by the mob, and before the end of May Shawar was once more in power.

With a Syrian army in Egypt, it was impossible for the King of Jerusalem to intervene in the north, and Nur-ed-din was at last free to embark upon a serious campaign against the Prince of Antioch. As soon as he learnt that Shirkoh was firmly established in Egypt, he left Damascus for Aleppo, and as he rode north he turned aside to harry the valley of the Eleutherus. But that raid nearly cost him his life, for the Hospitallers always maintained a powerful garrison in their great fortress of Le Crac, and sallying out they succeeded in surprising Nur-ed-din in his camp at La Bochée. As the Hospitallers rode in amongst the tents, the Saracens dashed to their horse-lines, and Nur-ed-din only escaped owing to the devotion of a faithful Kurd, who, waiting to sever the head-rope of his master's horse, was himself cut down by one of the Hospitallers.[3] In this engagement a body of Templars from Tripolis also took part under an English knight, Gilbert de Lacy, and another Englishman, Robert Mansel, greatly distinguished himself.

[1] See Lane-Poole's *Saladin*, p. 80.

[2] See Stevenson, *The Crusaders in the East*, p. 187.

[3] An account of this incident is given in Stevenson, *The Crusaders in the East*, p. 188.

Undeterred by this misadventure, Nur-ed-din continued his march to Aleppo, and joined the troops of the Emirs of Northern Syria and Mesopotamia, which had concentrated at Artah. The combined forces then advanced to Harenc (Harim) and laid siege to that famous fortress, the last bulwark of Antioch on the side of Aleppo. Prince Bohemond III was not unprepared for the attack, he had already been joined by Count Raymond II of Tripolis, Prince Thoros of Armenia and by Constantine Calamanos, the Byzantine Governor of Cilicia, as well as strong contingents of Hospitallers and Templars,[1] and at once marched to the relief of the threatened fortress. The battle that followed on 10 August was one of the most disastrous in the annals of the northern principality, the Christians suffered an overwhelming defeat, the Prince of Antioch and the Count of Tripolis were amongst the prisoners, and two days later Harenc surrendered. No barrier except the River Orontes was now left between the city of Antioch and the Moslem border. Satisfied with this brilliant success, and anxious not to provoke the Emperor Manuel to activity, Nur-ed-din returned to Damascus, ready to take advantage of any opportunities that the march of events in Egypt might present.

Meanwhile in that country Shawar no sooner found himself restored to power than he began to regret the lavish promises that he had made to the Syrians in the days of his exile. Shutting himself up in Cairo, he openly defied Shirkoh, declined to pay a dinar of the huge sums he had promised, and sent envoys to the King of Jerusalem to demand assistance in expelling his recent allies. But the Kurdish general was not the man to allow himself to be treated in this manner, and at once established a strict blockade of Cairo, sending his nephew Saladin with a covering force to hold Belbeis against the Christians. King Amaury anxiously watching for an opportunity to intervene, whilst Nur-ed-din was still absent in the north, was speedily on the march and before the end of July had once more laid siege to Belbeis, where Shirkoh had now concentrated all his forces. The siege dragged on throughout the summer and early autumn, and it looked as if the town must fall. But Nur-ed-din was now back in Damascus, and the northern borders of Jerusalem were defenceless, in the absence of the army in Egypt. To relieve the pressure on Shirkoh, Nur-ed-din struck at the frontier town of Bélinas (Banias), then held by a certain Walter Chesney. After a few days' siege Bélinas fell through treachery on 18 October, and its fortifications were levelled with the ground. The news of this disaster rendered the return of King Amaury to his own land imperative. He concluded a treaty with Shirkoh that both besiegers and besieged should evacuate Egypt, and on 27 October the 'Lion of the Faith' marched out of Belbeis with all the honours of war. He himself brought up the rear of the column, battle-axe in

[1] See *Les Hospitaliers en Terre Sainte*, p. 66.

hand, and as he passed by, one of King Amaury's knights asked him if he was afraid of being attacked, to which the fierce old veteran grimly replied, 'Rest assured, if you do attack, not one of my soldiers will go to Paradise until he has first sent an infidel to Hell.' The first phase of the struggle for Egypt had ended in a draw, but a draw distinctly in favour of the Syrians, who had used the opportunity to capture two of the most important of the Christian frontier fortresses, Harenc covering Antioch, and Bélinas in northern Palestine.

For two years longer the rival princes held each other in check, each longing to seize the helpless prey, but neither daring to make the first move. At last in January 1167 Shirkoh made a sudden spring upon Egypt with 2,000 picked horsemen at his back. Taking the desert route by the Wady el-Ghizlan or Valley of Gazelles, he successfully evaded the forces of King Amaury, who had advanced to Kadesh-Barnea in the hope of intercepting him. But he was delayed by a severe sandstorm, which gave time for the Christian army to arrive, and on reaching Egypt on 2 February[1] he turned south to avoid it, and crossed the Nile at Atfih, 40 miles south of Cairo. Meanwhile King Amaury after his abortive attempt to intercept Shirkoh had returned to Ascalon, and then on 30 January left for Egypt at the head of 374 knights and a body of Turcopoles. We are probably not far wrong in assuming that the majority of the knights were Hospitallers and Templars. The king followed hard on the heels of Shirkoh, but on reaching Atfih found that he had already crossed the river. Both forces then descended the Nile with the river between them, Shirkoh encamping at Ghizeh, and King Amaury facing him at Fostat. Here the king entered into a formal alliance with Shawar and his nominal master the Caliph, who agreed to pay him an immediate subsidy of 200,000 dinars, and a further sum of the same magnitude, when he had succeeded in driving Shirkoh and his Syrians out of Egypt.

The allies then descended the Nile to where it forked into two branches to form the Delta, and crossed by night unobserved by the enemy. Shirkoh as soon as he heard the news fell back rapidly upon Upper Egypt with King Amaury in hot pursuit. The chase continued for over 150 miles, and then the old Lion of the Faith turned at bay at El-Baban, 10 miles south of Minyah. According to William of Tyre[2] his forces had now increased to 9,000 men-at-arms, 3,000 archers and 10,000 Arab spearmen, but the latter can have had little fighting value. In the battle that followed on 18 April King Amaury and his knights drove Saladin off the field, but Shirkoh cut their Egyptian allies to pieces, and they were compelled to abandon their baggage and fall back upon Cairo. Shirkoh then rode rapidly northward to receive the surrender of Alexandria, and leaving his nephew Saladin with

[1] See Stevenson, *The Crusaders in the East*, p. 191, note 1.
[2] See Lane-Poole's *Saladin*, p. 89, footnote.

1,000 of his troopers as garrison, returned to Upper Egypt to plunder the country.

King Amaury and Shawar at once laid siege to Alexandria. It was Saladin's first independent command, he was now 29 years of age, and by his gallant defence he extorted the admiration of his enemies [1] and first revealed those great qualities which were ultimately to place him amongst the most famous of Moslem heroes. No preparations had been made for a siege in Alexandria, provisions were very scarce, the garrison was small for the defence of so great an area, and its cosmopolitan population was unreliable and soon rendered hostile by hardship and starvation. Nevertheless Saladin held out for seventy-five days, successfully beating back the incessant assaults of the enemy. At last came the welcome news that his uncle Shirkoh had returned from Upper Egypt and was besieging Cairo, and with that news the second phase of the struggle for Egypt was at an end, resulting like the first in another stalemate. Shirkoh realized that his attempt on Egypt had definitely failed, while the King of Jerusalem was anxious to get back to his own land, for the Lord of Damascus had not been idle in his absence, and on 4 August a treaty was signed by which both again undertook to evacuate Egypt. Alexandria was surrendered to Shawar, prisoners were exchanged and Shirkoh and Saladin rode back to Damascus with the remnant of their exhausted troopers, and 50,000 dinars of the subsidy paid by Shawar to his Christian allies. But when the King of Jerusalem returned to his own land he had an undertaking from Shawar to increase the annual subsidy from 33,000 to 100,000 dinars, and he left a resident in Cairo with a guard on the city gates.[2]

The operations of Nur-ed-din in Syria in the absence of King Amaury had not had such serious results as during the previous campaign in Egypt. Concentrating his forces at Hama in the spring for an attack on the County of Tripolis, on his way north he surprised Munaitera between Baalbec and Jubail. He then carried fire and sword into the valley of the Eleutherus, mercilessly ravaged the country round Arka, captured Safitha and Araima, dismantling their fortifications, and by the middle of June was back again in Homs, where he spent Ramadan. Marching south a month later he crossed the northern frontier of Jerusalem and advanced against Chateauneuf, now Hunin, on the opposite side of the valley to Bélinas (Banias). But the garrison evacuated the stronghold, and after destroying its defences, he returned to Damascus and disbanded his forces.

[1] During the negotiations preceding the treaty of 4 August Saladin was entertained as a guest or hostage in King Amaury's camp, where he struck up a friendship with Humphrey of Toron, Constable of the Kingdom of Jerusalem, and one of the most gallant knights of his day, and was probably knighted by him. See Lane-Poole's *Saladin*, pp. 387, 388.

[2] A detailed account of the events in Egypt during this period is given by Lane-Poole in his *Life of Saladin*, Chapter VI.

The activities of Nur-ed-din and more particularly the loss of Harenc, had rendered it necessary for Bohemond III of Antioch, now released from captivity,[1] to readjust his system of frontier defence. His most serious preoccupation would always in future be his exposed eastern frontier and the protection of his capital. He therefore decided to follow the policy adopted by the Count of Tripolis in 1142, and to hand over to the Hospitallers the guardianship of his southern frontier. Accordingly in January 1168 he ceded to the Master of the Hospital the fortress of Abu Kobais west of the Orontes, and Famiyah (Apamea), east of that river with all the lands dependent upon them.[2] But Famiyah can have had little value for its new owners, since it had been in the possession of Nur-ed-din ever since 1149. Shortly afterwards King Amaury in his capacity as Regent of Tripolis, for Count Raymond II was still a prisoner of war, handed over to the Hospitallers the fortresses of Arka and Hisn Akkar [3] south of the Eleutherus, which placed under their control the whole of the eastern defences of the county, except Tubania only granted to them in 1180.[4] In his treaty with the Master of the Hospital, the Prince of Antioch undertook never to make a treaty with the Saracens without the assent of the Hospitallers, and never to claim a share in any booty that they might take.

The Christian army had returned from Egypt rightly convinced of the ease with which that country could be conquered, and with its appetite for its immense wealth keenly whetted by the enormous subsidies paid over by Shawar for its assistance. They had seen its helpless government reduced to utter impotence by only two regiments of Saracen horse, and King Amaury must have returned to Jerusalem resolved upon a policy of conquest. The only obstacle in the way of success was Nur-ed-din of Damascus, and it was clear that the blow to be delivered must be hard and swift, to avoid giving time for a Syrian army to intervene. In any case Shirkoh's recent attempt on Egypt showed what must inevitably happen, if the Christians did not forestall him.

King Amaury had no more enthusiastic supporter for his policy of conquest than Gilbert d'Assailly, Master of the Hospital, and William of Tyre appears to have considered him more responsible for what followed than any other man. He at any rate pledged his Order to support the king up to the limit of its resources, and during the autumn of 1167 appears to have crossed the Mediterranean [5] for

[1] Bohemond III had been released from captivity by Nur-ed-din early in the summer of 1165, no doubt out of deference to his brother-in-law the Emperor Manuel, and partly according to William of Tyre, because he regarded him as too young to be dangerous.

[2] See *Cartulaire-Général,* Vol. I, No. 391.

[3] Ibid., No. 411.

[4] Ibid., No. 585.

[5] Ibid., Nos. 372, 404, and *Les Hospitaliers en Terre Sainte,* pp. 67–9.

the purpose of raising a loan from the bankers of Florence and Genoa. The king had married the Princess Maria Comnena, niece of the Emperor Manuel, immediately after his return from Egypt. In the following spring he sent William, the Archdeacon of Tyre, on a special mission to Constantinople to arrange for the co-operation of a Byzantine fleet in the proposed operations. But the invasion of Egypt, though ultimately necessary for the security of the Holy Land, was not so obviously a defensive measure as to gain unanimous support. The barons could not be compelled to take part in it against their will, and one of the most powerful of them all Philip de Nablus, Master of the Temple, flatly declined to have anything to do with it. However, by lavish promises of the territories and cities of Egypt the king succeeded in collecting together a considerable force, and in the autumn of 1168 there concentrated at El-Arish an army of probably five or six thousand men. The nucleus was furnished by the Hospitallers, who sent 500 knights [1] and 500 Turcopoles under their Master, Gilbert d'Assailly, the largest force that they had ever raised.

The rewards promised to the Hospitallers were in proportion to the value of the services they were rendering. In an agreement signed on 11 October [2] the king ceded to them the important city of Belbeis and all the territory to the north of it between Syria and the sea, sufficient to produce a revenue of 100,000 besants a year. From this it is clear that they were destined to assume what was now the usual rôle of the military Orders, the guardianship of the frontier of Egypt. In addition the king promised them a further revenue of 50,000 besants a year settled upon ten of the chief cities of Egypt,[3] and in each of these cities they were to receive the best house or palace after the king, and moreover they were to have a tithe of all the lands that should be conquered. Their share of the plunder was to be in accordance with the rules of war, but in all expeditions in which they alone were engaged, the whole of the plunder was to be theirs, unless the king were present in person.

By the middle of October the expedition was ready to start, a small naval squadron co-operating, but the hoped-for Byzantine assistance was not forthcoming. King Amaury after denouncing his treaty with Shawar must have left El-Arish on 21 October and ten days later was before Belbeis. The city was held for Shawar by his son Mahazan,[4] who refused the summons to surrender. Two days were spent in

[1] The term knight is here used with its original meaning of heavy armed cavalry, and includes both knights and serjeants, many of whom would be laymen, and not professed brethren of the Order.

[2] See *Cartulaire-Général,* Vol. I, No. 402.

[3] The ten cities were Cairo, Tanis, Damietta, Mehallet, Alexandria, Kus, Assouan, Behnesa, Atfih, Fayoum.

[4] A spirited description of the capture of Belbeis is given by the Abbé Vertot, *Les Chevaliers de Malthe,* Book II.

preparations, and then on 3 November the city was carried by assault. Its capture was followed by one of those abominable massacres, so painfully characteristic of Christian armies in their wars against the infidel. In accordance with his agreement King Amaury handed over Belbeis to the Hospitallers, who placed a garrison there, and the march on Cairo began. They reached the capital on 13 November, only to find that Shawar the previous day had adopted the desperate policy of burning the whole of the buildings outside the walls of the fortress, including Fostat, for three hundred years the capital of Egypt. In this ghastly conflagration which lasted for fifty-four days, before it completely burnt itself out, no fewer than 20,000 barrels of naphtha and 10,000 torches were employed, and its traces can be seen to the present day in the wilderness of sand heaps on the south side of Cairo.[1]

The dense fumes from Fostat rendered it impossible for King Amaury to occupy the usual camping-ground, the Birket-el-Habash or lake of the Abyssinians, and finding Cairo too strong to carry by assault, he settled down to a regular siege. But the investment was incomplete, for his naval squadron after capturing and plundering Tanis, found itself unable to ascend the Nile and withdrew. Shawar was in a critical position; if no help came the Christians must ultimately take Cairo, and his power and probably his life would be at an end. On the other hand, the only persons capable of rendering assistance were Nur-ed-din of Damascus and his general Shirkoh, whom he had grossly deceived and repeatedly defied, and who themselves had serious designs upon Egypt. However, he determined to risk the dangers involved in evoking Syrian aid, and sent an urgent appeal for help to Nur-ed-din, the young Caliph himself writing and enclosing some of his wives' hair, the strongest sign of distress in a Moslem.[2] Meanwhile Shawar to gain time had involved King Amaury in negotiations, by offering to pay him fabulous sums of money to stay his hand. He offered no less than two million dinars for peace with 100,000 paid at once as ransom for his son and nephew, who had been captured at Belbeis. To give time for the collection of such a sum, the king agreed to a suspension of arms, apparently having no suspicions of the appeal that had been made to Damascus, and it was not until nearly the end of December that he learnt that Shirkoh was once more on the march for Egypt.

Nur-ed-din as soon as he received Shawar's appeal decided upon intervention. A strong force was assembled at Ras-el-ma, south of Damascus, 2,000 of his personal guard and 6,000 Turks, and Shirkoh was once more placed in command. The expedition left on 17 December, and on Christmas Day King Amaury raised the siege of Cairo and marched eastward, determined to fight a pitched battle before Shirkoh could effect a junction with the Egyptian troops. But once

[1] See Lane-Poole, *Egypt in the Middle Ages*, p. 184. [2] Ibid.

more Shirkoh succeeded in evading the Christian army, and reached Cairo in safety. The united forces of Syria and Egypt far outnumbered the Christians, and King Amaury, realizing that all hope of success was at an end, withdrew the garrison of Hospitallers from Belbeis on 2 January, and retired to his own land. Shirkoh entered Cairo in triumph on the 8th, ten days later Shawar was arrested and executed, as was naturally to be expected, and the helpless Caliph appointed the Syrian general vizier in his place. But he was not destined to enjoy his new power for long, the old 'Lion of the Faith' loved too dearly the pleasures of this life, and two months later he died suddenly, the result of over-eating. His successor as Vizier of Egypt was his young nephew Saladin, who now entered upon his great career.

King Amaury was not the type of man to renounce his schemes of conquest merely because they had failed at the first attempt, and to leave the immense financial resources of Egypt in the hands of Nur-ed-din would inevitably be fatal to the Latin kingdom of Jerusalem. A special mission was sent to Europe, with the Archbishop of Tyre at its head, to visit the courts of Rome, Paris and London, and to represent the imminent dangers that now threatened the Holy Land. With this mission Gilbert d'Assailly sent a special representative of his own, William de Mauny, Preceptor of the Hospital, which sufficiently reveals how preponderant was the position of the Hospitallers at this time.[1] Plans were concerted with the Emperor Manuel for a joint expedition in the autumn, and negotiations were opened with the discontented faction in Cairo, whose opportunities of office and plunder had been seriously jeopardized by the accession to power of so vigorous a personality as Saladin.

The discontented faction was led by the chief black eunuch Nejah, and it was arranged that when Saladin marched out to meet the new invasion, Cairo should rise in revolt, and an attack be delivered upon his rear. But the conspiracy was discovered by Saladin in the summer, Nejah was executed in July, and the Sudanese troops upon whom the eunuch had relied were subdued after sanguinary fighting in the heart of the city, and sent away into Upper Egypt. When King Amaury began his new campaign in the autumn, all hopes of a native rising had passed away. Once more the nucleus of his force was to be furnished by the Hospitallers, 500 knights and 500 Turcopoles, and on 20 August he signed a fresh agreement[2] with Gilbert d'Assailly, in which he again guaranteed him Belbeis with sufficient additional territory to produce the revenue of 50,000 besants previously charged upon the ten chief cities of Egypt.

The campaign of 1169 differed entirely from those of previous

[1] See Delaville Le Roulx, *Les Hospitaliers en Terre Sainte*, p. 72.

[2] See *Cartulaire-Général*, Vol. I, No. 409.

years, and was unfortunately to form the model for all subsequent campaigns in Egypt. The fleet to be furnished by the Emperor Manuel was very large, 150 galleys, 60 transports and 12 larger vessels, and it was apparently intended that it should co-operate in an attack upon Cairo by ascending the Damietta branch of the Nile. It was therefore necessary first to capture the city of Damietta at the mouth of the river, the chief seaport of Egypt after Alexandria. The army of Jerusalem took up its position at the end of October, and three days later the imperial fleet arrived under the command of Andronicus the emperor's cousin. The siege that followed was pushed with vigour, and lasted fifty days, but was continually hampered by every form of misfortune. Provisions were short, there were constant heavy rains, the river rose and flooded the camp, and disease broke out amongst the troops. As usual Greeks and Latins were quite unable to co-operate harmoniously and Saladin incessantly harassed their outposts. In despair it was decided to abandon the siege, and on 19 December the retreat on Palestine began. But even then their misfortunes were not at an end, for a great storm arose and wrecked the Byzantine fleet, and few of its ships survived. So ended King Amaury's last attempt to conquer Egypt, but had Damietta fallen at once, it is more than doubtful if an army could have forced its way across the succession of rivers and canals that intersect the Delta, even with the support of a powerful fleet. Both King John de Brienne and St. Louis were to try the same route later, and in each case with disastrous results; the true line of invasion was that adopted in the previous campaigns.

King Amaury's failures to conquer Egypt were probably due to one cause only, that the resources of his little kingdom were totally insufficient for the purpose, but his offensive policy so far as we can now judge was perfectly sound, for if he did not conquer the country his most dangerous enemy Nur-ed-din was certain to do so. Throughout these campaigns Gilbert d'Assailly had been his most trusted adviser and most loyal supporter, and now that they had resulted in nothing but failure, a strong tendency became manifest to place the blame for that failure upon his shoulders. In fact William of Tyre seems to have regarded him as almost entirely responsible. Amongst the Hospitallers there was practically a revolt against the authority of their Master. They must undoubtedly have built the most extravagant hopes upon the benefits that were to accrue to their Order from the conquest of Egypt, and the corresponding reaction was equally violent. As the chief advocate of a policy that had failed so lamentably, and had left their Order embarrassed by a debt of over 200,000 besants, Gilbert d'Assailly found himself attacked from almost every quarter. Above all he was blamed for having committed the Order to far-reaching schemes of conquest without having first consulted the

Chapter, and there were some who even blamed him for the increased responsibilities that he had accepted on the frontiers of Tripolis and Antioch.

The leader of the disaffected party was Pons Blan, Preceptor of the Hospital, and his whole conduct gives the impression that he was not uninfluenced by the desire to succeed to the office of Master. He had only been recently appointed Preceptor by Gilbert d'Assailly, who at that time must have regarded him as a loyal and trustworthy subordinate. In the bitter controversy that had so soon after arisen, his true character stands revealed in a most unfavourable light. Deeply wounded by the disloyal and insubordinate attitude of so many of his brethren, the Master decided that it was best that he should retire from his high office. In vain King Amaury endeavoured to restrain his trusted councillor from so drastic a step. In vain the great dignitaries of the Order protested that their Chapter and their first superior the Pope had the right to be consulted in such an emergenoy. Gilbert d'Assailly stood firmly by his decision, released his brethren from their oath of obedience, laid down his office and withdrew to a hermitage.[1]

The Master's retirement automatically placed the supreme power in the hands of his lieutenant Pons Blan the Preceptor, pending the election of a new Master. But the Hospitallers were far from desiring that insubordinate chieftain for their head, as the event was to show, and there seems to have been no doubt felt as to his unsuitability for that exalted position. Eventually the Patriarch of Jerusalem, Amaury de Nesle, at the request of the great dignitaries of the Order and the chief ecclesiastics of the realm, decided to intervene, and summoning Gilbert d'Assailly to Jerusalem prevailed upon him to resume office on the understanding that his brethren should renounce their grievanoes, and again take the oath of obedience to him. But Pons Blan and his supporters were determined to make the Master's position intolerable, and demanded that he should give guarantees regarding his future conduct. To that humiliating request there could be only one reply from Gilbert d'Assailly, 'I wish to justify my actions, and then to resign, I am not prepared to resume office on such conditions'. But this time before finally resigning, he summoned a meeting of the Chapter, and directed it to elect a new Master in accordance with the statutes, and they elected not Pons Blan, but the Treasurer of the Order, Caste de Murols. The new Master at once appointed a new Preceptor in accordance with custom, and the old Preceptor found himself back in the ranks as a simple brother of the Order.

Pons Blan, with all his hopes and ambitions shattered, thereupon broke out into open rebellion, and flatly refused to recognize the new

[1] For the events that followed the resignation of Gilbert d'Assailly, see Delaville Le Roulx, *Les Hospitaliers en Terre Sainte*, pp. 76–8.

Master. He and his supporters declared that it was an impossibility for a Master to resign office without the authority of the Holy See, that the actions of the Chapter were therefore *ultra vires* and declared their intention of appealing to Rome. But the authority of the new Master was not thus to be defied with impunity. Pons Blan was simply ordered to hand over to his successor as Preceptor the staff and houses, equipment and other property that he held by virtue of his office, he was forbidden to present himself before the Pope and we hear no more of him. But his extinction did not put an end to the difficulties. The discontented brethren appear to have gone so far as to elect a rival Master, a certain Rostang,[1] whose seal as master is in existence, but of whom we know nothing further except that he had been Preceptor of the Hospital in 1162 under Arnold de Comps, and had not been re-appointed to that office at his death. Gilbert d'Assailly, much troubled at the intrigues and insubordination that had followed his resignation, began to doubt the wisdom and propriety of his action. The question was referred to a great assembly at Jerusalem, over which the Patriarch presided, and which included the Bishops, the great dignitaries of the Hospital, the Preceptor of the Temple, and the Barons and wise men of the realm. It was decided that Gilbert d'Assailly should proceed to Rome, and lay the whole matter personally before the Pope, who seems to have been satisfied simply to concur in his resignation and in the election of his successor.

We hear nothing further of Gilbert d'Assailly from the time he left the Holy Land in 1170, until his tragic death thirteen years later. In 1183 he visited King Henry II of England at Rouen, and was well received by him, afterwards leaving the court for England, presumed to be his native land. He embarked at Dieppe on 19 September in a vessel which proved to be quite unseaworthy, and 3 miles from land she foundered, only eight persons escaping. So far as we can now judge, Gilbert d'Assailly was an able and vigorous Master, in character proud and autocratic, a good soldier and filled with ambition for his Order. The official chronicle sums him up as a man of high purpose, under whom the Religion increased both in the number of the brethren, and in the quantity of its possessions. It was he who first appointed a Preceptor d'Outremer to act as his Lieutenant in Europe, and to coordinate the administration of the six existing Priors.[2] Probably the official chronicler is referring to this reform, when he states that he made good ordinances. Under his guidance the Order of St. John had made rapid strides in power and influence, and occupied a position of greater predominance in the Latin East than ever before. Gilbert d'Assailly must certainly rank amongst the most famous of the Masters

[1] See *Les Hospitaliers en Terre Sainte*, p. 81.

[2] The Priors of St. Gilles, Messina, Portugal, Navarre, England, and Aragon, and after 1169 Barletta.

of the Hospital during the two centuries that it fought and laboured in the Holy Land.[1]

APPENDIX

KING AMAURY'S GRANT OF LANDS IN EGYPT

Dated 11 *October* 1168 [2]

In the name of the Holy and Indivisible Trinity, Father, Son and Holy Ghost, Amen. Be it known to all the sons of Holy Mother Church, both present and to come, that I Amaury, by the grace of God-fifth King of the Latins in the Holy City of Jerusalem, have given, conveyed and granted to God and to St. John Baptist and to the poor of the Holy Hospital of Jerusalem, and to Gilbert then the venerable Master thereof, and to his successor and brethren forever: Bilbeis with all the appurtenances thereof, which the inhabitants of the city possess, and all the inhabitants on the land and of the land, and so much land cultivated and uncultivated, as stretches from the hither side of Bilbeis towards Syria and the sea, as shall furnish a revenue every year with Bilbeis itself of full 100,000 besants. And this aforesaid land, with all the men who are on the land or of the land, I give to God and the Holy Hospital, and to the Master and Brethren, freely and absolutely: and in ten cities of the land of Babylon (i.e. Egypt) 50,000 old besants,[3] that is to say, in Babylon (i.e. Misr. Old Cairo) 5,000 besants, and in Tanis 5,000 besants, and in Damietta 5,000 besants, and in the island of Mahalla 5,000 besants, in Alexandria 5,000 besants, in the city of Kus 5,000 besants, and in Suana (i.e. Assuan) 5,000 besants, and in When (Behnesa ?) 5,000 besants, and in Ahideph (Atfih ?) [4] 5,000 besants, and in Fun (Fayum ?) 5,000 besants: and in all the cities of the whole land the best house or palace after that of the King: and if God grant that the treasure of Mulan,[5]

[1] There is in the Chapter-Hall of the English Order of St. John at Clerkenwell a tablet to his memory of gilded bronze, bearing below his arms the following inscription: Fr. Gilbert d'Assailly, First English Grand Master, elected 1162, resigned 1170, drowned at sea off Dieppe 19 September 1183.

[2] The Latin text is printed in *Cartulaire-Général*, Vol. I, No. 402.

[3] 'Old besants' evidently refers to the original Arab dinars or besants, weighing each 65–3 grains, and worth therefore about 11*s.* 6*d.*: the besants of King Amaury's time were much depreciated weighing only 52–4 grains, and worth therefore about 8*s.*

[4] The cities of When, Ahideph and Fun are difficult to identify. Since the first five cities are in the Delta, and the next two go up the Nile on the right bank of the river, we should rather expect to find the next three descending the Nile on the left bank. Fun certainly appears to represent Fayum. Delaville Le Roulx suggests that When may be Behnesa on the left bank, representing the first part of a form Wehnesa, whilst he identifies Ahideph with Atfih on the right bank opposite Fayum, and Fun he identifies with Fau on the right bank north of Kus. See *Les Hospitaliers en Terre Sainte*, p. 71, note 1.

[5] The treasure of Mulan is presumably the treasure of the Caliph.

and of the other cities and towns shall come into my hands by the fortune of war, I have given and granted to the Master of the Hospital and to his brethren aforesaid one whole tenth both of the treasure of Cahira (i.e. Cairo) and of other cities and of all the stocks belonging to the land, by right forever, freely and absolutely, with good will and intent, without fraud, guile or trickery. Moreover I add this, that if land and the wealth on the land be captured at the point of the sword, in the organized distribution thereof the Master and Brethren of the Hospital shall receive their shares without deduction before any others, both of treasure and of other things, immediately after I have taken my half of the whole. And if it happen that the land be ransomed for money, the Master and Brethren shall receive their shares as for service done. And in return for all the things aforesaid the House of the Hospital, and the Brethren and Master of the same, must have in this first expedition 500 Knights and as many Turcopoles, well-armed, and these Knights and Turcopoles must be mustered at Larriz (i.e. El-Arish) before the Marshal or Constable. And if their numbers be in each case the whole number of 500, the things aforesaid shall be observed in their entirety to the said Hospital, but if less, the things aforesaid shall be diminished in proportion to the numbers wanting; and if more, the revenues and other things aforesaid shall be increased in proportion to the overplus. Moreover in whatsoever expedition the brethren of the Hospital shall henceforth take part, their banner shall divide the booty or spoils with no one, save only with myself, if I happen to take part therein. Otherwise whatever they can obtain shall be wholly and freely theirs in its entirety. And if land be taken, and cannot be brought under the faith of Christianity, what is said above with regard to the dividing of the banner shall remain firm and stable. And this was done in the year of Our Lord 1168, in the second Indiction, these being witnesses:

Frederick, Archbishop of Tyre
Aitard, Bishop of Nazareth
Ralph, Bishop of Bethlehem
and William, Bishop of Acre
Walter, Prince of Galilee
Hugh, Lord of Ibelin
The Lord Humphrey de Toron (the Constable)
William the Marshal
The Lord Milo de Plancy (the Seneschal)
The Lord Gormund de Tiberias
Guago de Neuville
Godfrey de Bremei
Guy de Maners.

Given at Jerusalem by the hand of Ralph, Bishop of Bethlehem, and the King's Chancellor, on the 5th day before the Ides of October.

CHAPTER VII

ROGER DES MOULINS AND THE RISE OF SALADIN

THE immense efforts made by the Hospitallers in the Egyptian wars must have strained their resources to the utmost, and have left their finances in a very embarrassed condition. Under these circumstances no better Master could have been elected than Caste de Murols, the Treasurer of the Order. He was a native of Auvergne from Murols in the Puy-de-Dôme, and as treasurer had been a Conventual Bailiff since 1163. His policy must necessarily have been one of peace and economy, with the restoration of harmony amongst the brethren and the placing of the finances of the Order once more on a sound basis. From the official chronicle we learn that he was a man of deep humility and great benevolence, noted for his kindness of heart, and that his reputation for rigid probity resulted in many great benefactions to the Religion throughout Europe. He held office for less than two years, and died in the spring of 1172. For some reason no doubt connected with the fact that Gilbert d'Assailly was still alive, the Hospitallers did not proceed at once to the election of his successor, and on 20 June we find Pope Alexander III writing [1] to the Preceptor of the Hospital directing the Order to elect a new Master, and definitely forbidding it to re-elect Gilbert d'Assailly, a contingency that was evidently regarded as very possible.

The two years during which Caste de Murols ruled over the Hospital were years of comparative tranquillity in the Holy Land. Saladin was engaged in consolidating his position in Egypt, where he was evidently aiming at complete independence, and Nur-ed-din was busy in the north, where the death of his brother, Kutb-ed-din of Mosul, had resulted in a considerable extension of his influence in northern Mesopotamia. But in December 1170 Saladin raided southern Palestine and laid siege to the border fortress of Darum held by the Templars under Ansel de Pass. King Amaury hastened down from Jerusalem with 250 knights, drawn from the Hospital and the Temple, and 2,000 foot. Saladin avoiding a battle slipped away under cover of darkness, and surprised and plundered Gaza, but failed to take the citadel held by Milo de Plancy. Returning to Egypt laden with plunder, he

[1] See *Cartulaire-Général*, Vol. I, No. 434.

OBVERSE

REVERSE

THE GREAT SEAL OF FR. CASTE DE MUROLS

ended up the year with the capture of Aila at the head of the Gulf of Akabah, an important post on the desert route between Damascus and Egypt, and a port of embarkation for the pilgrims for Mecca. The following year came the expected religious revolution in Egypt, when Saladin put an end to the Fatimite Caliphate, and proclaimed in the Mosques of Cairo that the Abbaside Caliph was the only true Commander of the Faithful. The delighted Caliph conferred upon Nur-ed-din the title of Sultan,[1] but ever the breach grew wider and wider between Saladin and his Master, and that for a time saved the Holy Land from the inevitable disaster that now hung over it like a cloud.

Forbidden to re-elect Gilbert d'Assailly, the Hospitallers on the receipt of the papal instructions in the summer of 1172 elected a certain Jobert to be their Master, probably a Provençal. It seems probable that his full name was Gerard Jobert, and that he belonged to the ancient family of De Jaubert well known in the Limousin and Languedoc. The arms attributed to him at a later date belonged to a branch of this family, and there is no serious reason for doubting the identification.[2] All that we know of his earlier career is that as far back as 1135 he had been selected by King Fulk for a mission to Europe of a highly confidential nature.[3] He proceeded in that year to the court of King Henry I of England in order to induce that famous knight Raymond of Poitou to come out to Syria, and marry the infant heiress of Antioch, the Princess Constance. Jobert succeeded in his delicate mission, in spite of the powerful influences working for its failure, and the following year he returned to Antioch safely with Raymond of Poitou, both of them in humble disguise, having narrowly escaped capture by King Roger of Sicily, the first cousin of Bohemond I of Antioch, who harboured designs of his own on the principality.

The rule of Jobert over the Hospital lasted just five years, and during that period there is little to record in the history of the Order. But it is none the less a period of the greatest importance, for Saladin was laying the foundations of his empire, which was to be the ruin of the Latin kingdom of Jerusalem. In May 1174 the great Sultan Nur-ed-din died, leaving as his heir a son Es-Salih Ismail, only 11 years of age, and Saladin's hour had come. Two months later, on 11 July, King Amaury died of dysentery at the early age of 38. He was not so popular as his brother Baldwin III had been, but he was a capable and energetic monarch, and a good soldier, and could ill be spared. His tastes were intellectual, and he was greatly interested in the historical works of William of Tyre, whom he made tutor to his only son, King Baldwin IV, who was just 13 years of age when he succeeded to the

[1] See Lane-Poole, *Life of Saladin*, p. 109.

[2] See *Les Onze Premiers Grand Maîtres, etc.*, of Viscount Oscar de Poli, in the *Annuaire du Conseil Heraldique de France*, 1892, pp. 71, 72.

[3] See Vertot, *Les Chevaliers de Malthe*, Book I.

throne. As promising and heroic a young prince as the great House of Anjou ever produced, his life was nothing but a martyrdom, for he had been cursed with the foul disease of leprosy from early childhood, and even his sword-arm was withered and his right hand incapable of grasping sword or lance. Milo de Plancy, Lord of Kerak and Montreal, assumed the guardianship of the young king during his minority, but he was assassinated at Acre a few months later, and his place was taken by Count Raymond II of Tripolis,[1] the most talented and capable of all the barons of Syria. He was a grandson of King Baldwin II, whose daughter the Princess Hodierna had married his father Count Raymond I, and he was suspected by many of having designs upon the throne.

Saladin was prevented from at once assuming the heritage of Nur-ed-din by a conspiracy in Cairo, and an attack on Alexandria by a powerful Sicilian fleet. No doubt had King Amaury lived he would have co-operated with the Sicilians, but without the help of the army of Jerusalem they could do nothing. In November Saladin began his policy of aggression against his late master's son by occupying Damascus, and then overran all Syria up to the gates of Aleppo, where the boy king Es-Salih Ismail had taken refuge. In the spring of 1175 Seyf-ed-din, the new Lord of Mosul, and now the head of the House of Zanki, sent an army into Syria to the assistance of his young kinsman, but Saladin won an overwhelming victory at the Horns of Hamah, and his position was thereupon regularized by the Caliph, who granted him investiture as Sultan of Egypt and Syria.[2] Next year the Lord of Mosul made one more effort to drive him back into Egypt, but was utterly defeated in the Battle of Tell-es-Sultan, 15 miles from Aleppo, and Saladin's position was at last secure, the foundations of his empire had been firmly laid.

During this struggle it was difficult to foresee on which side victory would ultimately rest, and Count Raymond as regent adopted a cautious policy of observation, there was nothing but the ordinary border warfare, and in 1175 he made a truce with the new Sultan. The real problem of the moment was the succession to the throne, for the poor young king was not likely to live long. His heiress was his sister the Princess Sibyl, and in 1176 she was married to William Longsword, son of the Marquis of Montferrat, who gave her a son Baldwin, but died before his birth. This marriage brought the guardianship of Count Raymond to an end, but the wretched health of the king rendered it

[1] Count Raymond had been taken prisoner by Nur-ed-din at Harenc in 1164; after nine years of captivity in Aleppo, he was released in 1173 owing to the intercession of Jobert, Master of the Hospital, in return for which he confirmed to the Order all the charters of his ancestors. See *Cartulaire-Général*, Vol. I, No. 467.

[2] See Stevenson, *The Crusaders in the East*, p. 210.

impossible for him to govern alone, although at 16 years of age he had reached his majority, and he appointed Reginald of Chatillon,[1] formerly Prince of Antioch, to be his procurator. This noble by his recent marriage with the widow of Milo de Plancy, Stephania de Nablus, was now Lord of Kerak, Montreal and St. Abraham (Hebron), and the most powerful baron in the Holy Land.

In 1176 the old plans of King Amaury and Gilbert d'Assailly for the conquest of Egypt, the basis of Saladin's power, were once more revived. The Emperor Manuel undertook to co-operate with a fleet, Philip Count of Flanders was to lead a new crusade to the East, and the old dreams of the Hospitallers of wide lands in Egypt began again to take shape. The Master Jobert deemed it prudent to obtain from the king a new charter,[2] definitely confirming to the order the grants made to it in Egypt by his father, and to ensure the co-operation of the Hospitallers the king increased the revenues, previously guaranteed to them on the territory of Belbeis, by a further 30,000 besants. But when in August 1177 the Count of Flanders arrived, he absolutely refused to take part in an expedition against Egypt, although the Emperor's fleet had already arrived at Acre. Under these circumstances the whole plan of campaign had to be abandoned, the Byzantine fleet returned to Constantinople in disgust, and the last opportunity was lost for ever of striking what might have been a fatal blow against Saladin, before his power had been consolidated.

Jobert died during the year 1177. His rule had been one of peace and tranquillity, and he is chiefly remembered for his charitable and religious services. His regulations concerning the conduct of certain offices of the church, and for the provision of white bread for the sick in the hospital are still in existence.[3] In the words of the official chronicle, 'he established good Statutes for the service of God and the Church, and for the benefit of our lords the sick'. In various disputes with the bishops he upheld with vigour and success the privileges of his Order, and with the Orthodox Church his relations were singularly cordial, for he handed over to the Greek Archbishop of Gaza the monastery of St. George of Jibelin, and received the Archbishop into the Order as a Confrater.[4]

The early history of the Hospitallers gives the impression that behind the scenes something like a struggle for predominance was in progress between what are for purposes of convenience best described as the religious and military elements, although both

[1] Reginald of Chatillon was taken prisoner by the Governor of Aleppo in 1160; after fifteen and a half years of captivity he was released early in 1176, owing to a temporary understanding between Antioch and Aleppo against Saladin.

[2] See *Cartulaire-Général*, Vol. I, No. 496.

[3] Ibid., Nos. 494, 504.

[4] See *Les Hospitaliers en Terre Sainte*, p. 85.

elements were equally composed of professed brethren of the Order. Under Raymond du Puy the military element had been continually increasing in importance, but none the less his two successors were ordinary monks rather than soldiers. With the election of Gilbert d'Assailly as Master, the military element was obviously in the ascendant again, for he was pre-eminently a soldier rather than a monk. The disputes that followed his retirement, and the intervention of the Pope to prevent his re-election in 1172, were probably due to the determination of the religious elements to assert themselves, and not to permit the original objects of their Order to be made secondary to its military duties. The two successors of Gilbert d'Assailly were again almost certainly monks of the usual type, but with the death of Jobert in 1177 the military element was once more predominant, and the Hospitallers elected as their Master a valiant soldier of Norman stock,[1] Roger des Moulins, a subject of King Henry II of England, probably belonging to the family of that name settled at Moulines in Lower Normandy, whose arms were attributed to him at a later date.[2]

We know absolutely nothing concerning his previous career in the Order, and his name is not to be found amongst its Bailiffs, which gives the impression that his service in it had not been very long. It is highly probable that his election was due to the influence of King Henry II of England, to whom as the head of the House of Anjou, there was always a tendency in the Holy Land to turn for advice and assistance. However that may be, no sooner was Roger des Moulins elected Master than Pope Alexander III considered it necessary to lay down [3] that the primary objects for which the Order existed were charitable, and to remind the new Master of the salutary principle of the Blessed Raymond du Puy that his knights must never draw the sword except when the standard of the Cross was displayed, either for the defence of the kingdom of Jerusalem, or in the siege of some pagan city. That letter was clearly written by the Pope because the military element was again in the ascendant, and he felt it essential to intervene, just as he had done in 1172, to prevent the re-election of the soldier Gilbert d'Assailly.

But the Holy Land had need of a good knight as Master of the Hospital, for the first of the great wars against Saladin had begun with the plans for the invasion of Egypt. The Count of Flanders had preferred a campaign in the north, influenced no doubt by the Count of Tripolis and the Prince of Antioch, and eventually decided to attempt the recovery of the important fortress of Harenc, which was in revolt against Es-Salih of Aleppo. King Baldwin sent troops to assist in the

[1] See *Les Hospitaliers en Terre Sainte*, p. 86.
[2] See *Les Onze Premiers Grand Maîtres, etc.*, pp. 72–5.
[3] See *Cartulaire-Général*, Vol. I, No. 527.

siege, which was grossly mismanaged and dragged on for four months. Antioch still worthily maintained its classical reputation as a city of pleasure, and its temptations were too much for the Christian knights who forgot their honour and their duty in the amusements of the city. In consequence reinforcements succeeded in entering Harenc, and in March 1178 the besiegers agreed to raise the siege in return for a suitable indemnity. Shortly after the Count of Flanders sailed for Europe, as the contemporary historian tersely remarks 'leaving behind him a memory that was in no wise blessed'.

With its main forces in northern Syria, the Latin kingdom was completely open to invasion from Egypt, and in November Saladin crossed the border with 8,000 [1] Mamelukes and 18,000 Sudanese foot, and on the 23rd reached Ascalon, into which King Baldwin had thrown himself a few days earlier with the scanty forces that he could collect. Next day the Saracens broke up into plundering parties, and scattered themselves over the country-side, burning Ramleh and Lydda, and penetrating even to the very walls of Jerusalem. On the 25th the heroic young king seeing the opportunity that the enemies' carelessness was giving, sallied forth from Ascalon with the whole of the garrison, and 80 Templars, who had just come up from Gaza under Odo de St. Amand, their Master. The king had under him less than 3,000 foot and only 375 knights, including Roger des Moulins and his Hospitallers, who had ridden down from Jerusalem after handing over to the women the guardianship of the Holy City and the Tower of David, as he tells us himself in a letter still existing.[2] King Baldwin the Leper fell upon the main body of the Saracens at Montgisart (Tell Jezer), near Ramleh, before they could form up for battle. Saladin in vain tried to get his men into some sort of order, his bodyguard was cut to pieces, his army dispersed, and he himself only escaped death or capture by the swiftness of the camel on which he was mounted. It was the most glorious victory that the Christians had ever gained over the infidels, since Godfrey's victory at Ascalon in 1099, and they were able to destroy at their leisure the scattered plundering parties of the enemy. What the pitiless Christian sword had begun, hunger, cold and heavy rains completed, and few of Saladin's army ever got back to Egypt. But the loss of the victors had been very heavy, and Roger des Moulins tells us in his letter that out of 3,000 men engaged, 1,100 were killed and that 750 of the wounded were taken into the Hospital of the Order in Jerusalem, and he tells how during the battle all the 950 sick persons

[1] The Mamelukes closely resemble the Turkish Janissaries of a later period, except that they were cavalry, and they were troops of a very high standard. They were recruited mainly from European or Turkish boys bought as slaves to be specially trained as soldiers.

[2] A letter of Roger des Moulins to a crusading knight crippled by his wounds in this battle, certifying that he had fought valiantly. See Rohricht, *Geschichte des Konigrechs Jerusalem*, 375–80.

then in the Hospital were on their knees praying to God to grant victory to His people.

The grave danger that now overshadowed the Holy Land rendered it not only desirable, but absolutely necessary, that there should be the most cordial co-operation between the two great military Orders of the Hospital and the Temple, which between them provided by far the most important part of the armies of the realm. But unfortunately the rapid development of the Hospital into a military Order had resulted in continual friction and controversy with the Templars, who could not forget that they were the first of the purely military Orders.

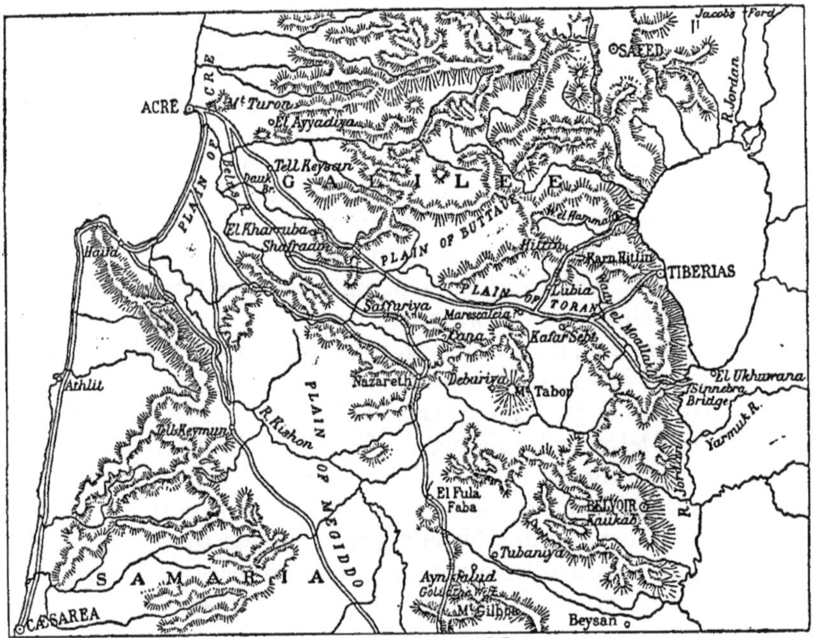

TIBERIAS TO ACRE

Scale of English Miles

0 5 10 15

MAP OF NORTHERN PALESTINE

No doubt originally the latter had been glad to welcome their brethren of the Hospital as comrades on the battlefield, but they had now long seen in them only dangerous rivals, whose power and influence were such that even in their own peculiar military sphere the Hospital was but little inferior to the Temple. Under Gilbert d'Assailly the military importance of the Hospitallers had increased enormously, they had formed the backbone of the Christian armies in Egypt, and the Templars had dropped for the moment into a secondary position, and had even declined to take any part in King Amaury's last campaigns in that country. The jealousy between the two Orders had become more and more bitter, and had now reached such a pitch, that it was said that a knight of the Hospital and a knight of the Temple could scarcely meet without fighting. Such a situation between two religious Orders was not only scandalous in itself, but was fraught with serious danger to the State, especially in a time of grave emergency, and Pope Alexander III brought all the weight of his great authority to bear upon the two Masters, to induce them to settle the outstanding differences between their two Orders, and to endeavour to ensure for the future those harmonious relations which ought to prevail between professed knights vowed to the service of their Saviour and His Holy Church. All through 1178 negotiations must have been in progress, and at last in February 1179 the two Masters, Roger des Moulins of the Hospital and Odo de St. Amand of the Temple, put their signatures to an agreement [1] by which every existing dispute was settled, and a system of arbitration adopted for the future. Under this agreement whenever a difference arose between the two Orders, either in Europe or the East, three brethren were to be appointed from each Order, by the Preceptors of the houses or provinces concerned, as arbitrators with full powers to settle. If they were unable to do so, they were to be reinforced by two of the more discreet brethren, and if they still failed to agree then the matter in dispute was to be referred to the Masters of the Hospital and Temple in Jerusalem, and they would settle the matter. The agreement was approved and confirmed by the Pope at Segni on 2 August 1179.

Meanwhile the war with Saladin was being fought out on the northern borders of the kingdom of Jerusalem. During 1178 the Sultan was occupied with the affairs of northern Syria, and King Baldwin on the advice of the Templars decided to take advantage of his pre-occupation elsewhere by building a new fortress at Jacob's Ford (Jisa Benet Jakub), south of Lake Huleh, to cover the frontier and take the place of Bélinas. The new fortress was begun in October, and took six months to finish. It was known as Chastellet or Castle Jacob, and was handed over to the guardianship of the Templars, in accordance with the now usual custom of making the military Orders responsible for the border castles. Having completed his work, the king moved north to raid the Moslem cattle grazing in the plain of Bélinas, but on 10 April 1179 was caught in an ambuscade with only a small force, by Saladin's nephew Ferrukh Shah, near Belfort (Shakif Arnun). The king only escaped owing to the personal gallantry of the Constable Humphrey de Toron, who paid for his devotion with his life, dying of his wounds at Castle Jacob twelve days later.

Saladin, desirous of avoiding a campaign in Palestine, offered King Baldwin 100,000 dinars, if he would destroy Castle Jacob. On the

[1] See *Cartulaire-Général,* Vol. I, No. 558, and for the papal confirmation No. 570. An English translation of both documents is in the Appendix to this chapter.

king's refusal, he established his headquarters at Bélinas, and sent out plundering parties in all directions. The king marching north through Safed and Toron, was joined by the Count of Tripolis, and attacked Saladin in the Mergion (Marj Uyun), 'the meadow of springs', on 10 June. In the battle that followed the Christians suffered a crushing defeat, and amongst the prisoners taken was the Master of the Temple, Odo de St. Amand. He refused to allow himself to be exchanged on the grounds that a Templar could give nothing for his ransom except his belt and his dagger, and died in a prison in Damascus the following year. He is described by William of Tyre as haughty and arrogant, having the breath of fury in his nostrils, neither fearing God nor regarding man. It is sometimes stated that the Master of the Hospital was also taken prisoner in the Battle of Mergion, but that is almost certainly due to confusion with the Master of the Temple.[1] At the end of August Saladin laid siege to Castle Jacob, which he captured on the 30th by mining, only five days after his arrival, and levelled with the ground. In the following spring a truce was concluded for two years.

It was now that the king consented to the marriage of his widowed sister the Princess Sibyl with a handsome young French knight, Guy de Lusignan,[2] whose brother Amaury had succeeded Humphrey de Toron as Constable. The marriage was one of unusual importance, for if Sibyl's infant son Baldwin should die she would become heiress to the throne, and her husband by virtue of his marriage would ultimately become King of Jerusalem. He was created Count of Jaffa and Ascalon, and almost at once began to act in many things for his brother-in-law the king, who was becoming crippled by the rapid ravages of his leprosy and was beginning to lose his sight. Unfortunately Guy de Lusignan had little but his good looks to commend him, and neither the exalted birth nor the solid ability necessary to fit him for such a position. The marriage was bitterly resented by the barons of the Holy Land, and by none more bitterly than by Count Raymond of Tripolis, the most powerful of the Christian princes and the ablest statesman and the most experienced soldier of them all.

The truce with Saladin was badly kept, and whilst regular military operations had ceased, there was little peace on the frontiers. In Antioch complete anarchy prevailed owing to the matrimonial vagaries of Prince Bohemond III, who was in consequence excommunicated by the Patriarch.[3] King Baldwin decided to intervene, and sent Roger

[1] See *Les Hospitaliers en Terre Sainte*, p. 90.

[2] Guy de Lusignan was the youngest of the six sons of Hugh de Lusignan, commonly known as Hugh the Brown, who came to the Holy Land on a pilgrimage in 1164, and was taken prisoner by Nur-ed-din. The family came from Poitou, and Guy's eldest brother Geoffrey was afterwards Count of La Marche.

[3] He first married Orgueilleuse of Harenc, by whom he had two sons; he then repudiated her in order to marry the Princess Theodora Comnena, a niece

des Moulins and his colleague Arnold de Torroge, the new Master of the Temple, to try to restore some sort of order. But neither Prince nor Patriarch was amenable to reason, though the forces of the former eventually prevailed. In the extreme south Reginald de Chatillon was quite uncontrollable. A typical robber baron of the period, greedy and unscrupulous, fierce and fanatical, his fifteen years of captivity in Aleppo had not tended to make his ways with the infidel any gentler. His two great castles of Kerak and Montreal (Shaubak) commanded the caravan route from Damascus to Egypt, as well as the pilgrim route to Mecca. He used his opportunities to the full, and the Sultan returned in 1182 from Egypt determined to resume the war.

This second war against Saladin began with an attempt to intercept him on the road from Cairo to Damascus. The feudal levy of Jerusalem, still headed by its gallant young king, the advances of whose hideous disease now compelled him to be carried in a litter, advanced to Petra. Saladin by skilful manœuvring avoided fighting a pitched battle, and safely escorted his unwieldy caravan to Damascus. Meanwhile in the absence of the Christian army Ferrukh Shah carried out a devastating raid through the Plain of Megiddo right up to the very gates of Acre, and on his return captured La Grotte (Habis Jaldek), the last Latin fortress beyond the Sea of Galilee. On the arrival of Saladin the combined forces of the Saracens crossed the Jordan in July by the wooden bridge of Sennabra, where King Baldwin III had gained his great victory over Nur-ed-din twenty-four years before, and advanced to Tiberias, sending out plundering parties in all directions. The Christian army now concentrated at Saffaria (Sepphoris), the strategic centre of Galilee, where all roads met, and the enemy moved south to Baisan. Eventually the two armies joined battle at the newly-built castle of Belvoir, north of Beisan, a fortress held by the Hospitallers, and which was known to the Moslems as Kaukab-el-Hawa, 'Star of the Air'. But the battle was not fought out to a finish, and Saladin withdrew across the Jordan, to appear a few weeks later at Beyrout, where the Egyptian fleet was ravaging the coast.

In the autumn the situation in Mesopotamia called the Sultan north, and gave the barons of the Holy Land the opportunity for a series of counter-raids on his southern dominions. The poor young king was no longer able to lead his army, not even from a litter, and the command was entrusted to his cousin Count Raymond of Tripolis, with whom he was now reconciled. Crossing the Jordan at the wooden bridge of Sennabra the Christian army during October carried fire and sword through the land as far as Bostra, recapturing La Grotte on its way home. Then in December just before Christmas it again crossed

of the Emperor Manuel. Growing tired of the princess, he sent her back to Constantinople with her daughter, and took a certain Sibyl to live with him, upon which the indignant Patriarch excommunicated him.

the frontier by Jacob's Ford, and advancing as far as Dariya close by Damascus ravaged all the rich country between the Abana and the Pharpar. But the most spectacular raid of all was that of Reginald de Chatillon in the south.[1] He formed the audacious plan of sacking Mecca and Medina, and dragging the body of the Prophet from his tomb. Seizing Aila at the head of the Gulf of Akabah, though he failed to take the castle on the Isle de Graye, he fitted out five galleys and a number of smaller vessels, and harried the Moslem shipping and the shores of the Hejaz as far as Aden. He himself landed at El-Haura in the spring of 1183 with his own followers and a body of Templars, assisted by 300 Bedouin, and marched on Medina. But in the gorge of Rabugh, a day's march from the city, he was overtaken by the Emir Hisham-ed-din Lulu, who had disembarked at El-Haura with troops from Egypt, and his force was cut to pieces. Reginald de Chatillon, with a handful of followers, escaped by land with great difficulty to his castle of Kerak. The Christian prisoners were taken to Cairo, and handed over to the fanatical populace to be tortured to death, but two were kept and taken to Mecca, where their throats were cut in the valley of Mina on the day of sacrifice, in expiation for the attempted sacrilege. When Saladin heard the news of this raid, he swore an oath that he would one day slay Reginald de Chatillon with his own hand, an oath that he was destined to keep.

In 1183 King Baldwin the Leper felt that his dreadful malady rendered it impossible for him to govern his realm any longer, and he appointed his brother-in-law Guy de Lusignan, Count of Jaffa and Ascalon, to be his procurator, retaining in his own hands only the city of Jerusalem, and a revenue of 10,000 besants a year. In June came the news that Saladin had captured Aleppo, and was now lord of all the lands of his old master Nur-ed-din. Although his relations with Mosul were the reverse of friendly, it was at last possible for the Sultan to turn his attention again to his southern dominions. During September his forces were assembling at Damascus, and on the 28th he advanced to the passage of the Jordan at Sennabra. Next day he crossed the river, and passing by the castle of the Hospitallers at Belvoir, reached Baisan, which he found deserted. On the 30th he moved up the Wady Jalud to Ain Jalud at the foot of Mount Gilboa, intercepting and destroying a Christian detachment on its way north from Kerak to join its main army.

Meanwhile Guy de Lusignan had assembled the forces of Jerusalem at Saffaria, as in the previous year. It was the largest army that had ever been raised in the Holy Land: 1,300 knights, as many Turcopoles[2]

[1] See Conder's *Latin Kingdom of Jerusalem*, pp. 140–2.

[2] The contingents furnished by the Hospitallers and Templars to the feudal levy of Jerusalem, may together be generally calculated at about one-third to possibly as much as one-half of the Knights, and as many Turcopoles.

and 15,000 foot, and even that included a body of Western crusaders. Nothing could reveal more clearly the weakness of the Latin kingdom of Jerusalem, and how dependent was its existence on the inability of the Moslems to unite against it. But at last they had found in Saladin a leader capable of uniting them, whilst the barons of the Holy Land were led by one whom they disliked, and only obeyed with the greatest reluctance. On 1 October, the day after Saladin reached Ain Jalud, Guy de Lusignan advanced to La Fève (El-Fuleh), just a mile from the enemy's position. There the two armies remained in observation of each other for nearly a week, there was constant skirmishing, and Saracen raiding parties plundered the country, but neither side would venture to attack, and so to bring on a decisive engagement. At last, on 6 October, Saladin fell back on Damascus through lack of supplies, and the crisis was over. But apparently it was thought by many that if the army had been handled more vigorously, a decisive victory might have been gained, and Guy de Lusignan was severely criticized for his inaction. Probably, however, nothing that he did would have seemed right in the eyes of the native-born barons of the Holy Land.

The year 1183 had witnessed a great weakening of Latin influence in the East generally, through the revolution in Constantinople. The Emperor Manuel had been succeeded by his young son Alexius II in 1180, but three years later his cousin Andronicus seized the reins of government by appealing to anti-Latin sentiment, and his rise to power was accompanied by a hideous massacre in Constantinople of the hated Latins. In this massacre the Hospitallers, whose possessions in the Imperial city were of considerable importance, thanks to the liberality and encouragement of the Emperor Manuel, suffered very severely. They possessed there two establishments of importance, the more famous hospital of St. Samson, between the Cathedral of St. Sophia and the Church of St. Irene, and also the hospital of St. John the Almoner. Urged on by fanatical Greek priests and monks the mob burst into the hospital, massacred indiscriminately the sick and the brethren of the Order, who ministered to them, and but few escaped to the Holy Land to tell the story of their sufferings.[1]

The inability of Guy de Lusignan to command the respect and obedience of the barons, had shown his unsuitability for his high position. It was still further shown, when he refused the wish of his unhappy brother-in-law and sovereign to take Tyre in exchange for Jerusalem. King Baldwin now a dying man, had still strength enough left to assert the dignity of the crown, and in November resumed once more the reins of government. By his directions his young nephew Prince Baldwin, though only 5 years of age, was crowned King of Jerusalem, to ensure that the throne should pass to him and not to his

[1] An account of the massacre, based upon William of Tyre, is given by Vertot, *Les Chevaliers de Malthe*, Book II.

stepfather, and in order to destroy any claims that Guy de Lusignan might put forward in the future, the king even proposed to dissolve his marriage with the Princess Sibyl, and summoned him to Jerusalem. But the princess and her husband shut themselves up in Ascalon, and openly defied the king, refusing to admit him to the city, and barring the gates against him.

With the downfall of Guy de Lusignan all real power passed into the hands of the king's cousin the Count of Tripolis, the natural leader of the native baronage. He was entrusted with the command of the force sent to relieve Kerak, which Saladin had been besieging since the end of October, and on 4 December compelled him to raise the siege. Early in the following year (1184) a great council met at Acre to consider the best course to take in view of the grave danger that now confronted the state, and how if possible to heal the differences by which it was so unhappily divided. For there were now two distinct parties in the kingdom, the European born aristocracy, and the native born, each with an entirely different policy. The former led by Guy de Lusignan and Reginald de Chatillon, supported by the Masters of the Hospital and the Temple, believed that the Holy Land could be held only by the sword. They were as a rule bitter fanatics, and considered that the Holy War should never cease so long as there was an infidel still left to slay. The national party on the other hand, led by Count Raymond of Tripolis, wished above all things to preserve their property and estates. They realized only too clearly that the Latin kingdom was helpless in face of the vast resources in men and money commanded by Saladin, and desired nothing better than to live at peace with their Moslem neighbours, until at least such time as Europe should again be prepared to pour out its strength upon Asia, as it had done in the First and Second Crusades.

At the Council of Acre King Baldwin IV presided in person, although now almost blind and unable to use either hand or foot, and the national party had things all their own way. Roger des Moulins, Master of the Hospital, and his colleague Arnold de Torroge of the Temple, supported by the Patriarch Heraclius, begged the king on their knees to pardon the Count of Jaffa and Ascalon. But he firmly declined to have further dealings with his brother-in-law, and they left the Council in great anger. The Count of Tripolis was then declared regent of the realm for ten years, that is until the boy-king Baldwin the Child should come of age, and he was allowed to occupy Beyrout as guarantee for any expenses that he might incur. The actual guardianship of the little king's person was entrusted to his great-uncle Joscelin III, titular Count of Edessa, and Seneschal of the Kingdom, and it was agreed that if he died, Count Raymond should remain regent until a new king had been selected by the Pope, the Emperor and the Kings of France and England. To pacify the military Orders and at the regent's request, all royal castles and fortresses were to be placed in the hands of the Hospitallers and Templars. Before the council broke up, it was decided to send the Patriarch and the Masters of the Hospital and the Temple on a special mission to the court of King Henry II of England, as grandson of King Fulk and head of the royal House of Anjou, to implore him to bring assistance to the Holy Land before it should be too late. The dying king, now only 23 years of age, had done all that was in his power to provide for the future government of his kingdom; within a year death at last put an end to his misery, and his nephew King Baldwin V, a child of six, reigned in his stead. There is no more pathetic or tragic figure in history than King Baldwin the Leper. With his body afflicted almost from earliest infancy, with the foulest and most loathsome and repulsive of all diseases, he exhibits, so far as his physical condition would permit, all the energy and capacity, the courage and high sense of duty of his race, and we see in him the gallant spirit of a true hero king rising superior to all the horror of his hideous doom.

During the summer of 1184 Saladin made another determined attempt to capture Kerak, which not only blocked the caravan route to Egypt, but was the home of his hated enemy Reginald de Chatillon, the sacrilegious unbeliever who had tried to defile the very tomb of the Prophet. He appeared before the walls of that impregnable fortress on 13 August, just when the Lord of Kerak was celebrating the marriage of his stepson, young Humphrey de Toron, grandson of the Constable, with the Princess Isabel, younger sister of King Baldwin the Leper. The chivalrous Sultan carefully inquired in which tower of the castle the young couple were spending their honeymoon, and gave orders that it should not on any account be bombarded. However, the siege did not last long; by the end of the month the army of Jerusalem was on the march, and successfully evading Saladin's covering force, entered Kerak on 3 September and the Sultan raised the siege. But on his way back to Damascus he took his revenge for the disappointment, sending a strong detachment across the Jordan under a renegade Templar Robert of St. Albans,[1] who plundered and burnt Nablus, Sebastiyeh and Jinin, before the Christian forces could get back from Kerak. This campaign ended the second war between Saladin and the Latin kingdom, both sides desired peace, and a truce for four years was concluded to be reckoned from the following Easter.

Meanwhile the Patriarch Heraclius and the Masters of the Hospital and the Temple had embarked at Jaffa in June for their mission to England. Landing at Brindisi, they first visited King William of Sicily, a personal friend of Roger des Moulins, and in November reached Verona, where they had interviews with the Pope and the Emperor Frederick Barbarossa. At Verona, Arnold de Torroge, Master of the

[1] See Stevenson's *Crusaders in the East*, p. 235, note 4.

Temple, fell sick and died. The Patriarch and the Master of the Hospital reached Paris in the middle of January, where they received the warmest welcome from the French king, and then proceeded to England. They arrived in London in February, and there on the 10th the Patriarch consecrated the Temple Church. They then proceeded to Reading, where King Henry II was holding his court. When the Patriarch and the Master of the Hospital had entered his presence, they placed in the king's hands the royal standard of Jerusalem with the keys of the Holy Sepulchre, the City and the Tower of David, the Patriarch exclaiming with deep emotion, 'Behold the keys of the kingdom, which the king and princes of the land have ordered me to give to thee, because it is in thee alone, after God, that they have hope and confidence of salvation.' The whole assembly was so deeply moved that it burst into tears, as the king reverently handed back the standard and keys to the Patriarch for safe keeping, until such time as he should have consulted the great council of the realm. The mission then returned to London, and on 10 March the Patriarch consecrated the new church of the Hospitallers in their Priory at Clerkenwell.[1] On 18 March the great council assembled at Clerkenwell in the hall of the Hospitallers to meet the king. But the prelates and barons, while ready to vote money for the Holy War, were very clear that it was the king's duty to govern his kingdom, and not to go campaigning in the East. There can never have been a more dramatic scene in the great hall of the Priory, than when the Patriarch, a violent, hot-blooded Frenchman from Auvergne, cried out in bitter disappointment, 'Not thus will you save your soul nor the heritage of Christ, we come to seek a king not money, for every corner of the world sends us money, but not one a prince.' And then losing his head entirely, he prophesied that the king would be henceforward forsaken by God, and his glory turned into disaster and shame. In spite of this painful scene King Henry rode down to the coast with Roger des Moulins and the Patriarch, on their way back to the Holy Land, reaching Dover on 10 April. To the disgust of the Master of the Hospital, the Patriarch was outrageously insulting to the king, and actually accused him of the murder of St. Thomas à Becket. They sailed on the 16th, and when the king once more expressed his regret that he could not go on crusade, owing to the danger he feared from his rebellious sons, the Patriarch could find nothing better to say than, 'No wonder, from the devil they came, and to the devil they will go.'[2] Seldom has a delicate

[1] Of this church, which had a round nave like the Temple Church, there now remains only the beautiful Norman crypt. At the west door of the existing church there is a notice reading: 'The Priory Church of the Order of St. John of Jerusalem. Consecrated March 10th 1185 by Heraclius, Patriarch of Jerusalem.'

[2] Alluding to the diabolic ancestry of the House of Anjou then currently believed.

RECEPTION OF THE PATRIARCH HERACLIUS AND THE MASTER OF THE HOSPITAL, IN READING ABBEY, BY KING HENRY II

From the Painting in Reading Museum

mission of importance been conducted with less tact, and greater folly, but for that Roger des Moulins was not to blame.

The Patriarch and the Master of the Hospital were probably back in the Holy Land by the autumn of 1185, to find King Baldwin the Leper dead, and Count Raymond of Tripolis now supreme in his capacity as regent for King Baldwin the Child. Under the new regime there was at last peace and security, almost for the first time since the death of King Fulk of Anjou. But the Templars had elected as their Master in the place of Arnold de Torroge a certain Flemish knight Gerard de Ridfort, well known to be a bitter personal enemy of the Count of Tripolis. When he first came out to the Holy Land as a young knight, he had desired to marry the Lady of Botron, a great heiress in the county of Tripolis. Count Raymond had forbidden the marriage, and Gerard de Ridfort had made his profession in the Order of the Temple, but he had ever after hated the Count with a deadly hatred that was shortly to bear very evil fruit. The Count of Tripolis was one of the few Christians in whose word it was possible for Saladin to have confidence, and the Sultan used the opportunity of a stable peace to settle his outstanding differences with Izz-ed-din [1] Lord of Mosul and head of the House of Zanki. In March 1186 a treaty was made with Izz-ed-din, who consented to acknowledge Saladin's suzerainty, and the Sultan was able to return to Damascus free from any future anxieties regarding his northern frontiers. This year, 1186, is also of importance in the history of the Hospitallers, for it is now that the famous castle of Margat came into their possession, so soon to be the headquarters of their Order.[2]

Peace and tranquillity were not to be of long duration in the kingdom of Jerusalem. Late in the summer of 1186 King Baldwin the Child died at Acre, and his body was taken by the Templars to Jerusalem for burial in the church of the Holy Sepulchre. His death was the signal for a fresh outbreak of strife, each party at once accused the other of having poisoned the young king, and the Master of the Temple began to organize a conspiracy for the overthrow of the Count of Tripolis. The regent called an assembly of the barons and notables at Nablus, no doubt to confirm his position, which had already been guaranteed by the Council of Acre, until such time as a new king should be chosen by the Pope and Emperor and the Kings of France and England. Gerard de Ridfort and the Templars were joined in Jerusalem by Count Joscelin of Edessa, Seneschal of the kingdom, by the Patriarch Heraclius and by Reginald de Chatillon. Then they suddenly summoned the Princess Sibyl to the Holy City and crowned her Queen of Jerusalem in the church of the Holy Sepulchre, and she

[1] Izz-ed-din Masud was a son of Nur-ed-din's brother Kutb-ed-din, and had succeeded his elder brother Saif-ed-din Gazi II in 1180.

[2] See *Cartulaire-Général*, Vol. I, No. 783.

immediately afterwards crowned her husband, Guy de Lusignan, as king, saying, 'Sire, take this crown, for I know not where I could bestow it better.' It was said that as the Master of the Temple took the hand of King Guy, he was heard to murmur, 'This coronation is well-worth the marriage of Botron.' In vain Roger des Moulins and the Hospitallers protested vigorously against these proceedings, which were contrary to the arrangement made at the Council of Acre, and could only have the most disastrous consequences for the country. The Master of the Hospital held one of the three keys of the treasury of the Holy Sepulchre, in which the royal insignia were kept, and without which the coronation could scarcely take place. For a long time he obstinately refused to surrender it, but the Hospitallers were helpless in face of the superior force of the conspirators, and he was eventually compelled to do so.

When the startling news of this *coup d'état* reached the Count of Tripolis and the assembled barons at Nablus, their first idea was to declare one of their own party, Humphrey de Toron, king, by virtue of his marriage with the Princess Isabel. But Humphrey de Toron had no ambitions for a throne, and stealing away to Jerusalem by night, gave in his allegiance to the new sovereigns. The Count of Tripolis then retired to his castle of Tiberias, which he held by his marriage with the widowed Princess of Galilee, and remained there quietly watching events, whilst the barons of the Holy Land, apparently unable to agree upon any definite policy, one by one accepted the *fait accompli*. The first intention of King Guy de Lusignan, urged on by the Master of the Temple, was to attack Count Raymond at Tiberias. But the Sultan of Damascus now began to exhibit a most disquieting interest in the affairs of the Latin kingdom, and advancing to Bélinas took up his position there with a corps of observation. It soon became known that if the new King of Jerusalem was so ill-advised as to attack the Count of Tripolis, then Saladin would undoubtedly march to the latter's assistance. In consequence wiser councils prevailed in Jerusalem, and actual civil war was avoided. But the Master of the Temple used the opportunity given by such an understanding, to brand the Count as a traitor ready to sell his country and his religion for gold, the friend of the infidel and a secret Moslem.

The coronation of Guy de Lusignan was fatal to the Latin kingdom of Jerusalem. Disliked and distrusted by the native barons, unrecognized by the most powerful of them all, he was quite unable to control those of his own party. Reginald de Chatillon resumed his old habits of levying blackmail upon Saracen merchants and pilgrims, as they passed his castles of Kerak and Montreal, entirely regardless of the truce, and early in 1187 captured a particularly rich caravan, with which a sister of Saladin is said to have been travelling. The indignant Sultan protested against such an infringement of the truce, and finding his protests were ignored, swore once more that he would yet slay Reginald de Chatillon with his own hands, and prepared for war. This time he was determined to drive the Christians out of Syria, not only was their religion objectionable to him, but as neighbours they were intolerable owing to their habits of brigandage, and no treaty could ever be relied upon. In the spring of 1187 the Holy War was being preached throughout all the realms of Saladin, and the forces of Islam were beginning to assemble.

No illusions were held in Jerusalem as to the serious nature of the blow that was about to fall. A great assembly of the barons was held there at Easter, and they insisted that there should be a reconciliation between King Guy and the Count of Tripolis. There could be no hope of success with their forces disunited. King Guy therefore agreed to send a special mission to Tiberias, where Count Raymond had remained ever since the king's coronation, to endeavour to arrange terms of reconciliation. The mission was to consist of the Masters of the two military Orders, Roger des Moulins of the Hospital, and Gerard de Ridfort of the Temple, with the Archbishop of Tyre and the Lords of Ibelin and Sidon. The two Masters left Jerusalem on 29 April escorted by 100 Templars,[1] and were to be followed by the remainder of the mission. They spent the night of 30 April at La Fève, and then next morning just as they were about to continue their journey, they heard that a strong party of Saracens was across the Jordan.

So far, war, though imminent and quite unavoidable, had not yet actually begun, and the relations between Saladin and the Count of Tripolis had up to now been consistently friendly, owing to their mutual aversion towards Guy de Lusignan and his friends. Apparently El-Afdal the Sultan's eldest son had asked Count Raymond's permission for a day's hunting on Christian soil. The required permission was granted on condition that the excursion should take place during the sunlight of one day only, and that the Saracens should pledge their word not to molest in any way any house or town they might pass. The Count of Tripolis then sent out a warning notice to the neighbourhood that this excursion would take place on 1 May, and to avoid the possibility of trouble instructed all Christian people to keep within their walls on that day.[2] It is evident from the conditions, which were most honourably kept by the Saracens, that the excursion can only have been a hunting party. Afterwards, however, a ridiculous story became prevalent, which was seized upon with avidity by the Master of the Temple and the Count's other enemies, that being a traitor and a secret Moslem he deliberately allowed El-Afdal to have a day's plundering on Christian soil. The idiotic nature of the story is sufficiently obvious from the fact that the lands of Galilee over which

[1] See *Les Hospitaliers en Terre Sainte*, p. 95, note 2.

[2] See Lane-Poole, *Saladin*, p. 202.

the excursion took place, were Count Raymond's own territory, owing to his marriage with the widowed Princess Eschiva of Galilee.[1]

As soon as the two Masters heard the news that a party of Saracens was over the border, their delicate mission of peace was entirely forgotten, and their fighting instincts took complete control. If infidels had had the effrontery to enter Christian lands, there was only one course open to the knights of the military Orders. Riding hastily on to Nazareth, they drew 40 knights from the garrison and about 400 infantry, and then set out to seek the intruders. Two leagues past Nazareth on the road to Tiberias, they found El-Afdal at the fountain of Cresson close by Kefr Kenna, the ancient Cana of Galilee. They at once attacked; during the mêlée that followed, a fresh detachment of Saracens came up from Kefr Kenna, and the Christians, surrounded and enormously outnumbered, were cut to pieces. Roger des Moulins fighting valiantly, fell in the midst of his enemies; repeatedly wounded by arrows, he was eventually run through the chest with a lance, and of the ten of his brethren, who had accompanied the mission, five fell by his side. The escort of Templars were all slain, except two and Gerard de Ridfort their Master, who hacked their way out of the press and so got away.[2] In spite of this attack El-Afdal kept his word, before the sun was set he was back in his own land, and no Christian town or castle or house had suffered any injury. It would have been better for the Holy Land had the Master of the Temple been amongst the slain in this engagement, for his insane hatred of the Count of Tripolis was to be the ruin of the Christian cause.

Roger des Moulins was perhaps fortunate in his death, for there could have been no better end for so stout a soldier and so gallant a knight, and he was spared the sorrow of witnessing the terrible disaster that was so soon to take place, and the loss of that Holy City, to whose protection he had devoted his life. His body was afterwards recovered by his brethren, and taken to Acre, where it was eventually buried owing to the loss of Jerusalem. The name of Roger des Moulins must always stand high on the roll of the greater heroes of the Order of St. John, and he appears to have been well deserving of the eulogies that have been lavished upon his memory by its historians.[3] A man of deep piety and sound judgment, he was wise in council, valiant in battle, and greatly esteemed for his knowledge of Oriental politics. No man's opinion was more respected in the Holy Land, and his free-

[1] He held the Principality of Galilee by right of his marriage, during the minority of his stepson Hugh de Tabarie.

[2] For an account of this engagement, see *Les Hospitaliers en Terre Sainte*, p. 95. The numbers attributed to the Saracens, namely 7,000, are no doubt greatly exaggerated by contemporary writers, as is usually the custom when estimating the strength of an enemy.

[3] The character and rule of Roger des Moulins are very completely summarized by Delaville Le Roulx in *Les Hospitaliers en Terre Sainte*, p. 96.

dom from prejudices and personal hatreds forms a pleasing contrast to the character of his colleague the Master of the Temple. Under his wise rule and firm hand the prestige and importance of the Hospitallers had continued to increase, and though before all things a soldier, his statutes [1] regarding the ceremonies of the church, and the care of the Hospital, show us that he never allowed himself to forget the original charitable objects for which his Order had been founded. His character is well summed up by the official chronicler, who tells us that 'he was a man of great wisdom, and vigorous in battle, a good man and pious and very high-minded, and he loved much his brethren, and our lords the sick '.[2] Roger des Moulins is the only Master of the Order of St. John, who was ever killed in action, and it is a very curious fact that so wealthy and famous an Order should never have been moved in all the centuries of its existence, to erect a monument on the spot where one of the greatest of its heroes fell fighting valiantly against hopeless odds in defence of the Christian faith.

APPENDIX

AGREEMENT BETWEEN THE HOSPITALLERS AND TEMPLARS [3]

Dated February 1179

In the name of the Father and the Son and the Holy Ghost. Amen. Be it known to all men, alike in future and present generations, that by the will of Almighty God and upon the admonishment of our Lord Pope Alexander, I Odo de St. Amand, humble master of the knighthood of the Temple, and I Roger des Moulins, humble master of the Hospital of Jerusalem, with the advice and assent of our Chapters, have made an agreement and peace concerning all the disputes which have up to this present day arisen between the House of the Temple and the Hospital, whether this side the sea or beyond the sea, both as regards moveable goods and real estate, and thus the whole of our disputes are set at rest, so that never again can they be revived nor repeated.

Moreover of all these disputes we have considered it advisable to set forth in words the following: the dispute concerning Le Crac, the dispute concerning the ill-deed of Mount Ferrand (Barin), the dispute concerning the plundering of the Bedouin of the Temple by the Turcopoles of Jibelin, the dispute concerning the land of the Marricii, which for the

[1] See *Cartulaire-Général*, Vol. I, No. 627, and the Statutes and Ordinances printed in Appendix E at the end of this work.

[2] 'The Chronicle of the deceased Masters' confounds Roger des Moulins and Geoffrey de Donjon, but there is no difficulty in making the necessary correction. See Appendix B at the end.

[3] Printed in Latin in the *Cartulaire-Général*, Vol. I, No. 558.

purpose of effecting this agreement is divided between the Temple and the Hospital, according to the right which is due to the Hospital therein, the disputes concerning the three casales,[1] Terra Galifa, Banna and Casale Bertrandimir,[2] whereof two, Terra Galifa and Banna are to remain with the Hospital quietly and peacefully with their appurtenances, whilst Casale Bertrandimir is to remain with the Templars with its appurtenances for ever. These are the complaints of the Templars against the Hospital. The following are the complaints against the Templars: the dispute concerning Gaza, the dispute concerning Castle Arnold,[3] the dispute concerning Aman,[4] the dispute concerning the House of Barolo.[5] All these disputes are settled and ended, and if there have been any other disputes, besides those named above, between the brethren of the Temple and the brethren of the Hospital, this side the sea or beyond it, they are all settled.

And if hereafter any dispute should arise again between us or our successors, or between our brethren, on this side the sea or beyond it, we decree that it shall be settled by three brethren from either party, as we are directed in the orders of our Lord the Pope, that is that the Preceptors of the houses or provinces, between whom the disagreement shall have arisen, whether it concerns land or money or a bequest or any other matter, shall each select two of the more experienced of their brethren, with the help of whom they shall do their best to solve the question at issue and preserve the peace between them, without guile, each endeavouring as much as in them lies to avoid injury to the other side. But if acting by themselves only they are unable to put an end to the dispute, they shall summon to their assistance mutual friends by whose advice and mediation the matter may be determined. And the decision shall be according as the majority of the brethren or friends agree, that is to say if one of my party agree with the view of the other party, the dispute shall be determined by that view, and unbroken peace and unimpaired affection shall endure for ever between our brethren.

But if it is impossible for them even by this means to agree, they shall send the complaint to us in writing, and we will determine the matter, if it be God's will, but they meanwhile shall keep the peace and live in goodwill towards each other. But if any of the brethren, which God forbid, shall break this peace and this keeping of the peace, let him know that he contravenes the commands of his Master and the ordinances of the Chapter of Jerusalem, and no way shall be open to him of expiating his offence, until he shall appear in person before his Master and the Chapter of Jerusalem. And to these provisions we add and strictly enjoin that the brethren of both Houses, wheresoever they shall be, shall hold each other in affection and honour, and with mutual goodwill en-

[1] The Casale was a hamlet of at least one hundred houses, taxed at about seven shillings a year. See Conder's *Latin Kingdom of Jerusalem*, p. 240.

[2] The land of the Marricii with Terra Galifa, Banna and Casale Bertrandimir cannot be identified.

[3] Castle Arnold midway between Jaffa and Jerusalem.

[4] Perhaps Calamon (Kusr Hajleh), south-east of Jericho.

[5] The House of Barolo is the Priory of Barletta, see *Les Hospitaliers en Terre Sainte*, p. 374.

deavour to study and promote each the interests of the other, so that though they may be by profession of two Houses, they shall in affection seem to be but of one.

And this peace and concord was made in the year of the Incarnation of Our Lord 1179, in the month of February, in the twelfth Indiction, in the presence of the Lord Baldwin, the sixth of the Latin Kings of the Holy City of Jerusalem; in the presence of the Lord Bohemond, Prince of Antioch; in the presence of the Lord Raymond, Count of Tripolis; in the presence of the Lord Albert, Count of La Marche; in the presence of the Lord Joscelin, the king's seneschal; in the presence of the Lord Balian; in the presence of the Lord Reginald of Sidon; in the presence of the Lord Humphrey, the king's constable; in the presence of the Lord Baldwin of Ramleh; and in the presence of the other barons of Eastern Christendom, all of whom laboured to bring about this agreement, and have confirmed it.

> I Baldwin the King was present at the drawing up of this agreement, and have confirmed this sheet with the apposition of my seal.
>
> I Bohemond, Prince of Antioch, was present, and have confirmed this sheet with the apposition of my seal.
>
> I Raymond, Count of Tripolis, was present, and have confirmed this sheet with the apposition of my seal.

CONFIRMATION BY POPE ALEXANDER III [1]

Dated 2 *August* 1179

Alexander, Bishop, Servant of the Servants of God, to his well-beloved sons the Master and brethren of the Knighthood of the Temple, sendeth greeting.

Exactly in proportion to the esteem in which your Order and the Order of the brethren of the Hospital of Jerusalem are held by God and man, ought we to rejoice and be glad that such a unity has been accomplished between you that henceforth the bond of affection will always bind you together in your zealous works. For this reason therefore we not only approve but do also ratify by apostolic authority the peace and concord which with their assent you have made with our well-beloved sons the Master and brethren of the Hospital, touching all those disputes which have for so long been maintained between your House and theirs, both concerning lands and estates and also concerning money and other things, and we decree that it shall endure firm unshaken for all time, which concord we here set forth word for word 'In the name of the Father, etc.' (here follows the previous document). And therefore we decree that no man whatsoever shall infringe this our act of confirmation or rashly dare to contravene the same. If any one, etc.

Given at Segni on the 4th day before the Nones of August (i.e. August 2nd).

[1] Printed in Latin in the *Cartulaire-Général*, Vol. I, No. 570.

CHAPTER VIII

THE LOSS OF JERUSALEM

THE death of the Master of the Hospital could not have occurred at a more inopportune moment, just as the last great war against Saladin was about to begin. There was no doubt as to the type of man required to fill the vacancy at such a time, he had to be above all things a good soldier. But circumstances rendered it impossible to summon a meeting of the Chapter, and the office of Master could not be filled immediately, but remained vacant for over a year. During the vacancy the powers of the Master were exercised according to the custom of the Order by William Borrell, Preceptor of the Hospital, who like the deceased Master was probably of Anglo-Norman stock. Of him we know only that he was appointed Preceptor by Roger des Moulins in February 1186, and that he was afterwards Marshal of the Order from 1193 to 1195. But he certainly succeeded in upholding the prestige and dignity of his Order, during a painful period of unmitigated disaster and tragedy.

When the Master of the Temple rode away from the slaughter by the fountain of Cresson, he made for Nazareth, where he met Balian, Lord of Ibelin, just arrived from Jerusalem. Together they rode on to Tiberias, and there had an interview with the Count of Tripolis. In face of the recent catastrophe and the approaching war, Count Raymond was prepared to lay aside all personal feelings, and agreed to a reconciliation with King Guy. The two met at Dothan, by the historic cistern into which Joseph was thrown by his brethren,[1] and there Count Raymond bent the knee in homage to King Guy, and the king raised him up and embraced him warmly. Before they parted they had agreed upon united action in the coming campaign.

During June the allied armies of Jerusalem and Tripolis concentrated at Saffaria, their usual place of assembly, when invasion threatened from Damascus. Every nerve was strained to place the strongest possible force in the field, and castles and towns were entirely stripped of their garrisons, with what ultimately proved to be fatal results. There finally assembled an even larger army than in 1183, 1,200 Knights,

[1] See Lane-Poole's *Saladin*, p. 203.

at least as many Turcopoles, and 18,000 foot,[1] although the number of Knights was slightly smaller, doubtless owing to 100 Templars having just been killed at the fountain of Cresson. Since the fighting value of a European force was considerably higher than that of a corresponding number of Oriental troops, the army should have rendered a good account of itself against Saladin, had it not been for one grave weakness, the bitter hostility existing between the two cliques of barons, which simply could not be terminated at a moment's notice by the outward reconciliation of their respective chiefs, however sincere that reconciliation may have been.

Meanwhile Saladin's army was concentrating at Tell Ashtera, south-west of Damascus, and by the latter half of June was ready to move. Its concentration had been much delayed by the late arrival of the contingents from Aleppo and Mosul, which had been engaged up to the last moment in operations against Antioch and Armenia. The total force amounted to about 25,000 men;[2] 12,000 of them the regular feudal contingents: all Turkish horse-archers of the Parthian type, the remainder auxiliaries drawn to the Sultan's standard by religious fervour or the desire for plunder. It was organized in three divisions under the Sultan, his nephew Taki-ed-din Omar, and Kukbury Emir of Harran. On 24 June Saladin held a grand review of his army, and on the 26th the advance began. Next day the Saracens crossed the Jordan at the usual crossing south of the Sea of Galilee, and went into camp at Sennabra. As the Christian army gave no sign of moving, Saladin firmly resolved on fighting a decisive engagement, advanced on the 30th to Capharsebti, 10 miles east of Saffaria. Still the Christian army remained stationary, and on the evening of 2 July Saladin attacked Tiberias, in the hope of tempting them to advance to its assistance. The town which was held by the Countess of Tripolis was easily captured, the Countess retiring with the garrison into the castle.

Saladin's action had exactly the result that he desired. That very night King Guy summoned a council of war at Saffaria, and Gerard de Ridfort, Master of the Temple, and Reginald de Chatillon strongly urged him to advance at once against the enemy. The Count of Tripolis on the other hand advised him to remain on the defensive, since the Saracen army was too strong to be attacked hastily, and the waterless state of the country would render any advance hazardous. Saladin, compelled by their presence to keep his army concentrated, must inevitably retire in a few days through lack of supplies, as he had done in 1183. The council of war having approved Count Raymond's advice by a large majority, broke up at midnight under the impression that its opinion had been accepted by the king. But Gerard de Ridfort and Reginald de Chatillon followed the king to his tent, and begged

[1] See Stevenson, *The Crusaders in the East*, p. 245, note 2.
[2] Ibid., p. 243.

him to remember that the Count of Tripolis was a false traitor in league with the infidel, a secret Moslem, a man capable of any iniquity whose advice must necessarily be bad. King Guy, by nature a weak man, allowed himself to be overpersuaded by Count Raymond's enemies, to whom he owed his crown, and finally issued fresh orders for an advance at daybreak.

Early in the morning on Friday, 3 July, the Christian army began its disastrous march on Tiberias, 16 miles away. It was organized in the usual three divisions. The troops of Tripolis and Galilee under Count Raymond formed the advance guard, the main body was under

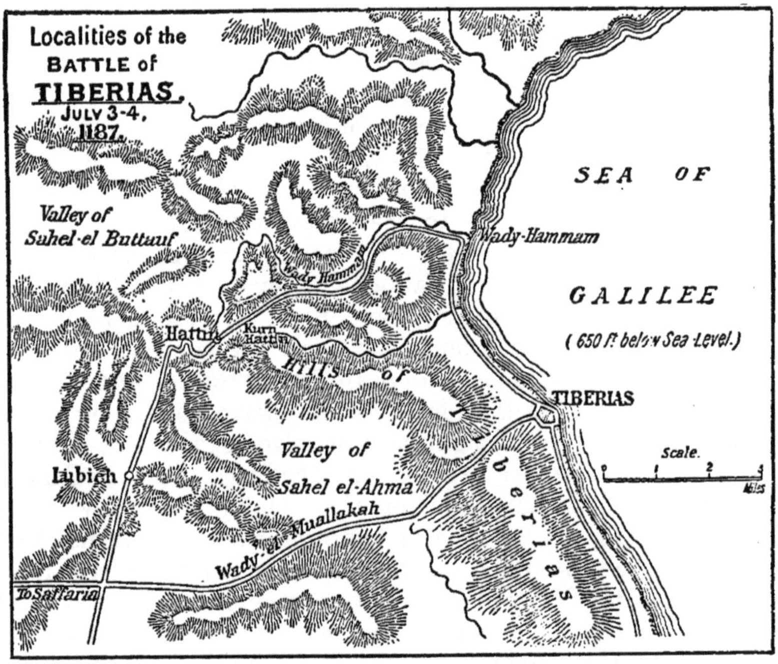

PLAN OF THE BATTLE OF HATTIN, OR TIBERIAS

King Guy and with him went the Bishop of Acre bearing the famous relic of the True Cross, whilst the Hospitallers under William Borrel their Preceptor and the Templars under Gerard de Ridfort their Master formed the rearguard. After marching about 9 miles along the shadeless, glaring limestone road they were surrounded by swarms of Turkish horse-archers, whose showers of arrows caused continual halts to enable the infantry to drive them off with their arbalests. By the time that the main body had reached the cross-roads south of Marescalcia (Lubieh), 6 miles from its destination,[1] the men weighed down by their heavy equipment under the heat of a July sun, were showing

[1] Marescalcia is probably the modern Lubieh. See Oman's *Art of War in the Middle Ages*, Vol. I, p. 327, note 1.

signs of exhaustion, and were already beginning to suffer from thirst. A message now came in from the Hospitallers and Templars in the rear to say that they were being heavily attacked, were unable to keep up with the column, and had been brought to a standstill. King Guy thereupon decided to halt for the night, and to encamp on the hill-side south of Marescalcia (Lubieh). Meanwhile the advance guard under the Count of Tripolis had descended by the Wady el-Muallakah into the valley and was barely 3 miles from the lake, in close contact with the main Saracen army holding the Hills of Tiberias. Count Raymond sent back to the king urging him to advance at all costs, as disaster was unavoidable unless he reached the lake before night. But the king held to his fatal decision to halt, and as the advance guard fell back upon the main body Count Raymond was heard to exclaim in the bitterness of his despair, 'Alas, alas, Lord God! the war is ended; we are all delivered over to death, and the realm is ruined'.[1]

The Christian army passed a wretched night in its bivouacs on the hillside, constant attacks rendered sleep impossible, there were no rations, hardly any water, and to add to their misery the enemy set fire to the dry grass to windward, causing clouds of acrid smoke to drift over them, rendering the torments of thirst almost unendurable. Next morning King Guy decided to abandon the direct road to Tiberias, and to take the road leading through the village of Hattin to Wady Hammam, where was the nearest water supply. Saladin thereupon made a flank march to his right, placing his main force astride the road. As King Guy deployed his army for attack under the heat of the midday sun, the infantry half mad with thirst began to waver and, swerving away to the left out of the battle, took refuge on the hillside leaving the cavalry on the road. Finding it useless to attempt to bring them into action, for they were now in a state of collapse, the king ordered the cavalry to endeavour to push their way through the enemy down the Wady Hammam. But the Saracens according to their custom again endeavoured to cut out the rearguard of Hospitallers and Templars, who were in consequence unable to keep up, and the king ordered a halt as he had done the previous day. All who were still able to fight grouped themselves round the True Cross, and then the king called upon the Count of Tripolis to make one final effort to burst through.[2] Count Raymond with the Preceptor of the Hospital,[3] the Lords of Ibelin and Sidon and young Raymond of Antioch his godson, at the

[1] The most detailed study of the Battle of Hattin, or Tiberias, as he prefers to call it, is to be found in Oman's *Art of War in the Middle Ages*, Vol. I, pp. 324–33.

[2] See Lane-Poole's *Saladin*, p. 212.

[3] The Preceptor William Borrel must have escaped from the battle with Count Raymond, since he was assisting in the defence of Tyre during the autumn.

head of their knights and retainers charged the Saracens to the north-west of the road, where their forces were very much weaker, hacked their way through and escaped northwards. The enemy closed round the remainder of the knights before they could follow, and King Guy and all that were left formed up for their last stand on the hill of Kurn-Hattin, on the very spot where more than eleven hundred years before Our Saviour had preached the Sermon on the Mount. They made one final desperate charge, but their horses were shot down under them, and then utterly exhausted they flung down their arms, and allowed themselves to be taken prisoners, and with them was taken the True Cross, the most precious and sacred relic in Christendom. The unfortunate infantry were in a state of collapse from thirst, physically incapable of any resistance, and lay about on the ground to be slain or captured according to the caprice of their enemies. So perished through utter mismanagement the finest army that the Latin Kingdom of Jerusalem had ever placed in the field.

As soon as the battle was over, Saladin had his tent pitched, and ordered King Guy and the chief barons to be brought before him. He received his prisoners in the most chivalrous and courteous manner, invited them to be seated, and cups of sherbet cooled with snow were handed round. But as King Guy passed his cup to Reginald de Chatillon, Saladin ominously remarked that he offered no hospitality to that man. Later in the day Reginald de Chatillon was summoned to Saladin's tent, and the Sultan formally offered him conversion to Islam, which was refused, and then he pronounced his doom: 'Twice have I sworn to kill him, once when he sought to invade the holy cities, and again when he took the caravan by treachery. Lo! I will avenge Mohammed upon thee.' Drawing his scimitar Saladin cut him down with his own hands in accordance with the oath that he had twice sworn. The other prisoners of noble birth were taken to Damascus, where they were well treated and held to ransom.

But for the Hospitallers and Templars another fate had been reserved. In the eyes of Saladin the military Orders were the relentless enemies of his faith, savage and merciless fanatics, who gave no quarter to their opponents, and should receive none from him. As they had treated others, so should they also be treated. An army order was issued directing every soldier, who held as his prisoner an Hospitaller or a Templar, to hand him over to headquarters, compensation being paid at the rate of 50 dinars a head.[1] There proved to be 230 knights of the Hospital or the Temple in Saracen hands. Two days after the battle on Monday, 6 July, they were taken out to meet their doom. Every knight was given the chance of saving his life by becoming a Mohammedan. To the everlasting honour of the military Orders, not a single man of them flinched before the ordeal, and the glorious crown

[1] See Oman's *Art of War in the Middle Ages*, Vol. I, p. 332.

of martyrdom was their reward. On the slopes of Kurn Hattin in the presence of the whole army they were publicly executed by the Sultan's bodyguard.[1] Only the Master of the Temple, at the special request of King Guy, was spared. There can be no spot in all the world more sacred to the members of the Order of St. John than the slopes of Kurn Hattin, where on that July day in 1187 such a multitude of their brethren, calmly and deliberately and in cold blood, gave their lives for the Christian faith, and it is a strange thing that no monument should mark the spot, where they died so gloriously.

The disastrous battle of Hattin was the end of the Latin kingdom of Jerusalem, as it had been constituted since the First Crusade. The whole country was completely paralysed by the irremediable nature of the disaster, and stunned at the loss of the True Cross. Except for a few frontier castles every city or fortress had been stripped of its garrison to strengthen the army, and after the battle further resistance was almost an impossibility, the kingdom simply collapsed like a house of cards. Saladin only had to appear before town or castle to receive its instant surrender. The day following the battle the Countess of Tripolis abandoned her castle of Tiberias, and was allowed by the Sultan to depart in peace with her children and attendants to join her husband. But Count Raymond had not many days to live, worn out by fatigue and strain and sorrow, the shock of such hopeless ruin was too great, and he died suddenly only fifteen days after the defeat. On 8 July Saladin appeared before Acre, and two days later the great seaport opened its gates to him, an example instantly followed by Haifa, Caesarea and Arsuf. Then the towns of central Palestine, Nazareth, Saffaria and Nablus followed suit, whilst the army of Egypt under the Sultan's brother El-Adil, whom the Christians called Saphadin, crossed the desert and stormed Jaffa. The strong castle of Toron stood a siege of only seven days before surrendering on 16 July, Sidon opened her gates to the Sultan on the 29th, and Beyrout fell into his hands on 6 August after resisting for seven days. Giblet (Jubail) in the county of Tripolis capitulated on condition that Hugh de Lembriac, its lord, taken prisoner in the recent battle, should be set free. In this universal débâcle only the city of Tyre stood firm, and she too would have followed the example of the rest, had it not been for the timely arrival from Constantinople of Conrad, son of the Marquis of Montferrat, with a small band of followers, only three days after the surrender of Acre. A man of resolute character and a good soldier, he at once took charge of the situation. There was no further talk of surrender in Tyre, and Saladin for the moment passed it by, since he dared not risk any delay in reaping the fruits of his startling victory.

From Beyrout Saladin marched south to the conquest of Judaea,

[1] See Stevenson, *The Crusaders in the East*, p. 248.

and he took with him King Guy and the Master of the Temple, who were to purchase their release by the surrender of certain fortresses.[1] After effecting a junction with the army of his brother Saphadin, the Sultan laid siege to Ascalon on 30 August. The 'bride of Syria', which had held out against Baldwin III for seven months in 1153, now made but a feeble resistance and surrendered on 4 September on condition that King Guy and certain other prisoners should be released at some future date, apparently after one year of captivity, since they were set free the following July. The Master of the Temple, so unlike his gallant predecessor Odo de St. Amand, appears to have purchased his liberty on the same conditions, by the surrender of Darum and Gaza.[2] Ramleh and Ibelin were taken, Jibelin the castle of the Hospitallers could make no resistance, and the armies of Syria and Egypt at last turned to the conquest of the Holy City.

Jerusalem was filled with refugees from all southern Palestine, but there were no fighting men left. In the convents of the Hospitallers and Templars there was not a single knight, and when Balian Lord of Ibelin and Nablus arrived to take over the command, he could find only two knights[3] in all the city, both of them fugitives from the Battle of Hattin. The siege began on 20 September. The Saracen army took up its positions on the west side of the city from the Gate of St. Stephen (Damascus Gate) to the Gate of David (Jaffa Gate). But on the 25th Saladin moved his camps to the Mount of Olives, and opened his attack on the north-east side from the Gate of St. Stephen to the Gate of Jehosaphat. It was from this direction that Godfrey de Bouillon had taken the city in 1099. Within a few days the barbican was undermined and captured, and there was clearly no possibility of offering any serious resistance. To save the city from the horrors of being taken by assault, Balian of Ibelin yielding to the urgent promptings of the Patriarch Heraclius regretfully consented to ask for terms. On 2 October the conditions of surrender were agreed, conditions so generous that they fill one with amazement as one thinks of the long-drawn-out pitiless massacres that followed the capture of the city by the Crusaders. The Christians were to pay a ransom and leave the city, and they might take with them their movable property, including even the treasures of their churches.[4] Queen Sibyl and her sister the Princess Isabel were permitted to leave free of all ransom, and the Queen was granted an interview with her husband at Nablus. When Saladin found that many elderly persons were too poor to pay any ransom, he finally proclaimed that they should be allowed to go free none the less. In the words of Ernoul, the esquire of Balian of Ibelin, who was present, 'Such was the charity which

[1] See Stevenson, *The Crusaders in the East*, p. 251. [2] Ibid., p. 252.
[3] See Archer and Kingsford, *The Crusades*, p. 278.
[4] See Stevenson, *The Crusaders in the East*, p. 253.

Saladin did, of poor people without number '.[1] There was not a prince in all Christendom who would have treated a helpless Moslem city as Saladin treated Jerusalem.

The exodus from the city lasted forty days, the citizens left in three parties, the first conducted by the Templars, the second by the Hospitallers, and the last by the Patriarch and Balian of Ibelin. But the Templars and Hospitallers in charge of them were only the chaplains and serving brothers of their Orders, for there were no knights present. Saladin provided an escort as far as the frontiers of the county of Tripolis, and since it was impossible for the Hospitallers to evacuate all the sick from their hospital, he permitted ten of the brethren to remain behind for one year to nurse the more serious cases.[2]

Concerning this exodus Balian's esquire Ernoul relates a picturesque incident of singular interest and beauty, that enables us to see more clearly the chivalrous and noble character of the great Sultan.

'Then I shall tell you of the great courtesy which Saladin showed to the wives and daughters of knights, who had fled to Jerusalem when their lords were killed or made prisoners in battle. When these ladies were ransomed and had come forth from Jerusalem, they assembled and went before Saladin crying mercy. When Saladin saw them he asked who they were and what they sought. And it was told him that they were the dames and damsels of knights who had been taken or killed in battle. Then he asked what they wished, and they answered for God's sake have pity on them; for the husbands of some were in prison, and of others were dead, and they had lost their lands, and in the name of God let him counsel and help them. When Saladin saw them weeping, he had great compassion for them, and wept himself for pity. And he bade the ladies whose husbands were alive to tell him where they were captives, and as soon as he could go to the prisons he would set them free. (And all were released wherever they were found.) After that he commanded that to the dames and damsels whose lords were dead there should be handsomely distributed from his own treasure, to some more and others less, according to their estate. And he gave them so much that they gave praise to God and published abroad the kindness and honour which Saladin had done to them.' [3]

Seldom has a victory been followed by such complete and overwhelming success. Within three months of the Battle of Hattin the whole land was in Saracen hands, and every city and fortress had been taken with the exception of Tyre and six frontier castles, whose garrisons it had been impossible to withdraw entirely, even for a great battle. In the extreme north Belfort (Shakif Arnun) in the valley of the Leontes (El-Bika), a castle then belonging to the Lord of Sidon,

[1] See Lane-Poole's *Saladin*, p. 232, and Stevenson, p. 253. He gave 1,000 to his brother Saphadin, who at once set them free; he gave 1,000 more to the Patriarch and Balian of Ibelin, who did the same. He then himself set free all the more elderly persons. Actually 18,000 people were released, but there remained behind a large number of children and young people, some say 15,000, others 11,000.

[2] See *Cartulaire-Général*, Vol. I, No. 847.

[3] See Lane-Poole's *Saladin*, pp. 232, 233.

but later to the Templars, was to hold out for nearly three years. Chateauneuf (Hunin) blocking the road to the sea-coast from Bélinas (Banias), was held by the Hospitallers, though with only a slender force, but Belvoir (Kaukab-el-Hawa) covering the road from the chief fort across the Jordan, they held firmly with a strong garrison. The Templars made a vigorous resistance in their famous castle of Safed, masking any advance from Jacob's Ford, and in the south the two castles in the desert, Kerak and Montreal, flatly declined to surrender, although ordered to do so by their mistress Reginald de Chatillon's widow. Saladin had released her son by her first marriage, young Humphrey de Toron, on condition that the castles were given up to him,[1] but their garrisons indignantly refused to carry out her unworthy instructions.

For six weeks after the fall of Jerusalem, Saladin was busily engaged in organizing the newly conquered territory, and was unable to leave the Holy City until the end of October. But by the middle of November he was free to undertake the reduction of Tyre, and arrived before that city on the 12th. He first tried to induce Conrad of Montferrat to surrender, by offering to release his father the Marquis of Montferrat, who was amongst the prisoners taken at the Battle of Hattin. When Conrad refused, he threatened to slay the Marquis, but the only reply to the threat was that Conrad would never presume to deprive his parent of the glories of martyrdom and the joys of Paradise. The siege began on 25 November, the army being assisted by a blockading squadron of the Egyptian fleet. It provided an entirely new experience for Saladin. Tyre was not only well fortified, but it was held by a strong garrison, for reinforcements were beginning to arrive from Europe, and above all its commandant was a man of very real capacity. As Ibn-el-Athir of Mosul the contemporary Arab historian tells us, 'this man called El-Markis, God's curse upon him, was a devil of a man in caution and watchfulness, and of immense bravery withal'.[2] In the defence of Tyre the Hospitallers played a very prominent part. William Borrel, the Grand Preceptor [3] of the Hospital, appears to have made it his headquarters after his escape from the disaster at Hattin. Here he was joined by one of the most important of the Bailiffs d'Outremer, Armengaud d'Aspe, Prior of St. Gilles and Castellan of Amposta, bringing with him strong reinforcements, amongst them two very notable knights, William of Auvergne and Pons de Baja.[4] Conrad of Montferrat in a letter to the Archbishop of Canterbury [5] speaks in

[1] See Conder's *Latin Kingdom of Jerusalem*, p. 155.

[2] See Lane-Poole's *Saladin*, p. 222.

[3] From this time onwards the Preceptor of the Hospital is generally spoken of as the Grand Preceptor or Grand Commander to distinguish him from the numerous Preceptors or Commanders appointed in the Priories.

[4] See *Les Hospitaliers en Terre Sainte*, p. 99.

[5] See *Cartulaire-Général*, Vol. I, No. 858.

the highest terms of the devoted services rendered by the Hospitallers, and how they had placed all their resources at his disposal. The siege dragged on all through December, but the Saracen army was growing restive. Like all Oriental armies of the period the men expected to get back to their wives to enjoy their booty, as soon as the campaigning season was over. On the night of 29 December Conrad gained a brilliant success over the blockading fleet, capturing eleven vessels with the Admiral of Alexandria and eight other emirs, the Hospitallers and Templars playing a prominent part in the engagement,[1] and on 1 January Saladin raised the siege and retired to Acre. It was the first check that he had received in his sweeping career of victory, and the dejected barons of the Holy Land began to regard Conrad of Montferrat as the only leader capable of restoring the kingdom.

Saladin, who very well knew that by now such a storm was brewing in Europe, as would shake his empire to its foundations, was determined to complete his conquests before the storm should burst. Leaving the siege of the frontier castles to detachments of his army, he moved north in the spring of 1188 for a campaign against Tripolis and Antioch. From Homs he descended into the valley of the Eleutherus, as Nur-ed-din had done twenty years before. But he found Le Crac and the other castles of the Hospitallers now strongly garrisoned, and could make no impression upon them. Advancing as far as the city of Tripolis, he was forced to abandon any designs that he may have had upon it, by the arrival of strong reinforcements sent by the King of Sicily, 500 knights and 50 galleys, and the Sultan turned towards Antioch. On his march along the coast he stormed Tortosa on 3 July, but failed to take the Tower of the Templars, and here he released King Guy and the Master of the Temple, as he had agreed the previous year. The county of Tripolis suffered no permanent loss as a result of the disaster of Hattin, and remained the most powerful Latin state in Syria.

In the Principality of Antioch Saladin was able to repeat his brilliant successes of the previous year. The campaign was one continuous victory, and town and castle fell with monotonous regularity, whilst Prince Bohemond III remained strictly on the defensive in his strong city of Antioch, whose walls he never quitted. On the frontiers of Tripolis the Sultan made no attempt against the powerful castle of Margat belonging to the Hospitallers, but he burnt their town of Valénie (Balanyas), and on 16 July occupied Zibel (Jabala). La Liche (Latakieh) surrendered a week later, and then turning inland he carried the castle of Saone (Sahyun) by assault on the 29th, after a siege of three days. During August the two fortresses on the Orontes, Bukas and Esh-Shugr were taken, then Sarmin fell, and on the 23rd Barzuya was stormed. The month of September was occupied in subduing the

[1] See *Cartulaire-Général,* Vol. I, No. 847.

castles covering the passes of Mount Amanus, Darbessac fell on the 16th after a siege of two weeks, and Gaston (Bagras), belonging to the Templars, on the 26th, and then Saladin marched upon the city of Antioch. But the Saracen army, gorged with plunder, was in no mood for further fighting, and as in the previous year the men wanted to get back to their wives and families. When Prince Bohemond sued for peace, Saladin granted him a truce on 1 October for eight months, and returned to Damascus well satisfied with a campaign which had resulted in the conquest of no less than twenty-five towns and castles.

During the Sultan's absence in the north his generals had made little progress in the sieges of the frontier fortresses. Chateauneuf (Hunin) held by the Hospitallers had fallen on 26 December 1187, after a siege of nearly six months, just before Saladin fell back from Tyre. It was not a particularly strong castle, and the Hospitallers had been unable to hold it against Nur-ed-din in 1167. But the five fortresses that remained offered a most obstinate and spirited defence, although their garrisons must have known well that relief was practically an impossibility. Kerak was starved out and surrendered to Saphadin on 24 October 1188, after resisting for a year and three months. The desperate garrison had expelled the women and children as useless mouths, and devoured the last of their horses before yielding.[1] The chivalrous Saladin restored their families to them, and sent them in safety to Christian territory. Upon Safed of the Templars and Belvoir of the Hospitallers the Saracen armies had made no serious impression at all, when the Sultan returned to Damascus. He at once took over the conduct of the siege operations himself, and at the end of a month on 6 December Safed surrendered, the garrison being allowed to depart to Tyre. The castle had held out for nearly a year and a half.

Saladin next turned his attention to the reduction of Belvoir. The defence of this castle 'set amid the stars like a falcon's nest' as Abu Shama, an Arab writer, poetically describes it,[2] 'the city of barking whose dogs ever yelped and bears growled', forms one of the most gallant episodes in the history of the Hospitallers. Its Castellan was a certain Bernard de Asinaria, who had been appointed to the command in 1186. He was a knight of wide experience, who must have served for many years in the Holy Land, since from 1163 to 1177 he had been employed in the Convent in Jerusalem on important administrative duties.[3] The siege of the castle began directly after the Battle of Hattin, but its garrison was evidently at full strength, and was handled with energy and vigour by Bernard its Castellan. Six months after the siege had begun, he sallied out on 2 January 1188 with all his men, and gained a brilliant little victory at Forbellet (Kefr Yebla), driving

[1] See Lane-Poole's *Saladin*, p. 249. [2] Ibid., p. 249.
[3] See *Les Hospitaliers en Terre Sainte*, pp. 347, 348, 413.

off the besiegers under Seyf-ed-din Mahmoud with heavy losses.[1] This success he followed up by the capture of two caravans employed in removing the arms and stores from the castle of La Fève,[2] so replenishing his own depleted magazines. The besiegers soon closed round the fortress again, but Bernard's active defence had attracted the personal attention of Saladin, who visited the siege works in March before leaving for his campaign in the north. When he returned in December after the fall of Safed, very little real progress had been made, though by now the garrison must have been much reduced by the casualties of a long siege. In spite of abominable weather with constant storms of wind and rain, which turned the soil into a sea of mud, the Sultan pressed on the operations with his usual vigour.[3] At last after suffering heavy losses a practicable breach was made in the walls, and then on 5 January 1189 after a resistance of eighteen months, the Hospitallers capitulated and marched out to Tyre with all the honours of war. Whether Bernard their Castellan survived the siege, we have no means of knowing, but his gallant conduct of the defence had been worthy of the best traditions of his Order.[4]

There were still two castles untaken by Saladin, Montreal in the desert north of Petra, and Belfort in the mountains of Lebanon. The former surrendered on 5 May 1189, starved out like Kerak, but Belfort held by Reginald of Sidon, resisted for yet another year. The baron was a diplomatist as well as a soldier, and talked Arabic and had studied Moslem literature. When Saladin appeared before his walls in April 1189, he gathered the definite impression that the Lord of Sidon was inclined to become a convert to Islam, and granted him three months' truce. The Sultan's intimate friend Boha-ed-din tells us that Reginald of Sidon discussed with them questions of religion with great moderation and courtesy.[5] However in July he was taken prisoner, but his castle still held out, and only surrendered on 22 April 1190 on condition that the Lord of Sidon was released. With the fall of Belfort, Saladin's conquest of the Latin kingdom of Jerusalem was complete, except of course for the city of Tyre. But already a year before the initiative had passed from his hands, and the reaction had begun with the siege of Acre. All Europe was once more aflame with religious zeal, and was preparing to pour forth her armies upon Syria in that attempt to recover the Holy City, which is known to history as the Third Crusade.

[1] See *Les Hospitaliers en Terre Sainte*, p. 99.

[2] See *Cartulaire-Général*, Vol. I, No. 847.

[3] See Lane-Poole's *Saladin*, p. 249.

[4] It is possible that he may be the same as the Bernard d'Avignon, who was Commander of Tripolis in 1198.

[5] See Conder's *Latin Kingdom of Jerusalem*, p. 159, footnote.

CHAPTER IX

GARNIER DE NABLUS AND THE THIRD CRUSADE

DURING the summer of 1188 it was at last possible for the Grand Preceptor, William Borrell, to summon a meeting of the Chapter, presumably at Tyre, for the purpose of electing a new Master of the Hospital, in succession to Roger des Moulins. The choice practically lay between two of the Bailiffs d'Outremer, Armengaud d'Aspe, Prior of St. Gilles and Castellan of Amposta, and Garnier de Nablus, Prior of England and Grand Preceptor beyond the seas. Since the former was actually present, and had greatly distinguished himself in the defence of Tyre, the choice not unnaturally fell upon him. Armengaud d'Aspe probably belonged to the well-known family of that name, and was therefore a native of Béarn,[1] from Aspe on the Aragonese frontier. He had been Castellan of Amposta since 1180, and in addition had been appointed Prior of St. Gilles in 1182. Holding the administration of all southern France and Aragon in his hands, he was one of the most influential dignitaries in the Order.[2]

Already there were signs of revival from the complete paralysis that had followed the disasters of the last twelve months. At Tyre Conrad, now Marquis of Montferrat, was beginning to take the offensive, and a Saracen force had to be stationed at Toron to hold him in check. At Tripolis King Guy was no sooner released than he began to collect an army, and to enrol under his banner the knights and men-at-arms continually drifting over from Europe in search of honourable adventure. By the spring of 1189 he found himself at the head of 700 knights and 9,000 foot, and marched to Tyre, the one city that still remained to him. But Conrad of Montferrat was a masterful man, and what he held he was determined to keep. He absolutely refused to admit the king, and declared that Tyre had been entrusted to him by Almighty God, and that he would be faithful to his trust. If the king

[1] See *Les Onze Premiers Grand Maîtres, etc.*, of the Viscount Oscar de Poli, in the *Annuaire du Conseil Héraldique de France*, 1892.

[2] The older historians of the Order knew practically nothing concerning Armengaud d'Aspe and Garnier de Nablus, except their names, and transposed their position in the list of Masters of the Hospital, but see Delaville Le Roulx, *Les Hospitaliers en Terre Sainte*, pp. 101, 102, 106, and J. H. Round, 'Garnier de Nablus', published in *Archaeologia*, Vol. LVIII.

wanted a resting-place, he must seek it elsewhere. King Guy was therefore compelled to remain outside the walls of Tyre, closely watched by Saladin, whose army was encamped in the Marj Uyun, 'the meadow of springs', west of Bélinas.

In August the king, who was being constantly reinforced from Europe, decided to attempt the recovery of Acre, the chief seaport of Palestine and the second capital of the kingdom. The city stood on a tongue of land jutting out into the Mediterranean, behind which lay its harbour. On the south and west it was washed by the sea, and its northern and eastern walls formed a right angle protected by a tower known as the Bloody Tower,[1] for the later new quarter known as Mount Musard had not yet been built. Its governor was Saladin's chief engineer Karakush, who had constructed the fortifications of Cairo, and the garrison was commanded by the Emir Ali el-Meshtub. On the 28th King Guy took up his position on Mount Turon, a low hill 90 feet high and about 1,400 yards east of the walls of Acre, and so began that famous siege, which was to last for nearly two years. The Saracen army arriving two days later, established what was practically a blockade of the besiegers, and on 14 September Saladin made an attack in force in order to cover the entry into the city of a large convoy under his nephew Taki-ed-din Omar. By the end of the month the besiegers were strong enough to complete the investment of the city from sea to sea, there had been a temporary reconciliation between King Guy and Conrad of Montferrat, and they were now in a position to make a serious attempt to drive back the main army of the Saracens, in what is known as the Battle of Acre.

At sunrise on 4 October King Guy led out his army to attack the Saracen camps 2 miles away on the hill of Ayadieh, rising about 250 feet above the plain. The army was in four divisions; the king commanded the right wing of French Crusaders and the Hospitallers under Armengaud d'Aspe their Master, the right centre was composed of Italians and the barons of the Holy Land under Conrad of Montferrat, and the left centre of Germans under Ludwig Landgrave of Thuringia, whilst the left wing was under Gerard de Ridfort, Master of the Temple, and consisted of the Templars and various French and German units. A reserve under the king's brother Geoffrey de Lusignan and James d'Avesnes held Mount Turon and the camp to its south, in order to prevent the garrison of Acre from intervening. The whole army probably numbered about 30,000 men, and was deployed on a front of 2 miles.[2]

To meet the attack Saladin drew up his army in the plain of Arab-el-Ghawarneh below his camp. The Saracens somewhat outnumbered

[1] See Conder's *Latin Kingdom of Jerusalem*, p. 410.

[2] The best account of the Battle of Acre is to be found in Oman's *Art of War in the Middle Ages*, Vol. I, pp. 333–40.

the Crusaders, and occupied a front of about 3 miles. The centre formed by the contingents from Mesopotamia was commanded by the Sultan in person, the two wings thrown well forward consisted on the left of veteran troops from Egypt, and on the right of Syrians under Taki-ed-din Omar.

The Templars on the Christian left opened the attack, and Taki-ed-din began to fall back before them. Saladin thereupon detached troops from his centre, and sent them to the assistance of his nephew, who was thus able to force the Templars back to the rising ground of Kisr-el-Hammar, where they re-formed their line. Then the Christian centre came into action under Conrad of Montferrat and the Landgrave. The Italian and German knights crashed into the Saracen light horse, which broke at once and, seized with panic, many of them were

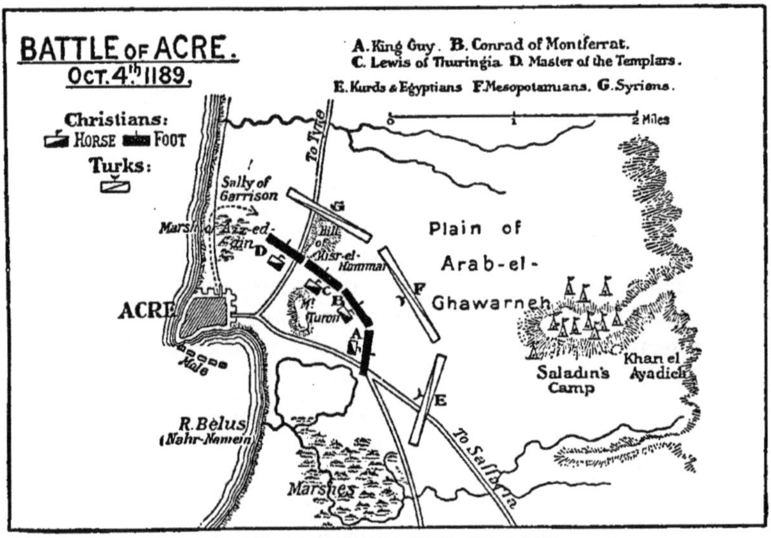

PLAN OF THE BATTLE OF ACRE

not heard of again until they were across the Jordan, and well on the road to Damascus. Unfortunately the victors, casting all discipline to the winds, broke their ranks for the purpose of plundering the Saracen camp. As they began to straggle back laden with booty, Saladin counter-attacked with all the men he could collect, and turned what should have been defeat into victory. King Guy and the Hospitallers, who had so far been fighting an indecisive engagement with Saladin's Egyptian mamelukes, became involved in the disaster to the centre, and were only saved from defeat by the arrival of the reserves under Geoffrey de Lusignan and James d'Avesnes.

Meanwhile the Templars were fighting an entirely separate action at Kisr-el-Hammar with the forces of Taki-ed-din. But when the Christian reserves intervened in the battle, they thereby released the garrison of Acre, which sallying out by the northern gate 5,000 strong fell upon the rear of the Templars. It was only with the greatest difficulty and terrible losses that the Crusaders here succeeded in cutting their way back to their camp. More than half the casualties sustained in the battle were at this point, and amongst the slain was Gerard de Ridfort, Master of the Temple. Urged by his comrades to join in the retirement, his reply was worthy of his exalted office, 'God forbid that men should say of me to the shame of our Order, that to save my own life I fled away leaving my fellows dead behind me'.[1] In his death he atoned, so far as it was possible to do so, for the grave misfortunes that his own turbulent nature had brought upon the Holy Land.

The Christian casualties in the Battle of Acre are estimated at 7,000 men killed, and the Saracens at only 1,500. But none the less Saladin was in no position to attack the camps of his enemy. The season for fighting was over, his men as usual were anxious to get back to their homes for the winter, and on 16 October he withdrew to El-Kharruba on the road to Sennabra, leaving the Christian army free to continue the siege of Acre almost unmolested. The city was now completely invested on the land side, and Armengaud d'Aspe and his Hospitallers took up their positions opposite the north wall,[2] the attack on which from the Bloody Tower to the sea was under the direction of Conrad of Montferrat. But Armengaud d'Aspe, for reasons unknown to us, does not appear to have been a success as Master of the Hospital, and during the winter resigned his high office, after holding it for barely one year. All that the official chronicle can tell us on the subject is that he was persecuted by the enemies of the faith, whatever that may mean, and that in his time Jerusalem was lost, and that he lived only a short time afterwards. Probably the Chapter of Tyre at which he was elected was not really representative, and the Hospitallers now continually arriving from all the countries of Europe resented the appointment, and desired to see at their head one whose wide experience in the Holy Land rendered him far more suitable for the office. Armengaud d'Aspe did not long survive his retirement; he was re-appointed Castellan of Amposta and died in the summer of 1191.

The new Master of the Hospital elected during the siege of Acre belonged to one of the most distinguished families in the Holy Land. Garnier de Nablus was a son of Henry de Nablus and a nephew of the Philip de Nablus who exchanged the lordship of Nablus for that of Kerak and Montreal, and after the death of his wife became Master of the Temple. His mother was Agnes daughter of Eustace Garnier, Lord of Sidon, and Constable of the Kingdom of Jerusalem. The house of Nablus was of Flemish origin, its founder being Payen de

[1] See Archer and Kingsford, *The Crusades*, p. 319.

[2] See *Les Hospitaliers en Terre Sainte*, p. 103.

Milly, upon whom King Baldwin I conferred the fief of Nablus, in which he was succeeded by his nephew Philip, son of his younger brother Guy de Milly.[1] Garnier de Nablus had had a career of the highest distinction in the Order. In 1173 he had become one of the Bailiffs of Syria on his appointment as Castellan of Jibelin. Four years later he was transferred to the Convent in Jerusalem as Grand Preceptor of the Hospital, a post which he held with a break of only two years, until he was appointed Prior of England in 1184, and whilst continuing to hold that office, he succeeded Geoffrey de Donjon (afterwards Master) as Grand Preceptor d'Outremer in 1187. When he was elected to the Mastership in succession to Armengaud d'Aspe, he was beyond all question the most prominent and the most distinguished knight in the Order. Garnier de Nablus must have received the news of his election in the Priory at Clerkenwell and left for the Holy Land almost immediately.

The fall of Jerusalem and the loss of the True Cross rang like a trumpet call through Europe. Men had talked for years of the necessity for a fresh crusade to save the Holy Land from disaster. But nothing had ever been done, in spite of repeated warnings from every quarter, and now the inevitable disaster had at last occurred. As usual when it was too late, men began to repent of their lethargy and inaction, and were horrified at the results of their want of zeal in the holy cause. With these feelings of horror and repentance came a fresh religious revival such as had accompanied the First Crusade. From every pulpit in Christendom the eloquent voice of the preacher pleaded with the people, to save Christ's Holy Sepulchre from the profanation of the infidel, and to repent for their sins, which alone had made such a disaster possible, until all Europe resounded with the clang of arms and the tramp of marching soldiers. The Third Crusade was the greatest of all the crusades, for it was led by the three most powerful monarchs of the West, the Emperor and the Kings of France and England, and in it every Christian country in Europe took part. But though all were united in a common cause, the recovery of the Holy Land, they were scarcely ever united in anything else, and the greatest military effort that Europe had ever made, was foredoomed to failure from exactly the same causes as had ruined the Second Crusade, and nearly brought the First to disaster, namely national rivalry and the personal jealousy and selfish ambition of the leaders.

The army of imperial Germany, as was fitting should be the case, was the first to assemble and the first to move, a full year before the armies of France and England. On 11 May 1189 the Emperor Frederick Barbarossa rode out of Ratisbon in Bavaria at the head of his

[1] For the family of Garnier de Nablus, see *Les Onze Premiers Grand Maîtres, etc.*, of the Viscount Oscar de Poli, in the *Annuaire du Conseil Héraldique de France*, 1892.

knights on his long march across Europe and Asia. The great Emperor, the very personification of the chivalrous and warlike spirit of his age, the natural leader of the armies of Europe, universally respected and admired, was the one man who had he lived might have brought the crusade to a victorious conclusion, but fate had ordained otherwise. He was now 66 years of age, and the most experienced soldier in Christendom. He had already served in the East under the Emperor Conrad during the Second Crusade, and he had decided to follow the same route across Europe, and Asia Minor, as he had previously traversed. The German army spent the winter at Adrianople, where as usual there was constant friction with the Emperor of the East, Isaac Angelus, who detested and feared the Emperor of the West. In the spring of 1190 soon after Easter they crossed the Bosporus, and took the same road as the Second Crusade as far as Laodicea. Here the Emperor turned east moving along the great Roman road through Apamea and Antioch-in-Pisidia on Iconium, the capital of the Turkish Sultan of Roum. There was heavy fighting at Apamea on 30 April and in the passes of the Borlu Dagh on 2 May, then followed twelve days' constant skirmishing up to the gates of Iconium, which was carried by assault on 17 May. In all this fighting the Germans lost remarkably few men, but the casualties amongst the horses from the Turkish arrows were enormous, and only 600 chargers were left in the entire army.[1] Peace was now made with the Turkish Sultan, and the Emperor descended by Laranda and the valley of the Calycadnus to Seleucia-by-the-Sea, and there on 11 June in fording the river he was thrown from his horse and drowned. The Emperor's entrails were reverently interred at Tarsus, and his body was carried to Antioch for burial in the Cathedral of St. Peter. So perished Frederick Barbarossa, one of the greatest and noblest of German heroes, and with him perished any possibility of a victorious termination to the crusade. His army melted away, some at once returned home, others marched to Antioch, where they were decimated by the plague, and when the Emperor's son, Frederick Duke of Swabia, reached the Christian camp at Acre, there were only 5,000 men left of the mighty host, which had marched away from Ratisbon seventeen months before.

King Richard Coeur-de-Lion of England and King Philip Augustus of France, who loathed and distrusted each other, and were by temperament as antagonistic as two men could well be, were not ready to start until the summer of 1190. The two kings had decided to transport their armies to Palestine by sea, King Richard embarking at Marseilles and the French king at Genoa. The armies wintered at Messina in Sicily, where the two kings quarrelled bitterly, an example that was loyally followed by their respective subjects, and the King of England also came to blows with the subjects of the King of Sicily,

[1] See Oman's *Art of War in the Middle Ages*, Vol. I, p. 250.

and stormed and sacked Messina. Already the great cause, which all professed to be serving, was being jeopardized by these national rivalries, and the two kings, on whose cordial co-operation everything depended, were by now on the worst possible terms. The King of France left Messina for Acre at the end of March, arriving there on 20 April 1191, but the King of England did not leave until ten days later, the force of circumstances caused him to conquer the island of Cyprus on the way, and he only reached Acre on 8 June. The strength of the English army in the Third Crusade is estimated at 8,000 men,[1] but a strong detachment under Baldwin, Archbishop of Canterbury, had sailed direct to Palestine the previous autumn.

Garnier de Nablus, Master of the Hospital, appears to have accompanied King Richard Coeur-de-Lion on his voyage to the Holy Land, no doubt as his chief adviser in Oriental affairs, and in much the same position as Everard des Barres, Master of the Temple, had occupied towards King Louis VII of France, in the Second Crusade. It is very probable that like Roger des Moulins he may even have owed his election to the Mastership to the fact that his sovereign was the head of the House of Anjou. We know that Garnier de Nablus was already with King Richard on his arrival at Messina,[2] and that at the beginning of the year he had been in Paris,[3] it is therefore almost certain that he had joined the king's staff on the journey through France, and embarked with them at Marseilles. When Cyprus was conquered, and its so-called Emperor Isaac Comnenus taken prisoner, he was handed over to Garnier de Nablus for safe-keeping, and sent by him to Margat, and the Master of the Hospital seems to have acted as a sort of Chief of the Staff to King Richard throughout the Third Crusade.

Meanwhile in the spring of 1190 the siege of Acre, which had degenerated into a mere blockade during the winter, was resumed with vigour, the Marquis of Montferrat arrived from Tyre, prepared to co-operate cordially in return for the grant of Tyre, Sidon and Beyrout, and Saladin having reassembled his army advanced to Tell Kisan on the main road south-east of the city. The Hospitallers and Templars continued to hold the sector of the lines of investment on Mount Musard facing the northern walls of the city, with the forces of Conrad of Montferrat on their right prolonging the line to the sea. Early in the year Ogier, Prior of St. Gilles, recently appointed Grand Preceptor by Garnier de Nablus, arrived to assume command of the Hospitallers,[4] pending the arrival of the new Master, who was now attached to the staff of the King of England. Active operations

[1] See Davis, *England under the Normans and Angevins*, p. 295.
[2] See *Les Hospitaliers en Terre Sainte*, p. 108.
[3] See *Cartulaire-Général*, Vol. I, No. 868.
[4] We know that Ogier was Grand Preceptor in October 1190 and Prior of St. Gilles earlier in the year. He was therefore appointed to his office by Gar-

opened on 27 April, when the besiegers succeeded in pushing up to the walls of Acre three great siege towers, constructed during the winter, and completely dominating the defences. They caused considerable dismay in the city, until the garrison succeeded in burning them on 5 May, and during the following month the citizens were still further encouraged, when the Egyptian fleet succeeded in forcing the blockade, and revictualling the fortress. In July Saladin began to grow uneasy concerning the expected arrival of the Emperor Frederick Barbarossa, and weakened his army considerably by detaching a large force to meet the Germans on their arrival in northern Syria. Knowing this, the Crusaders on 25 July made a serious attempt to drive back the Saracen army, which was holding them almost invested in their lines. The attack was delivered upon the enemy's right, but after hard fighting was repulsed by Saphadin with heavy losses, amounting to at least 4,000 men.[1] During this battle the garrison of Acre made a vigorous sortie from the northern gate. The brunt of the fighting here fell upon the Hospitallers, who covered themselves with glory and after a very sanguinary engagement drove them back behind their walls.[2] Three days later Henry Count of Champagne arrived from Europe with a reinforcement of 10,000 men, and took charge of the operations, in place of James d'Avesnes and the Landgrave of Thuringia, who had held the command by turns. This increase of strength rendered it impossible for Saladin to remain so close to the Christian lines, and forced him to draw back to the hilly country south-east of the city.

In spite of their increased strength and greater freedom of action, the besiegers made very little progress, and when the winter arrived the situation was practically the same as the previous year. On 24 September there had been an unsuccessful attempt to complete the blockade of the harbour by capturing the celebrated Tower of Flies, which covered the entrance, and a second attempt was made on 17 October, but was equally unsuccessful. Two days earlier the rams, which had only been brought into action with the greatest difficulty, had been destroyed by the garrison. During the same month, on 7 October the Duke of Swabia arrived from Antioch with all that remained of the German army, and on the 12th a part of the English army arrived under Baldwin, Archbishop of Canterbury, Hubert Walter, Bishop of Salisbury, and Ranulf Glanville the Justiciar, the remainder wintering with King Richard at Messina. But the French and German Crusaders were quite unable to co-operate harmoniously, and in the words of a contemporary writer, the latter

nier de Nablus, who would presumably at once send him out to the Holy Land to act as his lieutenant, since he was delaying his own arrival to travel with the King of England.

[1] See Archer, *The Crusade of Richard I*, p. 18.

[2] See *Les Hospitaliers en Terre Sainte*, p. 107.

'proved a cause of disagreement; for the French had an old and long-standing quarrel with Germany, since the kingdom and the empire contended for supremacy'.[1] The last fighting that autumn was the Battle at the Spring Head (of the River Belus) on 14 November, when Saladin inflicted severe losses upon a large force of Crusaders under Henry of Champagne and Conrad of Montferrat, as they were returning from an expedition to Haifa to bring in a convoy of provisions landed on the south side of the bay. After this both armies went into winter-quarters, and all active operations came to an end.

The second winter of the siege of Acre was a time of almost intolerable hardship and suffering. A continual stream of reinforcements from all countries had increased the army to a strength that can scarcely have been much less than 50,000 men, and may possibly have been even greater. For its supplies it depended almost entirely upon Europe, since the long war had swept the country bare. During the winter communications by sea were very difficult and quite unreliable. In consequence the commissariat broke down altogether, and the army for some months was in a state of semi-starvation. The mortality amongst the troops was terribly high, and the men died off like flies from famine and sickness. Under such conditions, combined with the enforced idleness of winter, the little discipline that had ever existed completely disappeared, and the Christian camp became a very sink of iniquity, whilst the leaders of the army were engaged in constant disputes and wrangling. The Archbishop of Canterbury's chaplain writing to his convent in England soon after his arrival, describes the situation at that time in the following words[2]:

> 'We found our army, I say it with grief and groaning, given up to shameful practices, and yielding to ease and lust rather than encouraging virtue. The Lord is not in the camp; there is none that doeth good. The chiefs envy one another, and strive for privilege. The lesser folk are in want, and find no one to help them. In the camp there is neither chastity, sobriety, faith nor charity, a state of things which, I call God to witness, I would not have believed had I not seen it.'

Out of the misery and suffering prevailing in the Christian camp arose two new military religious Orders, one of the greatest importance in the history of Europe, and the other destined to fade away in obscurity a century and a half later. Certain German merchants from Bremen and Lubeck, deeply moved by the sufferings of their fellow-countrymen, drew one of their vessels ashore, and turned it into a field-hospital for the use of German Crusaders. To this hospital the brethren expelled from the Hospital of St. Mary of the Germans in Jerusalem attached themselves, and eight years later these German Hospitallers were transferred into a new military religious Order

[1] See Conder's *Latin Kingdom of Jerusalem*, p. 259.

[2] The letter is printed in Archer, *The Crusade of Richard I*, p. 18.

generally known as the Teutonic Knights, and destined to play a great part in history. The English Order of St. Thomas Acon originated at the same time and from similar causes.[1] One of the English Crusaders, a certain priest named William, chaplain to Ralph de Diceto, Dean of St. Paul's, was horrified to see the numerous bodies of good Christian men lying about on the battle-fields of Acre, and deprived of the blessings of Christian burial. He and some of his comrades formed themselves into a religious society to ensure Christian burial to the dead Crusaders, taking St. Thomas à Becket as their patron saint. They were eventually transformed into a military religious Order and attached to the Templars, and died out in Cyprus towards the end of the fourteenth century.

There were many deaths amongst the leaders of the crusade during that terrible winter. Ranulf Glanville the Justiciar died only a few days after the arrival of the English army, and the Archbishop of Canterbury followed him to the grave on 11 November, bitterly lamenting the vice and corruption and wickedness that so dishonoured the sacred cause for which they were fighting. The German army was deprived of its chief, the Duke of Swabia, by his death on 20 January 1191, and many other great nobles and knights fell victims to the hardships of the siege. Early in the autumn Queen Sibyl died, having been predeceased by her children, and her death left King Guy in a most precarious position, for his right to the crown was only due to his marriage, and he was so hopelessly discredited that he had been unable to sustain his claim to command the allied forces in the siege, although the only crowned king present. The heiress to the throne of Jerusalem was now the Princess Isabel, wife of Humphrey de Toron, and the barons of the Holy Land were determined to use the opportunity to shake themselves free from King Guy. Their chosen hero was Conrad of Montferrat, his desires entirely coincided with theirs, and he was not the man to allow any mere marriage to stand in the way of his ambitions for a throne. The clergy were prevailed upon to pronounce the existing marriage of the Princess Isabel null and void, although the Archbishop of Canterbury vigorously protested against such an iniquity, and then Conrad, whom scandal alleged to have two wives already, one in Italy and the other in Constantinople, married the Princess on 24 November and laid claim to the crown of Jerusalem. The opinion of Humphrey de Toron on these proceedings appears to have been regarded as having no importance, and the Princess was ready enough to abandon him for Conrad.[2] There was now a fresh cause of dissension in the Christian camp already sufficiently divided

[1] See Archer, *The Crusade of Richard I*, pp. 114, 115.

[2] On this point the Norman monk Geoffrey de Vinsauf cynically remarks, 'for a female is always variable and changeable, her sex frail, her mind fickle, and she delights in novelty. So she lightly rejects and forgets those whom

by former quarrels, and half the army supported the claims of King Guy, and the other half those of Conrad of Montferrat.

When the spring arrived the Christian army had been reduced by famine and disease to only a shadow of its former self, whilst its leaders were more intent than ever upon their wretched personal feuds. Saladin meanwhile had used the winter months and the slackening of the blockade to refill the magazines of Acre, and during February had withdrawn its exhausted garrison, and replaced it by entirely fresh troops, but he retained Karakush and Ali el-Meshtub in command. When spring at last arrived Acre was stronger than ever, and the siege must almost certainly have ended in disaster for the Crusaders, had it not been for the arrival of the Kings of France and England. King Philip Augustus arrived on 20 April, but his troops were less numerous than had been expected, occupying only six large ships,[1] but none the less he was received ' with hymns and songs of praise and floods of tears, as though he had been an angel of God '.[2] On 8 June King Richard Coeur-de-Lion arrived with twenty-five galleys, and that night all the camps were illuminated in his honour so that ' the Turks thought that the whole valley was in a blaze '.[3] Unfortunately King Richard had been met in Cyprus by King Guy, who was by birth one of his subjects, and had pledged himself to support his claims to the throne of Jerusalem, whilst the King of France was equally determined to support those of Conrad of Montferrat. Their joint campaign was beginning under the worst possible auspices. However, with the arrival of Richard Coeur-de-Lion the last phase of the long siege of Acre begins, for the King of England in spite of continual friction with the King of France, was able to inspire the discordant elements of the crusading army with something of his own fiery zeal and energy, and the English army, devoted to its gallant hero-king, could always be relied upon in every emergency.

On 10 June, within two days of his arrival, King Richard had set up his great siege tower called Mategriffon, and his archers were able to look down into Acre. Then a line of battering-engines was brought into action against the curtain wall, and mining began on a large scale, the French at the same time pressing their attack on the Bloody Tower. Garnier de Nablus had now assumed command of the Hospitallers, and we are told that during the bombardment the machines manned by the Hospitallers and Templars were remarkable for their efficiency.[4] Whilst King Richard was prostrated with fever the King of France on 14 June much against his colleague's wishes

she knows, and willingly receives evil advice '. Quoted in Conder's *Latin Kingdom of Jerusalem*, p. 269.

[1] See Stevenson, *The Crusaders in the East*, p. 267, note 4.

[2] See Archer, *The Crusade of Richard I*, p. 56.

[3] Ibid., p. 82.

[4] Ibid., p. 87.

ordered a general assault, which failed, as did another three days later, Saladin on each occasion creating a diversion by attacking the camps of the besiegers. By the end of the month the defences of Acre were beginning to crumble under the continual bombardment and mining. On 3 July a large stretch of wall near the Bloody Tower fell to the ground, and next day the garrison offered to surrender the city, if they were allowed to go free. On the 5th another great breach was made, and on the 6th King Richard ordered a general assault, which was within an ace of succeeding. For a few days longer the garrison continued their resistance, and then on 12 July surrendered after a siege of one year and eleven months. The most important city in Palestine was once more in Christian hands, but at a price that had really been the ruin of their cause, for in only one year they are said to have buried no fewer than 124,000 dead bodies.[1] The conditions of the surrender were that Saladin should restore the True Cross, release 100 knights and 1,500 other prisoners taken in the Battle of Hattin, and pay an indemnity of 200,000 besants, on which the garrison of Acre would be set free. But Saladin would not trust the Christians to keep their word unless they gave him hostages; King Richard refused to agree to any of his suggestions, and on 20 August by his orders and those of the King of France's representative the Duke of Burgundy, the whole of these unfortunate prisoners to the number of 2,700[2] were led out to the plain at the foot of the hill of Ayadieh, and there massacred in the sight of the Saracen army, a few high officers alone being spared for the sake of their ransoms. It is worthy of note that Saladin, in whose hands were many hundreds of Christian prisoners, refrained from any reprisals.[3]

No sooner had Acre fallen than the King of France began to search for an excuse to abandon the crusade. A cold calculating far-sighted politician, he was determined not to lose the opportunities given to him in Europe by the absence in Syria of the King of England, and the recent death before Acre of the Count of Flanders. He sailed for Europe on 3 August on the plea of ill-health, in the words of Richard Coeur-de-Lion 'to the eternal dishonour of his kingdom'. His desertion was in reality no great loss to the crusade, for as a contemporary writer, speaking of the Kings of France and England, tells us, 'the two kings and peoples did less together than they would have done separately, and each set but light store by the other'.[4] During the siege of Acre the friction between the allies was so great that it had even been impossible for the two armies to fight side by side, and when the English attacked, the French guarded the camp and vice versa. Before his departure the King of France sent 100 knights and 500 men-at-arms

[1] See Archer, *The Crusade of Richard I*, p. 115. [2] Ibid., p. 126.
[3] See Lane-Poole's *Saladin*, p. 307.
[4] See Archer and Kingsford, *The Crusaders*, p. 329.

to the assistance of the Prince of Antioch,[1] King Richard doing the same, and he handed over to the Duke of Burgundy the balance of his personal following consisting of 500 knights and 1,000 foot.[2] The King of England was now nominally in supreme command of the Crusaders, but with little real authority over any part of the allied army, except the English contingent, whilst his policy and plans were continually obstructed by the disloyalty and intrigues of the French leaders.

The capture of Acre had brought to a head the rival claims of King Guy and the Marquis of Montferrat to the throne of Jerusalem, and had rendered some final settlement an absolute necessity. Pending a settlement the royal dues and revenues from the port and market of Acre were to be held in trust by the Masters of the Hospital and the Temple. The claimants submitted their case to the arbitration of the Kings of France and England, and were heard on 27 July. It was decided that King Guy should retain the crown for life, and that on his death he should be succeeded by the Marquis of Montferrat and the Princess Isabel. The royal revenues were to be equally divided between the two claimants, and the Marquis was confirmed in his possession of Tyre, Sidon and Beyrout,[3] but the two latter towns were still occupied by the Saracens.

On 21 August, the day after the massacre of the prisoners, the campaign for the recovery of Jerusalem was to begin. But the discipline of the Crusaders was as usual abominable, and it was difficult to induce the knights and soldiers to tear themselves away from the pleasures and amusements of Acre, and to concentrate in the camp established on the banks of the River Belus. The march south did not begin until the 25th, when Haifa was reached. King Richard had decided to take the coast road to Jaffa, and there to fortify a new base, before advancing on Jerusalem. The army was organized in twelve brigades, each composed of cavalry and infantry, and grouped in five divisions. It marched in three columns, on the right nearest the sea the transport mostly pack-animals and carriers, in the centre the cavalry, and on the left the infantry. The Hospitallers under Garnier de Nablus and the Templars under Robert de Sablé, their recently elected Master, formed the advanced guard and rearguard, changing position each day. The fleet carrying the heavy stores and supplies, moved parallel with the army, communicating at every possible landing place. There were no fortresses to be encountered, for Saladin had adopted the deliberate policy of destroying the fortifications of the captured towns and castles.[4] He had no troops to spare for gar-

[1] See Norgate, *Richard the Lion Heart*, p. 168.

[2] See Archer, *The Crusade of Richard I*, p. 118.

[3] See Norgate, *Richard the Lion Heart*, pp. 160, 167.

[4] In the summer of 1190, in expectation of the arrival of the Emperor Frederick Barbarossa, Saladin dismantled Sidon and Jubail, and soon afterwards

rison duties, and they had a deeply rooted dislike for being shut up in fortresses, a dislike greatly increased by the fate of the garrison of Acre.[1] The Saracen army, whose main strength as usual lay in its Turkish horse-archers, marched parallel with the Crusaders, continually harassing them day and night.

The European troops, burdened by their heavy armour, suffered terribly from the heat of the Syrian summer. They marched only in the early hours of the morning, and seldom more than 8 or 10 miles in the day, halting on each alternate day. It took no fewer than 19 days to cover the 80 miles between Acre and Jaffa. The skirmishing was incessant, the Turkish horse-archers returning to the attack again and again, as fast as they were beaten off. In the words of a writer, who was present:

> 'the Infidels not weighed down with heavy armour like our knights, but always able to outstrip them in pace, were a constant trouble. When charged they are wont to fly, and their horses are more nimble than any others in the world, one may liken them to swallows for swiftness. When they see that you have ceased to pursue them, they no longer fly, but return upon you: they are like tiresome flies which you can flap away for a moment, but which come back the instant you have stopped hitting at them: as long as you beat about, they keep off: the moment you cease, they are on you again'.[2]

All the time Saladin was keenly watching for a favourable opening for the general engagement, that could alone prevent King Richard from reaching Jaffa. At last on 7 September it seemed to him that his opportunity had arrived, and a determined effort to destroy the Christian rearguard brought on the decisive Battle of Arsuf.[3]

On 5 September King Richard marched from the Salt River (Nahr Iskenderuneh) to the river of Rochetaille (Nahr-el-Falaik), and there rested his army the following day. Early on the morning of the 7th he began his march on Arsuf, 6 miles distant. That day the Templars furnished the advanced guard, and Garnier de Nablus and his Hospitallers the rearguard. Ever since leaving the Salt River, the route had been flanked by one of the few forests in the Holy Land, the Forest of Arsuf. It was a thick oak-wood covering the lower slopes of the hills, with a mile or two of open country between it and the road, and completely concealing the movements of the Saracen army. From this forest Saladin had decided to launch his attack upon the Crusaders.

The Christian army had scarcely left its camp, before the battle

Latakieh, Tortosa and Beyrout. On 8 July 1191, when expecting the fall of Acre, he ordered Haifa to be dismantled, and shortly afterwards Tiberias, Caesarea, Arsuf and Jaffa. See Stevenson, *The Crusaders in the East*, pp. 264, 269, 276.

[1] See Stevenson, *The Crusaders in the East*, pp. 277, 283.

[2] Quoted in Oman's *Art of War in the Middle Ages*, Vol. I, p. 308.

[3] The best account of the Battle of Arsuf is to be found in Oman's *Art of War in the Middle Ages*, Vol. I, pp. 305, 317.

began. The Turkish horse-archers debouching from the forest engaged the marching columns all along the line, with their main body massed against the Hospitallers. It was Saladin's intention to bring the rearguard to a halt, thus creating a gap in the line of march, and then to surround and destroy it. Richard Coeur-de-Lion knowing

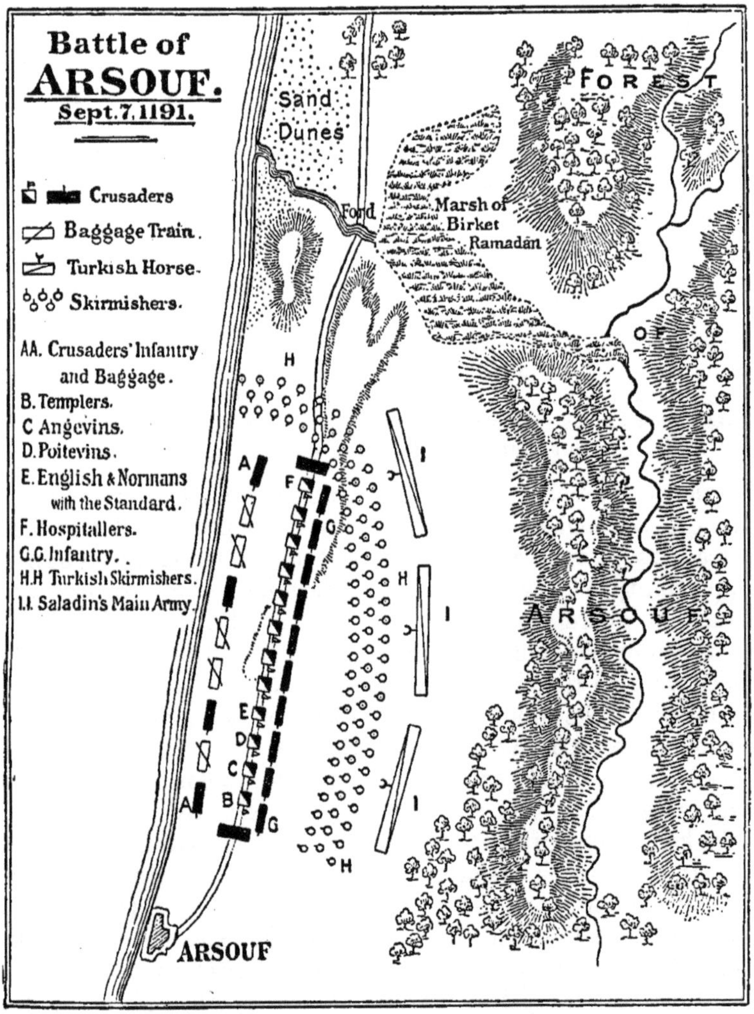

PLAN OF THE BATTLE OF ARSUF

well the danger of these tactics, had issued strict orders to Garnier de Nablus that on no account must the rearguard halt, however closely pressed it might be. He was hoping that Saladin would commit his elusive light horse to hand-to-hand fighting, and it was then his intention so soon as they were too closely engaged to break away, to overwhelm them in one decisive charge of his heavy cavalry. Until the trumpets should sound the charge, the whole army must continue to plod steadily along the road to Arsuf, the infantry with their cross-bows as far as possible protecting the horses of the cavalry from the Turkish arrows.

Gradually Saladin's horse-archers began to press the Hospitallers more and more closely. Squadron after squadron galloped up, discharged its arrows into the marching columns, and galloped away again. It was one incessant storm of arrows, and the horses of the knights began to suffer severely. We are told that the infantry of the rearguard were walking slowly backwards with their faces to the foe, discharging their cross-bows as quickly as they could load them. The strain had almost reached the breaking-point, and Garnier de Nablus, riding up to the King, protested vigorously: 'Great St. George, Sire, will you let us be crushed in this way? Christianity will perish if we do not give battle to these rascals.' But the hero-king, calm and confident, watching for the right moment for the decisive charge, simply replied, 'My dear Master, be patient, we must put up with it, I cannot be everywhere at the same moment'. At last the enemy began to close in, and one who was present tells us that 'they had laid their bows aside, and were now thundering upon the rearguard with their scimitars and maces like smiths upon anvils'. It was more than human nature could endure, two of the knights, the Marshal of the Hospital [1] and a Norman knight Baldwin le Carron losing their heads forced their way through the infantry, and flung themselves upon the Saracens. At once the whole of the Knights of the Hospital, as if it had been the signal, wheeled their horses to the left, raised a shout of 'St. George', and bursting through their foot charged home. Fortunately the decisive moment for which Richard Coeur-de-Lion was waiting had arrived, the trumpets sounded the charge all along the line, and the cavalry passing through the marching columns, dashed upon the infidels. The Saracens following their usual tactics at once fled, but great masses of them were now so closely engaged that it was quite impossible to break away. The Christian knights took a terrible revenge, and when their work was done 7,000 of the enemy lay dead upon the field, including 32 of their principal emirs. The losses amongst the Crusaders are said to have been only 700 killed, but amongst them was one of their most heroic leaders James d'Avesnes, who for a time had commanded the allied army in the siege of Acre. Pursuing the enemy too rashly, he was cut off and slain, but he sold

[1] The Marshal of the Hospital in 1188 was a certain Lambert, and in 1193 William Borrel, who had been Grand Preceptor during the interregnum following the death of Roger des Moulins, but when the latter succeeded the former is not known. It seems more probable that William Borrel was Marshal at the time of the Battle of Arsuf.

his life dearly, and when his body was discovered, no fewer than fifteen dead Saracens were found beside it.

The Battle of Arsuf was decisive of the fate of the Holy Land for another hundred years; it settled the question as to whether Saladin was strong enough to drive the Crusaders out of Syria, and he never ventured to engage them in another pitched battle. Richard Coeur-de-Lion continued his march to Jaffa, which he reached on the 10th, and Saladin took up a defensive position at Ramleh blocking the road to Jerusalem. As a measure of precaution he ordered the fortifications of every town and castle in southern Palestine to be dismantled, except Jerusalem and Darum, the last fortress on the coast-road to Egypt. A lull in the operations now followed, and King Richard whilst busily engaged in re-fortifying Jaffa, opened serious negotiations with Saladin for a partition of the Holy Land. But no compromise of that nature was as yet possible, Saladin would not consent to give up Ascalon, and the question of the Holy City seemed insoluble. In November negotiations broke down, and on the 22nd the Crusaders occupied Ramleh and Lydda, Saladin falling back upon Toron des Chevaliers (En-Natroun), on the edge of the hill-country. Six weeks later the march on Jerusalem began, and on 3 January 1192 Richard Coeur-de-Lion advanced to Bêtenoble (Beit Nuba) and En-Natroun. But the weather was now abominable, and the Syrian winter at its worst. Constant storms of wind and rain ruined the health and the morale of the army, and it became evident that if it ever reached Jerusalem, it would be in no condition for conducting a difficult siege. Garnier de Nablus of the Hospital and Robert de Sablé of the Temple with the barons of the Holy Land, combined in making urgent representations to King Richard on the hopelessness of the enterprise, until at last on 8 January he regretfully consented to order a general retirement upon Ramleh.

There could be no further advance upon Jerusalem until the spring, when reinforcements would arrive from Europe, and King Richard decided to strengthen his base on the sea-coast by occupying and re-fortifying Ascalon. On 19 January he evacuated Ramleh, and marching through Ibelin reached Ascalon the following day, and at once began the restoration of its defences. But his plans were continually hampered by the French who seemed far more intent upon thwarting the King of England than in recovering the Holy Land. The Marquis of Montferrat, disappointed at the result of the arbitration concerning the throne of Jerusalem, was also quite unreliable and always causing trouble. He had refused to co-operate with King Richard in the campaign that followed the fall of Acre, remaining at Tyre, and during the winter actually offered to assist Saladin against him, if he would only secure him in the possession of Sidon and Beyrout. Finally the Duke of Burgundy and the French, after trying to induce King Richard to pay them large sums of money to remain, deserted the army on 20 February, and went back to Acre, where they at once assisted the Marquis of Montferrat in an attempt to deprive King Guy of that city by force. This compelled King Richard to go in person to Acre to restore order, and he was unable to get back to Ascalon until 1 April, but his visit to the temporary capital of the kingdom seems to have convinced him that there would be no peace in the Holy Land until King Guy had abdicated in favour of the Marquis. At the end of April he sent his nephew Henry Count of Champagne to Tyre to inform the Marquis that he was now prepared to acknowledge him as King of Jerusalem, but that unscrupulous prince was not destined to enjoy the results of his intrigues, for on the 28th he was murdered by the agents of the Sheikh of the Assassins, commonly known as the Old Man of the Mountains, whom he had offended by his arbitrary conduct. The French Crusaders delighted at such an opportunity for blackening the character of Richard Coeur-de-Lion, chivalrously announced to the world that the assassins had been hired by him to do the work, an accusation which he treated with contempt. A week later on 5 May the Count of Champagne married the Marquis's widow the Princess Isabel, and was acknowledged as king of Jerusalem but only with the title of Lord of the Kingdom. The new monarch was popular with the barons of the Holy Land, he was not only King Richard's nephew, but he was also nephew to the King of France,[1] and there could have been no better ending to the wretched disputes concerning the crown that had so long agitated the crusading army.

Although he had at last realized how impossible Guy de Lusignan was as King of Jerusalem, Richard Coeur-de-Lion felt that he was in honour bound to make some suitable provision for his late protégé. A satisfactory solution to this problem was found in the island of Cyprus, his conquest of the previous year. King Richard had sold the island to the Templars for 100,000 besants, but their conduct had been so brutally oppressive, that in April it broke out into revolt from one end to the other, and the Master of the Temple begged the king to take it back again and return the purchase-money. He agreed to do so, and conferred the island upon King Guy, on the understanding that he should be responsible for the repayment of the 100,000 besants, and so was founded the royal dynasty of Lusignan, which was to rule over Cyprus for 250 years.

On his return to Ascalon from Acre King Richard was still occupied in consolidating his position there, and on 22 April seized and garrisoned the castle of Blanchegarde. In the following month the

[1] He was the son of Mary of France, a daughter of King Louis VII by Eleanor of Aquitaine, and therefore half-sister of King Philip Augustus and half-sister of King Richard Coeur-de-Lion.

Hospitallers and Templars carried out a brilliant raid [1] up to the walls of Darum, and then on 22 May King Richard stormed that fortress after a siege of only four days, and the whole sea-coast from Tyre southwards was once more in Christian hands. The time had now come for a fresh attempt against Jerusalem, and on 10 June King Richard again occupied Bêtenoble, which would form the advanced base of the army. His nephew the new King of Jerusalem was sent to Acre to try to round-up the numerous French stragglers, and for three weeks the army was kept waiting their arrival. Two days after the occupation of Bêtenoble, the King of England carried out a raid to Emmaus, and in his absence 200 Saracens attempted to surprise the camp. They were beaten back by the Hospitallers and Templars, and during this fighting an incident is recorded illustrative of the discipline of the military Orders.[2] A certain knight of the Hospital named Robert de Bruges rode out of the ranks of his brethren, contrary to the rules of the Order, to challenge to single combat a Saracen champion, whom he ran through with his lance and slew. Garnier de Nablus thereupon sternly ordered him to dismount from his horse, and to return to his tent under arrest, and there to await the punishment that his conduct deserved. It was only at the urgent request of the leaders of the crusading army, that the Master of the Hospital consented to pardon this breach of discipline.[3]

Apparently the Hospitallers and Templars and the barons of the Holy Land, that is all those who really knew the country, were still strongly opposed to a direct attack upon Jerusalem, and used the opportunity furnished by this period of waiting to impress upon King Richard that any such attempt was foredoomed to failure. They held the view that had been held in the Holy Land ever since the days of King Amaury, that its safety depended upon the conquest of Egypt, and that Jerusalem must be won on the banks of the Nile.[4] They eventually convinced King Richard of the soundness of their views, but he was quite unable to persuade the Duke of Burgundy to join them in a march upon Cairo. Rather than break with the French, he again agreed to attempt the capture of the Holy City, but declined to be responsible for the results. Just at this moment on 21 June the news arrived that heavy reinforcements for Saladin were on the road from Egypt, with an enormous convoy of stores. The king and the Duke of Burgundy rode out of the camp that evening to intercept it, and at

[1] See *Les Hospitaliers en Terre Sainte*, p. 113, note 2.

[2] See Archer, *The Crusade of Richard I*, pp. 251, 252.

[3] The Rule of the Templars, on which the military rules of the Hospitallers were modelled, reads: 'If a brother on an expedition pricks forward without leave and harm comes of it, he is liable to lose his habit. But if he sees a Christian in peril of death and his conscience moves him to go to the rescue he may do so.' See Curzon, *La Règle du Temple*, p. 243.

[4] See Norgate, *Richard the Lion Heart*, p. 234.

dawn on the 23rd surprised the convoy at the Round Cistern (Kuweilfeh) south-west of Hebron. The attack that followed was a brilliant success, 2,000 of the escort were killed, and the entire convoy captured, with 4,000 camels, and horses and mules too numerous to be counted. They returned to the camp at Bêtenoble on the 30th bringing with them King Henry of Jerusalem, and the long-expected reinforcements from Acre. But the constant quarrels between the French and the English became more violent than ever, the plans for the capture of the Holy City were abandoned, and on 4 July the army fell back upon Ramleh. Fresh negotiations for peace followed, and both sides were now in agreement on the general principles of a partition treaty. The Christians were to have the sea-coast, and the Moslems the hill-country and Jerusalem, in which special privileges were to be ensured to the former. But neither side would agree to give up Ascalon, the negotiations broke down on the 19th, and the war was resumed.

With Jerusalem safe from any likelihood of attack, Saladin so long on the defensive was at last in a position to take the offensive again. By the end of July the bulk of the Crusaders were once more in Acre, and on the 27th Saladin suddenly appeared before the gates of Jaffa. The attack was pressed vigorously, on the 31st a breach was opened in the walls, and the garrison retired into the citadel. On the morning of 1 August, just as they were about to surrender, a relieving force under the King of England arrived by sea from Acre, consisting of 55 knights and 2,000 foot. He at once drove the Saracens out of the town, and Saladin broke up his camp and retired. For three days King Richard was employed in repairing the walls of Jaffa, and then on 5 August the last battle of the Third Crusade was fought.

At daybreak Saladin attempted to surprise the camp outside Jaffa, having now learnt how very small the relieving force was. King Richard however was warned in time, and the Saracen horse in vain tried to break the steady line of Christian pikes and cross-bows. Then the king at the head of only ten knights,[1] for there were no horses for the remainder, charged out from behind the infantry, broke right through the Saracen army, and marvellous to relate succeeded in cutting his way back again. It was one of the most Homeric combats in all the warlike history of the Middle Ages. The enemy made another half-hearted attack about midday and then drew off, finally retiring to En-Natroun. The Crusaders are said to have had only two men killed, though many were wounded, and they claimed that the

[1] The names of the ten knights deserve to be recorded, they were King Henry of Jerusalem, the Earl of Leicester, Bartholomew de Mortimer, Ralph de Mauléon, Andrew de Chavigny, Gerard de Furnival, Roger de Sacy, William de Stagno, Hugh de Neuville, a most valiant serjeant, and Henry the German, who was the king's standard-bearer. See Archer, *The Crusade of Richard I*, p. 306.

enemy left 700 dead on the field and 1,500 horses, but these figures are generally regarded as exaggerated.[1]

The physical and mental strain of the operations for the relief of Jaffa proved too much for King Richard. A man of immense activity and energy, he always suffered from very bad health, and he now broke down completely.[2] Gradually it became evident that if he did not soon leave Syria, he would probably die there, and negotiations were once more opened with Saladin for a partition of the country. At last terms were agreed and on 2 September the Peace of Ramleh was signed, after a war of five years, which had devastated and depopulated the Holy Land from end to end. The terms were those that had already been under discussion ever since the Battle of Arsuf the previous year. The Christians were to keep the sea-coast and the lowlands from Tyre to Jaffa, and their border towns towards Jerusalem were to be Ramleh and Lydda. The Moslems were to have the hill-country with Jerusalem, but were to allow all Christian pilgrims to have free access to the Holy Sepulchre. Both sides agreed to drop all claims upon Ascalon, its fortifications were to be demolished, and it was to remain unoccupied. Darum had already been dismantled and abandoned by the Crusaders since the beginning of July. The treaty was to last three years from 22 September, and was to include the Count of Tripolis and the Prince of Antioch. On 9 October 1192 King Richard Coeur-de-Lion sailed for Europe, and the Third Crusade was at an end. The combined efforts of all the powers of Europe had failed to wrest Jerusalem from the hands of Saladin, and henceforward the Latin kingdom was to consist only of Phoenicia and the land of the Philistines with Acre for its capital, and for a time even Sidon and Beyrout remained under Saracen rule.

Garnier de Nablus Master of the Hospital did not live to see the Peace of Ramleh signed, but died on 31 August,[3] and presumably was buried in Acre. When the king went to the relief of Jaffa by sea, the Hospitallers and Templars co-operated by advancing along the coast-road. But they were unable to proceed beyond Caesarea, owing to the presence of a strong Saracen force under a son of the Sheikh of the Assassins, detached by Saladin to cover his attack on Jaffa. No doubt the strain of the summer campaign proved too much for Garnier de Nablus, as it did for the Duke of Burgundy and so many of the Crusaders. We really know nothing of his personality or rule beyond the facts that he was a very gallant knight and wise counsellor, held in the greatest esteem by his contemporaries. The official chronicle only tells us that he showed great courage in deeds of arms against the

[1] See Oman's *Art of War in the Middle Ages*, Vol. I, p. 319.

[2] For a study of Richard I see Hilaire Belloc, *A History of England*, Vol. II, pp. 214, 215.

[3] See *Les Hospitaliers en Terre Sainte*, p. 116.

enemies of the faith. Throughout the Third Crusade he had been one of King Richard's most loyal comrades and most trusted advisers. It was no doubt owing to his military reputation that he was elected to be Master of the Hospital during such a time of disaster in the Holy Land, and it is amongst its great soldiers, like his Anglo-Norman predecessors Gilbert d'Assailly and Roger des Moulins, that his name is remembered in the Order of St. John. England may well be proud of its only Prior, who was ever elected to be Master of the Hospital.[1]

There is a very beautiful mediaeval story linking the great name of Saladin with the Hospital of St. John in Acre, and if the story were fact and not a mere legend, it could relate only to Garnier de Nablus. The Minstrel of Rheims tells us[2] that Saladin, having heard of the boundless charity of the brethren of the Hospital, went to Acre disguised as a sick pilgrim to test their charity for himself. Pretending to be unable to eat the food provided, he at last told the distressed knight in charge that he had one impossible caprice, which alone could satisfy him. The knight urged him to make his request saying, 'A sick man here is given whatsoever he fancies, if gold can buy it; ask what you will and you shall have it.' So Saladin made his request, 'It is the foot of the Grand Master's famous horse Moriel that I desire to eat, and unless it be cut off in my presence, I can never touch food again.' When the Master of the Hospital heard the story of the knight, he ordered that the caprice of the sick man should be granted, 'Since it be so, take my horse; better that all my horses should perish than one sick man.' But as they were about to strike off the foot of Moriel in his presence Saladin suddenly announced that the desire had passed away, and that he would be content with the ordinary food supplied. And when he had returned to his own country, he sent the brethren of the Hospital a charter, sealed with his own seal, which is said to have read as follows:

> 'Let all men know that I Saladin, Soldan of Babylon, give and bequeath to the Hospital of Acre a thousand besants of gold, to be paid every year in peace or war, unto the Grand Master be he who he may, in gratitude for the wonderful charity of himself and his Order.'

Historically there is a certain slight foundation for this story. During the Saracen occupation of Acre after the Battle of Hattin, Saladin took for his own use the house of the Templars, formerly the palace of the Egyptian governors, and gave the house of the Hospitallers to the Moslem clergy, turning the bishop's palace into a hospital.

[1] There is in the Chapter-Hall of the English Order of St. John at Clerkenwell a tablet to his memory of gilded bronze, bearing below his arms the following inscription: 'Fr. Garnier de Nablous, Second English Grand Master. Elected 1190. Died in the Holy Land 31st August 1192.'

[2] See *Recits d'un Menestral de Reims*, edited by M. N. de Wailly for the Société de l'histoire de France, Paris, 1876.

He conferred rich endowments out of the spoils of his successful campaign upon both these institutions.[1]

APPENDIX

NOTE ON THE FATE OF THE TRUE CROSS

(*From Lane-Poole's 'Saladin'*, *p.* 304.)

'THE fate of the True Cross is obscure. When it was taken at the Battle of Hattin the sacred wood is described as mounted in red gold and adorned with pearls and precious stones. It was sent first to Damascus and then to Baghdad, where the Caliph buried it (4 June 1189) under the threshold of the Bab-en-Nuby to be trodden under Moslem feet: a bit of the gold could be seen. Yet Boha-ed-din says the True Cross was exhibited in Saladin's camp at Acre and included in the first instalment of the proffered indemnity. When the negotiations were broken off, the Cross was sent to Damascus and exposed to contempt in the Omayyad Mosque. It should be noted that as the Moslems hold the story of the Crucifixion to be an unworthy fable, contempt for what they regard as a superstitious forgery involves no disrespect towards the honoured name of Jesus, whom they reverence. From Damascus the Cross is said to have been sent as a gift to Isaac the Emperor of Constantinople. Yet the Bishop of Salisbury is reported to have seen it at Jerusalem by permission of Saladin in September 1192.[2] Ernoul moreover has a curious story of a Frank soldier who undertook to find it on the field of Hattin at the spot where he had buried it with his own hands during the battle; but after three nights' digging he gave up the search. Another presumed fragment was shown to Richard by the Abbot of St. Elias at Beit Nuba. There were doubtless several True Crosses, and imitations.'

[1] See Lane-Poole's *Saladin*, p. 244.

[2] Doubtless this is true, because the True Cross was returned by the Sultan El-Kamil in 1221, at the peace which terminated the Fifth Crusade. Only a fragment therefore can have been sent to Constantinople.

CHAPTER X

THE CONVENT AT MARGAT AND ACRE

WHEN the Order of St. John was driven from Jerusalem by Saladin, the brethren were allowed to take with them their archives and the treasures of their church, and were conducted under escort to the frontiers of the County of Tripolis. Here now lay the most important possessions of their Order in the East, centring round their two great fortresses of Le Crac and Margat. It was obvious that the Convent would have to be established in one of these two places, for there was no city available in the Holy Land except Tyre, which was in a state of siege, and shortly to be an object of contention between King Guy and Conrad of Montferrat. Le Crac as a frontier fortress, continually liable to attack, its garrison always on active service, was quite unsuited to be the seat of the Convent, and so William Borrell the Grand Preceptor decided, as we should naturally expect, to establish it at Margat, a decision which was evidently confirmed by Armengaud d'Aspe the following year on his election to be Master of the Hospital.

Margat, now known as Markab, was situated on the frontiers of Tripolis and Antioch, close to the sea covering the coast-road from La Liche (Latakieh) to Tripolis, and had only recently come into the possession of the Hospitallers. It stood on a spur of the Ansariyeh Mountains, jutting northwards from the main massif, with which it was connected to the south by a narrow neck of land. On this neck of land lay the castle, and to the north of it the town, the whole enclosed by a double line of walls.[1] It was one of the most formidable fortresses in Syria, and was probably of Byzantine origin. Margat was taken from the Saracens in 1140, and Prince Raymond of Antioch bestowed it as a fief upon Reginald le Mazoir, Constable of the Principality. On the death of the Constable in 1160, it passed to his son another Reginald, together with the important duty of holding in check the pestilent sect of the Assassins, now firmly ensconced in the mountains behind it.[2] When this Reginald died about 1183, his son Bertrand le

[1] For a detailed description of Margat, see Rey, *L'Architecture Militaire des Croisés en Syrie*, pp. 19–38.

[2] The Assassins belonged to the Moslem sect of the Ismailians, their headquarters were at Alamut, south of the Caspian Sea. By the middle of the

Mazoir apparently found the defence of so great a fortress too heavy a charge, and so in February 1186 he granted it to the Hospitallers, the grant being confirmed by the Prince of Antioch and the Count of Tripolis, and at the same time he granted to them the town of Valénie (Balanyas) with the consent of its bishop.[1] Margat had thus been in their possession little more than eighteen months, when it became the seat of the Convent and the administrative headquarters of the Order of St. John, but the military headquarters necessarily remained in Palestine during the Third Crusade and the campaigns for the recovery of Jerusalem.

What happened to the sisters of the Order of St. John, who ministered in the hospice for women pilgrims, is unknown to us. Doubtless after the fall of Jerusalem, they became scattered and ended their days in peace, attached to various commanderies, as was then the custom. Apparently certain houses of the Order in the early days had one or more sisters attached,[2] presumably for the benefit of sick women admitted to their hospitals. The system had obvious objections, and towards the end of the twelfth century, the sisters of the Order began to be collected together in separate establishments. The first house to be founded for the sisters was in England, where about 1186 [3] King Henry II presented to the Order of St. John for this purpose the house of Austin Canons at Buckland in Somerset, which had been forfeited to the Crown. Here all the sisters in England were concentrated under their first Prioress Fina, who ruled over them for no less than fifty-four years, dying at a great age in 1240, and leaving behind her a memory always held in the deepest reverence.

Two years after the foundation of Buckland, the most famous of all the houses of the sisters of the Hospital was founded by Queen Sancha of Aragon at Sigena, between Saragossa and Lerida. We are told that the Queen, deeply distressed by the misfortunes that had befallen the Holy Land, determined to found a nunnery for ladies of noble birth, in memory of the Knights of the Hospital who had fallen in battle fighting for the Christian faith. So lavish were the gifts of the Queen, and so generous her endowments, that it is said that the house resembled in appearance a palace rather than a religious establishment. After the death of her husband Alfonso II in 1196, Queen Sancha and

twelfth century they had established an independent state in Syria in the Ansariyeh Mountains, where they possessed nine strongholds of which Masyaf was their capital. Their Sheikh was known to the Crusaders as the Old Man of the Mountain, and was greatly feared owing to his systematic and successful use of murder as a political and financial weapon.

[1] See *Cartulaire-Général,* Vol. I, No. 783.

[2] See *Les Hospitaliers en Terre Sainte,* pp. 299, 300.

[3] The gift was to Garnier de Nablus, Prior of England, who only became Prior in 1185, and the date 1180 given in Hugo's *History of Mynchin Buckland,* p. 9, must therefore be incorrect.

ST. UBALDESCHA

one of her daughters entered the house of Sigena and took the vows, the Queen herself becoming the Prioress. The sisters of the Hospital were always required to give the same proofs of noble birth as the knights of the Order, but at Sigena the nuns were of such exalted and famous families as to render proofs of their nobility unnecessary,[1] and in memory of their royal foundress they were accustomed during divine service to carry silver sceptres.[2] The nunnery of Sigena still exists, but under a papal dispensation the sisters are no longer required to produce proofs of noble birth, and the house has ceased to be subject to the jurisdiction of the Grand Masters of the Order, whose place in this respect has now been taken by the Bishops of Lerida.[3]

Not many years after the foundation of Buckland and Sigena, a third house for the sisters was founded at Pisa in Italy in 1200,[4] an establishment that was at once rendered illustrious by the beautiful life of one of its inmates St. Ubaldescha, most famous and beloved of all the saints of the Order, after its founder the Blessed Gerard. St. Ubaldescha was born in the year 1136 in the castle of Calcinaja near Pisa, and from her earliest days was filled with the love of God, giving up her whole life to works of piety and devotion. At the early age of 14, as the result of a heavenly vision, she made her profession in the Order of St. John, afterwards entering the newly-founded house of the Order at Pisa. There by her continual austerities, her goodness and sweetness of disposition, and her devout life, she began to be regarded as almost a saint, whilst still living, and many said that miracles were performed by her. A party of women pilgrims even alleged that when at their request she had blessed some water, that they had begged of her, it was miraculously turned into wine. For this reason in her portraits she is generally represented carrying a little cruse of water, and sometimes with a palm-branch also, to show that she had died a martyr to her own self-devotion. St. Ubaldescha died on 28 May 1206, in the 70th year of her age.[5] Her head was preserved in the church of the sisterhood, together with the miraculous cruse, until the French destroyed their house in 1808.[6] Her body was interred in the Priory Church of Pisa (the church of the Holy Sepulchre), where it still is, but in 1586 a part of the relics were translated to the conventual church of the Order in Valletta. In an iron age of bitter fanaticism

[1] See Vertot, 'Traité du Gouvernement', Article I, in his *Histoire des Chevaliers de Malthe.*

[2] See Vertot, *Histoire des Chevaliers de Malthe,* Book II.

[3] See Delaville Le Roulx's Introduction to his *Cartulaire-Général.*

[4] See Boisgelin, *Malta, Ancient and Modern,* Vol. II, Appendix 9.

[5] For the life of St. Ubaldescha, see Bosio, *Istoria della Sacra Religione, etc.,* and *Les Vies des Saints de L'Ordre.*

[6] It stood in the street of San Giovannino near the church of the Holy Sepulchre, and the buildings of the commandery can still be seen there. See Delaville Le Roulx's Introduction to his *Cartulaire-Général.*

and callous cruelty, the sweet gentle life of Ubaldescha is like a fragrant breath from another world. In the eloquent words of the Abbé Vertot[1] 'Nature formed her generous and beneficent; grace rendered her charitable; she was the mother of the poor; the sick met with a relief always at hand in her assiduous care; there was no kind of misery but she brought a remedy for it, or gave consolation under it; and when her duties allowed her some moments to herself she spent them before the cross, and in a continual meditation upon the death and passion of our divine Saviour. It was in a continual exercise of these virtues that the blessed Ubaldescha died about the year 1206.'

Many houses were founded for the sisters of the Order during the following centuries. They all followed the Augustinian rule, and were subject to the Statutes of the Order of St. John, their regulations being based upon those of Sigena.[2] But these sisterhoods carried out no hospitaller duties, and constituted a purely contemplative order, engaged in works of piety and devotion.[3] The sisters wore a red robe,[4] and a black mantle, bearing the cross of the Order, and their houses as a rule were subject to the jurisdiction of the Prior of the province, unless coming directly under the Master of the Hospital.

The capture of Jerusalem by the Saracens marks the final turning point in the history of the Order of St. John. Since the Blessed Raymond du Puy had first instituted a class of military brethren, its military duties and liabilities had been constantly increasing, but none the less its great hospital for pilgrims in Jerusalem, containing 2,000 beds, always remained the primary object of its existence. As we have already seen there had been a gradually increasing tendency on the part of the military elements to assert their predominance, and in 1177 it had been necessary for the Pope to remind the Master Roger des Moulins that the real objects for which his Order existed were charitable and not military. But with the loss of their world famous hospital, and the events that followed, only military duties were left to the Order of St. John. During the five years' war against Saladin, the military brethren naturally and inevitably obtained complete control over the affairs of their Order, and although its original charitable objects were never allowed to be forgotten, from henceforward they were to play a very secondary part in its history. It is true that the Hospitallers always maintained an important hospital as a part of the establishment of their Convent, wherever

[1] See *L'Histoire des Chevaliers de Malthe*, Book III.

[2] The rule of Sigena is printed in the *Cartulaire-Général*, Vol. I, No. 859.

[3] See *Les Hospitaliers en Terre Sainte*, p. 300.

[4] See Vertot, *Histoire des Chevaliers de Malthe*, Book II; the red robe was only changed to black as a token of mourning after the loss of Rhodes, Boisgelin, *Malta, Ancient and Modern*, Vol. II, p. 229, and Helyot's *Histoire des Ordres Monastiques*, 1715, Vol. III, p. 128. Bosio in his *Life of St. Flore* also mentions this red robe.

THE CASTLE OF MARGAT

it might be, but none the less from the loss of their original hospital in Jerusalem, they became as purely a military Order as the Templars.

When the treaty of Ramleh once more brought peace to the Holy Land, the Hospitallers must have found themselves face to face with a financial crisis of extreme gravity. They had lost the whole of their once rich possessions in Palestine except along the sea-coast, and there their lands and property had been plundered and ravaged a dozen times and the countryside almost depopulated. Moreover, for five years they had been straining their resources to the utmost, in order to maintain the largest possible military force in the East. The long war can only have left the affairs of the Hospital in hopeless confusion, and their financial position in a state perilously near to bankruptcy. It was essential that the Master elected to fill the vacancy created by the death of Garnier de Nablus, should be a sound organizer and administrator rather than a soldier, and just as they had done after the collapse of Gilbert d'Assailly's Egyptian policy, they elected the former Treasurer of the Order to fill the vacancy.

The new Master, Geoffrey de Donjon,[1] was elected at a Chapter General held at Margat in January 1193. He is said to have been a Frenchman from Picardy, and from his previous record it is clear that he was by far the most experienced official of his day. As Treasurer of the Order he had been a Conventual Bailiff as far back as 1177. The following year he had been appointed to the high office of Grand Preceptor d'Outremer, a position which he appears to have held until again recalled to the Convent as Treasurer in 1187. Probably he held the latter office until superseded early in 1192 by Robert the Englishman, afterwards Prior of England, but what appointment he was filling at the time of his election is no longer on record.[2]

Two months after the election of Geoffrey de Donjon, Saladin died at Damascus, worn out by a life of incessant toil, and his empire was divided between his sons. The eldest, El-Afdal, took Damascus, El-Aziz was Sultan of Egypt, and Ez-Zahir Sultan of Aleppo, whilst the ablest member of the family, their uncle Saphadin, ruled in Mesopotamia. The inevitable civil war began in the following year, when El-Aziz marched against his brother of Damascus; driven back into Egypt he was only saved by the intervention of his uncle Saphadin, who became his vizier. Then in 1196 they drove El-Afdal out of

[1] The historian Bosio calls him 'de Duison', copying from a fourteenth-century chronicler, who probably identified him with this family out of compliment to John de Duison, then Grand Prior of France. Bosio's mistake was copied by Vertot. See Vicomte de Poli, *Les Onze Premiers Grand Maîtres, etc.*, in the *Annuaire du Conseil Heraldique de France*, 1892.

[2] For the career of Geoffrey de Donjon, see the list of Dignitaries given in the Appendix to *Les Hospitaliers en Terre Sainte*, a list that Delaville Le Roulx must have overlooked when he remarked that nothing was known of his past, except his presence in the Holy Land in 1185.

Damascus, and Saphadin became its governor in the name of his nephew El-Aziz. Such was the situation in Syria, when the Treaty of Ramleh finally came to an end, after having been renewed by El-Aziz for an additional year, and a fresh Crusade involved the impoverished barons of the Holy Land in an entirely useless war.

The Emperor Henry VI, son and successor of Frederick Barbarossa, filled with ambition for universal empire, had recently conquered the kingdom of Sicily, and was now anxious in the name of religion to add Syria to his dominions. At the bidding of Pope Celestine III he had gladly taken the cross, and in 1197 a German army was ready to attempt the recovery of Jerusalem. While the main body under the Emperor in person moved south into Italy and Sicily, the northern Germans under the Dukes of Saxony and Brabant were to sail from the ports on the North Sea, and a strong detachment of Germans and Hungarians under the Archbishop of Mainz and Queen Margaret of Hungary marched down the valley of the Danube to Constantinople, where they were to embark for Acre.

The news of a fresh crusade was no subject for rejoicing in the Holy Land, and its arrival was viewed only with apprehension by the enfeebled remnant of the Latin kingdom of Jerusalem. All that the ruined Christian population desired was to live on good terms with their Moslem neighbours, and to enjoy what was left of their property in peace. It was already clear that in Saphadin a worthy successor had been found to his brother's empire, and that it would be unwise for so weak a state to provoke him. Moreover the rough hard-drinking overbearing German soldiery, who despised every other race but their own, were detested by the Latins of the East.

The first of the German Crusaders to arrive was the contingent under the Archbishop of Mainz. They at once clamoured to be led against the infidels, and were filled with indignation to find that the barons of the Holy Land had no desire to begin hostilities, unless there were reasonable prospects of success. In vain Henry of Champagne begged them to await the arrival of the Emperor and the main body of their army. But they were quite uncontrollable and the conduct of their drunken troops was so abominable that the women and children were advised to take refuge in the houses of the Hospitallers and Templars. At last they marched out of Acre and began to plunder the lands of the Moslems, raiding as far as Nablus. But they were roughly handled by Saphadin, who had concentrated his forces at Jerusalem, and were driven back to Acre with heavy losses. Then Saphadin suddenly struck at Jaffa, and after a short siege captured the town on 5 September before help could arrive, and after completely destroying its fortifications left it in ruins. The new war had opened badly enough, and to add to the difficulties of the situation, five days later Henry of Champagne met his death in an accident at

Acre. He was giving audience to an embassy from Pisa, when the balcony of his palace collapsed, and he was killed by the fall. Count Henry was a very gallant knight, but circumstances had rendered it impossible for him to accomplish much for his sorely stricken kingdom. Although King of Jerusalem by right of marriage, he never underwent the ceremony of coronation, and even on his coinage is styled simply Count Henry. He had always longed for the day when he might return to his beloved France, but fate had ordained otherwise, and he died a martyr to his sense of duty.

In the midst of these disasters the North-German Crusaders arrived under the Dukes of Saxony and Brabant. They had stopped on the way to assist King Sancho of Portugal in his wars against the Moors, and had much distinguished themselves at the capture of Silves. With this reinforcement it was possible to assume the offensive, and on the advice of John d'Ibelin the Queen's half-brother [1] and Constable of the kingdom, it was rightly decided first to attempt the recovery of Beyrout, which was now the centre of a wedge of Moslem territory separating the county of Tripolis from the kingdom of Jerusalem. Gibelet (Jubail) had been already surrendered by its Emir to its former lord Hugh de Lembriac, called 'the Lame', the year after Saladin's death,[2] but at Beyrout the Saracens were steadily consolidating their position, and their shipping had become a serious menace to the Christian communications with Europe.

The Crusaders were not ready to move until the latter half of October, but they met with little serious opposition. A battle was fought with Saphadin on the 22nd as they were approaching the ruins of Sidon, but the attack was never pressed home by the Saracens, and at nightfall Saphadin, who had been slightly wounded, fell back on the road to Damascus. Next day the Crusaders occupied Beyrout without resistance. Saphadin despairing of holding the town, had ordered its fortifications to be dismantled, and the governor of the castle, which had been strongly fortified, abandoned his post. Beyrout was granted by Queen Isabel to her half-brother the Constable. Already Lord of Ibelin and Ramleh, and by his marriage with its heiress Lord of Arsuf also, John d'Ibelin thus became the most powerful baron in the Holy Land, and as the Old Lord of Beyrout was to play the leading part in its politics for the next forty years.

After spending a fortnight at Beyrout, the Crusaders returned to Tyre to refit, and were there joined by the remainder of the German

[1] Balian, Lord of Ibelin, the defender of Jerusalem against Saladin, had married King Amaury's widow, Queen Maria Comnena, by whom he had two sons John and Philip, afterwards Regent of Cyprus, and a daughter Marguerite, who married (1) Hugh de Tabarie, Prince of Galilee, and (2) Walter de Layron, Lord of Caesaréa.

[2] See Stevenson's *Crusaders in the East*, p. 295, note 6.

army under the Emperor's lieutenant Conrad of Wurzburg, Bishop of Hildesheim, Chancellor of the Empire. It was decided that they were strong enough to attempt the capture of the great fortress of Toron (Tibnin), which dominated all the country east of Tyre and north of Galilee. Built originally by the Christians to hold in check the garrison of Tyre, then in Moslem hands, under its new owners it continued to fill the purpose for which it had been designed, and there could be no real security for the coast lands so long as it was held by the Saracens. The siege began on 28 November, and dragged on all through December and January, but the Imperial Chancellor was unable to keep his army together owing to the demoralization caused by the news of the Emperor's death in Sicily. The different contingents began to straggle back to Tyre and Acre, eager to return to Europe, and on 2 February the siege was raised and the army fell back upon Tyre.

It was now necessary to consider who should be the future ruler over the kingdom of Jerusalem. Since the death of Henry of Champagne the nominal ruler had been the young Queen Isabel, who although she had already survived three husbands was still only 26 years of age, and there was no lack of claimants for her hand, and for the somewhat damaged throne that went with it. On the advice of the Imperial Chancellor, supported by Geoffrey de Donjon Master of the Hospital and his colleague Gilbert Horal of the Temple, the barons of the Holy Land decided to offer the hand of their Queen and with it the crown to Amaury de Lusignan, King of Cyprus.[1] No better selection could possibly have been made, for he was a very different man to his incompetent brother the late King Guy. He was now 52 years of age, and of all the Latin princes there was none with a wider experience of eastern warfare and eastern politics, and none who had gained a higher reputation or greater popularity, whilst in his organization of the recently conquered island of Cyprus he had displayed administrative ability of an exceptionally high order. And so the King of Cyprus came to Tyre, and after marrying Queen Isabel, was crowned King of Jerusalem under the name of Amaury II, and he showed his turbulent baronage that he intended to be master of his realm, when he declined to confirm John d'Ibelin in the possession of Beyrout, until he laid down his office as Constable.

Before the departure of the Imperial Chancellor and the last of the German Crusaders, an event of the greatest importance was still to take place. Up to this time French and Italian influence had been predominant in Syria, and Germans had played a very minor part in

[1] He succeeded his brother King Guy as Lord of Cyprus on his death in 1194. His lordship was raised to the dignity of a kingdom by the Emperor Henry VI in 1197, and he was crowned king at Nicosia by the Imperial Chancellor in September of that year, on his way to the Holy Land.

the Latin states. Within the sadly diminished boundaries of the kingdom of Jerusalem, the military Orders of the Hospital and the Temple were now all-powerful, for they supplied the only reliable forces for its defence. But whilst cosmopolitan in constitution, their actual membership was so overwhelmingly Latin, that German interests were likely to be more completely ignored than ever. Such a situation was not in accordance with the dignity of the Empire, and to the Germans it seemed necessary that they should have a military religious Order of their own, not inferior in importance to the older Orders, capable of looking after German interests in the East and of upholding the prestige of their race. The necessary instrument lay ready to their hands in the existing Order of German Hospitallers so long dependent upon the Order of St. John. And so on 5 March 1198 in the house of the Templars at Tyre [1] these German Hospitallers in the presence of the German Crusaders, of the Masters of the Hospital and the Temple, and the barons of the Holy Land, were solemnly proclaimed to be an independent military religious Order, to be exclusively restricted in membership to Germans of noble birth, and to be known henceforward as the Teutonic Knights of the Hospital of the Virgin Mary at Jerusalem. Their rule was based upon that of the Templars in all that concerned their military duties, and on that of the Hospitallers in all matters of charity. Under their first Master Henry Walpot von Bassenheim they established themselves in Acre. From the beginning they had greater military importance than the Order of St. Lazarus, but in the Holy Land they were never able to rival in power and influence the famous Orders of the Hospital and the Temple, since their field of action lay rather in Northern Europe.

After the last of the German Crusaders had sailed, the war against the Moslems was practically at an end. It was impossible for King Amaury to carry on hostilities against Saphadin with any prospects of success, unless his slender resources were swelled by European assistance. As for Saphadin, his position in Syria was still so insecure that it was essential for him to be free as soon as possible to turn his attention elsewhere. Accordingly there was no difficulty in coming to terms, both sides agreed to accept the existing situation, and peace was signed in June. It had been a singularly useless war. The Christians had lost Jaffa, which was to remain in ruins, and had recovered Beyrout in its place, and Saphadin agreed to recognize their occupation of Gibelet (Jubail). The treaty was to last for six years, unless a crowned king should come on crusade to the Holy Land, whose actions King Amaury would naturally be unable to control.[2]

Saphadin at once left for the north, and no sooner had he restored order in Mesopotamia, than he found himself face to face with the

[1] See *Les Hospitaliers en Terre Sainte*, p. 127.

[2] See Stevenson's *The Crusaders in the East*, pp. 295, 296.

crisis, which he had long foreseen. El-Aziz of Egypt suddenly died in November, leaving an infant son El-Mansour. At once the exiled prince El-Afdal seized Cairo, proclaiming himself regent, and entered into an alliance with his brother Ez-Zahir of Aleppo, for the purpose of depriving their uncle of Damascus. But Saphadin was too quick for his nephews, and was back in Damascus, before they had time to arrive. Then he drove El-Afdal out of Egypt, and assumed the regency. On the death in the following year of the baby Sultan El-Mansour, Saphadin declared himself Sultan, and two years later, in 1202, his remaining nephew Ez-Zahir of Aleppo acknowledged his supremacy. The empire of Saladin was at last re-united under the rule of a Sultan scarcely less capable than its founder. But there was this great difference between the two brothers, Saladin had always been determined to drive the Christians out of Syria, whereas Saphadin desired only to live at peace with them, and to avoid if possible provoking a fresh crusade, a policy which was followed by most of his dynasty.

After the loss of Jerusalem and the restoration of peace, Acre, the most important seaport in the Holy Land, naturally became the capital of the Latin kingdom, and the seat of government. It must have very soon become clear that Margat, far away in the north, was no longer a suitable position for the Convent of the Hospitallers. We do not know exactly when the Convent was transferred from Margat to Acre, but it seems evident that the transfer was made by Geoffrey de Donjon, or the Hospitallers could never have objected to his successor holding a Chapter General at the former place. The German Crusade necessarily compelled the Master of the Hospital to have his military headquarters at Acre, and probably the inconvenience of separating the military and administrative headquarters at this time, was the determining cause for the transfer of the Convent to the capital. The Hospitallers had maintained an important establishment in Acre since at least 1155,[1] and its Commander was one of the Bailiffs of Syria. It was situated in the north-west of the city, and during the Saracen occupation, Saladin had converted it into a college for the Moslem clergy ; it now, in or about 1197, became the seat of the Convent. The buildings were remodelled to meet the requirements of the headquarters of the Order, a Hospital scarcely inferior to that at Jerusalem was established there, and the conventual church eventually became so conspicuous a landmark that the city was later generally known from it as St. Jean d'Acre.[2] But the hospice for pilgrims was

[1] A certain Gerard was Master of the Hospital at Acre in 1155, see *Cartulaire-Général*, Vol. I, No. 237.

[2] See Conder, *The Latin Kingdom of Jerusalem*, p. 407. In his description of Acre that follows, he says that the Hospice ultimately became the Serai, and the church of St. John a Mosque, but it is certainly not a mosque at the present day.

established outside the old walls in the new fortified suburb that was now growing up on Mount Musard.

Scarcely had peace been established between King Amaury and Saphadin, than all the latent jealousy and rivalry that had so long existed between the Hospitallers and Templars suddenly burst forth into flame. A knight named Séguin [1] held lands of the Hospital situated between Margat and Valénie, upon which the Templars had certain claims. Unable to obtain satisfaction they suddenly expelled Séguin from his castle by force, and seized it, and he thereupon complained to the Castellan of Margat. The Castellan Peter d'Escurai,[2] one of the Bailiffs of Syria, furious at the high-handed conduct of the Templars towards a vassal of the Hospital, marched out with his garrison, carried the castle by assault, and replaced Séguin. Apparently there was considerable bloodshed, and no doubt both Hospitallers and Templars were each honestly convinced that the insolence of their rivals had become insufferable, and must be firmly checked. Excited with angry indignation, the high-spirited young knights of the two Orders suddenly broke away from all control, and forgetting their religious vows and the bonds of discipline, began to fight out their quarrel wherever they met. As if that were not sufficiently scandalous and disgraceful, the vassals and personal friends of the two Orders began to take a hand in the strife, until all Christian Syria was in serious danger of becoming involved in what almost amounted to civil war. What the two Masters had been doing to allow the situation to reach such proportions, we have no means of knowing, but it gives the impression of hopeless weakness. In the case of Geoffrey de Donjon, as we know, his past career had been administrative rather than military, and probably in such a crisis he lacked influence over the military brethren of his Order. Eventually King Amaury assisted by the Patriarch and the bishops was able to bring his influence to bear upon the angry knights, gradually common-sense obtained a hearing, until at last arms were laid aside, and the whole matter in dispute was referred for a decision to the Pope, the first superior of all religious Orders, the Hospitallers being represented at the court of Rome by Ogier, the Grand Commander d'Outremer,[3] and Digisio, Prior of Barletta.

Pope Innocent III, who had only recently ascended the throne of

[1] Vertot calls him Robert de Margat, see *L'Histoire des Chevaliers de Malthe*, Book III.

[2] For the name, see *Cartulaire-Général*, Vol. I, Nos. 1031, 1096.

[3] One of the most prominent knights of the Hospital at this period. He succeeded the Master Armengaud d'Aspe as Prior of St. Gilles in 1188. Garnier de Nablus appointed him Grand Commander in 1190, and for a time he commanded the Hospitallers in the siege of Acre. He was appointed Prior of France in 1191, and Grand Commander d'Outremer about 1198, dying about 1210, since Isembard succeeded him as Grand Commander d'Outremer before 1211.

St. Peter, gave his decision in a bull dated 8 February 1199.[1] After sternly rebuking the two Orders for the violence of their conduct, so utterly unworthy of their religious professions, he endeavoured to settle the dispute in such a manner as should leave behind it the minimum of ill-feeling, and should pave the way for a complete and genuine reconciliation. The Hospitallers were ordered to replace the Templars in possession of the holding from which they had so forcibly ejected them. At the end of one month Séguin might then commence legal proceedings against the Templars before a special tribunal, constituted in such a way as to give complete confidence to both parties. The judges were to be drawn from amongst the leading men of the Principality of Antioch and the county of Tripolis, and they were to be nominated by the Hospitallers, subject to the approval of the Templars. If they should decline to serve, as was very possible, for fear of exciting against themselves the hostility of either Order, then they were to be compelled to do so by the Patriarch of Antioch, the Archbishop of Nazareth and the Bishop of Valénie, under pain of ecclesiastical censure. In the event of their judgement being unacceptable to the losing party, an appeal might be lodged against it, but the decision of the Court of Appeal would have to be regarded as final. In conclusion the Pope urged the two Orders forthwith to settle all their outstanding disptues in accordance with the agreement come to by the Masters Roger des Moulins and Odo de St. Amand in 1179. The result of the legal proceedings was that the Templars were judged to have been wrong in the first instance, and were ordered to restore Séguin [2] to his holding. So terminated one of the most disgraceful episodes in the history of the two Orders, but the real blame for it must lie in the culpable weakness of the two Masters, who seem to have been completely incapable of controlling the turbulent hot-blooded young soldiers, supposed to be under their command.[3]

The recent treaty with Saphadin had guaranteed to the Christian princes at least six years of peace, in which it would have been possible for them to do much to consolidate and strengthen their new position. They chose instead to weaken that position, already weak enough, by plunging into civil war over the succession to the throne of Antioch. Turbulent and quarrelsome, disloyal to each other, incapable of honest co-operation against a common foe, never have any states more richly deserved the doom that ultimately befell them, than the Latin states of Syria.

When Count Raymond II of Tripolis died in 1187, a fortnight

[1] Printed in the Appendix to this chapter.

[2] A certain Séguin was Prior of the Hospital in 1207; the name is very uncommon, it might possibly be the same man.

[3] A very full account of this episode is given in Vertot, *L'Histoire des Chevaliers de Malthe*, Book III, and in *Les Hospitaliers en Terre Sainte*, pp. 125, 126.

after the disastrous Battle of Hattin, leaving no descendants, he was succeeded by his godson Raymond of Antioch, eldest son of Prince Bohemond III called the Stammerer, whose matrimonial irregularities had been the cause of so much trouble a few years earlier. The new count in 1194 married Alix a daughter of Rupen of the Mountain, Prince of Lesser Armenia, by whom he had a son Raymond-Rupen. But the count appears to have been of weak intellect, and before his death in 1197 became completely imbecile, his younger brother Bohemond the One-eyed governing the county in his name. On the death of his elder brother the latter, ignoring the rights of his young nephew, declared himself Count of Tripolis. The Prince of Antioch apparently acquiesced in his son's action in Tripolis, but declared his grandson Raymond-Rupen heir to the Principality, and it was arranged that he should also succeed to the throne of Armenia on the death of his great-uncle Leo II, usually known as Leo the Great, who had no sons, thus uniting Antioch and Armenia. But Bohemond the One-eyed, desirous of having Antioch also, protested energetically against his father's action. Finding that the Latins were in favour of his nephew the rightful heir, he began to intrigue with the Greek population, who hated the Latins, and entered into an understanding with Ez-Zahir of Aleppo. Leo the Great, who had just been raised to the dignity of King of Armenia by the Emperor,[1] in vain appealed to the Pope against the unscrupulous and criminal conduct of the Count of Tripolis, and it became increasingly clear that the death of Prince Bohemond III would be the signal for civil war. The Hospitallers declared themselves on the side of the legitimate heir, but the Templars had a feud against the King of Armenia, who had recaptured their castle of Gaston (Bagras) from Saladin in 1190,[2] and declined to give it up to them; and so took sides with the Count of Tripolis. Had only the two Orders acted together, the long civil war that followed could probably never have taken place.

In 1201 Prince Bohemond III died, and Bohemond the One-eyed, his son, seized Antioch with the assistance of the Templars, and proclaimed himself prince under the title of Bohemond IV. The little Prince Raymond-Rupen was however got away in safety, and conveyed to the court of his mother's uncle the King of Armenia. It was of the utmost importance to avoid a resort to arms, because at this moment a fresh crusade was being organized by Pope Innocent III. Generally known to history as the Fourth Crusade, the intentions of the Pope were that it should attempt the recovery of the Holy Land by the conquest of Egypt. From now onwards the policy originally put

[1] Lesser Armenia was raised to the dignity of a kingdom by the Emperor Henry VI at the same time as Cyprus, and Leo the Great was crowned king by the Archbishop of Mainz and the Catholicos Gregory in 1198.

[2] See Stevenson, *The Crusaders in the East*, p. 258, note 1.

forward by King Amaury I became an accepted principle, that the Holy Land was naturally dependent upon Egypt, and could only be held permanently by the rulers of that country. Accordingly the church took up the strongest attitude against the usurping prince, the Pope denounced his conduct in no unmeasured tones, and the Patriarchs of Jerusalem and Antioch combined in excommunicating him. But the Count of Tripolis cared nothing for public opinion or the thunders of the church, he was in occupation of Antioch, and there he intended to remain, unless superior military force should eject him.

Such was the situation in the summer of 1202, when Geoffrey de Donjon died, the Christians of Syria on the verge of civil war, whilst the armies of the Fourth Crusade were beginning to concentrate at Venice. Geoffrey de Donjon had ruled over the Hospital for nearly ten years, but is none the less little more than a name to us. To judge from his previous career, we may safely assume that he was a sound administrator, and that his experience as Treasurer enabled him to restore the financial position of his Order, so badly shaken by the disastrous wars against Saladin. The official chronicle tends to confirm this, when it states that he protected vigorously the endowments of the Hospital, and that he ruled over it with dignity.[1] But the sanguinary quarrel with the Templars, and his inability to control his knights, leaves the impression that Geoffrey de Donjon was a somewhat weak ruler, and a distinctly bad disciplinarian.

In their choice of a successor the Hospitallers made a very unusual selection, which adds to the impression that all was not well with their Order. They seem to have felt that the situation demanded a chief of altogether exceptional character, one who would restore the old stern discipline, who would brook no disobedience and whose reputation and standing were such as would command instinctively the respect of all. Accordingly they now elected as their Master, Alfonso of Portugal, who appears to have had no previous connexion with their Order.[2] He was an illegitimate son [3] of the first King of Portugal, the famous Affonso Henriques, whose heroic deeds against the infidels of Spain were celebrated throughout the length and breadth of Europe. But although a Portuguese by birth, like so many of the Portuguese nobles of that day, he was French in origin, tradition, and culture, since the father of King Affonso was Count Henry of Burgundy. In the eyes of the Knights of the Hospital he was quite as much a French-

[1] These phrases seem to relate to Geoffrey de Donjon, but at this point the Chronicle is in a somewhat confused condition. See footnote to Para. 11 of Appendix B at the end of this work.

[2] Had he had any previous connexion with the Order, he would almost certainly have risen to the rank of Bailiff, and his name would then have been on record.

[3] The natural sons of ruling princes were an exception to the rule that only persons of legitimate birth were eligible to be received in the Order.

man as his Anglo-Norman predecessors, and they never elected as their Master anyone but a Frenchman, until long after their expulsion from Syria. Whether he had ever served in the Holy Land, we have no record, but he was certainly in Europe when the news of his election reached him, and was at Corbeil early in 1203,[1] when his half-sister Matilda the Dowager Countess of Flanders presented certain lands to the Hospital.

By the time that Alfonso of Portugal reached Acre, it was apparent that the Fourth Crusade had completely miscarried, and had degenerated into a buccaneering expedition against Constantinople of a peculiarly disgraceful and scandalous nature. Its leaders, Boniface Marquis of Montferrat, a younger brother of the famous Conrad, and Baldwin Count of Flanders, had proved false to their honour and their religious vows, and had become the willing tools of the Doge of Venice in his policy against the East Roman Empire. The Fourth Crusade instead of entering upon the long expected campaign against the infidels of Egypt, had turned its arms against its fellow Christians at the bidding of Venice. Zara had been stormed and sacked in November 1202, and in July 1203 these so-called Crusaders and their Venetian allies were besieging Constantinople in the name of the dispossessed Emperor Isaac Angelus. Two small contingents alone remained true to the sacred cause to which they had pledged their faith, and arrived in the Holy Land in the summer of 1203, a body of knights from Champagne under Reginald de Dampierre, and a Flemish contingent under John de Nesle, Castellan of Bruges. But King Amaury was still at peace with Saphadin, and was only free to break the peace if a crowned king came on crusade to the Holy Land. So Reginald de Dampierre thirsting for adventure went north with eighty knights to assist the Count of Tripolis to deprive his nephew of Antioch, and fell into an ambuscade laid by the Emir of La Liche (Latakieh),[2] only one knight escaping to tell the tale. Shortly after John de Nesle, having quarrelled with King Amaury, also joined the Count of Tripolis, and that was all the help that the Fourth Crusade ever gave to the kingdom of Jerusalem.[3]

Before the year was out some Moslem ships from Sidon seized two Latin ships off Cyprus. By way of reprisals King Amaury raided Moslem territory, and war was resumed, only to be speedily checked by an outbreak of pestilence. In the following year King Amaury sent a squadron of twenty ships on a daring, but rather useless, raid

[1] See *Cartulaire-Général,* Vol. II, No. 1167.

[2] See Stevenson, *The Crusaders in the East,* p. 300, note 2.

[3] John de Nesle had with him a Flemish knight, who had married the daughter of Isaac Comnenus, the so-called Emperor of Cyprus. This knight claimed the kingdom of Cyprus on behalf of his wife, and in consequence he and John de Nesle, who supported him, were ordered by King Amaury II to quit the realm.

against Damietta. Then came the startling news that the army of the Fourth Crusade had stormed and sacked Constantinople, that Baldwin of Flanders had been declared Emperor of the East, and that the Crusaders were dividing up amongst themselves the rich towns and territories of the Byzantine Empire. Instantly every landless knight and soldier of fortune in Syria was embarking in haste for Constantinople to share in the plunder before it should be too late. Scarcely a lancer or bowman was left in the Holy Land. Under these circumstances there was nothing for King Amaury to do but make peace, and Saphadin alarmed by the fall of Constantinople had no desire to continue the war, and was even ready to make certain concessions. Accordingly in September 1204 peace was signed, and was to last until Easter 1210,[1] and Saphadin restored to the Christians Jaffa and Nazareth, and agreed to divide with them the revenues of Sidon, Lydda and Ramleh. King Amaury II survived the treaty only a few months, and died at the age of 60 on 1 April 1205, being followed to the grave by Queen Isabel shortly afterwards. He was one of the wisest and most capable of all the kings of Jerusalem, and in spite of many difficulties and disappointments did much to strengthen and consolidate what was left of the kingdom. His realms were divided at his death, Cyprus going to his eldest son Hugh I by his first marriage, and Jerusalem going to Queen Isabel's eldest daughter Mary by her second husband Conrad of Montferrat, whilst John d'Ibelin, the all-powerful Lord of Beyrout, became Bailiff [2] and regent for his young niece.

The conclusion of peace with Saphadin in the autumn of 1204 left the Master of the Hospital free to quit Acre for the north, where his presence was urgently needed. As we have seen the Count of Tripolis had seized Antioch in 1201, the Pope used all his influence to avert war, and the winter of 1202–3 was spent in negotiations. But they were hopeless from the first, the King of Armenia was not prepared to abandon his young kinsman the rightful Prince of Antioch, and the count was equally determined to cling to his ill-gotten gains. The war that followed swayed backwards and forwards, keeping all northern Syria in disorder, and neither side was able to obtain a final victory for nearly twenty years. In November 1203 the King of Armenia, as regent for the young prince, secured possession of Antioch, but was driven out four days later by the Count of Tripolis, who had won over the Genoese by important concessions, and the count threw the patriarch into prison. The king again attacked the following year, but was driven back by the count, with the assistance of Ez-Zahir of

[1] See Stevenson's *The Crusaders in the East*, p. 297.

[2] The Bailiff or Seneschal was the chief of the five great officers of state of the French court between the eleventh and thirteenth centuries, the others being the Butler, Chamberlain, Constable and Chancellor.

Aleppo. With the Templars bitterly hostile to King Leo, owing to his retention of Gaston, and therefore on the side of the Count of Tripolis, and with the Hospitallers warmly supporting the legitimate prince, there was grave danger of the latent rivalry between the two Orders resulting in further strife.

In 1205 the Pope again intervened, but without result, and King Leo once more secured possession of Antioch, but failed to capture the castle which remained in the hands of the count. Prince Raymond-Rupen now ten years of age made his state entry into the city, where he was warmly received, and was solemnly crowned by the Patriarch in the Cathedral of St. Peter. The burning question of the succession to the throne of Antioch seemed at last settled, when Alfonso of Portugal summoned the Chapter-General of the Hospitallers to meet at Margat in 1206 for the purpose of confirming new statutes and ordinances.

The Master of the Hospital was above all things a stern and rigid disciplinarian, and from the moment of his election he seems to have been inspired by one ideal only, to restore the old Spartan rules that had prevailed in the days of the Blessed Raymond du Puy. But that was no longer possible for times had completely changed. In the old days when the military brethren were first instituted, the knights were in the minority and became absorbed in the ordinary conventual life, instinctively following its established rules and customs. But during the long wars against Saladin, the situation had become entirely reversed as we have seen, the knights were now in an immense majority and all power had passed into their hands. Constantly on active service for many years, it had been impossible under such conditions to maintain the old conventual discipline, and the necessarily heavy casualties had had to be replaced by a constant stream of recruits, who had never known the old traditions, and had no real call for the conventual life. The recent sanguinary dispute with the Templars had thrown a lurid light on the changed tone and discipline of the Order.

The first task of Alfonso of Portugal had been to make a clear distinction between the professed knights, and the secular knights who had attached themselves to the Order,[1] whilst on crusade, making a donation for the privilege, and known later as Donats.[2] Whilst actually serving with the Order, he permitted them to continue to wear its dress, but he laid down clearly that they were only auxiliaries of the Order not members, and that when they ceased to serve with it, they must cease to wear its dress. It can have done little good to the reputation of any religious Order, to have had roystering young knights wearing its distinctive dress and in no way subject to its discipline, and their example was not likely to be very beneficial to the professed knights.

[1] See Vertot, *Histoire des Chevaliers de Malthe,* Book III. [2] See page 72.

His second task was to codify existing rules and customs, and to draft certain new rules for submission to the Chapter-General for its approval. But the man who attempts to restore a shaken discipline must inevitably incur unpopularity, until at any rate the beneficial nature of his work has become obvious, and it is evident from what occurred at the Chapter-General that Alfonso of Portugal was not popular amongst certain elements. No doubt he had summoned the Chapter-General to meet at Margat and not at Acre, because it was at that moment the political centre of events for the Order, and therefore the most convenient meeting-place. This was at once seized upon as a grievance, and an attempt was made to maintain that it was not lawful for the Chapter-General to meet anywhere outside the boundaries of the Kingdom of Jerusalem.[1] The subsequent proceedings were stormy in the extreme. Certain proposals of the Master were duly accepted, and became a part of the statutes of the Order. But when he went on to submit to the assembly rules and regulations concerning the daily life of the knights, that would have had the effect of restoring the primitive conventual discipline of the early days, there were vigorous protests that times had changed and that such rules were not possible for men almost continually on active service. The Master, unaccustomed to brook any opposition, sternly replied, 'I insist upon unquestioning obedience.' At this a wave of anger swept over the assembly, and one of the senior knights publicly rebuked the Master, saying that the Chapter-General of the Order was not accustomed to hear its superior address it as if he were an absolute monarch. Finding himself unable to carry the measures that he thought necessary, according to one account Alfonso of Portugal flung the great seal of the Order to the ground in the presence of the Chapter, and thereupon resigned the Mastership.[2] Whatever actually did take place, he certainly very shortly after resigned a position that he no longer regarded as tenable just as Gilbert d'Assailly had done, and returned to his own country. But he did not live many months longer, for apparently his return to Portugal was viewed with considerable apprehension by certain members of his family, and they arranged to have him poisoned on the journey.[3] Their efforts were crowned with success, and he died on 1 March 1207, and was buried in the church of St. Joao d'Alporao at Santarem, where his memorial inscription can still be seen.[4] There is no doubt that from this time onwards there was a very great improvement in the general tone and discipline of the Order, and we cannot be far wrong if we attribute it to the work and influence of Alfonso of Portugal.

[1] See *Les Hospitaliers en Terre Sainte*, p. 131. [2] Ibid.

[3] See 'The Chronicle of the deceased Masters', in Appendix B at the end.

[4] See *Les Hospitaliers en Terre Sainte*, p. 131, note 3.

APPENDIX

PAPAL DECISION ON THE QUARREL BETWEEN THE HOSPITALLERS AND TEMPLARS

Dated 8 *February* 1199

INNOCENT, Bishop, servant of the servants of God, to the Master and brethren of the Hospital of Jerusalem, greeting. To the loss of all Christendom, to the shame of the apostolic see, and to the peril of your own souls, the dispute which has arisen between you and our beloved sons the brethren of the knighthood of the Temple concerning certain possessions in the holding of Margat and Valénie has far exceeded all the disputes of this age in the magnitude of the harm done; inasmuch as it is harmful to all Christendom, injurious to ourselves, pestilent to the parties concerned, useful to the enemies of the Christian faith, to whom it furnishes weapons both for open attack and more insidious disparagement. We have seen Christians in arms against one another in this cause, Religious (if indeed they can be called Religious, who thus wrongfully avenge wrongs done to themselves) have been stirred up to do grave injury to other Religious, and have raised up their hands against each other, before whom fighting in defence of Christian folk the Saracen line of battle has so often given way. For it has not been sufficient for the parties concerned to decide their differences by legal process, but laying down the law each for themselves in their own cause, inflicting violence one upon the other, repelling force by force, not only not observing the moderation with which they might blamelessly protect their rights, but even rushing into revengeful excesses, they have fought together fiercely, and those who have been accustomed to assemble in one force to fight side by side against the enemies of the Christian faith, turning their backs upon the enemy, not only in words, but in deeds and in writings, have attacked each other furiously.

But when on the business of this dispute there came into our presence our beloved sons Digisio, Prior of Barletta, and Ogier, Commander of Italy,[1] your brethren, and on the other side Peter de Villeplane and Theodoric, brethren of the knighthood of the Temple, and presented to us a decision made between the parties,[2] by certain pilgrims together with the bishops of the land beyond the sea, although of right the matter belongs wholly to us, we have preferred nevertheless to intervene on the side of peace, and to settle this cause by friendly agreement rather than to end it by a legal judgement. Therefore calling together their brethren as well as yours, and discussing together this agreement, at their wish and in the presence and with the consent of Séguin the Knight, we have ordered the said properties with the fruits thereof, on the advice of our brethren, to be restored to the brethren of the knighthood of the Temple: on this condition however that, after they have taken peaceful possession thereof, they shall be bound on your summons to make answer

[1] He was Grand Commander d'Outremer, and therefore of Italy. For his career, see p. 171, note 3.

[2] Presumably terms of armistice pending a reference of the matter to Rome.

in your court to this same knight, who claims that these properties belong by right to him or to his sons, and that you on your side shall call together from the Principality of Antioch and the County of Tripolis men fitted to give judgement, who shall be men of whom the brethren of the knighthood of the Temple can have no reasonable suspicions. But if perchance they should have reason to regard any of them with suspicion, they shall have the right to object without arousing ill-feeling, so that the decision given may be above suspicion, more especially since we have charged them, as they would deserve our favour, to object to no one without good reason. But if they should fail to answer to your summons, as we have said, then you shall place the said knight or his sons in possession, reserving to them (i.e. the Templars) the right to take proceedings.

The men you call together as here laid down shall declare upon oath that, laying aside all hatred, favour or fear, they will hear the case without distinction of persons, and will give judgement in accordance with the accepted customs of the country. But if perchance they are unwilling to do this, we have given instructions to our venerable brethren the Patriarch of Antioch, the Archbishop of Nazareth and the Bishop of Valénie, to compel them to take this oath, by the censures of the Church without right of appeal, and we have forbidden the parties to the case to appeal against the court before sentence is given. But if after sentence either of the parties desires to appeal, and the appeal has been lodged and proceedings begun, we commit the hearing thereof to those of that province,[1] without further appeal, so that the said case may be decided in the best manner by those of the neighbourhood, who are best qualified to judge the merits of the case, and they guided by local custom, shall determine the said case as justice shall require. And with the help of the Lord we shall see that their sentence is carried out in its entirety.

And that which we have now commanded in the interests of peace, we do not intend to be to the prejudice of either of the parties. But let all other questions that you have or may have in dispute between you, be settled in accordance with the agreement made between you and them in times past,[2] and confirmed by Pope Alexander our predecessor, of blessed memory, and subsequently confirmed by us, to be determined harmoniously or by legal decision. And therefore by these apostolic letters we commit this matter to your discretion, and strictly enjoin, as you would obtain our favour and under pain of excommunication, in the Name of the Holy Spirit, and invoking the judgement of God, that you carry out these proceedings and any others that may be necessary with mutual respect and consideration, not striving one against another with violence and wrong, but reasonably submitting to judgement the case for each side. And be well assured that if either party shall dare to contravene this very plain injunction, upon that party we shall without fail lay our hands most heavily. Given at the Lateran on the sixth day before the Ides of February (i.e. the 8th), in the first year of our Pontificate.

[1] Presumably the appeal is to be to the ecclesiastical court of the province, that is the court of the Patriarch of Antioch.

[2] This refers to the agreement for permanent arbitration of all questions, made between Roger des Moulins and Odo de St. Amand in 1179, see pp. 121–3.

CHAPTER XI

GARIN DE MONTAIGU AND THE FIFTH CRUSADE

THE successor of Alfonso of Portugal was Geoffrey Le Rat, Castellan of Le Crac, probably a Frenchman from Touraine, where a very ancient family of that name is known to have existed.[1] He had long been one of the Bailiffs of Syria, having been Commander of Antioch for many years, and was appointed Castellan of Le Crac in 1202.[2] He ruled over the Hospital for a very short time, and died in the summer of 1207. According to the official chronicle he was in person strong and vigorous, and a vigilant protector of the possessions of the Religion.[3]

Whilst the opposition to the reforming policy of Alfonso of Portugal had been strong enough to force his resignation, it was not strong enough on the death of Geoffrey Le Rat to prevent the election of a successor, who had been one of his staunchest admirers and supporters. The new Master of the Hospital was Garin de Montaigu, Marshal of the Order. He is said to have been a Frenchman from Auvergne, belonging to the family of Montaigu-sur-Champeix, and no fewer than three of his brothers rose to positions of high distinction in the East. Peter de Montaigu was afterwards Master of the Temple, Eustorge was Archbishop of Nicosia, and Fulk Bishop of Limasol in Cyprus.[4] Garin de Montaigu had risen to the rank of Bailiff at the most only three years before his election to be Master and he must have been a man of unusual personality to have been promoted over the heads of so many of his seniors. The official chronicle tells us that he was a very upright man, and that he had been deeply distressed by the resignation of Alfonso of Portugal for whom he had a great affection on account of

[1] The family was still connected with the Order a century later, a certain Thomas Le Rat was Lieutenant to the Prior of France in 1280, and Simon Le Rat was Commander of Cyprus in 1303, and three times Marshal of the Hospital.

[2] We know him to have been Castellan in 1204, but his predecessor, Peter de Mirmande, was appointed Grand Commander in 1202, so presumably he succeeded to the post in that year.

[3] 'The chronicle of the deceased Masters' confuses the personalities of Geoffrey Le Rat and his successor, but the necessary correction is obvious. See Appendix B at the end.

[4] See *Les Hospitaliers en Terre Sainte*, p. 137, note 3.

his honourable character. It would seem probable that he was one of those younger men, whom a strong Master like Alfonso would naturally have selected for accelerated promotion, and this would no doubt account for the unusual length of his reign. But after the troubled period through which it had recently passed, the Order must have had need of a young and vigorous chief. We may safely assume that Garin de Montaigu continued to follow and develop the policy of reform initiated by the predecessor whom he so greatly admired, and that during his long reign those reforms were brought to their final completion.

A year after the election of the new Master the situation in northern Syria underwent a complete change. A triple alliance was formed against the King of Armenia by the Count of Tripolis, Ez-Zahir of Aleppo and the Turkish Sultan of Roum. Then the people of Antioch rose in revolt against their young prince and his Armenian supporters, the Count of Tripolis descended from the citadel, which he had never ceased to hold, and together they drove the troops of Leo the Great out of the city. The combination was too strong for the King of Armenia, and before the year was out he was forced to make peace. The treaty was to last for eight years, and he had to relinquish the claims of his young kinsman, and to surrender Gaston (Bagras) to the Templars.[1] Bohemond IV was now Prince of Antioch as well as Count of Tripolis, and he took an ample revenge upon those who had opposed him. The unfortunate Patriarch was deposed, thrown into prison and cruelly tortured, a Greek being nominated to fill his place, and the Hospitallers found in the new prince one of the bitterest enemies that they had ever possessed.

Meanwhile in the Kingdom of Jerusalem the old question had once more arisen, who was to marry its young queen, and reign over the land. Fate dealt very harshly with this unhappy kingdom, for over and over again its kings left no sons, but only young heiresses, when above all things it required strong and vigorous monarchs. Mary of Montferrat was now 15 years of age, and in 1208 the regent John d'Ibelin sent the Bishop of Acre and Aymar de Layron, Lord of Caesarea, on a mission to the French court to ask King Philip Augustus to select a suitable husband for their young queen. The king selected Count John de Brienne, one of the most renowned warriors of his day, and still full of vigour and energy in spite of his 60 years. The betrothal took place at once, and John de Brienne promised to raise an army that should restore to the Kingdom of Jerusalem its ancient boundaries. But next year an infinitely more attractive crusade presented itself against the heretic Albigenses of Languedoc, and the gallant chivalry of France preferred to seek the favour of Heaven by murdering and plundering their unhappy fellow-countrymen, who

[1] See Stevenson, *The Crusaders in the East*, p. 299, note 1.

OBVERSE

REVERSE

THE GREAT SEAL OF FR. GARIN DE MONTAIGU

Museum of the Order of St. John at Clerkenwell

dared to differ from them in doctrine, a pleasant pursuit in which great riches might be gained, rather than to make the arduous and unprofitable journey to the Holy Land. It was no longer possible for John de Brienne to raise a French army for a campaign in the East, and when he landed at Acre in September 1210, he had only 300 knights with him. His marriage to the young queen followed immediately, and then proceeding to Tyre, the usual place of coronation after the loss of Jerusalem, the sovereigns were solemnly crowned by the Patriarch. Again no son was born of this union, but only a daughter Isabel, sometimes known as Yolande, destined to be the indirect cause of much trouble and strife in the Holy Land, and two years after her marriage to her elderly and somewhat brutal husband, the Queen died, only 19 years of age.

Shortly before the arrival of King John at Acre the treaty with Saphadin expired, and so anxious was the Sultan to renew it that he offered to surrender ten castles. The Master of the Hospital supported by Herman von Salza, Master of the Teutonic Knights, urged strongly that the Sultan's offer should be accepted. But the civil war in Antioch had left the relations between the Hospitallers and the Templars very strained, and it was sufficient for the former to support a certain policy, for the latter to oppose it. Philip du Plessis, Master of the Temple, warmly advocated the renewal of war, and his view prevailed. But the new king arrived with a far smaller force than had ever been expected, and he was in no position to undertake a serious campaign. His raiding-parties from Acre were easily checked by Saphadin, who established a garrison for that purpose on Mount Tabor, under his second son El-Muazzam generally known to the Latins as Corradin.[1] In 1211 King John sent his cousin Walter de Montbéliard the Constable with 1,100 men on a rather futile raid against Damietta,[2] and the year after a fresh treaty was signed for five years.

It must never be forgotten that the Hospitallers and Templars were not only the chief bulwark of the Latin Kingdom of Jerusalem, but were also playing no unimportant part in the constant warfare against the Moors, that prevailed in the Spanish Peninsula. For this reason they were never able to draw much upon their resources in Spain for the use of the Holy Land. All through the twelfth century the Christians were steadily driving back the Moors, but in Morocco a new dynasty the Almohades had arisen, filled with the old religious zeal, and in 1195 their Sultan Yakub I came to the help of his countrymen in Spain. At a great battle at Alarcon on the River Jucar he inflicted a crushing defeat upon King Alfonso VIII of Castile, which gained for him the title of El-Mansour 'the victorious'. But the Moors made

[1] The prince's full name was El-Muazzam Sharaf-ed-din Isa, and Corradin was a corruption of his second name.

[2] See Stevenson, *The Crusaders in the East*, p. 298, note 1.

no permanent advance, and the Christians began once more steadily to push forward their frontiers year by year. At last in 1212 it became necessary for the Moors of Africa again to come to the help of their co-religionists, and the Sultan Mohammed III En-Nasir, the successor of El-Mansour, invaded Spain at the head of an immense army. The King of Castile had spent the intervening years in consolidating his position, and preparing to meet the new danger from Africa. As soon as a fresh invasion became imminent a crusade was organized against the Moors, and when the critical moment arrived, King Alfonso VIII found himself at the head of the united armies of the five kingdoms of Spain, reinforced by a body of Crusaders from the south of France. To this army the Hospitallers sent a powerful contingent, under the command of Walter d'Ermegild,[1] Prior of Castile, and covered themselves with glory in the campaign that followed. In the decisive battle of La Navas de Tolosa, just south of the Sierra Morena, the Moors suffered an overwhelming disaster, from which they never recovered, and which laid all Moslem Spain at the feet of the Christians. According to the exaggerated accounts of the day, no less than 200,000 infidels perished by the sword in this glorious victory. Within little more than a generation, almost the whole of Spain was once more in Christian hands, with the exception of the Kingdom of Granada.

The success of the Count of Tripolis in driving Prince Raymond-Rupen out of Antioch had naturally been a serious blow to the influence of the Hospitallers in that principality. But the generous gifts of the King of Armenia, in gratitude for the support that they had given to his young kinsman, more than compensated for their losses. In 1207 as regent of Antioch he had granted to the Hospitallers the town of Zibel (Jabala), and a little later the Château de la Vieille,[2] an important accession of territory rounding off the northern boundary of their great lordship of Margat. But no sooner had the Count of Tripolis secured control of Antioch than he conferred Zibel upon the Templars, so creating a fresh cause of dissension between the two Orders. The Hospitallers did not secure control of Zibel until 1210 [3] as it had been in Moslem hands ever since the conquests of Saladin, and the dispute with the Templars was not ended until 1221, when the Papal legate ruled that the two Orders must share it between them,[4] but the town seems like Sidon to have been in some way partitioned between the Christians and Moslems for many years.[5]

The gifts of Leo the Great in Armenia were on such a scale that it

[1] See Vertot, *Histoire des Chevaliers de Malthe*, Book III.

[2] See *Cartulaire-Général*, Vol. II, Nos. 1262, 1355. The Château de la Vieille is probably Kalaat-Mehelbeh, in the mountains north-east of Zibel. Rey's *Architecture Militaire des Croisés*, etc., p. 19.

[3] See *Cartulaire-Général*, Vol. II, No. 1358.

[4] Ibid., Vol. II, No. 1739.

[5] See Stevenson, *The Crusaders in the East*, p. 299, note 3.

was necessary to add to the numbers of the Bailiffs of Syria for the purpose of administering the new territory. In 1210 the king granted to the Hospitallers the important town of Selefkeh (Seleucia) in Western Cilicia with Chateauneuf and Camard, and made an agreement to hand over to them the town of Laranda beyond the mountains on the road to Iconium, as soon as it should be taken.[1] At the same time he gave them the right to make peace and war and to retain any booty that they might capture, conditions identical with those made by King Amaury I, when he granted them Belbeis and other Egyptian territory. It is evident that it was the intention of King Leo to make the Hospitallers the wardens of his western marches against the Sultan of Roum, just as they were the wardens of the marches of Tripolis against Hamah and Homs, and the wardens of the southern march of Antioch against the Assassins. For the few years that Selefkeh remained in the possession of the Hospital, its Castellan was amongst the most important of the Bailiffs of Syria ranking with the Castellans of Le Crac and Margat.

In this same year King Hugh I of Cyprus also granted territories to the Hospitallers of such extent that the Commander of Cyprus ranked as one of the chief of the Bailiffs of Syria. The most important of these grants was Colossi, south-east of Limassol, which became the residence of the Commander, and here the Hospitallers erected one of the strongest castles in Cyprus, of which the keep is still to be seen.[2]

The treaty between the King of Armenia and the Count of Tripolis, which was to have lasted for eight years, was speedily broken and soon the wretched civil war over the throne of Antioch was in full swing again. It was a war of little raids and counter-raids, of plunderings and burnings, which reduced the principality to misery and ruin, and left the Latins of northern Syria in such a state of weakness and poverty, as to render recovery impossible. At last early in 1216 owing to the treachery of Acharias the Seneschal of Antioch, who betrayed the city to the King of Armenia, Prince Raymond-Rupen was restored once more to his rightful throne. Almost his first act was to confirm the Genoese and Pisan merchants, the most important Latin element in the state, in the possession of all their ancient privileges. But the prince, now 21 years of age, was violent and headstrong, and had seemingly no feelings of gratitude towards the great-uncle, who had adopted him as heir to the Kingdom of Armenia, and to whose untiring efforts his present position was entirely due. There was a violent

[1] See *Cartulaire-Général*, Vol. II, Nos. 1344, 1349, 1350, 1351. Delaville Le Roulx identifies Camard with Demir-Capou on the borders of Syria and Cilicia, but this can scarcely be the case, since it forms part of the lordship of Selefkeh.

[2] It is not uninteresting to note that a part of the Castle of Colossi has recently passed into the possession of the British Order of St. John. See Report of the Chapter-General, year ending 31 December 1913, pp. 8, 9.

quarrel between the two, and Leo the Great left Antioch for ever. He never forgave the ingratitude of his nephew, and at his death the crown of Armenia passed to his daughter Isabel. Probably his folly would have cost Prince Raymond-Rupen his throne again sooner than it actually did, had not the attention of his rival the Count of Tripolis been drawn for a time elsewhere by the preparations for the Fifth Crusade.

Pope Innocent III had been deeply moved by the reports of King John on the deplorable weakness of the Kingdom of Jerusalem, but little could be done until the rival crusades against the Albigenses of Languedoc and the Moors of Spain had drawn to a close. That Europe in spite of so many disappointments, could still however be roused to enthusiasm for the Holy War in the East, was once more revealed by that curious outburst of religious revivalism known as the Children's Crusade. In 1212 in certain districts of France and Germany the children began to see visions and dream dreams, that they by their purity and innocence might accomplish what sinful soldiers had failed to do, and rescue the Holy Sepulchre from the infidels. Troops of children, many not more than twelve years of age, in spite of the protests of parents and friends, began to wander south towards the sea-ports singing the refrain, 'Lord Jesus, restore to us your Holy Cross', and living on charity. To those who asked what they were doing, they simply replied, 'We are going to Jerusalem, to deliver the sepulchre of Our Saviour.' It is said that in all as many as 50,000 children were affected by this religious frenzy.[1] Many of them lost their way or died of hunger, but helped and encouraged by those good people, who saw in their actions the inspiration of Heaven, and by unscrupulous rogues, who used them for their profit, great numbers succeeded in reaching the sea-ports. Of the German children 7,000 led by a child called Nicholas of Cologne actually crossed the Alps, and reached Genoa, only to be sent home again, and when asked why they had done it, they could only say that they did not know. The French children were less fortunate; a great horde of them, conducted by a shepherd boy named Stephen, came to Marseilles, firmly convinced that the Almighty would dry up the Mediterranean in order to give them a road to Jerusalem. Here two rascally merchants, Hugh Ferrers and William Porous, offered to transport them to the Holy Land, for the love of God free of all charge. They were so numerous that they filled seven ships, two of them sank in a gale with all on board, the remaining five took their young passengers not to the Holy Land, but to Egypt, where the two merchants sold them all into slavery at a very handsome profit. It is good to know that Hugh Ferrers and William Porous ultimately met the fate that they so richly deserved, for being con-

[1] The legend of the Pied Piper of Hamelin, who enticed the children away, probably has its origin in the Children's Crusade.

cerned some years later in a plot to murder the Emperor Frederick, they both perished miserably on the gallows, after first being cruelly tortured. The pitiful story of the Children's Crusade at least helped to awaken the conscience of Europe, and to prepare the ground for the Fifth Crusade, in the words of the Pope, 'The very children put us to shame, while we sleep, they go forth gladly to conquer the Holy Land'.

In the year 1215 at the command of the Pope, the representatives of all Europe gathered at Rome in the Fourth Lateran Council to deliberate on the state of Christendom. At this council the crusades against the Albigenses and the Moors of Spain were declared to be at an end, and a new crusade to the Holy Land was proclaimed, to begin two years later. Meanwhile all warfare between Christian princes was forbidden and the Truce of God decreed for the next four years, and all commerce with the Saracens was to cease forthwith. It was resolved that the first objective of the crusade should be Egypt, as had been intended in the case of the Fourth Crusade. Then the preachers went forth to summon Europe to arm herself once more for the Holy War, chief among them being Cardinal Robert Curzon the Englishman, and James de Vitry, soon to be Bishop of Acre. In the fervour of his enthusiasm Pope Innocent III had declared that he himself would lead the crusade in person, but he died in 1216. The young Emperor Frederick II took the cross, though it was to be many years before he fulfilled his vows, and so did King Andrew II of Hungary, and most of the great princes of Germany, but the King of England was a young child, and the King of France too busily occupied with more mundane affairs.

The armies of the Fifth Crusade began to assemble at Acre in the autumn of 1217, and in July Garin de Montaigu went to Cyprus,[1] on the instructions of the Pope, to be ready to meet the King of Hungary on his arrival in Eastern waters. By the end of October the contingents from Austria, Bavaria and Hungary had arrived, and the united army is said to have been even larger than that which was besieging Acre in 1192.[2] No fewer than four kings were present, Andrew of Hungary, John of Jerusalem, Hugh of Cyprus and Leo of Armenia, as well as the Dukes of Austria and Bavaria and the Count of Tripolis. But so many kings and magnates were a source of weakness rather than of strength, for there was no united command, and no one was prepared to subordinate himself to another, and as usual the Crusaders from beyond the seas made no effort to conceal their contempt for the barons and knights of Syria.

Winter was now near at hand, the contingents from Northern Europe had not yet arrived, having stopped to assist the Portuguese against the Moors, and the projected campaign in Egypt could not

[1] See *Cartulaire-Général*, Vol. II, No. 1580.

[2] See *Les Hospitaliers en Terre Sainte*, p. 142.

begin until the spring. A council of war was held in Acre, and it was decided to pass the time by a great raid through the enemy's country. Riding through the fertile plain of Megiddo past the Moslem garrison on Mount Tabor the Crusaders reached the Jordan at Beisan, and then turned northwards to the Sea of Galilee. Crossing the river at Sennabra, they took the road to Damascus through Khisfin and Nawa, burning and plundering the countryside. The Saracens under Saphadin's son Corradin, the ruler of Damascus, kept them under close observation but declined to risk a battle. Then the Crusaders turned north to Bélinas, where they spent three days, and so back to Acre gorged with plunder, after a highly successful raid that lasted just a fortnight.

Encouraged by this success a part of the army under the King of Jerusalem resolved upon an advance against Mount Tabor, which covered the main road inland from Acre, but the King of Hungary took no part in it. The siege began on 29 November [1] and the Crusaders gradually forced their way up the steep hill-side to the fortress on its summit. But the rumour spread through the army that a great Saracen host was about to cut them off, and suddenly on 7 December without any reason whatever the Crusaders abandoned the siege, and retired precipitately upon Acre. To retrieve this discreditable affair, a raid was organized a few days later into the hill country near Sidon. Five hundred horse rode north, and after plundering the unfortunate inhabitants of ruined Sidon, moved towards Belfort. But the troops suffered terribly from the intense cold, and on Christmas Eve a violent storm of rain and hail, which proved fatal to many of their horses, completed their discomfiture, and forced them to return to their base.

And now the army of the Fifth Crusade, so powerful in outward appearance, without having fought a single battle, or having embarked upon any serious military operation, began to show signs of disintegrating. There were too many kings and princes, all far too inclined to stand upon their dignity, and they were demoralized by the inclemency of the winter, and the weariness of enforced idleness. The most important of them all, King Andrew of Hungary, who had received disquieting news from his native land, openly announced his intention of returning home, and not even the Patriarch's threat of excommunication could shake his resolution, but he agreed to leave half his troops behind him. Soon after Christmas the Kings of Hungary and Cyprus with the Count of Tripolis left Acre for Tripolis, and the King of Armenia departed to his native land. At Tripolis the marriage was celebrated between Count Bohemond the One-eyed, now a widower, and the young Princess Melisende of Jerusalem, half-sister of King Hugh of Cyprus. But the wedding festivities were sadly

[1] For the date of this siege, see Stevenson, *The Crusaders in the East*, p. 302, note 2.

marred by the sudden illness and death of King Hugh, and a few days later the King of Hungary left for Europe by the overland route.

King Andrew II of Hungary has always been remembered with gratitude by the Hospitallers as one of their most generous benefactors. He seems to have been much attracted by the personality of their Master Garin de Montaigu, from the moment that he first met him in Cyprus. During his residence at Acre he stayed, not in the royal palace as we should expect, but in the Convent of the Hospitallers, where he was deeply impressed by his surroundings. There he was able to see for himself their works of charity, and in the great raid across the Jordan in which he took part, he observed with admiration their gallantry in the field. At his own request he was affiliated to the Order of St. John as a Confrater, sharing in all its spiritual privileges, and after his return from the raid he conferred upon the Hospitallers the customs duties of the port of Bobeth at Soprony (Odenburg), together with land between the Drave and the Csurgo, and wide privileges throughout his realm.[1] Then directly afterwards he granted to them the sum of 500 marks of silver [2] a year, secured upon the royal salt-works at Szalacs.[3] In the first of these grants he gives expression to his admiration for the Hospitallers in well-known terms, so elegantly paraphrased by the Abbé Vertot.

> 'Lodging in their house, we have seen them feed every day an innumerable multitude of poor, the sick laid in good beds and treated with great care, the dying assisted with an exemplary piety, and the dead buried with proper decency. In a word the knights of the house of the Hospital are employed sometimes like Mary in contemplation, and sometimes like Martha in action, and this noble knighthood consecrates its days either in the hospitals, or else in battle against the infidel Amalekites and the enemies of the Cross.'

From the marriage-feast of Tripolis, King Andrew departed on 12 January on a visit to the two famous Hospitaller castles of Le Crac and Margat. At the former he was received by Raymond de Pignans its castellan, and so delighted was he with his reception and all that he saw, that he granted to the Order of St. John a further 100 marks of silver a year, also secured on the salt-works of Szalacs,[4] and to be devoted to the defences of the fortress. From Le Crac he proceeded to Margat, where he was equally impressed, and granted yet another 100 marks of silver secured in the same manner, to be used for its maintenance.[5] The king left Margat on 18 January for Tarsus, where the Armenians generously bestowed upon him gifts, that seemed to him beyond all value, the head of St. Peter, the right arm of St. Thomas

[1] See *Cartulaire-Général,* Vol. II, No. 1590.

[2] The mark of silver, weighing eight ounces, was the equivalent of 25 white besants of Cyprus, or a little more than 7 besants of the ordinary type circulating in the East. Schlumberger, *Numismatique de l'Orient Latin.*

[3] See *Cartulaire-Général,* Vol. II, No. 1591. [4] Ibid., No. 1602.

[5] Ibid, No. 1603.

the Apostle, and most precious of all one of the seven water jars from Cana of Galilee, which had held the water which Our Saviour miraculously turned into wine. We know not at which to marvel most, at the childlike faith of the pious king, or at the cool assumption of the Armenians that their remarkable statements would be believed by their distinguished visitor.

After the departure of the three kings, there appears to have been a marked improvement in the morale of the crusading army. To prevent the troops from becoming demoralized by idleness, they were kept employed on military works during the remainder of the winter. Half the army under King John, the Duke of Austria and Garin de Montaigu of the Hospital reconstructed the citadel of Caesarea, while the other half under William de Chartres the new Master of the Temple, Herman von Salza of the Teutonic Knights and the Flemish knight Andrew d'Avesnes built a new castle at Le Detroit (Athlit) covering the road across Mount Carmel from Haifa to Caesarea. At this point the road was particularly liable to Moslem attack, and as the connecting link between the northern and southern halves of the kingdom of Jerusalem, the fortress almost at once became the most important in the Holy Land. Known as Château Pelerin [1] it was held by the Templars, until the final collapse of the kingdom in 1291.

With the return of spring, heavy reinforcements arrived from Europe, including the North Germans under the Count of Holland, who had been fighting the Moors in Portugal. The army was at last strong enough to undertake the conquest of Egypt, on the success of which the future of the Holy Land would depend. Unfortunately the plan of campaign was that adopted by King Amaury I in 1169, in spite of the fact that it had completely failed. In any attack upon Egypt, Cairo, the very heart of the country, is necessarily the ultimate objective. King Amaury I, based upon Ascalon, had repeatedly shown how easily it could be reached by land. But the Crusaders now had no suitable base in southern Palestine, and to feed their army they would be dependent upon river transport. They therefore decided to occupy Damietta as their base, no doubt because it was the nearest sea-port to the Holy Land, and because the Damietta branch of the Nile was the most suitable as a line of communications. But they either underrated, or regarded as unavoidable, the series of formidable obstacles constituted by the network of rivers and canals, over which they would have to pass.[2]

The army embarked at Acre, and on 29 May 1218 reached Damietta,

[1] This Château Pelerin must not be confused with the Château Pelerin built by Raymond of St. Gilles, Count of Toulouse, outside Tripolis, when blockading that city.

[2] A detailed study of the conditions governing a campaign in Egypt are given in Oman's *History of the Art of War in the Middle Ages*, Vol. I, pp. 265–9.

disembarking and pitching its camps on the west bank of the Nile, on the opposite side to the city. There are no reliable figures as to its strength, but it probably numbered between 20,000 and 30,000 fighting men. King John of Jerusalem was in command, and the most important of the contingents from the Latin East were as usual those

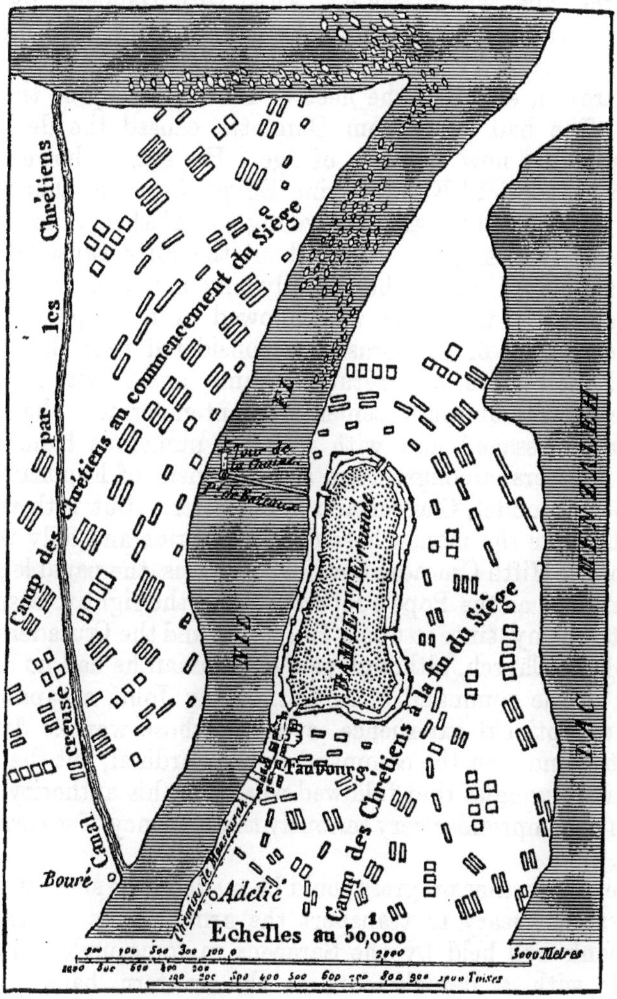

PLAN OF THE SIEGE OF DAMIETTA

furnished by the three military Orders of the Hospital, the Temple and the Teutonic Knights. We have no means of knowing exactly how many men the Hospitallers supplied for a campaign of this importance, but when we remember the large garrisons that they had to maintain in Syria, it is not probable that they could have furnished much more than 500 knights and 500 Turcopoles, as in the days of Gilbert d'Assailly. The contingent was commanded by the Master Garin de Montaigu, who had as his second-in-command Aymar de Layron, Marshal of the Order, and he appointed as his Lieutenant in Syria the Grand Commander Isembard.

The Crusaders began the siege by attacking the great tower on an island in the Nile, which was connected with Damietta by a bridge and a boom, completely blocking the river. After three months the tower was stormed by the Duke of Austria on 25 August, and the boom destroyed, enabling the fleet to come close up to the walls of the city. The bad news from Damietta caused the death of the Sultan Saphadin, now 75 years of age. His empire however passed quietly to his sons, El-Kamil taking Egypt, Corradin Damascus, and El-Ashraf Mesopotamia, whilst a young son of their cousin Ez-Zahir was reigning over Aleppo. Throughout the Fifth Crusade the three brothers supported each other loyally and acted in co-operation.

The capture of the tower was followed by a complete lull in the operations. Many of the Crusaders considered that they had now performed their vows, and returned home, and it was necessary to await the arrival of reinforcements. September was the month of the autumn passage,[1] and with it came numerous bands of fresh Christian warriors, amongst them a detachment of Englishmen under the Earls of Arundel, Chester and Winchester. But with these reinforcements came the man, whose obstinate pride and folly were to be the ruin of the Fifth Crusade, Cardinal Pelagius, the papal legate. He claimed at once as the Pope's representative the right to assume command of the army, since it was a Holy War and the Crusaders were the soldiers of the Church, although as a churchman he had no experience whatever in the command of armies. King John, a capable soldier of quite exceptional experience, even for those warlike days, flatly declined to hand over the command to the Cardinal, but the continual disputes and wrangles that followed weakened his authority to such a degree, as to compromise very seriously the efficiency of so cosmopolitan an army.

Before any further progress could be made in the siege of Damietta, it was first necessary to transport the army across the river. The eastern bank was held by the Saracens in force under their Sultan El-Kamil, with a detachment on the western bank, constantly harassing the Crusaders. It was in an engagement with this detachment that Aymar de Layron, Marshal of the Hospital, so greatly distinguished himself on 9 October 1218.[2] Attempt after attempt was made to get the army across the river, and a passage was only effected

[1] It was the custom for the pilgrims to the Holy Land to embark either in March or September, whether going out or returning home, and these were commonly known as the Spring or Autumn Passages.

[2] See *Les Hospitaliers en Terre Sainte*, p. 144.

in the end owing to the misconduct of the enemy. A Kurdish emir Imad-ed-din, son of Ali El-Meshtoub the gallant defender of Acre in the Third Crusade, formed a plot to depose the Sultan. El-Kamil, having discovered the plot and uncertain as to its extent, suddenly withdrew from the army at midnight. Next morning Imad-ed-din endeavoured to draw the leaderless army into revolt, and in the confusion that followed it was seized with panic, abandoned its camps, and retreated in disorder along the road to Cairo. The Crusaders at once took advantage of the situation, crossed the Nile on 8 February 1219,[1] and seized the Saracen camps with an enormous booty. The sudden retreat of the enemy they attributed to the personal intervention of the Almighty by a direct miracle from heaven. King John of Jerusalem was now able to draw his lines closely round the beleaguered city, the garrison of which had been unaffected by the panic that had seized the field army.

Shortly afterwards the Sultan El-Kamil, reinforced by the army of Syria under his brother Corradin of Damascus, once more advanced towards Damietta, in the hope of saving the city. Before leaving for Egypt, Corradin following the policy of his uncle Saladin, destroyed every fortress in the Holy Land, so that if the Christians should be tempted to advance from their coast towns into the interior, they would be incapable of holding the country. Mount Tabor had been dismantled by the orders of Saphadin, just before his death, and Toron and Bélinas in the autumn of 1218. During the winter Safed and Belfort (Shakif Arnon) were destroyed, and in March Corradin ordered the destruction of the walls of Jerusalem.[2] The interior of the Holy Land, once so prosperous under its Latin kings, was now nothing but a desolate waste, almost depopulated with only a few miserable villages, and never likely again to attract European colonization as in the days of the First Crusade.

All through the summer of 1219 King John pressed ever closer and closer the siege of the now doomed city, and never for one moment relaxed his blockade, in spite of all the efforts of the two Sultans. On 29 August, the day of the execution of St. John Baptist, an unsuccessful attack was delivered upon the Moslem camps at Fareskour, in which the military Orders lost heavily, thirty-three Templars being killed or taken prisoners, and among them Aymar de Layron the gallant Marshal of the Hospital, who was no doubt slain as he was never heard of again.[3] With the autumn passage there arrived in the crusading camp that most Christ-like of all the saints of the Church, Francis of Assisi, and he had come in the hopes of converting the two Sultans to the true faith. Deliberately allowing himself to be taken prisoner, he was brought before El-Kamil, and boldly preached

[1] See Stevenson, *The Crusaders in the East*, p. 304, note 1.

[2] Ibid., p. 305, note 1.

[3] See *Les Hospitaliers en Terre Sainte*, p. 144.

to him the way of salvation. The indignant mollahs begged the Sultan to order to instant execution the blasphemous unbeliever, but the Sultan listened patiently to the earnest discourse of the gentle saint, and then sent him back to his own people. After a visit to the Holy Land, St. Francis returned to Italy and died there six years later.

Meanwhile famine and plague had now descended upon unhappy Damietta, and were rapidly destroying garrison and civil population alike. The besiegers too suffered much from disease, and William de Chartres, Master of the Temple, died of the prevailing fever. In his place the Templars elected as their Master Peter de Montaigu, a brother of the Master of the Hospital, and so more harmonious relations were ensured between the two great military Orders, at least for a time. The Sultans, anxious if possible to save the city, and uneasy at the sensational news of the advance of Jenghiz Khan and his Mongols against the Chorasmian Empire, offered the most generous terms to the besiegers. It is said that they were ready to restore the Latin kingdom of Jerusalem to its original boundaries, with the exception only of the castles of Kerak and Montreal (Shaubak), so vital to the communications between Damascus and Egypt. King John and most of the northern Crusaders would gladly have accepted these terms, but Cardinal Pelagius and the Italians successfully urged their rejection, since the fall of Damietta was now imminent and would place them in a still stronger position for negotiating. In this view they were warmly supported by Garin de Montaigu and the Hospitallers.[1] And so the siege went on until on 5 November, the Crusaders carried the city by assault, nearly eighteen months after their landing, to find that out of a population of 70,000 people, only 3,000 were still alive, and they almost too weak from hunger to be able to stand. Damietta was at once handed over to the King of Jerusalem as part of his dominions, but there was great dissatisfaction over the distribution of the rich plunder found there, and in January 1220 the Italians broke out into such furious rioting, that they had to be driven out of the city by the Hospitallers and Templars.[2]

The capture of Damietta almost brought the Fifth Crusade to an end, and at the March passage of 1220 half the army returned home. The remainder after seizing Tannis, the only sea-port of any importance between Damietta and the Holy Land, began to consolidate their position and to settle down to the enjoyment of their new conquests. Meanwhile the Sultans of Egypt and Damascus, with their armies completely demoralized by their failure to relieve Damietta, established a strongly fortified camp at the junction of the Ashmoun Canal with the River Nile, covering Cairo, and apparently decided to undertake no offensive operations until they should be reinforced by the army of their brother El-Ashraf of Mesopotamia. But over all the

[1] See *Les Hospitaliers en Terre Sainte*, p. 145. [2] Ibid.

Moslem world there now hung the dark cloud that had so suddenly arisen in the East, for the Chorasmian Empire had collapsed before one of the greatest and most ruthless conquerors the world has ever known, and the Mongol hordes of Jenghiz Khan were already sacking the great cities of Bokhara and Samarcand.

In the summer of 1220 [1] the Sultans determined upon a demonstration in force against the Christian possessions in Palestine, in the hope of causing the crusaders to withdraw from Egypt, and Corradin returned for a time to Syria. He captured and utterly destroyed Caesarea, the lordship of Walter de Layron, in spite of a vigorous resistance by its Genoese garrison, and twice unsuccessfully attacked Château Pelerin (Athlit), the newly-built fortress of the Templars. These operations had the result of causing King John and the Master of the Temple to return to the Holy Land, leaving Cardinal Pelagius and the Master of the Hospital in charge at Damietta, but otherwise had no effect upon the march of events. Later in the year King John found it necessary to intervene in Armenia instead of returning to Damietta. Leo the Great had died the previous year, leaving his throne to his daughter Isabel, who soon after married Philip of Antioch, son of the Count of Tripolis. But Prince Raymond-Rupen of Antioch laid claim to the throne, since he had previously been adopted as King Leo's heir, and after obtaining help from the Crusaders at Damietta, invaded the country. He was surprised and taken prisoner at Tarsus by Constantine the Constable of Armenia, and died in prison two years later. King John then claimed the regency by virtue of his second marriage with Stephanie, another of King Leo's daughters, but finding the Constable Constantine too firmly seated in power, he returned to Acre, where his young wife died in 1221. Scandal alleged that her death was due to the brutality of her elderly husband, who is said in a moment of anger to have kicked her so violently with his spurred heels that she died of the injuries.

Cardinal Pelagius spent the year 1220 at Damietta, urging upon the Pope and the Emperor and all the princes of Europe, the need for a great combined effort in the spring, if the conquest of Egypt was to be completed. He was loyally supported by the Pope, and in the spring of 1221 fresh contingents from all Europe poured out to the East, chief amongst them the Duke of Bavaria at the head of 400 German barons and knights, but the Emperor whose presence had been expected was again detained in Europe. The Cardinal, who apparently had unlimited confidence in his own ability to command armies, would undoubtedly himself have conducted the new campaign, had not the soldiers led by the Duke of Bavaria flatly declined to obey a churchman, stating that they would serve under no one except the King of Jerusalem. In consequence Cardinal Pelagius had

[1] See Stevenson, *The Crusaders in the East*, p. 305.

to undergo the humiliation of asking his old enemy King John to come and assume the command. The king arrived on 7 July[1] and ten days later the army had completed its concentration at Fareskour in readiness for the march on Cairo, but it was dangerously late in the season for the Nile was rising fast, and the time had nearly arrived for breaking the dykes, and allowing the river to flood the fields.[2]

It is difficult to estimate the strength of the crusading army; contemporaries speak vaguely of 70,000 men, but even if approximately correct that would include a mass of camp followers, and probably even women and children. We know that it contained 1,200 knights, 4,000 bowmen and a large number of mounted troops besides the infantry,[3] and these figures give the impression of a force about the strength of that which fought at Hattin, namely 20,000 men. The march upon Cairo began under distinctly unfavourable auspices, for it had been forced upon King John and the more experienced soldiers against their better judgment, owing to the vehemence of Cardinal Pelagius and his supporters. A week's marching brought the army to the junction of the Ashmoun Canal with the Damietta branch of the Nile on 24 July, but they were unable to force the passage of the canal, and so fortified a camp on the north side facing the Saracen camp. The Sultan El-Kamil, who had been reinforced in February[4] by the army of Mesopotamia under his brother El-Ashraf, still desired peace at almost any reasonable price, for Jenghiz Khan was across the Oxus ravaging Khorassan, and none could foretell what his future movements might be. The Sultan again offered to restore the kingdom of Jerusalem to its ancient boundaries, except Kerak and Montreal, and even to allow the Crusaders to retain Damietta.[5] King John and the soldiers, who well knew the difficulties and dangers of their position, were only too anxious to accept such terms, but Cardinal Pelagius and his supporters in their folly and ignorance insisted upon war, their influence was predominant and the terms were rejected.

For nearly a month the two armies lay watching each other, separated by the Ashmoun Canal, and all the time the Nile was rapidly rising. Then on 18 August the Moslem fleet took the offensive, and of the Christian ships few escaped the blazing torrent of Greek fire that

[1] See Stevenson, *The Crusaders in the East*, p. 306.

[2] The first rise of the Nile caused by the heavy rains in Central Africa becomes perceptible at the beginning of June, and at Cairo by the middle of the month. Owing to the quantity of vegetation brought down, it is known as the Green Nile. A few days later the melting of the Abyssinian snows is felt, and red with fertilizing mud, the river becomes known as the Red Nile. About the middle of July the dykes are broken, and the river is allowed to flood the fields, by the end of September it reaches its greatest height, and then rapidly falls until in December it is once more confined to its original bed.

[3] See Stevenson, *The Crusaders in the East*, p. 306.

[4] Ibid., p. 306, note 2.

[5] See Michaud's *History of the Crusades*, English Edition, Vol. II, p. 257.

was poured upon them. The control of the river had now definitely passed to the enemy, the road to Damietta would soon be closed, the opening of the dykes had flooded all the land, and the position of the Crusaders was no longer tenable, whatever Cardinal Pelagius and the churchmen might think. On the night of 26 August they set fire to their camp, so revealing their intentions to the enemy, and fell back along the road to Damietta. There was fighting all through the following day bringing the retreat to a standstill, and on the 29th King John had no option but to ask for an armistice, preparatory to discussing terms of peace.

The Sultan El-Kamil like his father Saphadin was a statesman, who desired if possible to live at peace with his Christian neighbours, and above all things to avoid provoking fresh crusades. He therefore granted terms of a most magnanimous nature, considering that his enemy was starving and completely at his mercy. The treaty was signed on 30 August, the Crusaders might return to Acre provided that they surrendered Damietta, and he undertook to provide them with rations, all prisoners were to be given up on both sides, and doubtless in the hope of ensuring future peace the Sultan presented to them that most sacred and precious of all relics, the True Cross captured by his uncle Saladin at the Battle of Hattin. The treaty was to last for eight years, unless meanwhile a crowned king should come on crusade to the Holy Land. When the news was known at Damietta on 2 September, there was great indignation, and many declared that they would never surrender, but would resist to the bitter end. However, the disorders that they provoked were firmly suppressed by the Hospitallers and Templars,[1] and on 8 September the city was restored to the Sultan, after having been two years in Christian hands. On the site of the Sultan's fortified camp on the Ashmoun Canal a new town grew up, to which was given the name of Mansourah 'the city of victory', to be rendered still more famous a generation later by an even greater victory. So ended the Fifth Crusade in shame and ruin, when it might have ended so very differently had only common sense prevailed.

Whilst the Hospitallers had been fighting for three years in Egypt, their old enemy Count Bohemond of Tripolis had been consolidating his position in northern Syria, and had at last succeeded in his ambition of uniting the thrones of Tripolis and Antioch. Neither he nor his nephew and rival Prince Raymond-Rupen had taken any part in the invasion of Egypt, and in 1218 the county of Tripolis had suffered severely from a raid by El-Ashraf of Mesopotamia, who was trying to assist his brothers the Sultans of Egypt and Damascus, by making a diversion in Syria.[2] Descending the valley of the Eleutherus, El-

[1] See *Les Hospitaliers en Terre Sainte*, p. 145.
[2] See Stevenson, *The Crusaders in the East*, p. 308, note 1.

Ashraf ravaged all the countryside right up to the walls of Le Crac and the Templar fortress of Chateau Blanc (Safitha). Next year Count Bohemond's chance came, one of the citizens of Antioch, William de Farabel,[1] entered into communication with him, and treacherously opened the gates to his forces. Prince Raymond-Rupen only saved himself by flight, and went to Armenia to beg once more the assistance of his great-uncle King Leo. But the old king was now dying, and had never forgiven his nephew for his base ingratitude three years before. On his great-uncle's death the Prince of Antioch endeavoured to seize the throne of Armenia by force, but failed and died in prison in 1222 as we have seen. From 1219 the thrones of Tripolis and Antioch were definitely and finally united in the person of Prince Bohemond IV, but the long struggle had so ruined the once sturdy Norman principality that it had no powers of recuperation left, and was the first of the existing Latin states to fall into the hands of the infidel.

The new prince at once began to take further revenge upon the Hospitallers, whom he hated for their loyalty to his predecessor. Already the county of Tripolis had been under an interdict since 1212, owing to the violence of his actions against the Order of St. John, but Bohemond IV cared nothing for the spiritual weapons of the church. The papal legate had sequestered the castle of Antioch until the disputes over the throne should be settled, and had entrusted its guardianship to the Hospitallers.[2] It was held by one of their most distinguished knights, Feraud de Barras, one of the Bailiffs of Syria, formerly Castellan of Selefkeh, and soon to be Marshal of the Order. Prince Bohemond now evicted him by force, and then adopted so outrageous an attitude towards the Hospitallers, seizing their lands and property everywhere without the shadow of an excuse, that in 1224 the Pope went so far as to authorize them to draw their swords against the prince, and to resist his continual encroachments by force of arms.[3]

The failure of the Fifth Crusade was followed by an outburst of indignation against the fatal rôle played by Cardinal Pelagius, who was regarded by most as the real author of that disaster. But the Pope refused to listen to any complaints against his legate, and tried to place the entire blame for the failure upon the shoulders of the Emperor, whose repeated promises to assume command of the crusade in person had never been fulfilled. The enemies of the military Orders on the other hand used the opportunity to endeavour to stir up popular feeling against them, by suggesting that they had intercepted for their own use large sums of money intended for the support of the army. The accusations were as ridiculous as they were unjust, since both the Hospitallers and the Templars had as usual exhausted their own resources in financing the campaign. At the request of their

[1] See *Les Hospitaliers en Terre Sainte*, p. 148. [2] Ibid.
[3] See *Cartulaire-Général*, Vol. II, No. 1824.

two Masters the leaders of the crusade wrote to the Pope to impress upon him how devotedly and wholeheartedly the two great Orders had sacrificed both their lives and their property in the holy cause, and the Pope in his turn instructed the bishops to put an end to these abominable and baseless rumours, by making known the true facts in all their nobility, for said he, 'We wish you to hold them in honour and affection, and we order you to make known to all the world the innocence of these fearless defenders of the Christian faith.'[1]

The Emperor Frederick well knew that the unfortunate ending to the crusade was a grave reflection upon the manner in which he had carried out his duties as the temporal head of Christendom. In 1222 he had a meeting with the Pope at Veroli, and as a result it was decided to summon King John, Cardinal Pelagius, the Patriarch of Jerusalem, and the Masters of the Hospital, the Temple and the Teutonic Knights to Italy, for a conference with the Pope and the Emperor, on the state of the Holy Land and the prospects of a fresh crusade.

Accordingly in September 1222 King John with Garin de Montaigu, Master of the Hospital, and their companions embarked at Acre for Cyprus, where they spent Christmas. Before his departure King John, who was destined never to return to the Holy Land, appointed Odo de Montbéliard to be regent, and Garin de Montaigu left the affairs of the Hospital in the hands of the Grand Commander Gouffier. But Peter de Montaigu, Master of the Temple, remained behind in the Holy Land, and sent his Grand Commander William Cadel to represent him. The party landed at Brindisi in January 1223, and proceeded to Rome, and the following month the conference took place at Ferentino. Here the Emperor definitely pledged himself to lead a crusade to the East in 1225, and it was arranged that since he had recently become a widower he should marry King John's daughter the little Princess Isabel, now 11 years of age, and really Queen of Jerusalem in her own right. Before the conference broke up, it was decided that King John and the Master of the Hospital should go on a special mission to the courts of France and England to endeavour to arouse the interest of those nations in the forthcoming crusade.

The mission of King John and Garin de Montaigu was very similar to that of the latter's predecessor Roger des Moulins and the Patriarch Heraclius in 1185, but it could scarcely have taken place under more unfavourable circumstances. On their arrival in France King Philip Augustus lay dying, and they attended his funeral at St. Denis on 16 July, and the coronation of his successor King Louis VIII at Rheims on 6 August. The new king was fully occupied with plans against the heretic Albigenses, and preparations for war with England over Poitou and Aquitaine; it was decidedly not the moment for arousing enthusiasm in France for a new crusade. The King of Jerusalem and the

[1] See Vertot, *Histoire des Chevaliers de Malthe*, Book III.

Master of the Hospital left for England a month later, but there too they found a situation no more favourable to their mission than in France. King Henry III had just been declared of age, the barons were up in arms against his great minister Hubert de Burgh, who was trying to reduce them to order, and civil war seemed unavoidable. Under such conditions it was useless to talk about expeditions for the recovery of the Holy Sepulchre, and in December the King of Jerusalem returned to France.

Garin de Montaigu appears to have spent the winter in England, where he was naturally the guest of Robert de Dive, Prior of England, in the priory of Clerkenwell. The visit gave him the opportunity of investigating the administration of the affairs of the Order of St. John in its two western priories of England and Ireland. In the spring of 1224 he left for France again, and in April landed at Bordeaux, which enabled him to inspect some of the commanderies of his Order in Aquitaine. We next find him at Paris in June, where important business had to be transacted in connexion with the foundation of a new establishment of the Order at Corbeil, by Queen Ingilburgis the widow of King Philip Augustus, in memory of her late husband. The establishment was to consist of thirteen chaplains, whose principal duties would be to celebrate three masses a day for the repose of the soul of the king. So important was the commandery of St. Jean-en-l'Isle de Corbeil, as it is generally known, that the priors of France made it their residence, until they finally transferred their headquarters to the Temple at Paris after the suppression of the Templars.[1] It was the richest and most important commandery in the priory of France, and eventually became the appanage of the Grand Treasurer of the Order.

After his visit to Paris, we next hear of the Master of the Hospital at Orange in August, where William des Baux confirmed certain acts of his predecessor. He spent Christmas with the Emperor Frederick at Palermo, and in the spring of 1225 embarked for the East. In June he was at Tarsus, no doubt having again visited Cyprus on the way, and from Armenia he would presumably go overland through Antioch and Tripolis in order to visit Margat and Le Crac, and we first hear of his arrival at Acre in December 1225.[2] The Master of the Hospital had now been absent from the Holy Land for no less than three years, but this long residence beyond the seas had given him the opportunity of inspecting personally all the priories of England, France and Italy, and few Masters can have had so wide and intimate a knowledge of the affairs of his Order as Garin de Montaigu, when he at last returned to the Convent at Acre.

[1] See Delaville Le Roulx's Introduction to his *Cartulaire-Général*, p. 61.

[2] The probable movements of Garin de Montaigu have to be largely inferred from a few isolated references. See *Les Hospitaliers en Terre Sainte*, pp. 147, 148.

On his visit to Tarsus, Garin de Montaigu had been able to make himself personally acquainted with the troubled state of affairs in Armenia. Queen Isabel's husband, Philip of Antioch, was greatly disliked by the native nobility, who had risen against him and thrown him into prison, and the Constable Constantine was once more all-powerful. The weakness of Armenia since the death of Leo the Great had enabled the Turkish Sultan of Roum to make the country tributary, and the Constable was striving to obtain support against the Turks from the newly risen military power of Jenghiz Khan, a policy which was always rigidly followed by his successors. The wardenship of the western marches of Armenia for which the Castellan of Selefkeh was responsible, had undoubtedly become a heavy charge upon the resources of the Hospitallers, without any compensating advantages. In continuing to undertake this responsibility, they were in danger of dissipating their forces over too wide an area, and the situation was still further complicated by their difficult relations with the Prince of Antioch. From Tarsus it is only reasonable to suppose that the Master of the Hospital proceeded to Selefkeh to discuss the local situation with its Castellan Bertrand de Thessy,[1] and when he returned to Acre he must already have decided upon a policy of withdrawal.

The following year Philip of Antioch died, and Constantine the Constable resolved that Queen Isabel should marry his son Haithon, who would thus become King of Armenia. The Queen however appears to have objected strongly to this arrangement, and fled for refuge to Selefkeh. She was received hospitably enough by Bertrand de Thessy the Castellan, but she can scarcely have been a welcome visitor, for the Hospitallers had no desire to become embroiled in the politics of Armenia, or to incur the hostility of the Constable. Probably the Queen's presence brought the whole question to a head, at any rate in this year 1226 the Hospitallers withdrew from Selefkeh,[2] which was handed back to the Constable, and Queen Isabel married his son Haithon, so making him King of Armenia. The evacuation of Selefkeh was by no means the end of the connexion of the Hospitallers with that country, their possessions were still of sufficient importance to necessitate the presence of a bailiff, and right down to the loss of Malta a titular Bailiff of Armenia was one of the great dignitaries of the Order of St. John.[3]

[1] The Castellan's name is given simply as Bertrand, but since the future Master Bertrand de Thessy must almost certainly have been a Bailiff at this time, and this is the only Bailiff bearing his name, the two would seem to be identical.

[2] See *Les Hospitaliers en Terre Sainte*, p. 141.

[3] In the sixteenth century when the Bailiwicks *in partibus infidelium* had been distributed amongst the different nations or langues composing the Order of St. John, Armenia was allotted to England. See St. Allais, *L'Ordre de Malthe*, p. 162.

The mission to Europe of the King of Jerusalem and the Master of the Hospital had been a failure. The Kings of England and France were too occupied with their own affairs to interest themselves actively in the future of the Latin kingdom, and the situation in Italy in 1225 compelled the Emperor to request the Pope to agree to postpone the crusade for another two years. But in March 1225 the little Princess Isabel Yolande, now 14 years old, was crowned Queen of Jerusalem at Tyre, and sent to Italy to marry the Emperor. The marriage took place at Brindisi in November, and to the intense surprise and indignation of King John, his son-in-law at once deprived him of his throne, the Emperor declaring himself King of Jerusalem by right of marriage. The Bishop of Melfi was sent to Acre to claim the homage of the barons of the Holy Land, and Odo de Montbéliard was re-appointed regent in the name of the new sovereign. King John was really the last effective king of Jerusalem and in spite of his advanced years he had proved a capable and energetic monarch, and had undoubtedly made the best of a difficult position. He was now 77 years of age, and had just married another young wife, the Princess Berengaria of Castile, by whom he had several children. In 1229 this remarkable old man, then in his eighty-second year, was elected Latin Emperor of the East, as regent for the young Emperor Baldwin, and died in 1237.

No graver misfortune could have happened to the kingdom of Jerusalem, than to have the Emperor Frederick as its ruler, in spite of the fact that he was one of the greatest and most versatile men of the age, whom a contemporary goes so far as to describe as the Wonder of the World. The Holy Land thereby ceased to be an independent kingdom, and became merely an outlying province of a vastly more important realm, and a mere pawn in the mighty struggle for supremacy between the Emperor and the Pope, that was soon to begin. The news of the Emperor's succession to the throne was very badly received in the East, where the barons feared that as Emperor he would claim prerogatives far in excess of those to which he was entitled as king. They at once began to combine for the purpose of asserting their constitutional rights, and John d'Ibelin the Queen's great-uncle, now generally spoken of as the Old Lord of Beyrout, and the most powerful of them all, placed himself at their head.

In Egypt the Sultan El-Kamil viewed with considerable apprehension the possibility of a fresh crusade in 1227, and opened negotiations with the Emperor with a view to a final settlement of that troublesome question, the control of the holy places. He appears to have offered similar terms to those previously offered during the Fifth Crusade, namely to restore the kingdom of Jerusalem to its original boundaries on certain conditions. The Emperor sent the Bishop of Palermo on a secret mission to Cairo to explore the situation. Both monarchs were highly enlightened broad-minded men of the world, far in advance of the age in which they lived, and they undoubtedly arrived at some understanding.[1] None the less the crusading army, consisting mainly of Italians and Germans, began to concentrate in Apulia, and in July 1227 the Emperor sent the Count of Acerra to Acre as his lieutenant, to prepare for the arrival of the crusade. Meanwhile the poor young Queen Isabel, only 16 years old, had died in May in giving birth to a son Conrad, and the rightful King of Jerusalem was now an infant in arms. The Emperor sailed from Brindisi in September but was seized the next day by a severe attack of the prevailing fever that had been decimating his army, and was forced to return to Otranto three days later, leaving the bulk of the expedition to continue its voyage to Acre. The new Pope Gregory IX desirous of asserting his authority, chose to regard the Emperor as having wilfully abandoned the crusade, and excommunicated him. A violent quarrel naturally followed, and soon Europe was scandalized by the indecent spectacle of open war between the spiritual and temporal heads of Christendom, just as the latter was about to make a serious effort to recover the Holy City.

When it was known at Acre that the Emperor had postponed his arrival, many of the assembled Crusaders returned home. There remained a force of about 800 knights and 10,000 foot,[2] who would have to be employed in some way during the winter. Half the force was sent to southern Palestine to restore the fortifications of Caesarea, which had been demolished by Corradin in 1220, and afterwards to strengthen Jaffa. The other half was employed in the north in restoring the walls of Sidon, which now passed definitely into Christian possession. Ever since Saladin had destroyed its ramparts in 1190 Sidon had remained an open town, its revenues being equally divided between Christians and Moslems under the terms of the Treaty of Ramleh. Part of the northern force also assisted the Teutonic Knights in building their new castle of Montfort at Kurain, in the mountains between Acre and Tyre. Montfort or Starkenberg, as the Teutonic Knights preferred to call it, was their only castle of any importance in the East, here they placed their treasure and their archives, and the Treasurer of the Order was always its Castellan.[3] But already the Teutonic Knights were beginning to turn their eyes away from the East towards Prussia, where they first established themselves in the following year.

The troops engaged in restoring the fortifications of Sidon were under the direction of Garin de Montaigu and the Hospitallers. Their work began on 11 November 1227, and was finished by 1 March 1228.

[1] See Lane-Poole, *A History of Egypt in the Middle Ages*, p. 226.
[2] See Stevenson, *The Crusaders in the East*, p. 308.
[3] See Rey, *L'Architecture Militaire des Croisés*, etc., pp. 144–51.

Some time during that period the Master of the Hospital died,[1] and he presumably died a natural death at Sidon during the winter. Garin de Montaigu had ruled over the Hospital for twenty-one years, a longer period than any other of its Masters in the Holy Land, except of course the Blessed Raymond du Puy. One definite conclusion we can safely draw concerning his reign, was that he completed the work begun by Alfonso of Portugal in restoring the discipline of the Hospitallers, for we hear no more of open strife with the Templars, in spite of the delicate situation created by the two Orders supporting rival candidates for the throne of Antioch, and during the Fifth Crusade they worked together in entire harmony. The fact that two brothers were ruling over the Hospital and the Temple at the same time was undoubtedly a great advantage to both Orders, as we can see from the official chronicle, which tells us that the Master of the Hospital was able to purchase from his brother Peter de Montaigu the balance of the rights of the Temple over the Hospital for the price of a horse, probably about 160 besants.[2] Apparently the Templars up to this time had retained certain rights to eat at the table of the Hospitallers, the last remains of the original dependence of the Templars upon the Hospital.[3] That Garin de Montaigu was held in high esteem by the Emperor and the ruling princes of Europe is clear from the manner in which he was received everywhere during his long tour beyond the seas. During his reign there was a notable increase in the donations made to the Hospitallers, more especially in France and Germany, and it is very evident that there was no diminution in the prestige of the Order. In Garin de Montaigu we see one of the greatest of the Masters, who ruled over the Hospital in the Holy Land.[4]

[1] See *Les Hospitaliers en Terre Sainte*, p. 158.

[2] The official chronicle places this incident under William de Chateauneuf, an obvious error. The price of a knight's charger at this period was 80 French livres, the equivalent of 160 besants. See Joinville's *Chronicle* (Marzial's translation), p. 262.

[3] See p. 32 of this work, and also *Les Hospitaliers en Terre Sainte*, p. 210, footnote.

[4] For an estimate of the importance of the reign of Garin de Montaigu see *Les Hospitaliers en Terre Sainte*, p. 159.

CHAPTER XII

THE RECOVERY AND FINAL LOSS OF JERUSALEM

IN the summer of 1228 just before the long-expected arrival of the Emperor Frederick, the Hospitallers elected as their Master, Bertrand de Thessy, until recently Castellan of Selefkeh.[1] From his name he evidently is a Frenchman, though we know nothing of his family. If as is probable he succeeded Feraud de Barras as Castellan of Selefkeh in 1216, when the latter was placed in charge of the citadel of Antioch, then he had been one of the Bailiffs of Syria for the past twelve years. The Order had great need of a wise and discreet Master in the delicate situation that was about to arise out of the quarrel between the Emperor and the Pope.

On 28 June the Emperor sailed from Brindisi with 20 ships and 600 knights to join the forces already assembled at Acre, leaving the Duke of Spoleto to carry on the war against the Pope, whose troops were commanded by the ex-King John of Jerusalem, delighted to have the chance of avenging himself upon his imperial son-in-law. A month later the Emperor landed in Cyprus for the purpose of asserting his suzerainty over that kingdom. The Old Lord of Beyrout, regent for the boy King Henry I, who was only 10 years old, stoutly refused to recognize the Emperor's demands, and relations between them became dangerously strained. Both sides however desired to avoid a resort to arms, lest they should ruin the crusade, and at the end of six weeks a compromise was reached.[2] But it was very much in favour of the Emperor who took over the royal castles and nominated a commission of five barons to uphold his rights, and John d'Ibelin after doing homage for his fief of Beyrout sailed with him for Acre, where they landed on 7 September.

Meanwhile the Pope was determined that the Emperor should not lead the crusade, as it would be a scandal to the Church for

[1] Delaville Le Roulx appears to have overlooked the fact that Bertrand de Thessy and Bertrand the Castellan are almost certainly the same person, when he wrote that absolutely nothing was known of him previously. *Les Hospitaliers en Terre Sainte*, p. 161.

[2] The compromise was that the barons of Cyprus should recognize the Emperor as the over-lord of their king, but should do homage not to the Emperor direct, but only to their own immediate sovereign.

an excommunicated person to command in the Holy War, and if he should do so the Pope was equally determined to do everything that lay in his power to make it a failure. He had already forbidden him to go, until he should first be reconciled to the Church, but the Emperor had merely treated him with contempt. On learning that he had actually sailed, he again excommunicated him, and sent two Franciscan Friars to Acre to forbid the military Orders to serve under him. When the Emperor landed he was well enough received by the Masters of the three Orders and the other magnates of the realm. But a few days later the two Franciscans arrived with the papal instructions, and the whole situation changed immediately. Many abandoned the crusade rather than serve under an excommunicated leader. Bertrand de Thessy, Master of the Hospital, informed the Emperor that he must obey the Pope as his superior, and could take no part in a campaign under his orders. Peter de Montaigu of the Temple took the same course, but Herman von Salza of the Teutonic Knights was in a more difficult position. He was not only the head of a religious Order, owing obedience to the Pope, but also a prince of the Empire owing allegiance to the Emperor.[1] The Teutonic Knights were all German subjects, and they finally decided to remain loyal to their sovereign. But with the defection of the Hospitallers and Templars, who now provided the only military contingents of any serious importance in the Holy Land, the crusade must have come to an end, had it depended only on force of arms.

The Emperor however had long realized that it might be possible to settle the thorny question of the custody of the Holy Places by mutual consent, and had already been in communication with the Sultan El-Kamil on the subject. The Sultan on his side had shown clearly during the Fifth Crusade how gladly he would welcome some solution of the problem, which would put an end once for all to the danger and nuisance of these periodical crusades, so destructive to the commerce and prosperity of the East. The Emperor therefore had no intention whatever of embarking upon a campaign for the recovery of Jerusalem, and had in fact only brought a handful of troops with him. His intentions were to settle the question on what we should now call modern lines, by negotiation and compromise and common-sense. As the intentions of the Sultan were the same, within a short time of the Emperor's arrival at Acre, secret missions were passing backwards and forwards between the two sovereigns. But in so doing, both were acting in a manner totally at variance with the spirit of the age, and both were afterwards to be condemned for their conduct by their own subjects in the severest possible terms.

There had recently been a change in the political situation in Syria

[1] The Master of the Teutonic Knights had been raised to the dignity of a Prince of the Empire in 1226.

of some importance. The Sultan El-Kamil's brother Corradin of Damascus had died the previous November, and had been succeeded by his son David. But El-Kamil in his capacity as over-lord had other views, and during the summer occupied Palestine with an army. This at once brought his brother El-Ashraf of Mesopotamia south, nominally to protect his nephew David, and he reached Damascus just about a week before the Emperor disembarked at Acre.[1] All through the autumn therefore the Sultan of Egypt, whose headquarters were at Nablus, was engaged simultaneously in negotiations with the Emperor at Acre and with his brother at Damascus.

The Sultan moved south to Forbiya near Gaza about the beginning of November, and his brother El-Ashraf joined him on the 10th near Ascalon, their nephew David whose suspicions as to his own probable future must by now have been aroused, advancing cautiously to Nablus. Before the end of the month at a meeting at Tell Ajul, between Ascalon and Gaza, the two brothers decided upon the fate of Syria. El-Kamil was to take Palestine and El-Ashraf Damascus, and compensation was to be found elsewhere for their nephew David. But the latter strongly objected to this arrangement, and early in December his uncle El-Ashraf began the siege of Damascus, which did not surrender until 25 June 1229.[2] David was then compensated for its loss by the grant of the districts of El-Gor (i.e. the Jordan valley) including Beisan and Nablus, and El-Belka (i.e. Trans-Jordania south of the Jabbok) including Salt and Kerak, the latter place becoming his chief residence.

With the future of Syria decided, the Sultan of Egypt was in a position to come to definite terms with the Emperor, who now left Acre on 23 November, and marched to Jaffa, a more convenient situation for the detailed negotiations that were about to take place. There were naturally no hostilities, and no doubt this was fortunate because his excommunication rendered his position difficult for the Emperor. He could not even rely upon orders given in his own name being obeyed in his cosmopolitan force, and it was found necessary to issue army orders in the name of God and Christendom.[3] The Hospitallers and Templars would not even submit to this compromise, but followed the Emperor at a distance, in readiness however to intervene should hostilities actually begin. The spiritual head of Christendom in his hatred for its temporal head was certainly doing his utmost to render it impossible for him to recover the Holy City.

The negotiations continued through most of the winter, since many of the details were of a very delicate and complicated nature,

[1] See Stevenson, *The Crusaders in the East*, p. 310, note 3.

[2] For the movements and policy of the Moslem princes see Stevenson, *The Crusaders in the East.*

[3] See Michaud's *History of the Crusades*, English edition, Vol. II, p. 277.

and it was not until 18 February 1229 that the Treaty of Jaffa was at last signed. The Emperor meanwhile employed his troops in strengthening the fortifications of Jaffa, whose Count was Walter de Brienne, a nephew of his father-in-law the ex-King John. The new treaty restored to the Christians their three holy cities of Jerusalem, Bethlehem and Nazareth, the last of which had already been given up by Saphadin in 1210. But in Jerusalem the Moslems were to retain their own sacred area the Haram-esh-Sherif, containing the Dome of the Rock and the Mosque of El-Aksa, and were to have the right of free and uninterrupted pilgrimage. The border towns of Lydda and Ramleh were again restored, and the Christians were to have the villages on each side of the direct road from Jaffa to Jerusalem, and the two villages between Jerusalem and Bethlehem, but all the remaining villages round the Holy City were to remain Moslem. In the north the Sultan abandoned all claims over Sidon and Toron (Tibnin), which had been in ruins since 1218, and ceded the two Moslem villages between Acre and Nazareth. All prisoners were to be given up on both sides, there were certain clauses concerning the right to fortify, and the treaty was to last for ten years, but it did not include Antioch and Tripolis. The Treaty of Jaffa thus provided a sound common-sense solution of the problem that had so long troubled the peace of the East, but it was not a common-sense age and the treaty was bitterly denounced by Christian and Moslem alike, who regarded it as almost blasphemous to relinquish to their opponents one atom of their claims, and to the Christians it was soon known as the Evil Peace.

The Emperor made his state entry into Jerusalem on 17 March, just one month after the signing of the Treaty of Jaffa, and on the following day, a Sunday, his coronation as King of Jerusalem took place in the church of the Holy Sepulchre. It was the first coronation to take place there since that of King Baldwin the Child forty-five years before, and was to be the last. But the Patriarch Gerold of Lausanne had now arrived, and at once placed the city under an interdict, and no bishop or priest could perform the ceremony of coronation. And so the Emperor Frederick surrounded by his magnificent retinue himself took the crown from the high altar, and placed it on his head. Then the Master of the Teutonic Knights at his sovereign's command read out a solemn and dignified protest against the outrageous attitude adopted by the Church. The ceremony was at an end, and the Emperor left the Holy Sepulchre, but the Patriarch's action in placing Jerusalem under an interdict at the very moment that he entered, was too gross an insult to pass unnoticed. That very morning the Emperor had been discussing plans for the fortification of Jerusalem, but his interest in the matter was at an end, he left suddenly the next day without again referring to the subject, or making any arrangements for its defence.[1] He spent six weeks longer in the Holy Land, organizing its future government. But there were turbulent scenes in Acre, especially with the Templars, who the Emperor was convinced had endeavoured to betray him to the Saracens, and he never forgave their Order. He appointed Balian, Lord of Sidon, to be his regent, he was a nephew on his mother's side of the Old Lord of Beyrout, and imperial garrisons were placed in Tyre and Sidon. Then on 1 May the Emperor left Acre for Europe, where he speedily drove the papal armies out of his Italian dominions, and in August 1230 he became for a time duly reconciled to the Pope. But it was not long before the old struggle for supremacy between the temporal and spiritual heads of Christendom again broke out, and from that struggle the barons of the Holy Land were determined to obtain all the advantages possible, regardless of consequences.

The conditions prevailing in Jerusalem during the second Christian occupation were totally different from those prevailing during the first occupation. The city was now unfortified, its walls had been destroyed by Corradin in 1219, and had never been reconstructed. The Sultan it is true had agreed to the Emperor refortifying it, but it was claimed that this condition applied only to the Emperor personally, and he never made use of his right to do so. Under the terms of the Treaty of Jaffa the city was practically partitioned between the two religions, each retaining its own sacred sites, and an imperial governor was stationed in the Tower of David, but there was a Mohammedan governor to rule over his co-religionists. Had the Emperor fortified Jerusalem, as he undoubtedly originally intended, and placed a strong garrison there, things would have been very different, but an unfortified city in the midst of a hostile population, situated on the frontier between two religions, each liable to wild outbursts of fanaticism, could never give any real security for life or property, and could never hope to attract merchants and commerce on any considerable scale. Poverty-stricken and half populated, it was now simply and solely a holy city, the resort of pilgrims of both religions, but nothing more. Under such conditions it was impossible again to make Jerusalem the capital of the Latin kingdom, and the seat of government remained at Acre. It was equally impossible for the Hospitallers and Templars to transfer their Convents back to an unfortified Jerusalem, and in the case of the latter Order their buildings actually remained in Moslem hands, forming a part of the Mosque of El-Aksa. The original convent of the Hospitallers did come back into Christian possession, and their hospice for pilgrims was reopened, but it never again became the headquarters of their Order.

No sooner had the Emperor left for Europe than the kingdoms of Jerusalem and Cyprus were stirred up into open revolt against his

[1] See Stevenson, *The Crusaders in the East*, p. 314, note 6.

14

authority by the Old Lord of Beyrout. The barons of the Latin East seem to have been curiously devoid of the instinct of self-preservation, and to have been quite incapable of realizing that in the long run they could only hope to preserve their fiefs by presenting a united front to the Moslem. When Saphadin had left them in comparative peace, they could find nothing better to do than to complete the ruin of the Principality of Antioch by a long civil war of nearly twenty years. Now that the Emperor had secured peace for them with El-Kamil for the next ten years, they seized the opportunity to plunge once more into civil war by attacking the one man who was capable and willing to protect them. Rather than submit to any form of authority, they were prepared to destroy for ever the last possibility of once more reconstructing and welding together the shattered kingdom of Jerusalem. Seldom has there been a better example of the old proverb that those whom the gods intend to destroy they first drive mad. The long war that followed is usually known as the War of the Lombards, the name given to the Emperor's party, and it lasted for fifteen years, and was quite naturally followed by the most appalling disaster that the Holy Land had known since the Battle of Hattin.

The war started a month after the Emperor's departure, when John d'Ibelin of Beyrout landed in Cyprus, and attacked the imperial officials. They suffered a severe defeat at Nicosia on 23 June, and took refuge in the castle of St. Hilarion, better known as Dieu d'Amour,[1] where they held out until the following May and then surrendered. John d'Ibelin was now once more regent of Cyprus for the boy King Henry, as he had been prior to the Emperor's arrival. Then in the Holy Land Queen Alice of Cyprus, mother of King Henry, was proclaimed regent for the Emperor's son Prince Conrad, as the nearest of kin[2] to the rightful King of Jerusalem. This was a direct challenge to the Emperor's authority there also, and could only lead to further war, but for the moment the Emperor temporized, until he had come to terms with the Pope.

Such was the political situation when the Master of the Hospital died. The short reign of Bertrand de Thessy had been a troubled and anxious period. The Hospitallers and Templars by their refusal to co-operate with the Emperor in the Holy Land, though the cause for doing so lay with the Pope and not with them, had deeply offended him, and on his return to Europe he had sequestered the whole of their

[1] The castle of St. Hilarion in northern Cyprus, originally a Greek monastery, is more generally known as Dieu d'Amour, from the legend that when St. Hilarion first came there, it was haunted by the God of Love, who was driven away by the presence of so holy a man.

[2] Queen Alice of Cyprus was the daughter of Queen Isabel of Jerusalem, by her third husband, Count Henry of Champagne, and aunt to the Emperor's wife Queen Isabel II. In the event of Prince Conrad's death, she or her descendants would succeed to the throne of Jerusalem, as was ultimately the case.

property in his dominions in Italy and Sicily.[1] In Antioch the hostile attitude of Prince Bohemond IV towards the Hospitallers was becoming increasingly violent, the permission of the Pope to protect their property against him by force of arms was not a sufficient check, and at the urgent request of Bertrand de Thessy, Pope Gregory IX decided to use the last weapon of the Church, and on 5 March 1230 he pronounced the dread sentence of excommunication against the prince.[2] The misfortunes of this period culminated in the same year in a grave military reverse, when a punitive expedition sent by the Hospitallers of Le Crac against Hama met with a sanguinary defeat. It was in an atmosphere of gloom and disappointment that Bertrand de Thessy died shortly afterwards, but he may have lived just long enough to hear the good news that the Emperor on making peace with the Pope, had released the lands of his Order from the sequestration under which they lay.[3] His short reign of little more than two years had been full of difficulties and anxieties, quite beyond his control, and in no way reflecting upon his capacity. The official chronicle tells us that before his election to be Master, he was much esteemed for his upright pious and virtuous life, and that his reputation was greatly increased during his term of office. He is said by the same authority to have endowed the Hospital with much property in Syria, and to have taken the deepest interest in its charitable duties.

The Hospitallers elected as their new Master, Guérin, the Prior of France. We know nothing regarding his origin and family, or of his previous career except that he had been Prior of France for a considerable period, possibly as long as ten years.[4] He may have been a relative of a famous French Hospitaller of this period, Guérin afterwards Bishop of Senlis, a trusted minister of the French crown, who had greatly distinguished himself at the Battle of Bouvines in 1214, and died in this very year.[5] But this is nothing but a conjecture based upon the identity of name, and the fact that both were knights of the Hospital.

Within a few months of the election of Guérin the War of the Lombards spread from Cyprus to the Holy Land, and entered upon a new and more dangerous phase. The first preoccupation of the Masters of the Hospital and the Temple was to ensure that their two Orders should preserve an attitude of absolute neutrality. On no account

[1] See *Les Hospitaliers en Terre Sainte*, p. 165, note 4.

[2] See *Cartulaire-Général*, Vol. II, No. 1955.

[3] Ibid., No. 1967.

[4] We know that he was Prior of France in 1225, and that Imbert de Luquiers was Prior in 1220; he was therefore appointed at any time between these dates. He had ceased to be Prior in November 1230, no doubt owing to his having succeeded Bertrand de Thessy as Master.

[5] For an account of Guérin, Bishop of Senlis, see Combauld, *Histoire des ministres d'estat*, Paris, 1642.

must their knights draw the sword against their fellow Christians. This attitude was successfully maintained during the earlier years of the war, but in its final stages, when far greater bitterness had been engendered, the strain proved too great for both Orders. As usual they took opposite sides, and while the sympathies of the Hospitallers were with the Emperor, the Templars were violently opposed to him, and it was only with the greatest difficulty that the scandal of further fighting between the two Orders was avoided.

At the beginning of 1231 the Emperor, now at peace with the Pope and free to turn his attention to the East, sent out a strong force to the Holy Land under Richard Filangieri, the Marshal of the Empire, who was to succeed Balian of Sidon as regent, and whose orders were to restore the Imperial authority in Cyprus, and to deprive John d'Ibelin of his fief of Beyrout. The Marshal established himself in Acre, and at once began the siege of Beyrout; the town was taken without much difficulty, but the castle held out. In February 1232 John d'Ibelin crossed over from Cyprus to attempt its relief, and was immediately joined by the whole of the barons of the Holy Land, who considered the Emperor's action too high-handed and contrary to their constitution, as defined in the Assizes of Jerusalem. But Bohemond Prince of Antioch and Count of Tripolis declined to be drawn into the war, and preserved a strict neutrality.

While the Marshal was besieging his castle of Beyrout, John d'Ibelin occupied Acre, which revolted in his favour, seized the imperial ships and stores, and organized the city as a commune on the Italian model. He then prepared to attack Tyre, and established a fortified camp at Casale Imberti midway between that city and Acre. This brought the Marshal south, and caused the siege of Beyrout to be raised. But in the absence of John d'Ibelin, the Marshal surprised his fortified camp at Casale Imberti on the night of the 2/3 May, inflicting a crushing defeat, and nearly capturing the young King of Cyprus. John d'Ibelin then fell back upon Acre, and the Marshal carried the war into Cyprus overrunning the whole island except only the castles of Dieu d'Amour and Buffavento. Undismayed by these disasters, John d'Ibelin embarked at Acre for Famagusta, where he landed on 30 May, and securing the assistance of the Genoese colony, to whom he granted valuable privileges, within a fortnight completely reversed the situation. The Marshal retired before him towards his base at Cérines (Kyrenia) in the north, and on 15 June was utterly defeated in the Battle of Agridi. The siege of Cérines followed, and its capitulation in April 1233 was the end of the war so far as Cyprus was concerned. The second phase of the War of the Lombards was over, and all that remained to the Emperor of his kingdom of Jerusalem was the city of Tyre.

Meanwhile the Master of the Hospital had been engaged in settling the two most pressing of the problems, which he had inherited from his predecessor. The interminable dispute with the Prince of Antioch, and the relations of the Order with the Emir of Hama. Bohemond IV was now nearly 60 years of age, and hardened though he was to the censures of the Church, under which he had lived and prospered most of his life, the papal excommunication of 1230 appears to have weighed more heavily upon him than usual, no doubt because the prospects of entering into eternity were approaching so much nearer. The Hospitallers found the prince in a far more reasonable frame of mind than they had ever found him before, and on 27 October 1231 a series of agreements were signed at Acre, under which they abandoned all grants made to them by Prince Raymond-Rupen except Zibel (Jabala) and the Chateau de la Vieille, in return for which Prince Bohemond IV confirmed them in the possession of these two places, and granted them an annuity of 873 besants secured on the revenues of Antioch, and 316 besants secured on the revenues of Tripolis, in settlement of any claims that they might have against him for damages.[1] The long feud between the prince and the Hospitallers was now at an end, and on 10 April 1233 Cardinal Pelagius the papal legate annulled the sentence of excommunication,[2] but the prince died the following year and was succeeded by his son Bohemond V.

Although the Hospitallers had been confirmed in their possession of Zibel, they none the less had to divide their interest in it with the Templars under the agreement of 1221. Their first occupation of the town in 1210 had not carried with it absolute possession, and for many years they seem to have shared it with the Moslems, but in 1231 there was fighting between the Castellan of Margat and the Sultan of Aleppo,[3] apparently followed by a treaty under which Zibel passed definitely to the Hospitallers. The question then arose as to whether the Templars were bound by this treaty, and on 18 June 1233 an agreement was made between the two orders [4] to the effect that as co-proprietors of Zibel they were to be equally bound by all treaties with the Sultan of Aleppo, but that in their dealings with their nearest Moslem neighbour the Emir of Saone (Sahyun) they might act independently of each other.

There remained the question of the Order's relations with Hama to settle. Ever since their great bailiwick of Le Crac had been founded in 1142, the rulers of Hama had generally found it convenient to pay a subsidy to the Hospitallers to refrain from raiding their territory. There had no doubt been difficulty over the tribute in 1229, when the Castellan of Le Crac made a raid against Barin (Mont Ferrand) and sacked the town. In 1230 the Emir of Hama, Kilij-Arslan, a grand-

[1] See *Cartulaire-Général*, Vol. II, Nos. 1999–2003. [2] Ibid., No. 2048.
[3] See Stevenson, *The Crusaders in the East*, p. 314, note 4.
[4] See *Cartulaire-Général*, Vol. II, No. 2058.

son of Saladin's famous nephew Taki-ed-din Omar, died and was succeeded by his brother El-Muzaffar Mahmoud. The new ruler declined to pay the usual tribute, and in the summer the Hospitallers aided by the Templars sent a powerful punitive expedition against him consisting of 500 knights and serjeants and 2,700 foot.[1] But the expedition met with an overwhelming disaster, and was driven back upon Le Crac with heavy losses. It was not only the prestige of the Hospitallers that was badly shaken by this defeat, but the prestige of all the Christian states of Syria, and in 1233 when the Master of the Hospital organized a new expedition to restore Hama to obedience, contingents came to his assistance from all quarters. In October Guérin assembled a force of 500 knights and serjeants and 1,500 foot in the plain of La Bochée based upon Le Crac. They were joined by a contingent of Templars under their new Master Armand de Périgord, 80 knights from the kingdom of Jerusalem under Peter d'Avalon, 100 knights from Cyprus under John d'Ibelin, and 30 knights from Antioch under the prince's younger son Henry. In a short campaign lasting only eight days, El-Muzaffar Mahmoud was reduced to obedience without difficulty. He met with no sympathy from his kinsmen the Sultans of Egypt and Damascus, who desired peace with the Christians, in order to be free for a war against the Turkish Sultan of Roum, and the arrears of tribute were duly paid. This campaign is of interest, because it shows us exactly what force the Hospitallers could put into the field in case of emergency.[2]

We must now turn to another side of the work of the Order of the Hospital. For many years it had been just as much a military Order as the Temple, but none the less its charitable origins and the traditions belonging to it had never been forgotten, and from time to time we are suddenly reminded of that fact. The Hospital it is true was now mainly engaged in sending out a steady stream of muscular Christians ever ready to sacrifice their lives for the faith on the battlefields of the Holy Land, of whom one of the most famous in his day was doubtless that St. Nicasius of Palermo, who flourished in the twelfth century and whose memory is still preserved in Sicily.[3] But the Hospital of St. John of Jerusalem was equally able to produce heroes of a very

[1] Delaville Le Roulx in *Les Hospitaliers en Terre Sainte*, p. 171, note 4, suggests that this defeat may have been confused with the successful expedition of 1233, which does not seem possible, and which he himself contradicts on p. 165.

[2] For this campaign, see *Les Hospitaliers en Terre Sainte*, p. 172.

[3] Bosio in his *Vies des Saints*, etc., tells us that the image of St. Nicasius is to be seen in three of the churches of Palermo, and in the chapel of the Decollation of St. John in Valetta. He is represented with swellings on the neck, from which he is supposed to have suffered, and devout people thought that by invoking his name they would be cured of this complaint. Nothing else is known about him except that Hellwald in his 'Bibliography', p. 126, says that he belonged to the Sicilian family of Burgio, and flourished in the twelfth century.

different and much rarer type, gentle and saintly men, who tried to follow in the footsteps of Our Saviour, by devoting all their lives to prayer and the alleviation of human suffering and misery. In the very year of the victory over Hama, there died at Genoa one whose kindly and saintly life has made him as revered and loved in the Order of St. John as St. Ubaldescha herself.

St. Hugh of Genoa is described as a small lean man, very devout and very ascetic, kindly and considerate to all, generous and charitable, and in spite of his high and dignified position in the Order of St. John as Commander of Genoa, a very humble man.[1] It was his custom to perform personally in his hospital the most menial duties, washing the feet of the sick, and preparing the bodies of the dead for burial, and he always slept on a plank-bed just below the wards. His extreme austerities must have greatly shortened his life, for we are told that he always fasted as in Lent all the year round, and that during Lent he took no cooked food of any description. Round his waist he always wore an iron belt next to his skin, with a hair shirt, and the whole of his time, not given up to charitable duties, was spent in prayer and meditation, and at Mass he seemed often to pass into a trance. The goodness and piety of St. Hugh became famous throughout the countryside and even in his lifetime he was regarded by the people as a saint, and wonderful stories became current of the miracles performed by him. Two of the most famous are often represented in his pictures. Some women related how when washing clothes on a hot summer day, and worn out with carrying water from a distance, St. Hugh passed by and was filled with pity to see their weariness. And as he watched them working, he prayed and made the sign of the cross with his stick on a rock, and immediately a spring of water gushed out, which was still known in the days of Bosio as the Fountain of St. Hugh. The other story was told by some sailors of how during a storm their ship was in danger of sinking, as they tried to enter harbour, and St. Hugh seeing it waded out into the sea, and raising his eyes in prayer to heaven, made the sign of the cross in their direction, and immediately the wind dropped and the sea became calm. Many other miracles are related of St. Hugh, both in his lifetime and after his death. He died at Genoa on 8 October 1233, and was buried there in the church of St. John. Bosio tells us that in his day the anniversary of the death of St. Hugh was observed in all the churches of Genoa, and his relics carried in solemn procession.[2] No names have ever been held in such

[1] For the life of St. Hugh of Genoa, see Bosio, *Les Vies des Saints de l'Ordre.*

[2] The following special Collect was used in Genoese churches on St. Hugh's day: 'Deus qui dedisti servo tuo Hugoni, in nomine tuo, signo crucis de durissimo saxo scatere fontem aquae vivae, demones effugare, et infirmos curare; concede quaesumus, ut cujus exsequimur cultu, sentiamus effectum. Per Dominum nostrum, etc.'

deep veneration in the Order of St. John as those of its three most famous saints, St. Ubaldescha, St. Hugh of Genoa and the Blessed Gérard the founder.

His successful campaign against Hama, and the settlement with Bohemond IV of Antioch, were the great events of the reign of Guérin as Master of the Hospital, and the last three years of his life were passed in comparative tranquillity, except for an unfortunate dispute with the new Prince of Antioch, which led to a severe rebuke from the Pope. Apparently Guérin claimed rights of wardship over the fief of Maraclée adjoining the bailiwick of Margat, and when its old lord died and was succeeded by a child Meillour, he placed a garrison in the castle. Prince Bohemond V strongly objected to this as an infringement upon his own rights, and when the Pope in 1234 instructed the Bishop of Valénie to settle the matter, declined to submit to his judgement, on which the bishop left the Hospitallers in provisional occupation of the castle.[1] The dispute became more and more embittered, and the prince accused the Hospitallers and Templars to the Pope of having allied themselves with the Assassins against him. The fact that the Old Man of the Mountain paid tribute to the military Orders, just as the Emir of Hama did, gave a certain colour to the accusation, and on 30 April 1236 the Pope wrote to the Archbishop of Tyre and the Bishops of Sidon and Beyrout insisting that the military Orders should break off their compromising relations with the Assassins on pain of excommunication.[2]

Under the rule of Guérin the affairs of the Hospital in Europe continued to prosper, although the great days of rapid expansion were now definitely finished. There was no longer the same passionate interest in the safety of the Holy Land, which had prompted men to bestow great gifts of land and property in their admiration for its gallant defenders the Hospitallers and Templars. But in 1233 an arrangement was made with the city of Marseilles of unusual interest, because it throws light upon the maritime activities of the two great Orders.[3] Under this arrangement each Order was permitted to send one pilgrim ship from Marseilles to the Holy Land at the Easter or March passage, and one ship each at the August passage. They might each carry up to 1,500 pilgrims as well as merchandise, but were to call at no port in Provence until they reached Monaco. There were apparently no restrictions upon their ships other than merchant or pilgrim ships, which alone affected the carrying trade of Marseilles. In England there had been a curious dispute over a nunnery founded at Aconbury in Herefordshire about 1216 by Margaret de Lacey, wife of a great Anglo-Irish baron. Margaret de Lacey had given a rule and

[1] See *Cartulaire-Général,* Vol. II, No. 2094.
[2] This letter is given in the Appendix to this chapter.
[3] See *Cartulaire-Général,* Vol. II, No. 2067.

ST. HUGH OF GENOA

a distinctive dress to the sisters of her foundation, and then affiliated it to the Order of the Hospital; without realizing that it would have to conform to its statutes and ordinances. Guérin insisted that Aconbury should adopt the habit and rules of his Order, until the Pope intervened in 1233 to re-establish the original situation,[1] and finally in 1237 gave it complete independence.[2] Guérin died in the summer of 1236 ; he had deserved well of his Order, for he had assumed office in a time of serious depression, and during his six years' rule had once more restored its old prosperity and prestige. The official chronicle tells us that he was a man of simple habits who disliked the pomp and ceremony that had gradually attached themselves to his high office. He is said to have paid great attention to the finances of the Hospital, and through his policy of peace and his careful administration large reserve funds were accumulated in the Treasury.

Guérin was succeeded by Bertrand de Comps, Prior of St. Gilles since about 1230. He is generally regarded as taking his name from the town of Comps in Lower Dauphiné, and as belonging to the family of De Vesc, in which the family of De Comps had become absorbed.[3] In Arnold de Comps there had probably been a previous Master of the same family. We know nothing of Bertrand de Comps before his appointment to be Prior of St. Gilles, except that he was serving in the Holy Land in 1216.

The lull in the War of the Lombards, which had existed ever since the fall of Cérines in 1233, still continued, for the Emperor was far too occupied in Europe to be able to send troops to the Holy Land. But without reinforcements Richard Filangieri the Marshal could do nothing to restore his master's authority, and had to be content with holding Tyre. The Old Lord of Beyrout remained all powerful in Palestine, as he was in Cyprus, until a fall from his horse in 1236 put an end to his career. He was succeeded in Beyrout, and in the leadership of the barons of the Holy Land, by his eldest son Balian, his younger son John taking Arsuf. Great and successful though his personal career had been, it was fatal to the cause which he represented. His refusal to co-operate with the Emperor, and his reckless pursuit of his own immediate ends, regardless of the ultimate consequence for Christian interests as a whole, had finally sealed the fate of the Latin kingdom. John d'Ibelin of Beyrout and Bohemond IV of Antioch, had between them completed the ruin of the Christian cause in the East, and the end was only a question of time.

During the reign of Bertrand de Comps the peace with the Moslems remained almost unbroken except in Antioch, where the Templars, taking advantage of the recent death of the Sultan of Aleppo, attempted to recover Darbessac, which blocked the road between Antioch and

[1] See *Cartulaire-Général*, Vol. II, Nos. 2047, 2059. [2] Ibid., No. 2167.
[3] See *Les Hospitaliers en Terre Sainte*, p. 179.

their castle of Gaston (Bagras).[1] But on 24 June 1237 they were attacked by a relieving force from Aleppo, and suffered a grave disaster, having 100 knights and 300 cross-bowmen amongst the slain. As a result of this defeat, the Templars called for reinforcements from their establishments in Europe, and with the contingent from England there came also a contingent of Hospitallers under Theodoric de Nussa, Prior of England. The two bodies went out to the East together, and Matthew Paris the contemporary historian relates how

> 'they started from the house of the Hospitallers at Clerkenwell in London, and passed through the City with spears held aloft, shields displayed, and banners advanced. They marched in splendid pomp to London Bridge, and sought a blessing from all who crowded to see them pass. The brethren indeed uncovered, bowed their heads from side to side, and recommended themselves to the prayers of all'.[2]

But while the Hospitallers were for the moment resting on their arms in Syria, they were once more hotly engaged on the western front of Christendom against the Moors of Spain. The decisive battle of La Navas de Tolosa had left the Christians definitely in the ascendant, the Castilians under St. Ferdinand gradually completed the conquest of Andalusia, and King James I of Aragon pushed steadily south into Valencia. The King of Aragon, known to history as James the Conqueror, had driven the Moors out of the Balearic Islands in 1229, and in 1238 laid siege to the city of Valencia. But here the victorious advance of the king received a severe check, the Moors resisted gallantly, and it looked as if the siege would have to be raised, when the arrival of a strong reinforcement of Hospitallers, comprising a numerous body of knights and 2,000 foot under Hugh de Forcalquier, Castellan of Amposta, put fresh life into the besiegers. The attack was now able to be pressed more vigorously, and the city eventually surrendered. The fall of its capital was the end of the Moorish kingdom of Valencia, which was annexed to the crown of Aragon. King James openly gave the credit for the successful result of the campaign to the Hospitallers, and in recognition of their services granted to the Order the town of Cervera in Catalonia, with its dependencies of Ascola, Alcocever and the plain of St. Matthew.[3]

As we have seen during the previous reign there had already been a complaint to the Pope against the Hospitallers by the Prince of Antioch, which had drawn forth a severe rebuke. Perhaps encouraged by this result the Bishop of Acre now brought a complaint to the Pope against the Hospitallers in his turn. He saw with alarm that the Hospital was continually increasing its possessions in his diocese, and as its possessions were exempt from the payment of tithes, it meant

[1] See Stevenson, *The Crusaders in the East*, p. 315, note.
[2] See Addison, *The Knights Templars*, p. 166.
[3] See Vertot, *Histoire des Chevaliers de Malthe*, Book III.

a continual decrease in his revenues. But the bishop was not content merely to state his case for the decision of the Pope, but just as the Patriarch Fulcher had done in the days of the Blessed Raymond du Puy he tried to prejudice him against the Hospitallers by including a multitude of vague general charges of gross immorality, of abusing their privileges, and of breaking their vows of poverty.[1] Now the old high standards of conventual discipline, applicable to the monks of the original Hospital, represented an ideal too high of attainment for an Order composed so largely of high-spirited young soldiers, scattered in garrisons and detachments all over the country. The Order was therefore very vulnerable to some of these charges, and it is evident that the Pope considered that its morale and tone had been allowed to sink below what was excusable. He also objected to the friendly terms that they maintained with John Vatatses, the Greek Emperor of the East, the irreconcilable enemy of the Latin Emperor, whom the Pope regarded as under his protection. Accordingly on 13 March 1238 he addressed to the Master and brethren of the Hospital a letter of rebuke phrased in the sternest manner possible, in which he stated that unless they reformed their ways within three months, he would commission the Archbishop of Tyre as his representative, for the purpose of reforming the Order both in its head and in its members.[2] Never in all its long history has such a letter been addressed to a Master of the Hospital as the Pope addressed to Bertrand de Comps, and it presumably had the desired effect, as nothing further is heard of the matter.

The ten years' peace arranged between the Emperor and the Sultan under the terms of the Treaty of Jaffa was now drawing to a close, but there had been a change of rulers in Egypt and Syria. On the death of his brother El-Ashraf in 1237, the Sultan El-Kamil had annexed Damascus to Egypt, but had himself died the following year, and been succeeded by his worthless son El-Adil II. With the knowledge that war with the infidel was once more rapidly approaching, the Christians began the fortification of Jerusalem, rebuilding the citadel in which was included the Tower of David, and a new crusade to the Holy Land was organized in Europe under the command of Theobald, King of Navarre and Count of Champagne.

Just at this moment the Master of the Hospital died. The official chronicle speaks of him in high terms, and says that by his upright and wise handling of affairs he was able to recover control over much Saracen territory that had previously belonged to the Hospital, and that by a judicious use of the great treasure, amassed by his predecessor Guérin, he was able to gain many increased privileges. It records one fact of exceptional interest when it tells us that it was

[1] See Vertot, *Histoire des Chevaliers de Malthe*, Book III.

[2] For a copy of this letter, see Appendix to this chapter.

Bertrand de Comps who put the finishing touches to the complete militarization of the Order by giving to the military brethren precedence over the clerical brethren.[1] The statement is to a certain extent confirmed by our knowledge that the codification of that great collection of regulations known as the 'Judgements and Customs of the Order', very probably took place at this time.[2] But the reign of Bertrand de Comps is irretrievably tarnished by the grave accusations brought against the Hospitallers by the Pope, and the veiled threat to remove the Master from his office unless within three months some reform took place.

The new Master was one of the Conventual Bailiffs, Peter de Villebride, the Grand Commander of the Hospital throughout the previous reign. His name is a corruption of the words Vieille Brioude, a town in Auvergne, to which province his family evidently belonged.[3] He had been serving in the Holy Land as far back as 1216, but we know nothing further of his previous career. Much of his short reign was to be spent as a prisoner of war in Egypt.

The King of Navarre, accompanied by the Dukes of Brittany and Burgundy and a great number of French barons and knights, landed at Acre on 1 September 1239. It was two months before they were ready to move, but reinforced by the Hospitallers and Templars and the knights of the Holy Land, on 2 November they marched south to join Walter de Brienne, Count of Jaffa, and no doubt at his suggestion decided to reoccupy Ascalon, which had lain in ruins ever since the Third Crusade, and to restore its fortifications. Meanwhile the Saracen army concentrated in southern Palestine under the command of David of Kerak, Corradin's son, but in the north the Sultan's uncle Ismail of Baalbec, a younger brother of El-Kamil, broke into revolt as soon as the crusade arrived, and on 27 September seized Damascus,[4] in the absence of its governor Ayoub, a son of El-Kamil, who was with the army in Palestine.

While the Christian army was halted at Jaffa, the Duke of Brittany carried out a brilliant raid up to the walls of Damascus, and returned to Acre loaded with booty. Excited by the news of this success the Duke of Burgundy and the other French nobles determined upon a raid to Gaza. With that complete lack of discipline so characteristic of the crusades, they ignored the protests of the King of Navarre, who objected to the whole proceedings, and on 13 November marched out of Jaffa. After crossing the frontier the Count of Jaffa, who knew the country well, urged them to halt for a rest, but they rode gaily on until

[1] See Appendix B.

[2] For the date of the 'Esgarts et Usances de l'Hôpital', see *Cartulaire-Général*, Vol. II, p. 536, footnote.

[3] See *Les Hospitaliers en Terre Sainte*, p. 183.

[4] See Stevenson, *The Crusaders in the East*, p. 316.

they found themselves in a hollow surrounded by hills, and there decided to halt for a meal. Apparently they took no precautions, and while so engaged were surprised by the Saracens from Gaza, and practically annihilated, although the Duke of Burgundy and the Count of Jaffa managed to get away. They are said to have had 1,800 killed, and 80 knights and 250 soldiers taken prisoner, and amongst the latter was Peter de Villebride, Master of the Hospital.[1] The King of Navarre, who had advanced to Ascalon in support of the raiders, fell back upon Jaffa, and then retired to Acre for the winter.

Encouraged by his victory at Gaza, David of Kerak followed it up by an attack on Jerusalem, and no attempt was made to come to its assistance by the Crusaders. After a siege of three weeks the newly built citadel was carried by assault on 7 December, and six days later its keep the Tower of David was captured. Then after having completely ruined its defences, David of Kerak withdrew from the city.

The campaign of 1240 was entirely governed by political considerations. The Sultan El-Adil was deposed in May, and on 17 June his brother Ayoub, the former governor of Damascus, became Sultan in his place. This alarmed his uncle Ismail, who well knew that the new Sultan would never permit him to retain Damascus. He therefore naturally opened negotiations with the Latin kingdom for an alliance against Egypt, offering to surrender Belfort (Shakif Arnun) and Safed,[2] with the lands dependent upon them. But in the chaotic state of the kingdom there was no one to speak with authority, and so Ismail entered into an alliance with the Templars and handed over to them Belfort and Safed, though the King of Navarre and certain other magnates also signed the treaty. As a result the allied armies assembled at Jaffa, to meet the expected invasion from Egypt. But as usual the Christian forces were rotten with dissension and strife. The Hospitallers, now under the leadership of William de Senlis the Grand Commander, objected strongly to the treaty with Ismail. They advocated an arrangement with the Sultan Ayoub, because in their opinion he would probably reconquer Damascus, and in any case it would certainly result in the release of the prisoners taken at Gaza, including Peter de Villebride their Master. They found considerable support in the army for their policy, including the King of Navarre, who had apparently changed his views, and all those who favoured an alliance with the Sultan abandoned the camp at Jaffa, and returned to Acre. There was now again an open breach between the Hospitallers and the Templars, and at the end of September the King of Navarre left for Europe, utterly disgusted with the continual bickerings and

[1] See Stevenson, *The Crusaders in the East*, p. 318.

[2] Belfort had formerly been a part of the fief of Sidon, and Safed a part of the fief of Tiberias.

jealousies and intrigues that destroyed any possibility of successful action.

Within a few days of the King of Navarre's departure, an English crusade arrived under Richard Earl of Cornwall, a brother of King Henry III, and on 8 October disembarked at Acre. The Earl of Cornwall took up his residence in the house of the Hospitallers, but declined to commit himself either to their policy or to that of the Templars, persuading them to unite in the fortification of Ascalon. At Jaffa he was met by envoys from the Sultan Ayoub, who adhering to the regular policy of his dynasty desired peace with the Christians, and then the Earl of Cornwall decided to be guided by the views of the Hospitallers. On 8 February 1241 the Sultan signed a treaty of peace, of which the details are not clear, but under it the prisoners taken in the battle of Gaza were to be released, and the occupation of Ascalon, Belfort and Safed were recognized and confirmed.[1] But the Templars held firmly to their treaty with Ismail of Damascus, whose troops allied with the Templars remained stationed on the Egyptian frontier, and under such conditions the treaty with the Sultan was doomed to ultimate failure. A situation in which the Templars were at war with Egypt, and the Hospitallers at peace, was obviously impossible. In consequence of the attitude of the Templars, the defence of Ascalon was not entrusted to them as they had hoped, but it was handed over to a representative of the Emperor, who passed it on to the Hospitallers two years later.[2] After completing the fortifications of Ascalon, the Earl of Cornwall returned to Acre. On 23 April the prisoners taken at the battle of Gaza arrived, including Peter de Villebride the Master of the Hospital,[3] and ten days later the Earl of Cornwall embarked for his own country.

The departure of the English Crusaders was followed by a period of anarchy and confusion worse than anything that the Latin kingdom of Jerusalem had ever yet known. The relations between the Hospitallers and the Templars, always inclined to be delicate, were by now strained to breaking-point, and there was serious danger of open war between the two Orders. For a time the Templars even went so far as to establish a blockade of the Convent of the Hospitallers at Acre, preventing the entry of provisions, and stopping the brethren from coming out to bury their dead, and they treated the Teutonic Knights in the same manner. That open fighting did not result from this, is perhaps due to the restraint of Peter de Villebride. Then in May 1242 the Sultan advanced from Gaza against Ismail of Damascus, and his

[1] See Stevenson, *The Crusaders in the East*, p. 320.

[2] See *Les Hospitaliers en Terre Sainte*, pp. 186, 193, 208.

[3] See Stevenson, *The Crusaders in the East*, p. 320. Since the Master of the Hospital, released in 1241, can only have been Peter de Villebride, it enables us to place the death of his predecessor Bertrand de Comps in 1239.

allies the Templars, but was heavily defeated. This caused him to come to an understanding with David of Kerak, on which in October the garrison of Jaffa surprised and plundered David's town of Nablus, and so provoked retaliation on Christian territory.[1] The helpless condition of Jerusalem still nominally in Christian possession, but totally unfortified and without a garrison, caused it to be almost deserted. It was probably at this troubled time, or else when the Chorasmians sacked Jerusalem two years later, that the famous mitre-shaped reliquary discovered in 1893, was hidden by the Hospitallers in the block of masonry under the high altar in their conventual church.[2]

To make confusion worse confounded, the wretched War of the Lombards, which had now been quietly smouldering for many years, suddenly burst forth into flame. Richard Filangieri, the Marshal of the Empire, leaving his headquarters at Tyre, secretly entered Acre, in order to arrange with his friends the Hospitallers, for the re-establishment there of the Emperor's authority. Philip de Montfort,[3] a nephew of the Old Lord of Beyrout, who had just arrived from Europe, heard of the plot, and at once warned his cousin Balian d'Ibelin of Beyrout. The two then invested the Convent of the Hospitallers, under the impression that the Marshal had taken refuge there, and maintained the investment for the next six months. When Peter de Villebride, the Master, returned from Margat, where he had been engaged in operations against the Sultan of Aleppo, they actually refused to allow him to enter his own convent, until he had formally declared his disapproval of the intrigues of the Marshal. The indignant Master bitterly denounced the outrage to which he had been subjected, in having his palace treated like an enemy's castle, which he said would be inexcusable, even if his knights in his absence had been guilty of the intrigues suggested. To this Balian d'Ibelin replied that he had no feelings whatever against the Hospitallers personally, and that he only wanted to catch the Marshal.[4]

In the midst of all this turmoil and strife we are suddenly once more reminded of that gentler, kindlier, more spiritual side of the Hospitallers, which is always quietly working in the background, carrying on the traditions of the Blessed Gerard. Two of the brethren, famous throughout the Order for the goodness and holiness of their lives, died in this year 1242, and were afterwards beatified and revered as saints.

[1] See Stevenson, *The Crusaders in the East*, p. 321.

[2] See Appendix to this chapter.

[3] Philip de Montfort was a son of Guy de Montfort by Héloïse, sister of the Old Lord of Beyrout, and widow of Reginald of Sidon: his father, Guy de Montfort, was a brother of the great Simon de Montfort, the conqueror of the Albigenses, and Philip de Montfort was therefore a first cousin of the English Simon de Montfort, Earl of Leicester.

[4] See *Les Hospitaliers en Terre Sainte*, pp. 186, 187.

The Blessed Gerard Mecati was born at Villemagne near Florence in 1174, and was received into the Order of St. John as a Serving Brother. From his very childhood he was conspicuous for his humble and devout piety, and his extreme goodness and charity to the poor. In course of time the desire came to him to retire from the world, and to seek and serve God in a life of solitude. St. Francis of Assisi personally conferred upon him the habit of his own new Order of Friars Minor, but sewn on to the grey robe of the Franciscans the Blessed Gerard Mecati always wore the white cross of the Hospitallers. Eventually he adopted the life of a hermit, giving himself up entirely to prayer, devotion, fasting and meditation and continually mortifying the flesh by the severest austerities. So holy did his reputation become that men spoke of him as the new St. Anthony and as the St. Hilarion of their time. Bosio states that in his day men could still show a favourite spot to which he used to go at night to pray, crawling there nearly 3 miles on his knees, and they could even show the marks of his hands and fingers on a great stone, against which he used to lean. Many miracles are related of him both during life and after death, and amongst others there is a famous story of how when dangerously ill a great desire for cherries was miraculously satisfied. He begged his sister who was nursing him, to go to a certain cherry-tree and pick the fruit; but since it was the month of January, she thought that he was raving in delirium. Eventually to satisfy him she went to the tree, to find that it was bearing ripe fruit as if it were summer. For this reason the Blessed Gerard Mecati is always represented with a bunch of cherries in his hand. He died on 13 May 1242, and his body in an open coffin was placed temporarily in a great oak tree close by his hermitage. But such a crowd of people came to see the body and to cut off pieces of his clothing as relics, that the republic of Florence had to place a guard of soldiers there. The incident is generally shown in his pictures. Eventually a church was built for him at Villemagne, and Bosio states that his body was still entire and incorrupt, and was exhibited to the people once a year on his festival, the second day of Pentecost.[1]

The Blessed Gerland was a contemporary of Gerard Mecati, and is generally spoken of as Gerland of Germany, but sometimes as Gerland of Poland. A knight of the Order of St. John, he was at one time attached to the court of the Emperor Frederick II, but he spent the latter years of his life at Calatagirona in the district of Alicata in Sicily. There he became famous for his goodness and piety, and his great charity and kindly sympathy to the poor and afflicted, who we are told loved and respected him like a father. At his death in 1242 he was universally mourned, and it is said that many sick people and

[1] See Bosio, *Les Vies des Saints de l'Ordre*, etc. The town of Villemagne no longer exists.

THE BLESSED GERARD MECATI

cripples were cured at his tomb. Then owing to a series of disasters that befell the neighbourhood the place of his tomb was forgotten, but 84 years after his death St. Constantine revealed in a vision to a certain James Calatasini of Calatagirona that he would find the body of the knight in the ruined church of St. Mary of the Temple outside the town. On digging there the body was discovered on 18 June 1327, and was translated to the church of St. James the Apostle at Calatagirona. St. Gerland there became very famous for the number of miraculous cures for sick people and cripples effected at his shrine, where it was the custom to bathe the parts afflicted with wine, in which the relics of the saint had been dipped. Bosio tells us that a book was preserved in the archives of the town recording ninety-six authentic miracles. The festival of the saint was always celebrated on 18 June, the day when his body was discovered.[1]

Not long after the siege of the Convent by Balian d'Ibelin and Philip de Montfort, Peter de Villebride died after a reign of only three years,[2] of which half the time had been spent in captivity in Cairo. He gives the impression of being a man of tact and moderation, who under circumstances of great provocation had kept his Order from coming to blows with the Templars, and preserved it from being dragged into the prevailing civil war. This view is confirmed by the official chronicle, which says of him that his upright and straightforward character gave him great influence, and that he was a strict disciplinarian. The same authority also tells us that under him there was a considerable increase in the possessions of the Hospital, and that three new Houses were established.[3] It was during the reign of Peter de Villebride that the troublesome question of Maraclée was finally settled. In 1238 the Pope had written to the Patriarch of Jerusalem directing him to terminate the affair,[4] but nothing came of it until 1241, when a satisfactory compromise was arranged. Peter de Villebride abandoned the rights of the Hospital over Maraclée and La Chamelle (Homs), the Prince of Antioch in compensation guaranteeing an annuity of 1,300 besants secured on the revenues of Tripolis, and Meillour de Maraclée on reaching his majority was to be given his choice as to whether he would hold his fief of the Prince or the Hospital.[5]

Since the death of Garin de Montaigu in 1228, less than fifteen

[1] See Bosio, *Les Vies des Saints de l'Ordre.*

[2] He died some time before 31 May 1243, because on that date William de Chateauneuf was already Master, but since we do not know how long before that he was elected, and since it took some time to assemble the Chapter-General for an election, we can conclude that Peter de Villebride probably died in 1242.

[3] The three new Houses were probably the Priories of Auvergne, Poland and Capua.

[4] See *Cartulaire-Général,* Vol. II, No. 2184.

[5] Ibid., No. 2280.

years had elapsed, but there had been no fewer than four Masters of the Hospital, which suggests that the office had been filled by somewhat elderly men. Such a succession of short reigns can only have been detrimental to the best interests of the Order, and from now onwards the Hospitallers appear to have elected younger men to fill the office of Master, if we can judge from the much greater lengths of their reigns. To fill the vacancy they elected one of the Conventual Bailiffs, William de Chateauneuf the Marshal of the Hospital. From the form of his name he was probably a Frenchman from the north of France, but as to which of the families of that name he belonged, we have no knowledge. He was serving in the Holy Land in 1233, and sometime between that date and the year 1241 he succeeded Arnold de Montbrun as Marshal, on the latter's appointment to be Castellan of Le Crac. Within a short time of his election the War of the Lombards was at an end.

On 25 April 1243 the young Prince Conrad attained his majority, and succeeded to the throne of Jerusalem, in the place of his father the Emperor, and sent to demand the oath of allegiance from the barons of his kingdom. At an assembly held at Acre on 5 June the barons declined to give the oath of allegiance unless King Conrad should come in person to the Holy Land to receive it, and they proclaimed Queen Alice of Cyprus regent during the king's absence, as next heir to the throne. Then having taken the oath of allegiance to Queen Alice and her husband Raoul de Soissons, they demanded the surrender of Tyre in their names. On the refusal of the governor Lothaire Filangieri, a brother of the Marshal, the barons laid siege to the town assisted by the Venetians. The Marshal in trying to run the blockade was taken prisoner, and to save his life Tyre surrendered after a siege of twenty-eight days. And that was the end of the war, for neither King Conrad nor his father the Emperor ever made any further effort to assert their authority in the Holy Land, they were too fully occupied by their long struggle for supremacy with the Pope, and Conrad was never more than nominally King of Jerusalem.

The state of anarchy prevailing amongst his Christian neighbours seems to have shaken the confidence of Ismail of Damascus in the value of their assistance against his powerful nephew the Sultan of Egypt, and in 1243 he endeavoured to arrive at an understanding with him. But the negotiations came to nothing, David of Kerak was also suspicious of the Sultan's intentions, and their common danger drove the two princes into a league against him. They then endeavoured to induce the Latin chiefs to join their alliance, by the offer of concessions so attractive that they were not likely to be refused. The whole of the remaining revenues of Tiberias, that is all the principality of Galilee, were to be surrendered, all control over Jerusalem to be given up, and the occupation of Ascalon to be confirmed. In fact all Palestine was being offered except the districts of Nablus and Hebron, which belonged to David of Kerak, and Jericho connecting them with his possessions beyond Jordan.[1] After a little hesitation and delay the terms were accepted by the Latin chiefs early in 1244, and all friendly relations with Egypt broken off. The policy so long advocated by the Hospitallers was now finally rejected, the policy of the Templars was triumphant, and the barons of the Holy Land had thrown in their lot with the losing side.

The Christians at once took possession of the places ceded to them. In the north Odo de Montbéliard, who had married the heiress of Galilee, began to refortify Tiberias, and in the south the Templars, with the assistance of David of Kerak, occupied and fortified Gaza, as an outpost against Egypt. The Moslems abandoned Jerusalem entirely, those that remained were driven out, and their sacred area the Haram-esh-Sherif once more passed into Christian hands. The Templars were now at last able to re-occupy what remained of their original Convent in the Mosque of El-Aksa, for the first time since the loss of the city, but the greater part of it in the Temple area had been destroyed by Saladin. The Patriarch Robert and his clergy with many Christian people returned to Jerusalem, the churches were reconsecrated, and the Hospitallers and Templars set to work to refortify the Holy City. For the moment it seemed as if a new era was about to begin.[2]

The Sultan Ayoub thoroughly alarmed at the dangerous alliance formed against him, which might end in depriving him of his throne, began to look round for assistance, and turned his eyes hopefully in the direction of Mesopotamia. After the collapse of the Chorasmian Empire before the arms of Jenghiz Khan, the first great Mongol invasion had ebbed away, and the heroic young Shah Jelal-ed-din had temporarily recovered his ruined realm. But in 1231 Ogotai the son and successor of Jenghiz Khan had sent another great Mongol host into Persia under Chormaghun, and Jelal-ed-din had been defeated and slain. This time the collapse of the Chorasmian Empire was final, and for twenty years the Mongols under Chormaghun and his successor Baidu systematically devastated Persia and western Asia. All organized government disappeared before the storm, and civilization itself almost ceased to exist in Mesopotamia. The Chorasmian army broke up on the death of Jelal-ed-din, and a detachment under Ertughrul taking service under the Turkish Sultan of Roum, became the founders of the Ottoman Empire. The remainder joined the wandering hordes of nomads engaged in ravaging Mesopotamia. In

[1] See Stevenson, *The Crusaders in the East*, p. 322, note 2. One account says that Beisan was excepted, and another account Jericho, but it must obviously have been the latter.

[2] See Addison, *The Knights Templars*, pp. 168–72.

the year 1244 a great horde of these Chorasmian Turks, 10,000 strong, under a certain Barbeh Khan, was terrorizing the country north of the Euphrates. To these savages the Sultan Ayoub turned in his hour of need, took them into his pay, and summoned them to join the Egyptian forces.

Crossing the Euphrates in the early summer, the Chorasmians rode south along the valleys of the Orontes and Leontes, plundering, burning and killing throughout the entire length of Syria, as was their wont. The country round Tripolis was badly ravaged, the districts of Safed and Tiberias devastated, and then on 11 July they arrived before Jerusalem. Both William de Chateauneuf, Master of the Hospital, and Armand de Perigord, Master of the Temple, had reached the Holy City a few days before, and had endeavoured to put it into a state of defence, but it was only partially fortified. The Chorasmians succeeded in breaking into the Armenian quarter, and entering the Armenian Convent of St. James, massacred every living soul, who had taken refuge there. Then the military Orders made a sortie in force, but were driven back, the imperial governor and William de Senlis, Grand Commander of the Hospital, being amongst the slain.[1] The city was obviously untenable, and on 23 August it was decided to evacuate the civil population, about 7,000 in number, and escort them to Jaffa. As soon as they had left the city, the Chorasmians entered and either in mockery, or with the intention of deceiving, began to wave Christian banners from the walls and to ring the church bells. At once a rumour ran through the mob of refugees swarming down the road to Jaffa, that the Chorasmians had been repulsed, and they turned back to the city, only to be massacred without pity by their relentless foes. It is said that out of 7,000 people, but 300 succeeded in escaping to Jaffa. Some women and children and old people took refuge in the Church of the Holy Sepulchre, but the Chorasmians bursting in, murdered them at the very entrance to the tomb of Our Saviour, and cut the throats of the priests at the high altar. Then they turned to the desecration of the most holy monument in Christendom, the marble shrine enclosing the sepulchre of Christ was shattered to pieces, and the carved columns at its entrance sent to Medina to decorate the grave of the Prophet, the tombs of the Latin kings were destroyed, the relics of the saints and martyrs defiled and scattered, and every loathsome abomination committed that their foul minds were capable of conceiving. Having plundered the Holy City at their leisure, they rode on to Gaza which they carried by assault, and there waited for the arrival of the Sultan's army from Egypt.

The Masters of the Hospital and the Temple, after escorting to Jaffa the remnant of the refugees from Jerusalem, rode north to Acre

[1] See *Les Hospitaliers en Terre Sainte*, p. 191.

to take counsel with the magnates of the realm concerning the approaching campaign. The Christian forces slowly assembled at Acre, the most important contingents as usual being those of the great military Orders. The Hospitallers furnished rather more than 350 knights[1] and a body of Turcopoles, who may have been more numerous, making the entire force about 1,000 strong. The contingent of the Templars would probably have been slightly larger than that of the Hospitallers, and that of the Teutonic Knights very much smaller, perhaps 250 of all ranks. The total strength of the army cannot have been great; if the full levy of the old kingdom could only produce 20,000 men for the Battle of Hattin, it is difficult to see how the now shrunken kingdom could produce much more than 8,000 men, even if they stripped the garrisons as at Hattin, which circumstances would certainly not permit of their doing. We know that one of the three divisions of the army was 2,000 strong,[2] it is not likely that the others differed greatly, and in that case the two divisions furnished by the Christians numbered together about 4,000 men. The morale of the army was very high, they knew themselves to be far better fighting men than the enemy, but the weak spot was the absence of a commander-in-chief, for which a feudal council-of-war could scarcely be regarded as an efficient substitute. At Acre the Christians were joined by the Syrian contingent, 2,000 strong, under the Emir El-Mansour of Homs, a famous warrior with a great reputation, described by Joinville as 'one of the best knights of paganism', and on 4 October the allies began their march south for the decisive battle of Gaza.

Meanwhile the Sultan's army 5,000 strong had crossed the desert under the Emir Beybars, destined in the future himself to be one of the most famous of the Sultans of Egypt, and had joined Barbeh Khan and his Chorasmians at Gaza, but showed no signs of taking the offensive. At a council-of-war of the allies, now concentrated at Ascalon, the same question was debated as had been debated on the eve of Hattin, whether to advance to the attack, or whether to remain on the defensive until the enemy attacked, or the lack of supplies should cause them to disintegrate. The Emir El-Mansour and the wisest of the Christian barons strongly advocated the latter policy since they they were heavily outnumbered, but the majority clamoured for instant battle, and on the morning of 17 October the allies marched on Gaza. The battle took place on almost the very same ground, where David of Kerak had defeated the Duke of Burgundy in 1239. The enemy about 15,000 strong were drawn up with the Chorasmians on the right under Barbeh Khan, and Beybars with his Mamelukes on

[1] 325 knights were killed, and 16 got away; how many were prisoners we do not know.

[2] The Syrian division was 2,000 strong, see Joinville's *Chronicle* (Marzial's translation), p. 269.

the left. The allies were in three divisions, probably numbering about 6,000 men. The centre under the Master of the Temple was composed of the Templars and the barons of the Holy Land, with whom went the Patriarch bearing the True Cross. The right wing was composed of the Syrians under El-Mansour, and the left of Hospitallers under their Master William de Chateauneuf, and the troops of Walter de Brienne, Count of Jaffa.[1]

The battle lasted two days, which means that on the first day the Christian heavy cavalry failed to get to close quarters with the elusive horse-archers of the enemy, and lost a large number of their chargers. On the second day the enemy concentrated their attack on the allied right under El-Mansour. The Syrians fought gallantly enough, and it was not until 1,700 of them had fallen that the Emir of Homs and the 280 troopers left rode off the field.[2] Then the enemy surrounded the two Christian divisions, and cut them to pieces. The army was practically annihilated, the Hospitallers had 325 knights and 200 Turcopoles killed, only 16 knights escaping from the slaughter.[3] Of the Templars 33 knights got away, and of the Teutonic knights only 3. The Master of the Temple was killed fighting to the last, and amongst the prisoners were the Master of the Hospital and the Count of Jaffa. The disaster was as complete and overwhelming as the Battle of Hattin, and from it the Latin kingdom never recovered. Never again were the barons of the Holy Land able to put an army into the field, never again did they venture to fight a pitched battle, from now onwards they stood definitely on the defensive behind the walls of their fortified towns and castles, until the end came.

APPENDIX

1. PAPAL OBJECTIONS TO THE POLICY OF THE HOSPITALLERS

Letter dated 20 *August* 1236 [4]

Gregory the Bishop, servant of the servants of God, to his venerable brethren the Archbishop of Tyre and the Bishops of Sidon and Beyrout, greeting. Would that the Master and brethren of the Hospital of Jerusalem had the wisdom to understand, as it is written that the prophet [5] said in rebuking King Jehoshaphat, 'Shouldest thou help the ungodly,

[1] See Michaud's *History of the Crusades*, English Edition, Vol. II, p. 329.

[2] See Joinville's *Chronicle* (Marzial's translation), p. 269.

[3] See *Les Hospitaliers en Terre Sainte*, p. 191.

[4] Printed in Latin in the *Cartulaire-Général*, Vol. II, No. 2,149, a similar letter was sent concerning the Templars.

[5] The prophet Jehu, the son of Hanani, see 2 Chronicles xix. 2.

and love them that hate the Lord, then shall wrath be upon thee from before the Lord,' that they should not in any way strive to aid the enemies of the Catholic faith against the sons of the Christian faith. Nevertheless, as we are informed by the Noble Prince of Antioch and Count of Tripolis (i.e. Bohemond V), giving no consideration to the harm done to their Religion before God and man, they have determined in support of the Assassins, the enemies of God and of the Christian name, who formerly dared to slay treacherously Raymond [1] of blessed memory, brother and bailiff of that same prince in Antioch, and many other magnates and Catholic princes, and are striving to overcome our faith by force, to place themselves in opposition to the said Prince, who is desirous of waging war against them, and when the said Assassins have need of their help against his attacks to the peril of their own souls they will defend them, and what is far graver still the aforesaid Assassins, on account of the promise made by the aforementioned Master and brethren to support and protect them from Christian attacks, have undertaken to pay them a certain sum of money every year. Therefore we have sent them orders in writing to desist from defending these same Assassins, and from any opposition of any kind to the said Prince. And so we now charge you that if the said Master and brethren should fail to observe this our command, you shall compel them to abandon this understanding by the censures of the Church, without right of appeal, after giving them due warning. And if all of you should be unable to take part in the execution of these instructions, then two of you at least should do so, notwithstanding the regulation concerning two days' journey laid down in the General Council, provided always that the second of you, who thus acts, shall not be drawn away from his diocese beyond the third or fourth day. Given at Rieti on the 13th day before the Kalends of September (i.e. 20 August) in the tenth year of our Pontificate.

2. POPE GREGORY IX SEVERELY REBUKES THE HOSPITALLERS

Letter dated 13 *March* 1238 [2]

Gregory the Bishop, servant of the servants of God, to the Master and brethren of the Hospital of St. John, greeting. We have heard with distress reports of you concerning which we write to you in sorrow, that you lead immoral lives, keeping women in your casales on fixed agreements, that you presume to possess private property contrary to your rules, that you constitute yourselves the protectors of all those who, on payment of four deniers a year or more, become your Confratres, and that you are accustomed to receive brigands and murderers of pilgrims and heretics in your houses and casales. That you are not ashamed to give aid against the Latins in horses and arms to Vatatses,[3] the enemy

[1] Raymond of Antioch, son of Prince Bohemond IV, was murdered by the Assassins at Tortosa in 1219.

[2] Printed in Latin in the *Cartulaire-Général*, Vol. II, No. 2,186.

[3] The Greek Emperor John Ducas Vataces, 1222–54.

of God and the Church, in return for which he has granted to you lands and casales. That you diminish your customary alms to the poor, that you alter fraudulently the testaments and last wills of persons dying in your Hospital, and that you do not permit the sick lying there to be confessed, without your special authority, by any priests other than your brethren and your own paid chaplains, and that you commit many other enormities, whereby God is offended and scandal raised in the eyes of the people. Moreover it is said that many of your brethren are with good reason suspected of heresy, on account of which and because a tiny particle of corruption may infect a mighty mass, we have good grounds for fearing lest this pest should spread to others. Therefore we charge you, within three months of the receipt of these presents, to amend your mode of life, and to take care to correct thoroughly and to reform what is set forth above, and all other things needing correction in the said Hospital, in accordance with the will of God and the Statutes of your Order, otherwise we shall give instructions in writing to our venerable brother the Archbishop of Tyre to go down to you in person, unless he has meanwhile received proof of such correction, and to hold full enquiry into what is set forth above and all other matters, considering only God's will, and to correct and reform on the spot both your head and your members, in accordance as he may deem the duty of correction and reformation to be necessary. Given at the Lateran, on the third day before the Ides of March (i.e. 13 March), in the eleventh year of our Pontificate.

3. NOTE ON THE HOSPITALLER RELIQUARY

Discovered in the Church of Mar Hanna

This reliquary, now in the Treasury of the Greek Patriarch in the Church of the Holy Sepulchre, was discovered in 1893 by workmen digging near the high altar in the church of Mar Hanna, formerly the Conventual Church of the Hospitallers. It is often suggested that it was hidden there by the Hospitallers, at the time when Saladin captured Jerusalem, but this is not at all probable, since the evacuation of the city was carried out in an orderly manner, and the Christians were permitted to remove the sacred treasures of their churches. It is far more likely to have been hidden there in a time of sudden danger and confusion, such as when David of Kerak occupied Jerusalem in 1242, or when the Chorasmians sacked it in 1244.

Monsieur Spyronides, the architect of the Greek Orthodox Convent in Jerusalem, referring to the Greek custom of depositing a relic under the high altar when erecting a new church, gives an entirely different opinion, and says, 'This Mitre was deposited under the sanctuary of the Church of St. John, at the time of its dedication, soon after the Crusades.' [1]

The reliquary is of crystal in the shape of a mitre set in a framework of gilded bronze, decorated with gems and filigree-work. Enclosed in it is a tablet of wood, overlaid with thin plates of gold, set with jewels, and holding on each side a series of relics. On one side, decorated with

[1] In a letter to Major Keith-Roach dated 13 December 1928.

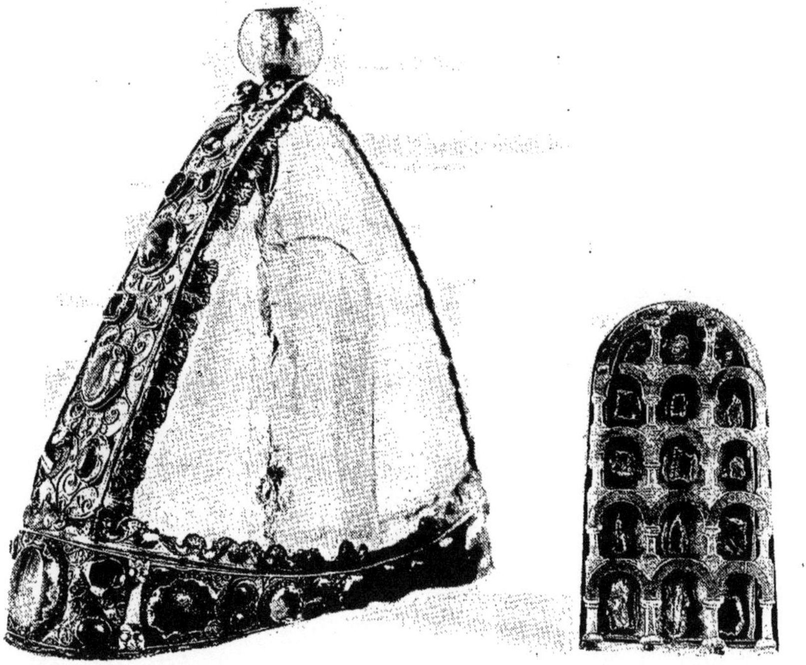

THE ANCIENT RELIQUARY FROM THE CHURCH OF MAR HANNA

Treasury of the Patriarch in the Church of the Holy Sepulchre

two patriarchal crosses, is a piece of the True Cross, and in the place of honour on each side of it, relics of St. Peter and St. John Baptist. On the other side, arranged in five rows of three each, are relics of the following fifteen saints: Andrew, Paul, James the Apostle, Philip, Bartholomew, Matthew, Thomas, James the Lord's brother, Simon and Jude, Mark, Matthias, Vitus, Laurence, Stephen, and King Oswald.

On the framework in front of the mitre, at the bottom, is an inscription now almost illegible, of which the following reading has been suggested: .........PIO.......RONSIO.......NAVIT, but at the end of it can be read the words D (omi)N (u) S JEJUNAVIT. Probably this inscription relates to a piece of stone inserted in the framework, and coming from the mountain of the Quarantaine, where Our Saviour fasted forty days and forty nights.

For an account of this reliquary, see Clermont-Ganneau, *Recueil d'Archéologie Orientale*, II, pp. 234–9; Vincent et Abel, *Jérusalem Nouvelle*, p. 667, note 1; Enlart, *Les Monuments des Croisés dans le Royaume de Jérusalem*, Vol. I, pp. 197, 198.

CHAPTER XIII

ST. LOUIS AND THE LAST CAMPAIGN IN EGYPT

WHILST the Hospitallers and the Templars were laying down their lives for the Christian faith by hundreds on the battlefield of Gaza, far away at Pontoise in the north of France, King Louis IX, whom the world was afterwards to know as St. Louis, lay unconscious and to all appearances dying. His mother Queen Blanche kneeling by his bedside, in her despair vowed that, if her son were restored to her, he should make the pilgrimage to the Holy Land, and there return thanks to God for his recovery at the tomb of Christ. And as she prayed consciousness suddenly returned to the king, and he was heard to murmur, 'The dayspring from on high hath visited me, and hath lifted me up out of the shadow of death.'[1] A little later he asked for the Bishop of Paris, and told him to fix the cross of a Crusader upon his shoulder. All present, wife, mother, bishop and attendants, begged him not to take so grave a step without further reflection, but the sick man said that he would touch neither food nor drink until the bishop had given him the cross, and from the moment that he had taken it he began slowly to recover. In later days men loved to tell the story of how the saintly king as he lay unconscious and sick unto death had seen in a vision the slaughter of Gaza, and vowed himself to the Holy War, but of these things St. Louis never spoke and he alone could have known. The king was now 30 years of age, a tall man and strong, an accomplished knight, very religious and devout, a little cold by nature, but kindly and considerate, and rigidly just in all things, soldier and saint he is the ideal of a mediaeval king. From this time onwards the recovery of the Holy Sepulchre was the chief interest of his life.

Meanwhile the crushing defeat of Gaza had not been followed by the same disastrous consequences for the kingdom of Jerusalem as had followed the Battle of Hattin. The Sultan Ayoub was mainly intent upon restoring his suzerainty over Moslem Syria, and in punishing the rebellious members of his own house. So far as the Christians were concerned he was content to follow the traditional policy of his dynasty, and merely to deprive them of the fruits of their alliance

[1] See Perry's *St. Louis*, p. 132.

with his rebellious relatives. Their terrific losses in the late battle had completely emptied the Convents of the Hospitallers and Templars, and until reinforcements could reach them from Europe with the March passage, both Orders were more impotent than they had ever been before. The Templars elected William de Sonnac to be their Master in the place of Armand de Perigord, whilst the Hospitallers during the long captivity of their Master were ruled by John de Ronay, the Grand Commander, in his capacity as Lieutenant-Master. John de Ronay had succeeded William de Senlis as Grand Commander, after the death of the latter in the defence of Jerusalem against the Chorasmians, and prior to that had been Commander of Tripolis.[1]

Directly after the Battle of Gaza the Chorasmians marched on Jaffa, taking with them Count Walter de Brienne their prisoner. Fastening the count to a cross close up to the city walls, they told him to order the citizens of Jaffa to surrender on pain of death. But the fearless count instead cried out to the citizens, 'Your duty is to defend a Christian city, and mine to die for you and Jesus Christ.' After enduring every insult and indignity, he was sent as a prisoner-of-war to Cairo, and was there murdered in prison.

When Queen Alice of Cyprus the Regent of Jerusalem died in 1246, she was succeeded as regent by her son King Henry I of Cyprus, who took the title of 'Lord of the Kingdom of Jerusalem', reserving however to King Conrad his legitimate rights to the throne, should he ever consent to reside in his kingdom. One of the first acts of King Henry was to confer the vacant fief of Jaffa upon John d'Ibelin, the famous legal authority, who compiled the Assizes of Jerusalem, and a son of Philip d'Ibelin, formerly Regent of Cyprus. At the same time he conferred the royal city of Tyre as a fief upon Philip de Montfort, Lord of Toron, a cousin of the new Count of Jaffa, and so every Christian city in Palestine except Acre was in the hands of the House of Ibelin and its relatives.

Finding that Jaffa and Ascalon could only be taken at the cost of sieges, which might prevent him from reaping the full fruits of his victory, the Emir Beybars without further delay occupied Hebron, Jerusalem and Nablus, and secured control over all Moslem Palestine. In March 1245 he laid siege to Damascus, and six months later on 1 October the city fell. Then the Chorasmians, dissatisfied with their share of the plunder, turned against their paymaster the Sultan. Ismail at once seized his opportunity, and joining forces with the Chorasmians and his nephew David of Kerak, attacked Damascus in May 1246. But[2] now the princes of northern Syria rallied to the banners of the Sultan Ayoub, and marched to his assistance. The Chorasmians were beaten in two engagements, their leader Barbeh Khan was slain, and the

[1] See *Les Hospitaliers en Terre Sainte*, pp. 193, 194.
[2] See Stevenson, *The Crusaders in the East*, p. 324.

remnants of his followers dispersed, and are heard of no more. With the defeat of his allies, the political career of Ismail was ended, and the Sultan Ayoub ruled supreme over the realms of his father El-Kamil.

Having successfully asserted his authority in Syria, the Sultan was free to deal with the Christian states, which he had no intention of leaving in possession of the territories ceded to them by his uncle Ismail. During the early part of 1247 the Emir Fakhr-ed-din was engaged in ravaging the territories beyond Jordan belonging to David, to whom Kerak alone was left. But in June he marched into Galilee, and on the 16th occupied Tiberias.[1] The siege of Ascalon followed, and the city was stoutly defended by the Hospitallers. During a storm, which caused the Egyptian fleet to seek shelter, Balian d'Ibelin of Beyrout ran the blockade, and reinforced and revictualled the garrison. But the city was bound to fall ultimately, as there was no field army capable of driving off the besiegers, or of making any effective intervention, and on 15 October 1247, after a gallant resistance the Hospitallers capitulated.[2]

The Sultan made no effort to recover Safed from the Templars, but he declined to restore to the Christians the privileged position in Jerusalem, granted by his father to the Emperor Frederick, and the Holy City was never again to pass into Christian hands until Lord Allenby, himself a Knight of St. John, drove out the Turks in 1917. But although the original Convent of the Hospitallers, so well known at the present day as the Muristan, now passed finally from the possession of the Order of St. John, the Hospital none the less continued to be used for many years for the purposes for which it had been constructed. When it ceased to be so used we do not know, but the German pilgrim, Ludolph von Suchem, who resided in the Holy Land from 1336 to 1341, in his description of Jerusalem makes the following statement.

> 'Near the Church of the Holy Sepulchre once dwelt the brethren of St. John of Jerusalem, and their palace is now the common hospital for pilgrims. This hospital is so great that 1,000 men can easily live therein, and can have everything that they want there by paying for it. It is the custom in this palace or hospital that every pilgrim should pay two Venetian pennies for the use of the hospital. If he sojourns therein for a year he pays no more, if he abides but for one day he pays no less.' [3]

Just as the fall of Eddessa in 1144 and the loss of Jerusalem in 1187 had provoked the Second and Third Crusades, so the Sixth Crusade [4] was caused by this second loss of Jerusalem. But it differed

[1] See Stevenson, *The Crusaders in the East*, p. 324.

[2] See *Les Hospitaliers en Terre Sainte*, p. 193.

[3] See Palestine Pilgrims' Text Society, Vol. XII, pp. 106, 107.

[4] Opinions differ widely as to how the crusades should be numbered, in this work that system of numbering has been adopted, which has been rendered familiar to all English-speaking people by Gibbon in his *Decline and Fall of the Roman Empire*, chapters 58 and 59.

entirely from the other two crusades, in that it was not an international undertaking led by the Emperor and preached by the Pope, but was a purely national crusade due to the pious enthusiasm of one man, St. Louis, and prosecuted only with the nominal approval of the Pope, who grudged anything that might weaken his own private crusade against the Emperor Frederick. In June 1245 the representatives of Europe at the bidding of the Pope, gathered together once more in the Council of Lyons, to consider the troubles in the East, the danger from the Mongols, and the dispute with the Emperor. But the latter question was the real cause of the meeting, and the only one that really interested the Pope. The Emperor in his absence was judged and sentenced, he was solemnly cursed by the Pope and the Bishops, condemned in this world and the next, deprived of his throne, and a crusade proclaimed to enforce the sentence, if possible. Then the question of a crusade for the recovery of the Holy Sepulchre was considered and approved, but with the Pope concentrating all his energies on the destruction of the Emperor, the Sixth Crusade was necessarily left in the hands of the laity.

St. Louis threw himself heart and soul into the prosecution of the new crusade. In October 1245 the French Parliament met at Paris, the necessary arrangements were sanctioned, and the great magnates of the realm took the cross. Negotiations with the Pope followed, and all through 1246 St. Louis was striving to make the peace between Pope and Emperor, but all in vain, and the Pope actually forbade the preaching of the crusade in Germany, lest it should interfere with his own private war.[1] At the end of the year supply officers were sent out to Cyprus to establish a base for the army, and to accumulate the necessary stores, and instructions were issued for improving and strengthening Aigues Mortes, the king's only harbour on the Mediterranean. At Mid-Lent in 1247 the king summoned Parliament to meet at Paris to settle the affairs of the kingdom in his absence, his mother Queen Blanche was appointed Regent, and the king announced his intention to start within a year of the approaching Nativity of St. John Baptist. But there was much friction during this year with the Pope, who was draining France of money for his own war. At last on 12 June 1248 St. Louis received the sacred banner of the Oriflamme[2] and his pilgrim's staff from the papal legate in the church of St. Denis, and after returning to Paris to hear Mass in Notre Dame, left for the East. On his way south he paid a final visit to the Pope at Lyons,

[1] See Perry's *St. Louis*, p. 143.

[2] The King of France was one of the vassals of the Abbey of St. Denis for the fief of the Vexin; it was in his quality of Count of the Vexin that he possessed the privilege of bearing the Oriflamme, which was the sacred banner of that great monastic foundation. Hassall's *History of France*, p. 106. The Oriflamme was a square banner of red silk with three points, borne on a gilt staff; it was last used on the battlefield, at Agincourt, in 1415.

begging him to be reconciled with the Emperor, and when he refused declared that if the crusade was a failure, the Pope alone would be to blame. On 28 August St. Louis embarked at Aigues Mortes for Cyprus with his brothers the Counts of Artois and Anjou, and with them went all the noblest chivalry of France. The size of the force is not exactly known, the fleet included 38 large ships, besides those carrying the horses, servants and stores, but several thousand men were left behind for lack of transport, to be brought on later by the king's other brother, the Count of Poitiers.

The French army arrived off Cyprus on 17 September and disembarked at Limassol, where stores had been steadily accumulating for nearly two years, and which had been prepared as their base. Here the king was received by the Masters of the two great military Orders, John de Ronay of the Hospital, and William de Sonnac of the Temple. The intentions of St. Louis were to follow the now generally accepted principle that the Holy Land could be successfully held, only if Egypt were first conquered. His plan of campaign was the same as that of King Amaury I in 1169, and King John de Brienne in 1218, but the results were to be infinitely more disastrous. Damietta was to be occupied as an advanced base, and the army was then to march on Cairo, supported by a flotilla moving parallel with it up the Nile. St. Louis would have liked to have begun the invasion of Egypt at once, but the whole army was not contained in the fleet that sailed from Aigues Mortes, and there were many contingents still to come in. The army could not be ready to move until the spring, and the king was perforce compelled to winter in Cyprus.

Meanwhile in Syria war had just broken out between the Sultan of Egypt and the Sultan of Aleppo, who had seized the town of Homs. Finding that the French intended to winter in Cyprus, the Sultan Ayoub established his headquarters at Damascus in November, and sent his troops to lay siege to Homs. But the town resisted vigorously, the Sultan was in very bad health, and the necessity for returning to Egypt to meet the French invasion, caused him to abandon the siege in the spring, and to come to terms with the Sultan of Aleppo, to whom he relinquished Homs. He was carried back to Cairo in a litter in April 1249, already a dying man.

The French fleet sailed from Limassol for Damietta on 13 May. It consisted of 120 large ships, and an enormous quantity of small craft amounting to 1,800 vessels all told, and there were 2,800 knights on board,[1] from which it seems possible that the army may have been about 50,000 strong. But a violent storm sprang up the following day, scattering the fleet, and when the king finally sailed on the 30th he had only one-third of his force with him.[2] They arrived off Damietta on 4 June and on the following day landed on the west bank of

[1] See Joinville's *Chronicle* (Marzial's translation), p. 172. [2] Ibid.

the Nile, opposite the city, at the same spot where the Fifth Crusade had landed in 1218. They were at once attacked by the Egyptian army under the Emir Fakhr-ed-din, but successfully beat them off, and the enemy, demoralized by a rumour that the Sultan was dead, fell back upon Mansourah behind the Ashmoun Canal, where the Sultans El-Kamil and Corradin had held King John de Brienne at bay in 1221. The garrison of Damietta finding themselves abandoned by the field army, withdrew during the night, and the next day 6 June the French occupied the city practically without resistance.

Had St. Louis been able to march upon Cairo at once, before the enemy had had time to recover from their initial demoralization, it is just possible that the Sixth Crusade might have ended in a brilliant success. But the storm off Cyprus had ruined its prospects from the very first, it had caused the army to land a fortnight too late, and the Nile was already beginning to rise. For this reason and partly also because only about one-third of his still scattered army had yet arrived, St. Louis decided to wait at Damietta until the inundation of the Nile was over, which meant a delay of five months before the advance could begin. This long delay was the ruin of the campaign.

By the end of October 1249 the whole of the French army was assembled at Damietta, including the last contingents from France under the king's third brother the Count of Poitiers, which had brought up the total to about 50,000 men. There was serving with the army a detachment of troops furnished by the barons of the Holy Land under John d'Ibelin Count of Jaffa, and the Hospitallers and Templars sent their usual contingents, the former commanded by John de Ronay the Lieutenant-Master, and the latter by their Master William de Sonnac. Each contingent no doubt consisted approximately of 1,000 men, namely 500 knights and serjeants and 500 Turcopoles, which may be regarded as the normal field force of each Order. There had also been a reinforcement of 200 English knights under William Longsword, Earl of Salisbury, a grandson of King Henry II and the Fair Rosamond. But the English and French as usual were on the worst possible terms, and were quite unable to work together without continual friction. The weak spot of the French army, as of all feudal armies, was its utter lack of discipline, not improved by the long period of waiting; each of the great barons desired to occupy the most prominent position, all were resentful of any form of authority, and none were ready to subordinate themselves for the good of the whole, the worst offenders being the king's own brothers, especially the Count of Artois. The Nile was now falling rapidly, and the campaigning season was near at hand. But a strong party amongst the French barons was advocating an expedition against Alexandria, the second port of Egypt, where much plunder was likely to be obtained. However, at a council of war it was finally decided to adhere to the original plan of campaign, since only by seizing Cairo could the conquest of Egypt and that of the Holy Land be effected, and on 27 November St. Louis began his march up the right bank of the Nile, along the road previously followed by King John de Brienne.

Six days before the French advance began, the Sultan Ayoub died, and his son and successor Turanshah was far away in Mesopotamia. The late Sultan like most of his race had been a strong and capable ruler, and his death under such circumstances might well have been the signal for disastrous strife amongst the leading Emirs. But there was in his harem a woman of very remarkable character, a Turkish or Armenian slave-girl by name Sheger-ed-durr, 'the spray of pearls', and she took charge of the situation. For three months she concealed the Sultan's death from all except Fakhr-ed-din and a few other trustworthy Emirs, until Turanshah arrived from Mesopotamia. His meals were regularly taken into the Sultan's rooms, orders were issued in his name, and Sheger-ed-durr continued to interview generals and ministers on behalf of her sick master, exactly as if nothing had happened, and she even watched over the discipline of the army until the decisive battle had been fought and won. During all this critical winter only the wit and intelligence of the dead Sultan's favourite slave-girl stood between Egypt and disaster.[1]

The French army moved slowly and took just three weeks to cover the 50 miles between Damietta and the Ashmoun Canal, or the Canal of Rexi as they called it, from the village of Dereksa close by.[2] The advance was not unopposed, there was fighting at Sharemsah on 7 December and at Faramoun on the 13th, and it was not until the 19th that they found themselves opposite the Egyptian position at Mansourah, with the canal between them. To pass this formidable obstacle it was decided to construct a causeway right across the stream, but as fast as the causeway advanced, the Egyptians dug away the bank on the other side, so continually providing a new channel for the Rexi, and no real progress was made for nearly two months. At last certain Bedouin for a price of 500 besants revealed the existence of a ford some distance down-stream, and on the night of the 7/8 February 1250 St. Louis with the whole of the mounted troops, making a wide detour, crossed by the ford, with the intention of establishing a bridge-head on the enemy's side of the Rexi, opposite the unfinished causeway, and so brought on the Battle of Mansourah.[3]

The French cavalry were organized in three divisions, with an advance guard composed of the military Orders under William de

[1] See Lane-Poole's *History of Egypt in the Middle Ages*, p. 237.

[2] It is of course nothing to do with the Rosetta branch of the Nile. See Lane-Poole's *Egypt in the Middle Ages*, p. 233, note.

[3] See Oman's *Art of War in the Middle Ages*, Vol. I, pp. 340–52.

Sonnac of the Temple and John de Ronay of the Hospital.[1] The leading division was commanded by the Count of Artois, with whom were William Longsword and his English knights and the mounted cross-bowmen, then came the division under the Count of Anjou, and lastly came the division commanded by the king in person. After crossing the ford and driving off 300 Saracen horse, who were watching it, the Count of Artois at the head of his division began to press forward upon the advance guard of Templars and Hospitallers. William de Sonnac, Master of the Temple, after vainly protesting against such conduct, was forced to conform to it, and the advance guard and the leading division rode on apparently intermingled. The enemy was taken completely by surprise, their men were without their armour

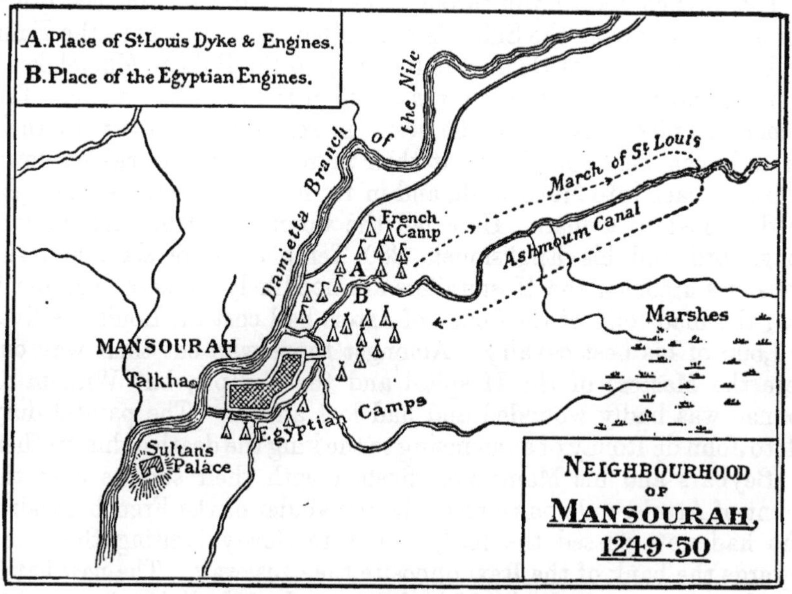

PLAN OF THE BATTLE OF MANSOURAH

and their horses unsaddled, when the French suddenly charged right through the camps east of Mansourah, inflicting tremendous casualties. At the moment of the attack the commander-in-chief Fakhr-ed-din was in his bath, and he was cut down as he rode up unarmed trying to rally his men. So far no harm had come of the undisciplined and impetuous conduct of the Count of Artois.

Beyond the captured camps across a stream lay the town of Mansourah, and beyond the town were encamped other bodies of troops. After a short breathing space the Count of Artois ordered a fresh advance into Mansourah, without waiting for the arrival of the other

[1] For the part played by the Hospitallers in the Battle of Mansourah, see *Les Hospitaliers en Terre Sainte*, p. 195, note 2.

two divisions under King Louis. The Master of the Temple begged him to give time for the rest to come up, but received in reply the sneering taunt that all the world knew the Templars and Hospitallers to be secret traitors, who dreaded the reconquest of the Holy Land, lest it should destroy their predominance. Then William Longsword joined his protests to those of the Master of the Temple, only to be grossly insulted with the remark that since all Englishmen had tails, they would doubtless show them to the enemy that day.[1] 'I shall go to-day where you will not dare to keep level with the tail of my horse,' retorted the indignant Earl of Salisbury, and lowering his visor and couching his lance, he led the charge into the narrow streets of Mansourah to meet his doom.

The French rode right through the town, and out on the other side almost as far as the Sultan's palace beyond. But here the Emir Beybars, the victor of Gaza, was forming up the Bahrite Mamelukes,[2] a force of heavy cavalry, the *corps d'élite* of the Egyptian army. The French knights arriving on the scene in scattered groups with their horses blown were completely at their mercy, they were ridden down or driven back into Mansourah, and in its narrow streets were slaughtered almost to a man. Here fell the Count of Artois and William Longsword and his Englishmen, 280 Templars were slain and the casualties amongst the Hospitallers are not likely to have been much less; the mad folly of the Count of Artois had cost St. Louis the lives of 1,500 of his best cavalry. Amongst those who cut their way out were the Masters of the Hospital and the Temple, but William de Sonnac was badly wounded and had lost an eye. The painful duty fell to John de Ronay of announcing to the king the death of his brother.

Beybars and his Mamelukes flushed with their success over the Count of Artois, rode on to meet the remainder of the French cavalry, who had now passed the ford, and were slowly fighting their way towards the bank of the Rexi opposite the causeway. The new battle was fiercely contested, the Mamelukes at first declining to come to close quarters, and pouring a continuous flight of arrows upon the French, who were unable to reply owing to the loss of their mounted cross-bowmen under the Count of Artois. Hundreds of knights were dismounted through the heavy losses of horses under the arrow-flight, and when at last the Mamelukes charged home, it looked as if victory was within their grasp. But by this time the French infantry under the Duke of Burgundy had succeeded in throwing a bridge over the

[1] An insolent reference to the insulting and idiotic story that all Englishmen were cursed with tails as a punishment for the murder of St. Thomas à Becket.

[2] The Sultan Ayoub paid great attention to his Mamelukes, and the body of picked horsemen that he placed in barracks on the island of Roda in the Nile opposite Fostat, were from this fact known as the Bahrite Mamelukes, from bahr meaning river.

Rexi from the head of the causeway. The cross-bowmen pouring across formed up on the opposite bank, and the Mamelukes unable to endure their deadly missiles drew off. King Louis had been saved from the defeat that had at one time seemed imminent, the object of the battle had been gained, the canal had been bridged, and the bridge-head was at once strongly fortified. But the success had been purchased at a price far beyond its value, the victory was little better than a defeat, half the cavalry had been lost, of the remainder hundreds were without horses, and the initiative had passed definitely into the hands of the enemy.

The Saracens well knowing how hopelessly crippled the French were by their terrific losses, regarded the battle as a victory, and followed it up by a determined night attack upon the bridge-head, which was only beaten off with difficulty. Three days later on 11 February the second Battle of Mansourah was fought, when the whole Saracen army was brought into action in an attempt to destroy the half of the French Army that was now encamped on the south side of the Rexi. For the moment the fate of the battle hung in the balance, when the enemy broke the French right under the Count of Anjou, and burst into the fortified camp. But St. Louis the hero of the day led the counter-attack in person that drove back the enemy, and the line was successfully restored. The centre, where the military orders were stationed, was the scene of desperate fighting, and the remaining Hospitallers and Templars were practically annihilated, but thanks to their gallantry the line stood firm. Here William de Sonnac, Master of the Temple, already severely wounded in the previous battle, was blinded and slain, and the whole of the Hospitallers including John de Ronay the Lieutenant-Master were killed, except five who were taken prisoners.[1] Repulsed all along the line, towards evening the Saracens withdrew, but their two costly victories had deprived the French of any power of resuming the offensive, and the only course open to them was to fall back upon their base at Damietta, while there was yet time.

But St. Louis could not bring himself to admit failure, and to give the orders for retreat, hoping to retrieve the situation by negotiations on the basis of exchanging Damietta for the kingdom of Jerusalem, the offer made by the Sultan El-Kamil in 1221 to King John de Brienne. The Saracens meanwhile were content to blockade the French camps until the arrival of the new Sultan Turanshah from Mesopotamia on 27 February. The French now began to suffer terribly from sickness, their camps astride the Rexi were surrounded by thousands of putrefying corpses, and the canal itself so choked with them that it took a week to clear it. Scurvy, dysentery and enteric fever attacked the army, the troops began to die off like flies, and when on 15 March the

[1] See *Les Hospitaliers en Terre Sainte*, p. 196. Amongst the dead was another Conventual Bailiff, Martin Sanchez the Drapier.

new Sultan placed a flotilla of galleys on the Nile, cutting the river route to Damietta, their fate was sealed. On 1 April St. Louis withdrew all troops to the north side of the Rexi, and after a last attempt at negotiations, on the afternoon of the 5th gave orders for the retreat to begin. The king himself insisted on accompanying the rearguard, although unable any longer to bear arms and so ill with dysentery that his knights thought him to be actually dying. By dawn on 6 April the pursuing cavalry came up, and rode in upon the retreating columns. The troops weary, disheartened and weakened by sickness, could make little serious resistance. His devoted followers carried the king into a wayside hut to die, where he was found by a Saracen Emir. The main body kept up a running fight as far as Fareskour, but by three o'clock in the afternoon had been broken up and dispersed. When the sun set on 6 April the French army had ceased to exist, the rank and file were almost all massacred, the knights and nobles alone being spared for their ransoms, and the Sultan Turanshah himself wrote that 30,000 Crusaders had been slain. So ended the Sixth Crusade, the most disastrous and tragic of them all.

St. Louis recovered from his illness, and did not long remain a prisoner of war. The Sultan Turanshah, like his grandfather El-Kamil, consented to terms of a most reasonable nature. Damietta was to be restored, there were to be no territorial changes, the king was to pay an indemnity of one million besants, the equivalent of 500,000 French livres,[1] all prisoners taken on both sides since the Treaty of Jaffa in 1229 were to be released, and the treaty was to last for ten years. But the chivalrous Sultan was so struck by the dignified and kingly bearing of St. Louis that he remitted one-fifth of the indemnity, saying, 'By my faith, this Frank is so large-hearted not to have haggled over so great a sum, that I give him 100,000 livres towards the payment.' But no sooner had the terms been agreed, than the Sultan was assassinated by the Bahrite Mamelukes, whose power he was attempting to break, and the Emir Beybars struck the first blow. Prior to the Sultan's arrival from Mesopotamia, the Mamelukes had learnt to trust and admire the Sultan Ayoub's favourite slave-girl Sheger-ed-durr, and they took the curious step of making her their queen, until the Caliph of Baghdad sent the significant message that if there was no man in Egypt, he would send them one. Then Sheger-ed-durr married her commander-in-chief Aybek, making him Sultan, but she first compelled him to divorce his existing wife, and she retained all power in her own hands. The *coup d'état* had for a moment placed the lives of St. Louis and the French prisoners in the gravest danger, for the Mamelukes were drunk with excitement and fanaticism. But three days later the Emirs confirmed the treaty, Damietta with a first instalment of the indemnity was handed over on 6 May and St. Louis

[1] See Joinville's *Chronicle* (Marzial's translation), p. 220.

embarked for Acre. To prevent the Christians from ever again using Damietta as a base of operations against Egypt, the city was afterwards razed to the ground, and rebuilt further inland.[1]

On his return to Acre, St. Louis felt that he could not return to France until the treaty had been fulfilled and all prisoners released, but he allowed his brother and the other French nobles to return. The political situation enabled him to bring pressure to bear upon the Egyptians, for the Sultan En-Nasir of Aleppo, head of the House of Saladin, seized Damascus on 9 July and announced his intention of avenging the death of Turanshah. In October 1250 the Egyptians fearing that St. Louis might come to some arrangement with the Sultan of Aleppo sent back 800 of their prisoners, including William de Chateauneuf, Master of the Hospital, and 25 of his knights, most of whom had been prisoners ever since the battle of Gaza in 1244.[2] William de Chateauneuf, after his six years' absence in captivity, returned to his convent at Acre to find it almost empty, his lieutenant, John de Ronay, dead and with him nearly every knight, who had followed the standard of the Hospital to Egypt with St. Louis. During the short interval since the death of the Lieutenant-Master, the Hospital appears to have been ruled by Hugh Revel, his successor as Grand Commander.

St. Louis spent the winter at Acre, strengthening its fortifications, and there received an embassy from the Old Man of the Mountain. The envoy had the insolence to arrive in his presence bearing the significant emblems of daggers and a winding-sheet, and demanded gifts for his lord, or at least that the king should use his influence with the Masters of the Hospital and the Temple to free him from the tribute that he paid them. The king dismissed the envoy until the following day, and then received him with William de Chateauneuf of the Hospital seated on his one side, and Reginald de Vichier of the Temple on the other side. Most unwillingly he repeated his message of the previous day, and was told by the two Masters to meet them at the Convent of the Hospitallers. There they told him that had it not been for the king they would have drowned him in the sea for his insolence, and that he was at once to convey their orders to the Old Man of the Mountain to send to the king within fifteen days such gifts as should be a worthy atonement for the insult. The envoy returned before the expiration of the stated period bearing the Old Man's shirt, as the outward sign that St. Louis was nearer to him in his affection than any other king, as well as rich and appropriate gifts. In return St. Louis sent an embassy also bearing suitable presents.[3]

[1] See Lane-Poole's *History of Egypt in the Middle Ages*, p. 239.

[2] See Stevenson, *The Crusaders in the East*, p. 330, note 1. There were 100 secular knights, 25 Hospitallers, 15 Templars, and 10 Teutonic knights.

[3] See Joinville's *Chronicle*, pp. 248–50.

In the early spring of 1251 St. Louis made the pilgrimage to Nazareth, and in March having completed the fortifying of Acre transferred his headquarters to Caesarea, where he was nearer to the Egyptian frontier. The Mameluke Sultan Aybek had just inflicted a crushing defeat at Abbasa on 3 February upon the Sultan of Aleppo, who had invaded Egypt, compelling him to fall back upon Damascus. The king remained over a year at Caesarea, trying to secure a revision of the Treaty of Damietta, and spent the time refortifying the town, which was held by John L'Allemand, by his marriage with its heiress Marguerite de Layron. During the king's stay at Caesarea there was an unfortunate brawl between the Hospitallers and some French knights, who were hunting gazelle, and the consequences might have been serious. The Frenchmen for reasons unknown to us were driven away by the Hospitallers with considerable violence, and thereupon lodged a complaint with the Master of the Hospital. William de Chateauneuf condemned his knights to the punishment of the Quarantine,[1] that is confinement to quarters for forty days, during which period they fasted, receiving on Wednesdays and Fridays bread and water only, and also undergoing flagellation on the bare back on these days during the recitation of the psalm 'Deus misereatur nostri'. All meals in the dining-hall had to be eaten seated upon their mantles on the ground. St. Louis' famous companion, the Sire de Joinville, relates the incident in his memoirs, and how he eventually prevailed upon the Master of the Hospital to remit the remainder of the sentence.[2] It furnishes an interesting example of how discipline was maintained amongst the Hospitallers during this period.

At last in March 1252 the Sultan Aybek agreed to revise the Treaty of Damietta on the lines proposed by St. Louis, in return for an alliance against the Sultan of Aleppo and Damascus. The political situation was in fact very similar to what it had been on the eve of the battle of Gaza, but this time the Christians allied themselves with Egypt. The conditions were practically identical with those granted by Ismail of Damascus in 1244: all Palestine west of Jordan was to be restored to the kingdom of Jerusalem except four fortresses,[3] St. Louis was to be allowed to send his agents into Egypt to search out Christian captives, and the treaty was to last for fifteen years. The allied armies were to effect a junction in May, the Christians advancing to Jaffa, and the Egyptians to Gaza. But the Sultan of Aleppo forestalled his enemies by occupying Gaza with a strong force, so preventing any advance from Egypt. St. Louis however in spite of the fact that his

[1] It must have been the Quarantaine, and not the Septaine, since under the rule of Raymond du Puy, the former was the penalty for striking a blow.

[2] See Joinville's *Chronicle*, pp. 262, 263.

[3] Ibid., p. 265; and Perry's *St. Louis*, pp. 210, [211. The four fortresses were Gaza, Darum, and presumably Nablus and Hebron, as in the treaty of 1244.

little army never exceeded 1,400 men,[1] advanced to Jaffa, where he spent a year in refortifying the town. The Sultan Aybek courteously invited him to make the pilgrimage to Jerusalem, but the French king following the precedent set by King Richard Coeur-de-Lion declined to do so, lest his example should influence other kings in the future to be content with making the pilgrimage, instead of reconquering the city.[2]

The Caliph of Baghdad, in terror of a fresh advance of the Mongols, now intervened to make peace between the two Sultans, and En-Nasir of Aleppo having failed in a fresh attack upon Egypt, in April 1253 came to terms with the Sultan Aybek, ceding to him Palestine west of Jordan, and withdrew his forces to Damascus. St. Louis' new treaty with Egypt, still unratified, thereupon fell to the ground and is heard of no more, but a great multitude of captives had been released, including over 3,000 men, of whom some had been many years in bondage.[3] On its way north the Syrian army, 30,000 strong, plundered Sidon, and massacred 2,000 of its inhabitants, but made no attempt against the citadel. On 29 June St. Louis marched north to restore the fortifications of Sidon, detaching a strong force against Bélinas (Banyas), which was sacked by way of reprisals. Eight months were spent in fortifying Sidon, where St. Louis' work can still be seen, and then after a visit to Tyre, the king returned to Acre. It had long been evident that there was no enthusiasm left in Europe for this unfortunate crusade; even in France the only sign of real interest was an outbreak of religious revivalism amongst the peasantry in 1251, resembling in certain respects the Children's Crusade, and known as the Shepherds' Crusade,[4] which became so tumultuous and violent in its manifestations that it had to be put down by force. The Queen Regent had died in November 1252, the king was now badly needed in France, and after concluding a treaty of peace with the Sultan of Aleppo and Damascus for two years and six months, St. Louis embarked at Acre for Europe on 24 April 1254, leaving Geoffrey de Sergines with a hundred knights as his Lieutenant in the Holy Land. In this year the Emperor Condra IV, nominally King of Jerusalem since 1243, died and was succeeded by his son Conrad, more generally known as Conradin and still only a child. The year before King Henry I of Cyprus had also died, and been succeeded by his son Hugh II an infant in arms, who like his

[1] See Joinville's *Chronicle*, p. 271.

[2] Ibid., p. 275.

[3] See Perry's *St. Louis*, p. 209.

[4] The leader of the Shepherds' Crusade was an Hungarian monk, identified by some as the Stephen, who had led the Children's Crusade forty years before. He claimed that he was sent by the Virgin Mary to call upon the shepherds and countryfolk to rescue the Holy Sepulchre from the infidel, and that she would grant success to the humble and weak, where strong and mighty armies had failed owing to their sinfulness.

father took the title of 'Lord of the kingdom of Jerusalem', so long as the rightful king should be absent. But none of these changes made any actual difference, for none of the people concerned exercised any real authority in the Latin kingdom of Jerusalem.

There was now a definite treaty of peace with Damascus, but relations with Egypt were governed by the Treaty of Damietta, which had almost been cancelled by subsequent negotiations. However, in 1256 the treaty was renewed for a further ten years and ten months,[1] and then with peace finally assured to them the Christians of the Holy Land could find no better way of utilizing it, than to plunge once more into a ferocious civil war, in accordance with what might almost be called their invariable custom. The commercial rivalry of the Italian republics of Genoa, Pisa and Venice, who had long monopolized the trade between Europe and the Levant, was the cause of the war. The relations between Genoa and Venice had been greatly embittered by the increasing predominance of the latter since her conquest of Constantinople in 1204. In Acre the Venetian and Genoese colonies held the church of St. Saba in common, in 1256 a quarrel over its ownership, accompanied by serious rioting and bloodshed, brought things to a head, and a war followed, which lasted for nearly twenty years. The Pisans joined the Genoese, all the barons of the Holy Land became involved, the new Prince of Antioch, Bohemond VI, favoured the Venetians, and so did the Count of Jaffa, chief of the great House of Ibelin. But Philip de Montfort, Lord of Tyre and Toron, supported the Genoese, and took the opportunity to expel their rivals from Tyre, where they held inconvenient privileges, and owned one-third of the city. The family of Lembriac, Lords of Gibelet, also supported the Genoese, because of their hatred for the Prince of Antioch, and even the military Orders were unable to maintain complete neutrality, the Hospitallers supporting the Genoese, and the Templars the Teutonic Knights and the Orders of St. Lazarus and St. Thomas supporting the Venetians. The war raged all along the coast of Syria, by sea and land, thousands lost their lives, and fortifications intended as a protection against the common foe, were uselessly damaged or destroyed. Whilst the Christians were thus madly tearing themselves to pieces, revolutions were taking place in Egypt and Asia that were to settle their future for ever.

In the midst of all this welter of confusion and bloodshed and folly, William de Chateauneuf died. He was still probably ruling over the Hospital as late as February 1258, but even that is not quite certain,[2] and he must have died soon afterwards. Nominally he had been Master of the Hospital for the unusually long period of sixteen years, but of the first eight years no fewer than six had been spent as

[1] See Stevenson's *Crusaders in the East*, p. 332.
[2] See *Les Hospitaliers en Terre Sainte*, p. 201.

a prisoner of war in Cairo, and it is only on the last eight years of his reign that he can be judged. The official chronicler is not of much assistance to us; he tells us that he was an example of upright conduct, and of many and courageous activities, and then goes on to attribute to him an incident that can only have belonged to Garin de Montaigu.[1] Just before his release from prison in 1250, a house for the sisters of the Hospital was founded at Alguayre in Catalonia in the district of Lerida, which exists to the present day.[2] There were the usual acquisitions of property, particularly in Syria, where after the failure of the Sixth Crusade there became visible a gradually increasing tendency on the part of landowners to dispose of their property to the military Orders. The most important acquisition was the fortified monastery of Mount Tabor, belonging to the Benedictines, but long completely ruined by the Saracens. The monastery with all its possessions was granted to the Hospitallers in 1255 by Pope Alexander IV, on condition that they refortified it, and stationed forty knights in garrison there, and also made provision for the dispossessed Abbot and monks.[3] Mount Tabor was the frontier fortress protecting Nazareth, and was to fulfil the same rôle in southern Galilee as the Templar fortress of Safed in northern Galilee; a certain knight called Joscelin was appointed its Castellan. A year later in 1256 the Benedictine nunnery of St. Lazarus at Bethany was also conferred upon the Hospitallers with all its possessions,[4] on condition that provision was made for the Abbess Philippa and her nuns, but there seems no military reason for this transfer, since the nunnery was in Saracen territory, and the transfer was cancelled five years afterwards.[5] Just before his death William de Chateauneuf was able to settle the outstanding question of the expenses of the defence of Ascalon. When the Hospitallers took over the responsibility for its defence from the Emperor in 1243, it was on the understanding that the cost should be refunded to them. The question had now dragged on for nearly ten years after its loss, but in 1257 William de Chateauneuf at last came to a final settlement with John d'Ibelin, Count of Jaffa and Ascalon, to whom the now unfortified town belonged.[6]

[1] See Appendix B at the end of this work.

[2] The House of Alguayre was transferred to Barcelona in 1699, and recently to San Gervasio de Cassolas near the town. See Delaville Le Roulx's Introduction to the *Cartulaire-Général*, p. 224 (1894).

[3] See *Cartulaire-Général*, Vol. II, No. 2,726.

[4] Ibid., No. 2,781.

[5] Ibid., Vol. III, No. 2,993.

[6] Ibid., Vol. II, No. 2,845.

CHAPTER XIV

THE MOSLEM COUNTER-ATTACK AND THE REFORMS OF HUGH REVEL

THE successor of William de Chateauneuf was Hugh Revel, the Grand Commander, long one of the most prominent of the Bailiffs of his Order. In 1243 he was Castellan of Le Crac, an appointment which he resigned in 1248, presumably to take charge of the Convent, when John de Ronay, the Lieutenant-Master, joined St. Louis in Cyprus. After the death of John de Ronay in the second battle of Mansourah, it seems almost certain that he must have been acting as Lieutenant-Master until the release of William de Chateauneuf, who appointed him Grand Commander. Hugh Revel, the Reformer as he was afterwards called, was a Frenchman from Dauphiné, and a man of quite unusual capacity and strength of character. His long reign is remarkable for a series of such important and far-reaching reforms as to influence the whole subsequent history of the Order. So impressed was the Abbé Vertot with his personality that he made the mistake of thinking that it was Hugh Revel, who obtained from the Pope for the heads of his Order the title of Grand Master, a mistake in which he is followed by Boisgelin.[1] But the Masters of the Hospital did not receive the official title of Grand Master until long after the loss of the Holy Land.

Almost at the moment that Hugh Revel was elected Master of the Hospital, but whether just before or just after the election we cannot tell, the war between the Genoese and the Venetians came to a head so far as Syria was concerned. In June 1258 the Hospitallers and the troops of Philip de Montfort, Lord of Tyre, were waiting in the outskirts of Acre for the arrival of a Genoese fleet to give them control of the city. The Genoese with 50 galleys arrived off Acre on the 24th; they were at once engaged by the 40 Venetian galleys already there, and severely defeated with a loss of 1,700 men. The Genoese colony was then expelled from Acre, and took refuge at Tyre. The success of the Venetians left their ally the Prince of Antioch free to attack his enemy the Lord of Gibelet. He was assisted by the Tem-

[1] See Vertot, *Les Chevaliers de Malthe*, Book III, and Boisgelin's *Ancient and Modern Malta*, Vol. II, pp. xxi, xxii.

FR GARIN DE MONTAIGU

FR. HUGH REVEL

THE MASTER'S SEAL IN WAX

From Casts in the Museum of the Order at Clerkenwell

plars, and opposed by the Hospitallers, the old enemies of his house, and the Lord of Botron. This little war was ended by the death of Bertrand of Gibelet, who was murdered in the environs of Tripolis by the agents of the Prince of Antioch.[1] But it resulted in a terrible conflict between the Hospitallers and Templars, whose ancient rivalries and animosities had been excited to fever heat by the civil war. The Templars, with the Knights of St. Lazarus and the Knights of St. Thomas Acon, made a united attack upon the Hospitallers, and a pitched battle between the military Orders followed. The Hospitallers were completely successful in this disgraceful affair, and killed every knight of the three Orders present except one Templar, who alone got away to tell the tale.[2] But the Templars are likely to have given as good as they received, and the Hospitallers must have lost very heavily. The Convent of the Templars was so depleted that a General Citation was issued to their priories in Europe, summoning out to the East all available brethren. It was the worst clash that had ever taken place between the two great Orders, and it was mercifully the last. The Hospitallers in their new Master, Hugh Revel, had a strong man at their head, and the Templars also had a recently elected Master in Thomas Berard an Englishman, and between them they prevented this miserable conflict from having any further evil results. A new treaty was made between the Hospitallers, the Templars and the Teutonic Knights on 9 October 1258, under the terms of which all disputes in Syria, Cyprus and Armenia were to be submitted to arbitration,[3] and this appears to have marked the end of the civil war in what was left of the kingdom of Jerusalem.

Ever since Jenghiz Khan crossed the Oxus in 1220, and carried fire and sword through northern Persia, the dire menace of the Mongol fury had hung like a dark cloud over all Western Asia. Now the second Mongol storm had burst, and all the land lay trembling under the blood-dripping sword of Hulagu Khan. In 1251 the celebrated Mangu Khan had succeeded to the throne of his mighty ancestor, and to commemorate his accession decreed two great military expeditions, one against China under his brother Kubilai Khan, whilst Hulagu Khan, his younger brother, was to conduct a campaign in Western Asia. Hulagu Khan did not arrive in Persia until 1256, and first extirpated the parent branch of the pestilent sect of the Assassins at Alamut, south of the Caspian Sea. Then in 1258 he turned upon the Caliphate of Baghdad, and the most revered and time-honoured institution in Islam, comparable only to the Papacy itself, disappeared in such an orgy of bloodshed and horror as has rarely been witnessed in the history of mankind. The plunder of Baghdad lasted an entire

[1] See *Les Hospitaliers en Terre Sainte*, p. 212.
[2] See Vertot, *Les Chevaliers de Malthe*, Book III.
[3] See *Cartulaire-Général*, Vol. III, Nos. 2,902, 3,565.

week, and in the pitiless massacres that accompanied it one million human beings are said to have perished, regardless of age and sex, and the Commander of the Faithful tied up in a sack, was trampled to death under the hoofs of the Tartar horses. The fertile land of Iraq was reduced to a desert, by the destruction of its complicated system of irrigation, and to the present day it has never recovered from the terrible visitation of Hulagu Khan.

Meanwhile in Egypt there had been a palace revolution the year before the fall of Baghdad. The Sultan Aybek desired to take unto himself a new wife, but to this the imperious Sheger-ed-durr had the strongest objections. She had no intention of seeing a rival installed in the harem, and enticing her husband into the Citadel, she had him murdered in his bath. In the confusion that followed she fell into the power of the Sultan's first wife, whom she had forced him to divorce. That injured lady ordered her slave-girls to beat Sheger-ed-durr to death with their wooden clogs, and the naked body of one of the most remarkable of Moslem women, the saviour of Egypt, was flung into the castle ditch to be devoured by dogs like Jezebel of old.[1] The Sultan Aybek was succeeded by his son Ali, a boy of 15, and then two years later in November 1259, when the armies of Hulagu Khan were concentrating on the Euphrates, the Emir Kutuz, a Chorasmian Turk, grimly remarking that it was no time for boy-puppets and that Egypt had need of a fighting king, installed himself on the throne of Saladin.

The long-expected invasion of Syria began at the end of 1259. Hulagu Khan was called back to Central Asia by the disorders that followed on the death of his brother Mangu Khan, and the Mongol host was placed under the command of his lieutenant, Ketbogha. The power of the Sultan En-Nasir of Syria collapsed before the storm like a house of cards. Aleppo was occupied at the beginning of 1260, Damascus was taken on 1 March, though its citadel held out until the summer, and the invaders swept through Syria up to the frontiers of Egypt. The invasion was accompanied by all those ghastly horrors that made of Mongol warfare a thing of unspeakable terror even in that iron age of brutal cruelty. The Christian states, which had long been angling for Mongol support against the enemies of their faith, suffered equally with their Moslem neighbours, and were reduced to appealing to Egypt for assistance.[2] The Sultan Kutuz at the head of the Egyptian army entered Palestine on 10 August, and the Mongols concentrated at Ain Jalut in the historic plain of Megiddo. Here on 3 September the decisive battle was fought that saved Syria. The Mongols suffered an overwhelming disaster, Ketbogha their general was slain, and the victorious Sultan of Egypt driving his enemies out of Syria, was able to reunite under his own sceptre the entire empire

[1] See Lane-Poole's *Egypt in the Middle Ages*, pp. 260, 261.
[2] See Stevenson, *The Crusaders in the East*, p. 333.

of Saladin. But he did not live long to enjoy the fruits of his glorious victory. Beybars the most powerful of his Emirs demanded the governorship of Aleppo, but was refused an appointment which would inevitably have meant a fresh partition of the now united empire. Probably fearing that he would have to pay for his ambitious request with his life, Beybars assassinated the Sultan on 23 October, and was himself instantly proclaimed Sultan in his place. With the accession of the new Sultan began the great counter-attack against the Christians, which within a generation was to drive them for ever from Syria and the Holy Land.

The Sultan Beybars El-Bundukdari, so frequently spoken of by contemporary Christian writers as Bendocdar, was by birth a Circassian from beyond the Caucasus. A tall ruddy complexioned man with blue eyes, one of them disfigured by cataract, he had originally been a mameluke of the Emir El-Bundukdar 'the crossbowman', from which fact he takes his second name.[1] He first became famous by his great victory at Gaza in 1244, then he saved the army of Egypt from disaster in the battle of Mansourah, and had greatly contributed to the recent victories over the Mongols. As we have seen he had also successfully arranged for the assassination of two of his predecessors. Beybars was by far the greatest of the Sultans of Egypt after Saladin, and stories concerning him are still current amongst the people even to the present day. He completely reversed the policy of the successors of Saladin towards the Latin kingdom of Jerusalem. They had always been content to regard it with a certain toleration as part of the accepted state of affairs, doing their utmost to avoid anything that might provoke fresh crusades. They had even allowed it to extend its narrow boundaries over the lost territory between Tyre and Tripolis, and all the land of Galilee. But the entirely unprovoked attack upon Egypt by St. Louis had greatly exasperated Moslem opinion, and had been followed by a persecution of the Christians in that country, accompanied by the destruction of 115 of their churches.[2] Moreover, the constant efforts of the Latin kingdom to play off the newly-risen Mongol power in Persia and Mesopotamia against the Sultans of Egypt now constituted a danger of the greatest magnitude. For whenever their armies were campaigning in Northern Syria, they were always liable to be attacked in flank by the Christian princes, and to have their communications with their base destroyed. And so the Sultan Beybars, above all things a soldier, ascended the throne of Egypt, with the fixed determination of extirpating the Christian states root and branch.

But before he could take up again the life work of Saladin and resume the Holy War, the new Sultan had first to consolidate his own authority. A rival Sultan had already been proclaimed in Damascus,

[1] See Lane-Poole's *Egypt in the Middle Ages*, p. 263. [2] Ibid., p. 241.

but he was crushed without difficulty in January 1261, and a campaign in northern Syria in the autumn secured the submission of Aleppo. Before leaving the north the Sultan revealed clearly his future policy towards the Christian states by ravaging the territories of Prince Bohemond VI of Antioch, whose principality had long paid tribute to the Mongols. As he passed south on his return to Egypt, the barons of the Holy Land made overtures of peace, and treaties were signed with John d'Ibelin, Count of Jaffa, and with his namesake John d'Ibelin, Lord of Beyrout. But no agreement could be arrived at with the Hospitallers and Templars, and the Sultan gave orders for their lands to be raided. There still remained the question of the Caliphate to be settled, which had been in abeyance since the sacking of Baghdad. El-Mustasim, a refugee of the House of Abbas, had been installed in Cairo as Commander of the Faithful in June 1261, and provided with troops for the recovery of Baghdad. But Beybars apparently distrusting his protégé, abandoned him to his own devices, and he was slain by the Mongols the following year. The new Caliph El-Hakim was definitely established in Cairo, and from that time onwards the Caliphs ceased to be independent, but remained purely spiritual authorities, occupying a position very similar to that of the Patriarchs in Constantinople. In the same year Beybars concluded an alliance with Baraka Khan, who ruled over the Mongols of the Golden Horde beyond the Caucasus, with a view to preventing any intervention in Syria by Hulagu Khan, and the Sultan was now free to prosecute the Holy War.

The Christians of the Holy Land had no illusions as to the storm that was about to burst upon them, and they prepared to face it with a feeling of hopelessness that made defeat inevitable. As usual there was no leader to whom all were ready to subordinate themselves. The nominal King of Jerusalem since the death of Conrad in 1254, had been his young son Conradin, who like his father never even visited his kingdom. The King of Cyprus as next of kin claimed the regency, but King Hugh II was only a child, and such little authority as existed was exercised in his name by his cousin the regent Hugh of Antioch. The Hospitallers and Templars provided the only military force of any importance, and they would submit to no authority other than that of their own Masters. Between them they could put from 2,000 to 3,000 good troops in the field, but beyond that there was nothing but the garrisons of the fortified towns and castles. The Christian states could do nothing but stand on the defensive, and their fortresses from this time onwards fell one by one into the hands of the Moslem conqueror with monotonous regularity until all was lost.

To meet the rising storm a serious effort was made to secure some sort of unity. The Hospitallers and Templars had already settled their differences, and in 1262 Prince Bohemond VI of Antioch signed a treaty of arbitration with the former Order. But the prevailing despair is clearly revealed, when we find the Archbishop of Nazareth disposing of his property in Galilee to the Hospitallers, and Balian d'Ibelin, Lord of Arsuf, transferring his lordship to them in 1261.[1] In the same year Julian of Sidon followed the example of Balian d'Ibelin and handed over Sidon and the Castle of Belfort (Shakif Arnon) to the Templars. To consolidate their position the Templars renounced all claims and rights in the districts of Margat and Valénie, on condition that the Hospitallers made a similar renunciation in the lordship of Sidon.[2]

Beybars began his first campaign against the Christian states in March 1263. As usual the barons of the Holy Land could not rely upon each other's loyalty to their common cause, and the Count of Jaffa on the flank of the enemies' advance, at once abandoned the league, and hastened to ensure his own neutrality by renewing his existing treaty with Egypt.[3] The Sultan established himself at Mount Tabor, and there received envoys from Hugh Revel Master of the Hospital, Thomas Berard Master of the Temple, and the other barons. But he declined to listen to them, overwhelmed them with sarcastic insults, and dismissed them with contempt. The church of Nazareth, one of the most revered in the Holy Land, was then destroyed, all southern Galilee was ruthlessly ravaged, and during the month of April the Sultan carried fire and sword up to the very gates of Acre. Before returning to Egypt he destroyed the strongly fortified monastery of Mount Tabor,[4] which had been in the possession of the Hospitallers since 1255. The garrison normally included 40 knights, but we hear of no resistance having been offered, and it seems probable that Hugh Revel withdrew the garrison, regarding the fortress as untenable in the face of the main Saracen army. It was in fact impossible to defend successfully the inland castles, if the Sultan were determined upon their capture. Their fall was only a question of time, since there was no field army to relieve them. Successful resistance was only possible for the fortresses on the sea-coast, which could be relieved, so long as the Christians continued to retain their command of the sea.

During the following year there were no serious operations, since the Sultan was fully occupied with the internal affairs of his empire, and did not leave Cairo. But there was fighting between the Saracens of northern Syria and King Haithon of Armenia, and in January the Hospitallers and Templars carried out a successful raid towards Ligon (El-Lejjun). During the early spring there was a truce in Palestine, but in April the castle of Shakif Tirun was restored, a source of considerable annoyance to its Christian neighbours. In June the Hospital-

[1] See *Les Hospitaliers en Terre Sainte*, pp. 214, 215. [2] Ibid., p. 217.
[3] See Stevenson, *The Crusaders in the East*, p. 336.
[4] See *Les Hospitaliers en Terre Sainte*, p. 218.

lers and Templars made another successful raid south to Ascalon, and Beybars in retaliation ordered the territory of the Lord of Caesarea, and of the Templars of Chateau Pelerin (Athlit) to be ravaged. November saw another raid of the two military Orders, in which they completely destroyed Beisan, but such warfare could produce no results of any real value, and the hopeless weakness of the Christian cause was again demonstrated to the Moslem world, when the long war between the Venetians and Genoese once more blazed up on the coasts of Syria, and the former actually blockaded the city of Tyre, which was only saved with difficulty by Philip de Montfort its lord.

In 1265 Beybars resumed the Holy War with his accustomed vigour, and delivered the first of that series of crushing blows, which brought the Latin kingdom of Jerusalem tottering to its fall. Before the end of winter and the beginning of the usual campaigning season, the Saracen army suddenly appeared in Palestine. The Sultan had selected Caesarea as his first objective, the city of John l'Aleman, who had married its heiress Marguerite de Layron. A night march brought the Saracens unperceived to the city walls, and at dawn on 26 February Caesarea was surprised and carried by assault. Its citadel held out for a week, and then its garrison escaped under cover of darkness.[1] After destroying the fortifications of the captured city, and plundering Haifa and the territory of Chateau Pelerin, Beybars turned south against Arsuf, now held by the Hospitallers, and opened the siege on 21 March. There were 90 knights in the garrison, the finest fighting men in Europe, all pledged to give their lives for the Christian faith, but the troops serving under them could not be relied upon. The demon of despair had seized upon the Christian population of the Holy Land, they regarded their fate as already sealed, and there was no more fighting spirit left in them. In vain their leaders sacrificed their lives again and again for the holy cause, as noble knights and gallant gentlemen as were ever seen in the East, but not a fortress however impregnable could be trusted to defend itself for more than a month. The knights of the Hospital, the name of their commandant is unknown to us, fell one by one in the defence of Arsuf. By the end of April the Saracens had opened a practicable breach in the walls, and on the 30th the city was stormed. One thousand of the inhabitants took refuge in the citadel, and then surrendered on condition that their lives should be spared.[2] Having utterly destroyed the city and its fortifications and ruined the countryside, in accordance with his usual policy of rendering the conquered territory unfit for reoccupation, Beybars satisfied with the brilliant result of the campaign returned to Cairo.

The Sultan's next blow was to be delivered against the Templars,

[1] See Addison, *The Knights Templars*, pp. 207, 208.
[2] See Stevenson, *The Crusaders in the East*, p. 338.

but he did not begin the campaign until somewhat late in the following year, and only left Cairo on 8 May. Safed, the key to northern Galilee, and one of the strongest fortresses in Palestine, regarded as almost impregnable, had been selected for attack. The campaign opened with a series of demonstrations against the coast towns, whilst a strong force from Homs moved down the south side of the valley of the Eleutherus into the county of Tripolis, and captured the castles of Kulaiat, Halba and Arka.[1] In the middle of June Beybars concentrated his forces at Jacob's Bridge, and on the 30th began the siege of Safed. The castle was one of the most important possessions of the Templars, and had held out for a year and a half against all the forces of Saladin. Strongly fortified, provisioned for at least a year, and with a numerous garrison, we should have expected a long and desperate defence. Instead it fell on 23 July, after a siege of little more than three weeks. We are told that the garrison was embarrassed by the presence of 2,000 refugees in the castle, and no doubt this was the reason for what occurred. The Templars repulsed three assaults, losing heavily in doing so, and then the Commander tamely capitulated, presumably being forced to do so by the mob of refugees. The conditions of the surrender were that the lives of all should be spared, and that they should be sent in safety to Acre. But Beybars, following the Christian doctrine that no faith need be kept with infidels, had no intention of showing mercy. All were given the chance of becoming Moslems, but inspired by the exhortations of the Commander of the Templars, and two Franciscan friars, all but one remained true to the faith, and at sunrise the following morning, 1,500 prisoners were massacred on the hill facing the castle, the Commander and the two friars being first flogged and then flayed alive. Two alone were spared: an Hospitaller, who was sent to Acre to tell the news, and a Templar who was false to his vows, becoming a Moslem and taking service with the Sultan.[2] The capture of Safed was followed by the occupation of Chateauneuf (Hunain) and Ramleh without resistance, and contrary to custom all three places were refortified and garrisoned. Then after a successful autumn campaign in the north against Haithon of Armenia, in which his capital, Sis, was taken and plundered, the Sultan returned in triumph to Egypt.

No sooner had the Egyptian army withdrawn, than the Hospitallers in co-operation with the other military Orders, assisted by reinforcements sent by Hugh of Antioch, Regent of Cyprus, organized what was intended to be a serious raid towards the valley of the Jordan. They probably expected to meet no real resistance in the early stages, but the Moslems warned of the coming raid, unexpectedly sent forward a strong force to intercept the raiders. The expedition had scarcely

[1] See Stevenson, *The Crusaders in the East*, p. 339.
[2] See Addison, *The Knights Templars*, pp. 209, 210.

left Acre on 28 October, before it met with overwhelming disaster.[1] The advance guard apparently pushed too far ahead, never imagining that the enemy was close at hand, and isolated at Carroblier (Tell-el-Kharruba), was surrounded and cut to pieces. Then too late the main body came up, and in its turn suffered a crushing defeat. It is evident that the expedition had been abominably led, and thoroughly deserved the fate that it met. The losses of the Hospitallers were particularly heavy, 45 knights were killed and amongst them Stephen de Meses, the Grand Commander.

The year 1267 saw a lull in the operations, but the castle of Kakun in southern Palestine, between Caesarea and Nablus, was rebuilt by the Saracens and regarrisoned, to hold the Christians in check. On 1 May the Sultan attempted to surprise Acre, and two regiments of horse, one in the uniform of the Hospitallers, and the other in that of the Templars, displaying the respective banners of the two Orders, tried to obtain an entry into the city by the east gate. The ruse was discovered in time, but the Saracens made a horrible slaughter of the helpless civilians living outside the walls.[2] Overtures of peace were now once more made, and Beybars used the opportunity to divide his enemies. A treaty to last for ten years was granted in June to Isabel d'Ibelin the heiress of Beyrout, and to Philip de Montfort of Tyre. The Hospitallers also opened negotiations. Apparently the Master Hugh Revel was anxious to have a treaty to cover his northern possessions, presumably in order to concentrate the strength of the Order in Palestine. Beybars consented to a truce with the Castellans of Le Crac and Margat, but for no definite period and liable to be denounced at any time, on condition that the Hospitallers renounced the tribute paid to them up to now by the Assassins, and by the Emirs of Hama, Shaizar, Famiyah and Boukbis.[3] It meant a serious loss of revenue and prestige for the Hospitallers, and Hugh Revel would never have accepted such terms, if he could have seen any other alternative. Perhaps the reason that he desired to be free from complications in the north, was the war between the Genoese and the Venetians, which was once more afflicting the Holy Land, and in August the Genoese made an unsuccessful attack upon Acre, and fought a naval battle there against their rivals. Even in face of the certain destruction that now overhung their cause, the Christians were still unable to present a united front to their common foe. Their hatred for each other was greater than their hatred for the Moslem.

Next year Beybars delivered a second deadly blow against the

[1] See *Les Hospitaliers en Terre Sainte*, p. 219.

[2] See Addison, *The Knights Templars*, p. 211.

[3] See *Les Hospitaliers en Terre Sainte*, p. 220, but the Emir of Ain-Tab can scarcely have been tributary. Hama paid 4,000 besants a year, Boukbis 800, and the Assassins 200 besants and a heavy tribute of corn.

remnants of the Latin kingdom. After raiding up to the walls of Acre, he suddenly appeared before the city of Jaffa on 7 March 1268. His treaty with John d'Ibelin had expired with the death of the Count in 1266, and had never been renewed with his son and successor Guy d'Ibelin. Jaffa like Caesarea was taken completely by surprise, and carried by assault within a few hours.[1] There was the usual massacre, the city was destroyed, and the historic county of Jaffa and Ascalon in a day had ceased to exist. The Sultan then marched north against Belfort (Shakif Arnon), which was now in the possession of the Templars. It was an exceptionally powerful fortress, and after the Battle of Hattin had defied the mighty Saladin for nearly three years. The town had been invested by the Saracens at the same time as Jaffa, but Beybars did not arrive before it until 6 April. Twenty-six large siege engines were employed to batter its walls, and within nine days of the Sultan's arrival it capitulated. The main defences of Belfort were two citadels, one held by the Templars and the other by native soldiery. The latter abandoned their post after setting fire to it, and the Templars after inflicting heavy losses upon the assaulting columns apparently found the fortress no longer tenable, and had no option but to surrender. The garrison marched out with all the honours of war, and withdrew with the civil population to Tyre.[2] Philip de Montfort of Tyre was so alarmed by the situation, and so despaired of the future that he wrote to St. Louis asking him to confer fiefs in France upon his son and heir, to replace possessions that he foresaw must inevitably be lost before many years were past.

After razing Belfort to the ground, Beybars flushed with victory carried the war into northern Syria. Marching into the county of Tripolis, he ravaged the country-side for the first ten days in May, whilst Prince Bohemond VI, powerless to intervene, could only witness the destruction of his possessions in helpless impotence. Then concentrating at Homs the Sultan suddenly swooped down upon the great city of Antioch, the ancient queen of Syria. The attack was so utterly unexpected that Prince Bohemond was still in Tripolis. Detaching a force to occupy Port Simeon so cutting off the doomed city from the sea, Beybars marched down the valley of the Orontes, arriving before Antioch on 16 May. The governor was killed in a sortie, a series of fierce assaults followed, and on the 19th the Saracens secured a footing on the ramparts, and from thence poured down into the streets. The garrison 8,000 strong, retired into the citadel, and then surrendered on the 21st on condition that the lives of all should be spared.[3] So fell the city of Antioch after a siege of only five days. It was well fortified, it had a numerous garrison, and had held out against the first Crusaders

[1] See Stevenson, *The Crusaders in the East*, p. 340.
[2] See Addison, *The Knights Templars*, p. 212, and Stevenson, p. 340.
[3] See Addison, *The Knights Templars*, pp. 213–16, and Stevenson, p. 341.

for nearly nine months, falling at the last only through treachery. Nothing could reveal more clearly the utter demoralization of the Christians of Syria, they were now a decadent race and there was no more fighting spirit left in them. The plunder was enormous, for Antioch was one of the richest cities in Syria, and its population is said to have been over 100,000. The prisoners were so numerous as to be a positive drug in the slave-market, a strong boy fetching only 12 pieces of silver and a little girl five. Beybars burnt the city to the ground, and from the destruction that he wrought it has never recovered. Antioch, for long one of the most famous cities in the world, is now represented only by a miserable poverty-stricken village.

One ghastly story is told of the sack of Antioch, which closely concerns the Order of the Hospital.[1] There was in the city a convent of the sisters of the Order, which had been recently established there, about the year 1260. It is said that the Mother Superior, when she knew that the city had fallen, called her nuns around her, and warned them what they must expect at the hands of the licentious Moslem soldiery. And then, since even under such circumstances suicide was a sin unpardonable, she showed them the one way of escape, to render their countenances so horrible and loathsome, that the brutal enemy in disgust would slay them instantly, and so send them pure and undefiled to join their Saviour in Paradise. And it is said that these brave sisters of the Order, following the example of their Mother Superior, cut off their noses and tore their cheeks to ribbons with the points of their scissors, and so, horrible to look upon and covered with blood, awaited the glorious crown of martyrdom, which mercifully was not long delayed to them.

This brilliant victory consolidated the power of the Sultan in his northern dominions. The Templars at once evacuated their castle of Gaston (Bagras) and their other fortresses in the now lost principality, whilst the Hospitallers withdrew from the coast town of Zibel (Jabala).[2] King Haithon of Armenia also hastened to make his peace by surrendering Behesna, Darbessac, Raban and other places on the frontier. On his return south Beybars plundered the territories of Philip de Montfort of Tyre, and in July returned to Egypt in triumph from the most successful campaign that he had yet waged. In a few months he had destroyed two of the most important of the Christian states, the county of Jaffa and the principality of Antioch.

During this year of disaster Conradin, the legitimate King of Jerusalem died, after a purely nominal reign of fourteen years. Defeated and taken prisoner by Charles of Anjou, King of Sicily, in the Battle of Tagliacozzo, he was beheaded on 29 October 1268. Like his father

[1] See Boissat de Lixieux, *Histoire de l'Ordre de St. Jean*, edition 1643, Vol. I, p. 47, also Boisgelin, *Ancient and Modern Malta*, Vol. II, Part II, p. 218.

[2] See Stevenson, *The Crusaders in the East*, p. 342, note 6.

Conrad he never visited his kingdom, and never exercised any influence over it. King Hugh III of Cyprus, who had succeeded his cousin the boy-king Hugh II the previous year, was now acknowledged as rightful king of Jerusalem, and was solemnly crowned at Tyre on 21 September 1269. The first coronation to take place in the Holy Land since that of the Emperor Frederick forty years before. But unfortunately the succession to the crown of this moribund kingdom even in its present desperate condition was still a subject for dissension. King Hugh had a rival in his aunt Mary of Antioch, the daughter of the Princess Melisende of Jerusalem, and from this rivalry much mischief was still to arise, for she had the enthusiastic support of the Templars and of those lawless elements in the Holy Land, who objected to any form of discipline or control.

The old crusading spirit had now long been dead in Europe, and there was but little sympathy or interest in the troubles of the Latin colonists in Syria, whose luxury and falseness and lack of fighting spirit were regarded with utter contempt by the hardier aristocracy of the lands beyond the seas. But there still remained one monarch, who had preserved whole and undefiled the noble and glorious ideals of a past age, and that was Louis IX the saintly King of France. He almost alone had never ceased to dream the old dreams of some day rescuing the Holy Sepulchre of his Saviour from the profanation of the infidel, and of re-establishing the Kingdom of God in the Holy Land. Once more he endeavoured to fan into flame the dying embers of religious enthusiasm and fierce fanaticism for a lost cause, which constant disaster and disillusionment had rendered incapable of stirring any longer the deeper emotions of Christendom.

Greatly moved by the disastrous news continually arriving from the Holy Land, after consulting with Pope Clement IV, St. Louis publicly took the cross before the French Parliament in the spring of 1267. His example was followed by his brother Charles of Anjou, King of Sicily, by the Spanish kings, and by Prince Edward of England the heir to the throne of that country, but the princes of Germany deeply resenting the seizure of Sicily by Charles of Anjou, and his subsequent murder of Conradin its rightful king, declined to serve in any expedition which included that monarch. It was realized that the preparations for the Seventh Crusade, and above all the complicated political negotiations required to free so many kings and great nobles for a distant campaign of this nature, would occupy a long period of time, and St. Louis announced that he should not leave for the East until 1270. But there was no real enthusiasm for the crusade, the news of the king's intentions had been received with deep sorrow throughout France, and St. Louis' great friend and devoted admirer the Sire de Joinville expresses his views on the subject in the frankest possible manner: 'I held that all those who advised the king to go on this expedition committed mortal sin'.[1] Of the other reigning monarchs pledged to the crusade, the King of Navarre gave his life for the holy cause, but the most important the King of Sicily, was inspired only by the most sordid of worldly motives, and the Kings of Castile and Portugal made no attempt to fulfil their vows. James the Conqueror, King of Aragon, too impatient to wait, despite the fact that his services had been rejected by the Pope, owing to his sinful life, sailed from Barcelona on 4 September 1268, with 30 ships and 2,800 troops on board. But his fleet was scattered by a storm off Majorca, and he himself wrecked on the coast of Languedoc. Only a handful of the knights of Aragon, under the king's natural son, succeeded in reaching Acre.[2]

The objective of the Seventh Crusade remained in doubt up to the last possible moment. It was naturally assumed that the old plans for the conquest of Egypt would be revived, and that the Latin kingdom of Jerusalem would be re-established in its ancient frontiers, by the occupation of Cairo and the destruction of the power of the Sultan Beybars at its source. But behind the scenes powerful influences were at work to divert the armies of the crusade from their real objective, and to utilize them in the name of religion for the furtherance of the selfish ambitions of one man. St. Louis' brother Charles of Anjou, King of Sicily, a worldly-minded prince devoid of all scruples, was bent upon making the King of Tunis tributary to his crown, and for that purpose the crusade appeared to him a heaven-sent opportunity that must be utilized to the full. Knowing well that religious sentiment was the weak spot in his brother's character, his agents skilfully prepared the mind of St. Louis for an expedition against Tunis. The French King was told that the King of Tunis was ready to become a Christian with all his people, if only the crusade would land in his territory, that he would have the glory of restoring the ancient Church of Africa, that the sea-route to Palestine would thus be made safe, and that a deadly blow would be struck against the power of the Sultan Beybars, who was said to rely greatly upon Tunis for money, military stores, and men and horses.

The French Parliament met at the beginning of 1270, and arrangements were made for a regency. Then in March the king, following the same procedure as at the Sixth Crusade, went to St. Denis to receive the sacred banner of the Oriflamme and his pilgrim's staff, returning to Paris to hear Mass in Notre Dame, before proceeding to Aigues Mortes, where the armies of France were to assemble. But the troops were slow to arrive, there was no enthusiasm for the crusade, and the fleet was not ready to sail until 4 July. The expedition was to concentrate at Cagliari in Sardinia, where St. Louis was joined by

[1] See Joinville's *Chronicle*, p. 320.
[2] See Michaud's *History of the Crusades* (English Edition), Vol. III, p. 30.

his brother the Count of Poitiers and Theobald, King of Navarre. Here a final council of war was held to decide upon the objective, but whilst there was violent opposition to the plans against Tunis on the part of many of the greatest of the French barons, the result was in reality a foregone conclusion, since it was well known that the King of Sicily would not co-operate unless Tunis were the objective, and that without his co-operation the crusade would be a failure.

The French army sailed for Tunis on 18 July, and arrived off the African coast two days later. Disembarking near the ruins of Carthage, they entrenched themselves in a strongly fortified camp, to wait for the arrival of the King of Sicily. It was a fatal decision, the army suffered much from the heat of the African sun, the provisions were of bad quality, the enforced idleness was destructive to discipline, and worst of all dysentery at once seized upon the troops, causing frightful mortality. Amongst the dead were the Papal Legate, and the king's young son Tristan, Duke de Nevers, who had been born at Damietta during the Sixth Crusade. Then on 3 August St. Louis, whose health had long been very fragile, was taken ill, and from the first it was evident that he could not recover. His thoughts dwelt continually upon the Holy War, and the dream of his lifetime—the reconquest of the City of God upon earth. Death came to him on the afternoon of 25 August, in the fifty-seventh year of his age, the last words that he was heard to murmur being: 'O Lord, I shall enter into Thy house, and shall worship Thee in Thy holy tabernacle.'[1] Except for our own King Alfred, there has been no monarch in all history of so noble and beautiful a character as St. Louis; devout though he was, he was no mere monkish saint, but a manly man, a vigorous and capable king, who loved justice and truth above all things. Twenty-seven years later he was canonized by Pope Boniface VIII, and his position in contemporary opinion is worthily summed up in the opening words of the bull of canonization: 'House of France, rejoice at having given to the world so great a prince; rejoice, people of France, at having had so good a king.'[2]

The very day that St. Louis died, his brother Charles of Anjou, King of Sicily, at last arrived, and immediately assumed command of the crusading army. Sincerely grieved though he was at the death of a brother, whom he dearly loved, it did not prevent him from using his position of authority for his own purposes. Active operations were begun against the King of Tunis, and in a series of engagements the European troops showed themselves so immensely superior to the native levies, that the Moslem prince was not long in suing for peace, to the immense disgust of the Sultan of Egypt. The French nobles were already tired of the useless campaign, St. Louis' son and suc-

[1] See Michaud's *History of the Crusades*, Vol. III, p. 46.
[2] Ibid., p. 56.

cessor Philip III was naturally anxious to return to France, and the King of Sicily had secured all that he desired, now that the King of Tunis was prepared to pay him tribute. A truce for ten years was signed on 31 October, under the terms of which the Christians obtained many privileges in Tunis, whilst its king undertook to pay to the King of Sicily 40,000 besants a year, as well as an indemnity of 210,000 ounces of gold. The expedition terminated in a terrible disaster. The army embarked for Trapani in Sicily on 18 November, but just as it was reaching its destination a terrific storm burst, and 18 ships sank with 4,000 troops on board and a great number of horses. Charles of Anjou did his utmost to keep the Crusaders together during the winter, in the hope of inducing them in the spring to repeat the abominable crime of the Fourth Crusade, and to join with him in another attack upon Constantinople. But shortly after his arrival at Trapani the King of Navarre died of dysentery contracted during the campaign, and the King of France and his nobles were determined to return to their native land, salving their consciences by an empty promise to renew the crusade four years hence. With the dispersal of the armies of the Seventh Crusade, the last possibility of restoring the Latin kingdom of Jerusalem was ended, and the only person to benefit from all the blood and treasure wasted on this futile campaign was the astute and unscrupulous King of Sicily.

The real hero of the Seventh Crusade was Prince Edward of England, just as his great-uncle Richard Coeur-de-Lion had been the hero of the Third Crusade. Tall and athletic, of noble and dignified presence, he had proved his worth in the Barons' War, and was now 31 years of age. Inspired by the example of St. Louis, in June 1268 he had taken the cross at Northampton in the presence of the papal legate Ottoboni. He sailed from Southampton for the Mediterranean in August 1270, having with him 300 knights and a fleet of 13 small vessels, and with him went his devoted wife Eleanor of Castile. Calling in at Sardinia he heard of the death of St. Louis, and then sailing to Carthage, arrived in the camp of the Crusaders just after the truce had been signed. So disgusted was he with the obvious lack of sincerity and bare-faced hypocrisy of his fellow Crusaders, that he absolutely declined to take any part in their councils. He spent the winter in Sicily, and in the spring of 1271 he sailed for Acre, the only one of the leaders who kept his vows and did not break his pledged word. He was accompanied by his brother Prince Edmund, and the Count of Brittany, and had with him his own 300 knights, 500 Frisians who placed themselves under his standard, and various small contingents, bringing his total force up to 1,200 men. And that was all the help that the Holy Land ever received from the Seventh Crusade.

Since the capture of Antioch the Sultan Beybars had been compelled by the force of circumstances to refrain from active operations against the Christian states, although the usual border warfare of raids and counter-raids never ceased. In 1269 he made the pilgrimage to Mecca, and the threatening attitude of the Mongols of Persia, who had defeated his ally Baraka Khan of the Golden Horde, caused him considerable anxiety, and compelled him to spend the winter in Syria. He returned to Egypt in the spring to complete his preparations for the expected invasion by the armies of the Seventh Crusade, and only when that threat was removed by the death of St. Louis and the dispersal of the Crusaders, was he free to resume his career of conquest.

The Sultan had always regarded Bohemond VI of Antioch as his chief adversary, since he was the most powerful of the Christian princes, and was capable of being dangerous owing to his alliance with the Mongols. Having deprived him of Antioch, he determined to complete his downfall by the capture of Tripolis. But before he could lay siege to that city it was first necessary to capture the outlying fortresses, Le Crac the great stronghold of the Hospitallers, Château Blanc (Safitha) one of the chief establishments of the Templars in the county, and the castle of Hisn Akkar. The Templars appear to have withdrawn from Château Blanc, doubtless because they regarded its ultimate fall as inevitable, since no relieving force would be available, at any rate the Sultan occupied it without difficulty,[1] and then turned to attack the famous castle of the Hospitallers.

Le Crac, more generally known at the present day as Crac-des-Chevaliers or Kalat-el-Husn, was almost certainly the most powerful fortress in Syria. It had been granted to the Hospitallers as far back as 1142 by Count Raymond I of Tripolis, it was their proudest possession, and for 130 years they had been continually adding to and strengthening its defences, until they had made of it what it still remains, one of the most perfect examples of mediaeval castle-building in existence. Le Crac stood upon a peak overlooking the valley of the Eleutherus, dominating the pass leading through the mountains that divide the county of Tripolis from the Moslem states in the valley of the Orontes. Its strategic position was one of the utmost importance, it was the chief bulwark of the county, and no Sultan not even Saladin himself had yet dared to attack it. The castle like most of the castles of Syria had been greatly damaged by the terrible earthquake of 1202, and the Hospitallers appear then to have completely reconstructed it. Probably the Master Alfonso of Portugal was responsible for the plans adopted. Le Crac, as it was then remodelled, was a concentric castle, having two complete lines of defence, one entirely within the other. In shape it is roughly triangular, with its base the most vulnerable part facing south, and its rounded apex pointing north. We have no knowledge as to who was Castellan of Le Crac at this time, nor as to the strength of its garrison, but it is not

[1] See *Les Hospitaliers en Terre Sainte*, p. 223.

likely to have been inferior to that of Margat, which we know included 200 knights and serjeants and 200 infantry.

The siege of Le Crac [1] began on 18 February, although the Sultan Beybars did not arrive until the 23rd. The first objective of the Saracens was the little town nestling under the castle walls, and this fell on 6 March. On the same day strong reinforcements arrived for the besiegers under the Emir of Hama. With the capture of the town, the Saracens began to get their battering engines into position against the outer defences of the castle, and by 14 March a systematic bombardment had begun. Seven days later on the 20th the outer defences were carried by assault, and it is very evident that the troops serving under the Hospitallers had no great fighting value. Beybars was so elated by his success, that he now had a special post prepared from which he personally might shoot at the garrison. It was perhaps at this time that his esquire Sheikh Osman was killed, whose tomb is in the cemetery close by, where are also buried two of the Emirs killed in the siege.

The defence of the inner walls of the castle was as weak and feeble as that of the outer walls had been. On 30 March, nine days after the outer line had fallen, one of the towers was brought down by the besiegers, and the Saracens swarming forward to the attack, stormed the breach and the castle was won. There appears to have been no very obstinate fighting, and it almost looks as if with the exception of the Hospitallers themselves, the garrison flung down their arms and surrendered. At any rate they were very well treated by the Sultan, who not only spared their lives, but actually set them free, which gives the distinct impression that treachery may have been at work. Such of the Knights of the Hospital as were left retired fighting to the great tower in the midst of the western wall of the inner line, and there prepared to sell their lives as dearly as possible. The Saracens thereupon brought their battering engines into the inner courtyard of the castle, in readiness to demolish the last refuge of the defenders. But the Sultan was anxious to complete the capture of Le Crac with as little damage as possible to its fortifications, and so he sent in to the garrison a forged letter, purporting apparently to come from the Master of the Hospital, and ordering them to surrender. In consequence the Hospitallers opened negotiations with the Sultan, terms of surrender were arranged on 7 April, and the following day they marched out to Tripolis with all the honours of war.

And so Le Crac, the pride of the Hospitallers, a first-class fortress upon which for over a century they had been lavishing enormous sums of money, fell after a siege of only seven weeks. The same fate had befallen its garrison as had befallen the Templars at Belfort and Safed.

[1] The best description of Le Crac, and of the siege, is contained in Rey, *L'Architecture des Croisés en Syrie*, pp. 39–67.

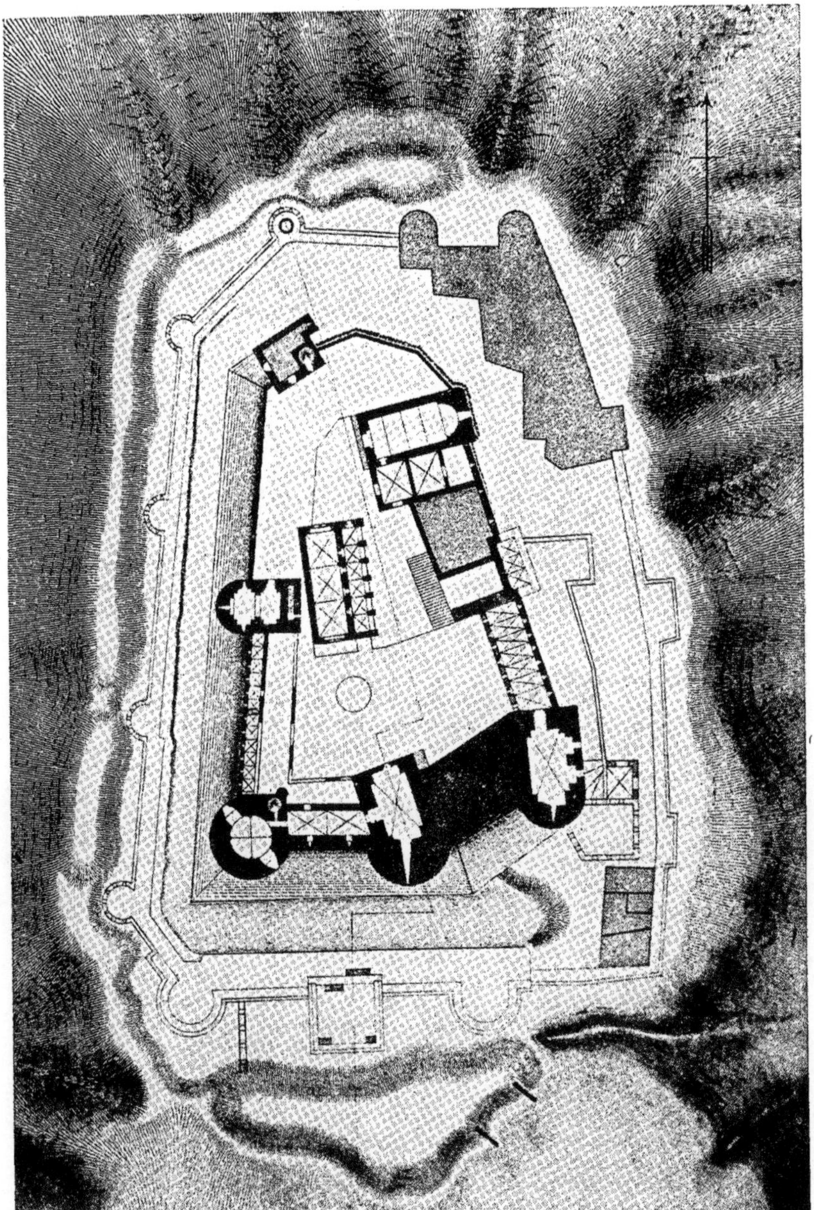

PLAN OF THE CASTLE OF LE CRAC

Upon the courage and honour of the Knights of the Hospital and the Temple no reflection can ever be made, but it was their misfortune to have serving under them troops who had no heart left in them, and upon whose loyalty and fighting spirit no reliance could ever be placed for a single day, when once invested by a besieging army. But it was none the less a dreadful blow to the prestige of the Hospitallers. and one that envelops in an atmosphere of gloom the reign of the Master Hugh Revel, able and capable though we know him to have been.

The Sultan had a peculiar sense of humour, it was his habit to write sarcastic letters of commiseration to his defeated adversaries, and to the Master of the Hospitallers he wrote:

> 'May the Lord include thee amongst the number of those who do not struggle against their destiny, but who fear to offer resistance to the master of Victory! We announce to thee what God has done for us on this occasion. Thou hadst fortified this place, thou hadst entrusted its defence to a picked force of the brethren of thine Order. Well, all that has not been of the slightest assistance to thee, thou hast merely hastened the death of thy brethren, and their death will be thy loss.' [1]

Le Crac was refortified by Beybars as a base of operations against Tripolis, and to commemorate its restoration he placed upon its ramparts the following inscription:

> 'In the name of God, the merciful and compassionate, the repair of this castle has been ordered in the reign of our master the Sultan Beybars, the conquering king, wise and just, the champion of the Holy War, the pious defender of frontiers, the victorious pillar of the world and of the faith, the father of victory.' [2]

From Le Crac the Sultan marched against Hisn Akkar, the last of the ring of fortresses covering Tripolis. He began the siege on 29 April and the castle fell on 12 May. The ground was now cleared for the siege of the great and flourishing seaport of Tripolis, but it was saved from the fate of Antioch by the news that Prince Edward of England had landed at Acre on 9 May. Concluding a treaty of peace for ten years with Bohemond VI, the Sultan marched south to meet this remnant of the Seventh Crusade, and took up a position of observation at Safed. But Prince Edward had not sufficient troops at his disposal to risk an advance against the main Saracen army, and Beybars laid siege to the castle of Montfort or Starkenburg (Kurain), the most important possession of the Teutonic Knights in the East, and a constant threat to the Moslem garrison of Safed. But as usual the native soldiery could not be relied upon, a handful of knights could not hold a great fortress with discontented troops behind them, and on 12 June, after a siege of only seven days, Johann von Sachsen the

[1] See *Les Hospitaliers en Terre Sainte*, p. 223.
[2] See Corder's *Latin Kingdom of Jerusalem*, pp. 392, 393.

Castellan was forced to surrender. The Teutonic Knights had fared no better than their brethren of the Hospital and the Temple. It was the last conquest that Beybars was to make against the Latin kingdom of Jerusalem.

Meanwhile Prince Edward had succeeded in getting together a force of between 6,000 and 7,000 men at Acre, but except for the troops from Europe, their fighting value must have been very low. In the hope of preventing the barons of Cyprus from joining him, the Sultan had sent a fleet against that island, but it was wrecked off the coast in a storm. In June, Prince Edward and King Hugh advanced to Nazareth, probably hoping that Beybars would raise the siege of Montfort, and the Crusaders massacred every Moslem they could find in the town. In July the Sultan was called back to Egypt, and Prince Edward at once carried out a raid to Ramleh and Lydda. The one hope of the Crusaders was to induce the Mongols to attack the Saracens, and their threatening attitude kept the Sultan in northern Syria during the autumn. Taking advantage of the absence of the Egyptian army, the Crusaders made another successful raid to Kakun in November, but were repulsed in an attack on the castle. There was a suspension of hostilities during the winter, and then in the spring serious negotiations for peace were opened. A definite treaty was finally signed on 22 April 1272 to last for ten years, ten months, ten days and ten hours. It secured the rights of Pilgrimage to Jerusalem, Bethlehem and Nazareth, and applied to the city and territory of Acre, that is to all that was nominally under the direct rule of King Hugh of Jerusalem and Cyprus. Treaties had already been concluded between the Sultan and the Masters of the Hospital and the Temple the previous year after the loss of Le Crac and Château Blanc,[1] and also with Prince Bohemond VI and John de Montfort the new Lord of Tyre, whilst other treaties were in existence with the few remaining lordships.

The new treaty was honourably observed by the Sultan, who for the remainder of his reign was sufficiently occupied by his wars against the Mongols and their ally the King of Armenia. But the long war of nine years had almost destroyed the Latin kingdom of Jerusalem, which had lost the city of Antioch, the towns of Jaffa, Caesarea and Arsuf, all the sea-coast south of Mount Carmel, all the land of Galilee, and the great fortresses of Mount Tabor, Safed, Belfort, Le Crac, Château Blanc and Montfort. All the villages and farms had been destroyed, the cultivated lands turned into desert, and no possibility of recovery any longer existed.

Prince Edward remained in the Holy Land all through the summer of 1272, and two months after the signing of the treaty the famous attempt to assassinate him was made. On the evening of 18 June

[1] See Stevenson, *The Crusaders in the East*, p. 343.

a Moslem messenger bearing a letter was admitted to his presence, and as the prince opened it stabbed him with a poisoned dagger. The prince at once kicked him over before he could repeat the blow, causing him to drop the dagger, and seizing it stabbed him to death with it. As soon as his wound had been dressed, he made his will, and summoned to his presence Hugh Revel and Thomas Berard, the Masters of the Hospital and the Temple, to witness it.[1] The popular story is well known of how his life was saved by the devoted love of his wife Eleanor of Castile, who is said to have sucked the poison from the wound. Her action has been picturesquely described by the old chronicler, who says:

> 'When no medicine could extract the poison, she did it with her tongue, licking daily, while her husband slept, his rankling wounds, whereby they perfectly closed, yet she herself received no hurt. So sovereign a medicine is a wife's tongue, anointed with the virtue of lovely affection.'[2]

It has never been certain by whom the would-be murderer had been sent, whether by the Emir of Jaffa or by the Sheikh of the Assassins. The Sultan Beybars indignantly denied any knowledge of the dastardly attempt, and sent a formal embassy of congratulation to the prince on his escape.

As soon as he had recovered from his dangerous wound, Prince Edward left the Holy Land, sailing for Europe on 22 September, and in Sicily he heard of the death of his father, and that he was now King of England. His crusade had been by no means a wasted effort, for if he had been unable to recover any of the lost territories of the Kingdom of Jerusalem, at least by his presence in the Holy Land he had been able to secure a period of peace for what little was left. He was the last European monarch to lead a crusade to the Holy Land, and he left a great reputation behind him, second only to that of his mighty ancestor Richard Coeur-de-Lion. Just as the Latin colonies in Syria a century earlier had always looked hopefully to King Henry II for assistance, so in their despair they were always hoping for fresh intervention by King Edward I, until the end came.

For a moment the possibility of yet another crusade brought fresh encouragement to the Holy Land, when a crusading pope was elected to fill the chair of St. Peter, now vacant for nearly three years, since the death of Clement IV in 1268. There had come out to the East with the Frisian contingent serving under Prince Edward of England, a certain distinguished churchman of Italian birth, Theobald Visconti, Archdeacon of Liége. He had shown such sincere and devoted zeal for the holy cause, as to gain universal confidence, and when in the late autumn of 1271 the news arrived that he had been elected Pope, there was the wildest enthusiasm amongst the Christians of the Holy Land.

[1] See Porter's *Knights of Malta*, Vol. I, p. 155, footnote.

[2] See Conder's *Latin Kingdom of Jerusalem*, pp. 391, 392.

Before leaving Acre for Rome, Gregory X as the new Pope was called, gave a farewell address to the assembled people, promising them that their cause should ever be his first consideration, and his last words to them taken from the 137th Psalm were: 'If I forget thee, O Jerusalem, may I myself be forgotten amongst men'.[1]

On reaching Rome and taking up the reins of his exalted office, Pope Gregory threw himself heart and soul into the cause of the Latin East, and as a first instalment of his promise, a strong reinforcement was sent out at his own expense to the garrison of Acre. The Pope then set to work systematically to organize a fresh crusade, all his influence was brought to bear upon the sovereigns of Europe to maintain peace amongst themselves, and to persuade them to assume the cross, and another great council of the Church was summoned to meet at Lyons in 1274. There were present the Patriarch of Jerusalem, the ambassadors of the Emperors of the East and the West, the envoys of every reigning monarch of any importance, and more than a thousand archbishops and bishops. Amongst those present were the Masters of the Hospital and the Temple, Hugh Revel and William de Beaujeu, who had succeeded Thomas Berard the previous year. It is interesting to notice that at the council the Masters of the Hospital and the Temple were given precedence above the Cardinals and ambassadors, immediately after reigning monarchs.[2] The Council of Lyons in accordance with the wishes of the Pope solemnly decreed a fresh crusade for the restoration of the kingdom of Jerusalem, and Rudolph of Hapsburg, now recognized by the Pope as the rightful Emperor of the West, undertook to lead the armies of Europe to the Holy War. But nothing came of it all, the age of universal crusades had long passed away, the Pope alone was sincere, and when he died in 1276, nothing more was heard of the project. The fate of the Latin kingdom of Jerusalem had ceased to be of serious interest to Europe.

There had been peace in the Holy Land since the Treaty of 1272, not because the Sultan had the slightest intention of keeping his word, but because he was too much occupied elsewhere. The only move he ever again made against the Christians was in 1275, when he seized the castle of Kusair, the residence of the Latin Patriarch of Antioch, who had abandoned his flock in the hour of trouble, and now met the death he had formerly evaded.[3] In 1273 Beybars completed his conquest of the Assassins, so long the terror of Syria, and reduced them to a harmless religious sect of somewhat peculiar tenets. Then followed another war with the Mongols, which culminated in a great victory at Abulusteyn in the spring of 1277, and the temporary occupation of Caesarea in Asia Minor. A few weeks later on 1 July, the

[1] See Michaud's *History of the Crusades*, Vol. III, p. 59.
[2] See Taaffe's *History of the Order of St. John of Jerusalem*, Vol. II, p. 176.
[3] See Michaud's *History of the Crusades*, Vol. III, p. 19.

great Sultan, 'the father of victory', now at the height of his power, died suddenly at Damascus, through accidentally drinking a cup of poison, that he had prepared for one of his Emirs.[1] His end was curiously typical of the man, for though a brave, wise and capable monarch, he was utterly unscrupulous, false and brutal, he prided himself on his powers of deception, and his word and his oath were alike devoid of the slightest value, yet he was loyal to those who served him well, and was a popular Sultan, whose bravery and generosity are remembered in the East to the present day. He was the most dangerous enemy the Christians had known since the death of the noble and chivalrous Saladin.

A few weeks before the Sultan's sensational end, Hugh Revel died in the Convent at Acre, after ruling over the Hospital for the unusually long period of nineteen years. It was his destiny to be set over his Order during stormy times, when disaster followed upon disaster in rapid succession, without one single ray of light, and the holy cause was already obviously lost beyond hope of redemption, for which the Hospitallers had laboured and suffered and died for so many weary years. He had had to relinquish Mount Tabor, Arsuf had been lost with heavy casualties, the tribute received from the Assassins and other Moslem states had been given up, Zibel (Jabala) had been evacuated, and worst of all Le Crac, the pride of the Hospitallers, had surrendered to the infidel under circumstances that had brought no credit to the Order, however unavoidable that surrender might have been.

But none the less Hugh Revel has ever been regarded as one of the greatest of the Masters of the Hospital in the Holy Land. In a time of unrelieved gloom, he had never despaired of his Order, he had kept at bay the demoralization that might well have seized upon it, and during his long reign he strengthened and completely revised its administration, so that to future generations he was always known as 'the Reformer'.[2] Between 1262 and 1270 the Chapter-General of the Order met at Acre on no fewer than six occasions to discuss and approve the reforms of their Master. The great bulk of these reforms were for the purpose of restoring and maintaining discipline, which was evidently showing signs of breaking down under the strain of continual misfortune and failure. There had evidently also been a serious decline in the class of recruits admitted to knighthood in the Order, for Hugh Revel thought it necessary to define clearly and precisely in a new statute [3] the qualifications necessary for knights in

[1] See Lane-Poole's *Egypt in the Middle Ages*, p. 272.

[2] See *Les Hospitaliers en Terre Sainte*, p. 229.

[3] See Statutes of the Order, Title II, Para. 17. This Statute was still more closely defined in the first half of the sixteenth century by the Grand Master John d'Homèdes, in a new Statute, XIX, 37, which runs, 'The term Parent,

future. 'Such as desire to be admitted knights, must prove by authentic evidence that they are born of parents noble both by name and arms.' So runs the new statute of Hugh Revel. From this time onwards, any candidate for admission as a knight had to show that on both his father's and his mother's side he was entitled to bear arms. At a later date such knights, since they were duly qualified, were known as Knights 'of Justice', to distinguish them from those few, who not being so qualified, were occasionally admitted none the less by favour, and were therefore termed Knights 'of Grace'. These distinctions, which have their origin in this new statute of Hugh Revel, have always been rigidly observed in the Order down to the present day.

With this effort to improve the standard of recruiting for knighthood in the Order, must be associated the Bull of Pope Alexander IV of 1259, granting a special distinctive dress for the Knights, whether in the Convent or on active service. Until this time all the brethren of the Order, knights, chaplains and serving brothers alike, had worn the black monastic *cappa clausa,* with the white eight-pointed cross upon the breast. And they had worn this garment not only in the Convent, but also over their armour, when on active service, as we know from the Bull of Pope Innocent IV of 1248,[1] which granted to the brethren the right to substitute for the *cappa clausa* over armour a wide surcoat similar no doubt to that worn by lay knights, but presumably of the same colour as before, since no change of colour is mentioned. But apparently from the wording of the Bull of Pope Alexander IV,[2] the Knights strongly resented having to wear the same dress as their humbler brethren. Accordingly the Pope now sanctions for them a special dress of their own, a black mantle to be worn in the Convent, to distinguish them from the other brethren, and a red surcoat with a plain white cross, of similar design to their Standard, to be worn over armour on active service. Some twenty years earlier the Master Bertrand de Comps had given the finishing touch to the militarization of the Order, by granting the knights precedence over the clerics, and this new rule sanctioning for them a distinctive dress, to be worn by them alone, was but its logical development and the outward visible sign of the absolute predominance of the Knights in their Order. But the rigid application of this new rule was found to be undesirable for various reasons, and in a Chapter-General held the year after Hugh Revel's death, permission was given for the Serjeants or

in the proofs of the Brother Knights, takes in the father, mother, grandfather and grandmother on both the father's and the mother's side,' so insisting upon four quarterings of coat armour. Certain nations were not even content with this, and the Germans insisted upon sixteen quarterings, the French upon eight, and the Italians upon four quarterings each of 200 years' standing.

[1] This Bull is printed in the Appendix at the end of this chapter.

[2] Ibid.

Serving Brothers-at-Arms to wear the red surcoat in time of war, and a black mantle was authorized for all the brethren.

Not the least important amongst the reforms of Hugh Revel are those concerning finance. The Order depended for its revenue mainly upon the produce of its great estates scattered all over Europe, now that its once rich possessions in the East were being rapidly lost beyond hope of recovery. Each Commander was supposed to send the whole of the revenue of his Commandery, known as 'Responsions', to his Prior for transmission to the Convent, after deducting only what was absolutely necessary for the support of his establishment. In theory this system would provide the maximum possible revenue, provided always that the Commanders were strictly conscientious in the performance of their duties. In practice it was quite unsound, for it took no account of human nature. Different Commanders would necessarily have different standards as to what was absolutely necessary for the support of their establishments, and it was quite certain that all were not likely to be equally conscientious in the performance of their duties. By this time the system had broken down, and the Order had no fixed definite revenue from Responsions, upon which it could rely. Hugh Revel completely changed the system by laying down that Commanders must in future pay over a certain fixed proportion of their revenues as Responsions.[1] The sum was generally calculated at one-third of the gross receipts. In these financial reforms the moving spirit was probably the Englishman Joseph de Cancy, the Treasurer of the Order. He came of a distinguished family holding lands in Yorkshire and Lincolnshire, and tracing back its origin to the days of King Stephen.[2] Joseph de Cancy must have been one of the most experienced financial administrators that the Order ever had, for he held the office of Treasurer from 1248 until his appointment to be Prior of England in 1273, and returned again to the East seven years later to resume his old office in the Convent.

There are conflicting statements as to the exact date of the death of Hugh Revel the Reformer. But probably he died in May 1277, since he was known to have been still alive in April, and his successor had been elected by August.[3] The ancient chronicle of the Order[4] speaks of his administration in the highest possible terms and since it represents the opinion current in the Order only two generations later, its value can scarcely be questioned. In the words of this chronicle:

[1] See Vertot, *Les Chevaliers de Malthe*, Book III.

[2] The head of the house was the Baron of Skirpenbeck in Yorkshire. See *A Crusader's Letter from the Holy Land*, pp. 5, 6, in Volume V of the Library of the Palestine Pilgrims Text Society. In King Edward's letter printed on p. 14 he is called by the modern form of his name, Joseph de Chauncy.

[3] See *Les Hospitaliers en Terre Sainte*, p. 228.

[4] The Chronicle of the deceased Masters', printed in Appendix B at the end of this work.

'He was a man remarkable for the soundness of his judgement and his capacity, and he placed the affairs of the House on a sound basis. For the other Masters, his predecessors, had made no reforms, but had merely maintained the good customs of the House. But he laid down everything afresh, not only by codifying the Statutes of others, but by ordaining new and useful Statutes of his own.'

APPENDIX

DOCUMENTS RELATING TO THE DRESS OF THE ORDER

1. Bull of Innocent IV defining the form of the Surcoat

Dated 1 *July* 1248

Innocent, Bishop, servant of the servants of God, to the Master and Brethren of the House of the Hospital of Jerusalem, greeting, and apostolic benediction. A humble petition has been made to us on your behalf that we would of our pity have a care to provide for you a remedy for the fact that when you are wearing the *cappa clausa* over your armour, which hampers both your hands and your arms, it makes it easier for your enemies in attacking you, and more difficult for you in defending yourselves. Being desirous therefore of acceding to your petition, we by these presents grant you this indulgence, that when it shall so happen that you are dwelling in or passing through suspect places, it shall be lawful for you to wear wide surcoats, bearing upon the breast the sign of the cross. Therefore let no one, etc. Given at Lyons on the Calends of July in the 6th year of our Pontificate.

2. Bull of Alexander IV granting a distinctive dress to the Knights [1]

Dated 11 *August* 1259

Alexander, Bishop, servant of the servants of God, to our beloved sons the Master and Brethren of the Hospital of St. John of Jerusalem, greeting and apostolic benediction. Whereas the Lord Almighty has built up your Order upon the foundation of obedience, as an immovable pillar in His Church, for the defence of the Holy Land, of which you are the renowned and stalwart champions, and the chosen protectors, and for the defence of which you have girded yourselves with the glorious armour of the cross of salvation, to fight the battles of the Lord against the blasphemers of His Name; and whereas you are the elect people of God, a princely race and earnest congregation, a council of righteous men and a gathering of mighty men of the King of kings, in whose hands verily are two equal swords and burning lights, to execute vengeance upon the nations and to protect the city of the Lord; so therefore we intend to strengthen with suitable gifts and to encourage with worthy favours,

[1] This translation, with slight modifications, is taken from Porter's *Knights of Malta*, Vol. I, Appendix 8.

your Order and yourselves also, who are the soldiers of Christ, in whom the Lord has aroused in those parts the spirit of the mighty Maccabees and of other similar warriors of old, and to grant to you such things as are known to redound to the advancement of your Order, and the protection of the Holy Land.

Since it has come to our knowledge that amongst the brethren of your Order, both Knights and others, there is no distinction or diversity of dress, contrary to the usual custom in most other similar institutions, on which account it comes to pass that the love of many brethren of noble birth grows cold, who casting aside the temptations of the world, under the habit of your Order, have chosen to devote their lives to the defence of the Holy Land: we therefore being earnestly desirous that your Order, by God's help, may still continue to be enriched with fresh donations, and may grow and increase in the votive offerings which it shall receive, do hereby grant to you by the authority of these presents, permission to decree unanimously and hereafter to maintain inviolate this rule, that the Knights, who are brethren of your Order, shall wear black mantles, in order that they may be distinguished from the other brethren of the said Order. In war however and in battle they shall wear jupons and other military surcoats, which shall be of a red colour, having sewn upon them a white cross, exactly as upon your Standard, so that thus by the uniformity of outward signs the identity of your souls may be easily apparent, and that in consequence the safety of your persons may be ensured. Therefore let no one infringe upon this Statute of our concession. For if anyone shall presume upon such an attempt, let him know that he will fall under the indignation of Almighty God, and of his blessed apostles, Peter and Paul. Given at Anagnia, on the 3rd day before the Ides of August, in the 5th year of our Pontificate.

CHAPTER XV

THE FALL OF ACRE AND THE LOSS OF THE HOLY LAND

THE successor of Hugh Revel was Nicholas le Lorgne, Commander of Tripolis, who had been Castellan of Margat as far back as 1250,[1] and must therefore have been a man of advanced years. He came apparently of a Provençal family,[2] but nothing else is known of his origin, and the older writers were not even certain of the correct form of his name, both the Abbé Vertot and Boyssat de Lixieux making the mistake of calling him Lorgue. During the twelve years immediately preceding his election as Master he had been holding the most important offices in the Order, he had been appointed Marshal of the Hospital in 1266, Grand Commander in 1271, Marshal again in 1273, and in 1275 Commander of Tripolis.

Nicholas le Lorgne succeeded to his high office in the midst of the profound peace which had reigned between Christian and Moslem ever since the treaty with the Sultan Beybars in 1272. It was the last period of peace and security that the Latin colonies were to know, before their final expulsion from the Holy Land. But they could find no better use for it than to resume the bitter quarrels and strife, which had been their curse for nearly a hundred years, and had done more than anything else to ruin their cause. Mary of Antioch, King Hugh's aunt, had never ceased to prosecute her claims to the throne of Jerusalem.[3] Urged on by the Templars, who hated the king, she had appealed unsuccessfully to Rome, and now early in 1277 sold her so-called rights to Charles of Anjou, King of Sicily. Meanwhile the Templars had stirred up so much trouble for the king in Acre, that he had withdrawn to Cyprus the previous year, disgusted with the continual intrigues and turbulence that poisoned the life of the city. The King of Sicily was not long in making good his claims to the kingdom

[1] See *Les Hospitaliers en Terre Sainte*, p. 230.

[2] See Harot, 'Essai d'armorial des Grands-Maîtres', p. 15. That his name is le Lorgne is clear from his letters to King Edward I of England, printed in the *Cartulaire-Général*, Vol. III, Nos. 3,766, 3,781.

[3] Mary of Antioch claimed to be the nearest relative to the late King Conradin, as the daughter of the Princess Melisende, third daughter of Queen Isabella. King Hugh claimed to be the rightful heir to the throne as grandson of the Princess Alice, second daughter of Queen Isabella.

THE GREAT SEAL OF FR. NICHOLAS LE LORGNE

THE GREAT SEAL OF THE CONVENT

of Jerusalem, and on 7 June 1277 a Sicilian fleet of six galleys under Roger de San Severino, Count of Marsico, sailed into the port of Acre. King Charles was duly proclaimed King of Jerusalem, and the Count of Marsico taking possession of the citadel and driving out the followers of King Hugh, assumed the duties of regent. After a period of hesitation, during which King Hugh made no effort to assert his rights, the barons of Syria including Bohemond VII of Tripolis, reflecting that a powerful and ambitious monarch like the King of Sicily was more likely to be of real assistance to them than the King of Cyprus, decided to take the oath of allegiance to King Charles. The following year King Hugh landed at Tyre with 700 knights, and attempted to get into touch with his supporters in Acre. But he could accomplish nothing, and after a few months returned to Cyprus, contenting himself with a formal protest at the court of Rome against the conduct of the King of Sicily. He took his revenge however upon the Templars, who were the real cause of all the trouble, by confiscating their lands in Cyprus. The Hospitallers following their usual policy had preserved an attitude of strict neutrality to the great annoyance of the King of Sicily.

Tripolis like Acre was equally torn by internal strife. Count Bohemond VI had died in 1275, leaving his widow Sibyl of Armenia as regent for their young son another Bohemond, duties in which she was to be aided by Bartholomew, Bishop of Tortosa, an able and respected prelate. But the Countess Sibyl was detested by her mother-in-law the Dowager Countess Lucia, widow of Bohemond V, a Roman woman, who endeavoured to get the power into her own hands by placing herself at the head of the numerous Italian residents, a policy in which she was vigorously assisted by her brother Paul, Bishop of Tripolis. The Templars as usual could not refrain from intervening, and took the side of the Dowager Countess and the Italian party, who were also supported by the most powerful baron in the county, Guy de Lembriac, Lord of Gibelet (Jubail). A bitter civil war followed, causing widespread ruin. Eventually Bohemond VII, who had now attained his majority, drove the Bishop of Tripolis out of the country, and in 1282 captured Gibelet, so putting an end to this senseless conflict, and Guy de Lembriac was thrown into prison, where he died.[1]

Meanwhile in Egypt the Sultan Beybars had been succeeded by his eldest son Es-Said, a weak, pleasure-loving lad of nineteen, who was contemptuously pushed aside by his Emirs two years later. His young brother Selamish, aged 7 years, nominally reigned for one hundred days, and then in 1279 the regent Kalawun, a Turk from beyond the Caucasus, seized the throne. Five months later a rival Emir Sunkur-el-Ashkar proclaimed himself Sultan in Damascus, and appealed to the Mongols for assistance. Kalawun struck quickly

[1] See Stevenson, *The Crusaders in the East,* p. 348.

and in June 1280 defeated his rival at El-Gesura near Damascus, and captured that city. The Mongols did not cross the Euphrates until the autumn, and in October seized Aleppo. The Christian states at once entered upon negotiations with them for a joint campaign the following year, and the Hospitallers opened hostilities against the Saracens by a raid from their great fortress of Margat.

At the head of 200 knights and serjeants the Castellan rode south for the Valley of the Eleutherus, and the road to Homs, plundering and ravaging on every side. Then as the enemy began to gather in force to oppose him, he turned home again laden with booty. A great horde of Turcoman horse, which with their customary exaggeration the Christian writers estimated to be 5,000 strong, followed hard upon his heels. From Château Blanc (Safitha) onwards the pursuers pressed closer and closer, until at Maraclée the Castellan was forced to turn at bay. Once more the Christian knights showed their immense superiority as fighting men over the native levies, and the 200 Hospitallers charging home drove the Saracens off the field with terrific casualties, losing themselves, so it is said, only a single serjeant. From this brilliant little affair the Castellan of Margat returned in triumph to his impregnable fortress.[1]

The Moslem Emir of Le Crac, Seif-ed-Din Balban, one of whose duties it was to hold in check the garrison of Margat, was determined to have his revenge. In February 1281 he marched north against the Hospitallers with 7,000 horse, and a great host of foot. The Castellan of Margat, justly confident in the superior fighting value of European troops, sallied out from his fortress with 200 knights,[2] and serjeants, and 200 infantry, and advanced to meet the enemy in the open. His boldness received the reward that it deserved, and he gained another victory even more brilliant than that of the previous October, the Hospitallers losing only one knight and twelve serjeants. It is deeply to be regretted that the name of so fine a soldier as the Castellan should not have been preserved to us.

The Sultan Kalawun had spent the winter in preparations for a decisive campaign in the spring for the recovery of Aleppo from the Mongols, and it was essential to him if possible to secure peace in southern Syria. He therefore recognized Sunkur-el-Ashkar as ruler of Damascus, granting him in addition Antioch and other towns in the north. Then on 3 May 1281 a treaty for the usual ten years, months, weeks and days was made with the Hospitallers,[3] and on 16 July with Bohemond VII of Tripolis, leaving the Sultan free to concentrate all his forces against the Mongols. But the Christian princes had not the slightest intention of keeping the treaties they had

[1] See *Les Hospitaliers en Terre Sainte*, pp. 231, 232.

[2] For the numbers see *Les Hospitaliers en Terre Sainte*, p. 232, note 3.

[3] See Stevenson, *The Crusaders in the East*, p. 347.

so recently signed, and none the less began to concentrate their forces at Tripolis, in readiness to join the Mongols as they advanced south. The King of Cyprus was late in arriving, but Bohemond VII of Tripolis and Nicholas le Lorgne, Master of the Hospital, were ready to move, when the rapid advance of Kalawun to Homs, thus placing his army between them and the Mongols, rendered a junction impossible.[1]

The expected battle was fought at Homs on 30 October, 1281, and resulted in a victory for the Saracens, which if not glorious, at least saved Syria from the invaders, and ensured the ultimate destruction of the Latin colonies. Both armies consisted entirely of cavalry, that of the Saracens being estimated to be about 50,000 strong, and that of the Mongols, under Mangu-Timur, brother of the Ilkhan Abagha,[2] at about 40,000 including their Armenian and Georgian allies. Their right commanded by King Leo III of Armenia drove the Saracen left off the field, and rode after them in hot pursuit. The Mongol left, under Mangu-Timur in person, forced back the Saracen right beyond their camp, but without dispersing it, and then began to attack the centre under the Sultan. The temptation however to plunder the Saracen camp was too great for the Mongols, who gradually drifted away from the battle for this purpose. Since the only idea of the plunderers was to get their booty safely home, Mangu-Timur could do nothing further with his ill-disciplined troops. The Sultan was thus left the nominal victor of a battle, which he had practically lost. King Leo of Armenia in spite of his local success, on the dispersal of the main army, could only retreat hastily to his own land, where he was harassed so badly by Turcomans, that the Master of the Hospital sent 100 horse to his assistance, composed as usual of 50 knights and serjeants and 50 Turcopoles.[3]

We are indebted for a most detailed account of this battle to the Englishman Joseph de Cancy, so long the Treasurer of the Hospital. In a letter to King Edward I of England dated 31 March 1282[4] he sums up the results of this battle in the following words:

'So neither the one nor the other held the field; but because the Sultan was the last to retreat, men thought the victory ought to belong to him. But well may one say with truth that never since the first conquest of their country

---

[1] See Palestine Pilgrims Text Society, Vol. V, *A Crusader's Letter from the Holy Land*, p. 7.

[2] The Mongol rulers of Persia took the title of Ilkhan, meaning provincial or dependent khan, since they nominally owed allegiance to the Khakhan or Great Khan, in China. The Ilkhan Abagha and Mangu-Timur were sons of Hulagu Khan.

[3] See Pal. Pil. Text Soc., Vol. V, *A Crusader's Letter from the Holy Land*, p. 12.

[4] See *Cartulaire-Général*, Vol. III, No. 3,782, written in old French. A translation is printed as *A Crusader's Letter from the Holy Land*, in the Pal. Pil. Text Soc., Vol. V.

have the Saracens received so great a check or been so completely cowed as they were then and are still.'

Joseph de Cancy had resigned the Priory of England either at the end of 1280, or early in the following year, since his successor William de Henley had been appointed by February 1281. He must have returned almost at once to the Holy Land to resume his old office as Treasurer of the Hospital, since the Master Nicholas le Lorgne in a letter to King Edward written in September 1281,[1] refers to his having arrived there. In his own letter to King Edward, Joseph de Cancy ventures the opinion that the Holy Land had never been so easy of conquest as at that time. This was perfectly true, since the Saracens had destroyed nearly every fortress in the country, but for this very same reason it would have been as difficult to hold, as it was easy to conquer. Whether Joseph de Cancy ever returned to England is unknown, although in a letter written to him by King Edward dated 20 May 1282,[2] he urges him to do so. It is evident from the tone of the letter, that the king had a very real affection for him, and it must have been the outcome of a friendship formed during the time that he was himself a Crusader in the Holy Land. Joseph de Canoy is one of the most distinguished Englishmen who ever made his profession in the Order of St. John, for he was not merely Prior of England for seven years, but as Treasurer was one of the Conventual Bailiffs of the Order for the unusually long period of nearly thirty years. There long remained a memorial of him in the Lord Prior's Chapel, which he added to the Priory Church at Clerkenwell, during the time that he was Prior of England.[3]

The result of the Battle of Homs had done little to lessen the Sultan's anxiety regarding the Mongols, and he was glad to sign a treaty with the Templars of Tortosa in April 1282, and with Odo Poilechien the Lieutenant of King Charles of Jerusalem in June 1283. But there was one ominous clause in all these treaties, that no fortifications should be added to, or strengthened. When King Hugh of Cyprus landed at Beyrout in August 1283, to endeavour to recover his lost kingdom of Jerusalem, his cavalry were surprised by the Saracens and cut to pieces, no doubt in accordance with the new treaty with Odo Poilechien, and King Hugh returned to Cyprus, vowing vengeance against the Templars, whom he suspected of having incited the Saracens. Meanwhile the Ilkhan Abagha had died in April 1282, and been succeeded by his brother, who assumed the name of Ahmed and the Mohammedan faith. In the summer of 1284 he sent a friendly embassy to Damascus, and the Sultan Kalawun was henceforward free from

[1] See *Cartulaire-Général*, Vol. III, No. 3,766.

[2] See Pal. Pil. Text Soc., Vol. V, *A Crusader's Letter, etc.*, p. 14.

[3] See Porter's *History of the Knights of Malta*, Vol. II, p. 282, but Porter calls him 'De Chauncy', the more modern form of the name.

anxiety regarding his northern frontier, and could devote the remaining years of his life to completing the work of Beybars, and driving the Christians out of Syria.

The Sultan's first objective was the famous fortress of Margat, covering the northern frontiers of the county of Tripolis.[1] It had been in the possession of the Hospitallers since 1186, for a time it had been the seat of their Convent after the loss of Jerusalem, and for a century they had been lavishing enormous sums of money upon its fortifications. Now that Le Crac had fallen, it was almost certainly the most powerful fortress in the East, with the possible exception of Château Pelerin (Athlit). It must have required a large garrison to hold the castle and town, but the only definite information that we possess on the subject, is that it included 200 knights and serjeants, and 200 infantry, and we must presume that it was provisioned for a year, as was the custom in the castles of the Holy Land. The name of the Castellan is unknown to us. For the events that followed the one thing to be remembered is that the 200 knights and serjeants were probably the only part of the garrison that could really be relied upon.

The Sultan, who had made great preparations for the siege, arrived before Margat on 17 April 1285. Establishing his camp on the slopes of the mountains to the south of the fortress he opened his attack on the south-eastern side of the castle itself, where it is more easy of approach and covered by a deep ditch. After a few days' bombardment by the military engines, the Saracens forced their way into the ditch, and began to mine under the walls, eventually on 15 May bringing down the advanced tower, known as the Tour de l'Espérance,[2] at the end of the spur on which the castle stands. An immediate assault followed, which was beaten back with heavy losses. The Saracens then recommenced their mining operations, and within eight days had succeeded in running galleries under the keep, so that its walls were only supported by the wooden props inserted in the mines. Then Kalawun, anxious to capture the fortress, without the necessity for destroying its defences, summoned the Castellan to surrender, and permitted his representatives to inspect the mines. They reported that the castle was no longer tenable, and on 25 May the Castellan surrendered. The garrison marched out to Tripolis with all their belongings on 55 mules, together with 2,000 pieces of gold, and so Margat the impregnable, after a siege of only thirty-eight days, was delivered up to the enemy. Whether the surrender was justifiable, is now difficult to judge, but probably most of the knights were dead, and the soldiers declined to fight any longer. But even though no blame attaches to the Hospitallers, it was another dreadful blow to their prestige, and the manner in which their two great castles

[1] For a description of Margat, see pp. 159, 160 of this work.
[2] See *Les Hospitaliers en Terre Sainte*, p. 235, note 3.

of Le Crac and Margat had been lost, brought no glory or credit to their Order.[1]

From the capture of Margat the Sultan turned against Bartholomew de Maraclée,[2] a noted robber baron of the day, who had long lived upon plundering the Saracens. But his castle of Maraclée built upon an island in the sea, and held by a garrison of a hundred men, was unassailable. The Sultan therefore informed his suzerain Bohemond VII, of Tripolis, that unless he ordered the castle to be dismantled and abandoned, he should make war upon the county of Tripolis, and to save his shrunken realm from utter ruin the Count gave the necessary instructions. Bartholomew de Maraclée afterwards murdered his only son in the streets of Acre, and fled to the Saracens. There he took service under the Sultan, and adopting the Mohammedan faith, became one of the bitterest enemies of his former co-religionists.[3]

According to the older historians, the disastrous condition of affairs in the Holy Land, was the cause of the death of Nicholas de Lorgne,[4] and the fall of Margat may well have been his death-blow. We do not know exactly when he died, but his successor had been appointed by September 1285, so that he probably died some time early in that summer. Little can be said of the reign of Nicholas le Lorgne, except that it marks a short respite in the inevitable march of fate, culminating in the crushing blow to the Hospitallers of the loss of Margat. The old chronicle has nothing to tell us, except that he passed many good statutes, thus bringing to completion the work of his great predecessor Hugh Revel. He held meetings of the Chapter-General in 1278 and 1283, and as we have seen extended to all the brethren the right to wear the black mantle in the Convent, and the red surcoat in war. It was he too who ordained that the military brethren should have the arms of the Order painted upon their shields,[5] a custom which was retained until shields were abolished, and he also laid down that deceased brethren should always be buried wrapped in their mantles.[6] But probably his most important statute was that instituting the Great Seal of the Master and Convent, for attachment to all charters and documents requiring the consent not only of the Master, but also that of the Conventual Bailiffs.[7] Until then the Master's Great Seal had been used for all important documents alike, whether emanating from him personally, or from the Convent collectively.

[1] The best account of this siege is in Rey's *L'Architecture Militaire des Croisés en Syrie*, pp. 36, 37.

[2] He is apparently the same person as Meillour III de Ravendel, Lord of Maraclée. See *Les Hospitaliers en Terre Sainte*, p. 236, note 1.

[3] See Michaud's *History of the Crusades*, Vol. III, pp. 68, 69.

[4] See Boyssat de Lixieux, *Histoire de l'Ordre de St. Jean*, Vol. I, p. 51.

[5] 'The Chronicle of the deceased Masters' in Appendix B at the end of this work.

[6] See *Cartulaire-Général*, Vol. III, No. 3,670.

[7] Ibid., and Appendix C at the end of this work.

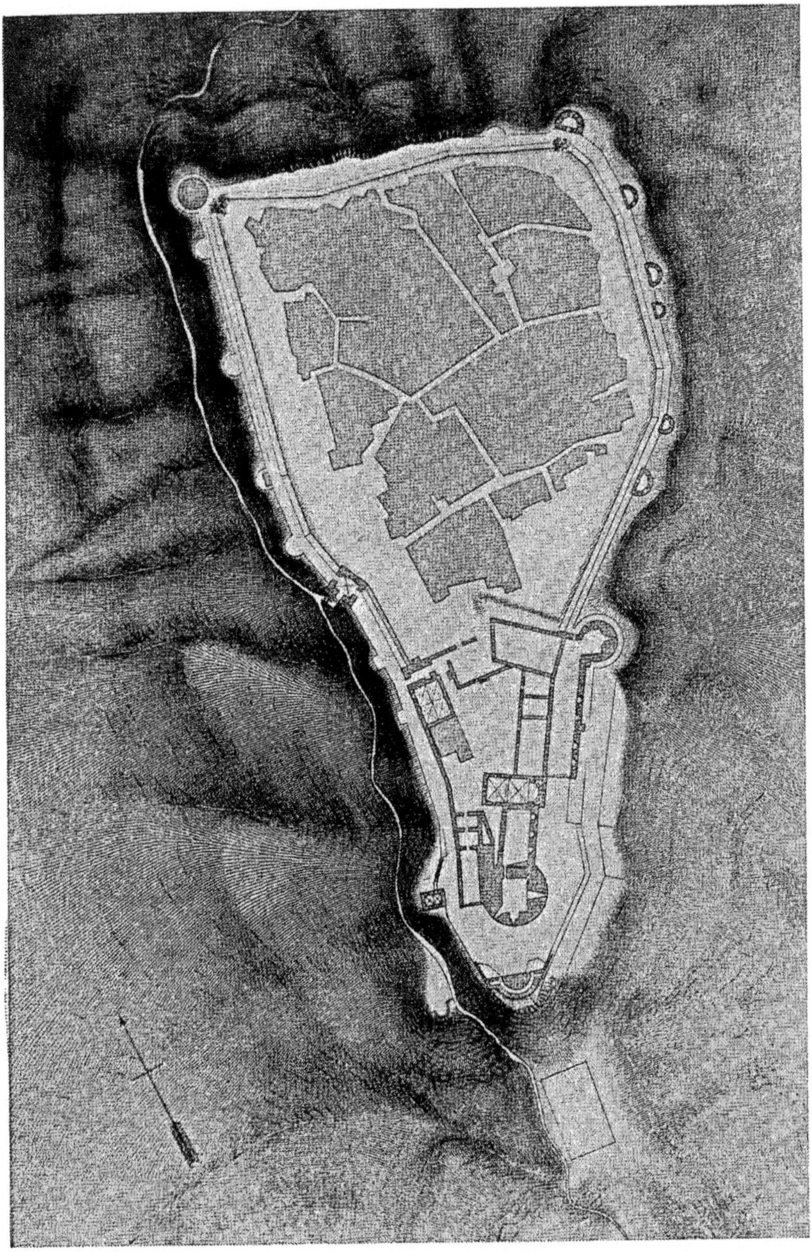

PLAN OF THE CASTLE OF MARGAT

The new Master of the Hospital was John de Villiers, Prior of France. We know little of his previous career in the Order, except that Hugh Revel had summoned him to the Convent in 1269, and that in 1277 he succeeded Nicholas le Lorgne as Commander of Tripolis. He was probably appointed Prior of France in 1280, when we find Thomas Le Rat acting as Lieutenant for an absentee Prior. John de Villiers was certainly Master of the Hospital in September 1285, but is not likely to have been elected much before that date, as he could scarcely have delayed his arrival in the Holy Land more than a year in such critical times, and he only went out to Acre in the autumn passage of 1286.

Important political changes had recently taken place in the Holy Land. King Hugh III of Cyprus had died in 1284, and his son and successor King John I had died in the following year, being succeeded by his younger brother King Henry II. At the beginning of 1286 King Charles of Jerusalem and Sicily died, having done nothing whatever to succour the Holy Land, and his rival the new King of Cyprus at once prepared to seize what little was now left of the kingdom of Jerusalem. King Henry landed at Acre on 24 June 1286, and five days later Odo Poilechien, King Charles's seneschal, surrendered with the Sicilian garrison. The new king was solemnly crowned at Tyre on 24 August, amidst great rejoicings, the last coronation of a King of Jerusalem that the Holy Land was destined to witness.

After his capture of Margat and Maraclée, the Sultan Kalawun had made a treaty of peace for the usual period of ten years with Marguerite de Montfort of Tyre, the widow of John de Montfort, and a similar treaty with King Leo III of Armenia, in return for an enormous tribute of a million besants a year.[1] In spite of his treaty with Bohemond VII of Tripolis the Sultan in 1287, whilst engaged in hostilities against Sunkur-el-Ashkar in northern Syria, attacked the town of La Liche (Latakieh), all that remained of the lost principality of Antioch. But since the town was tributary to Sunkur-el-Ashkar,[2] the Sultan presumably regarded it as Moslem rather than Christian property. An earthquake had shaken the walls, and badly damaged its principal defence, the Tower of the Pisans, covering the entrance to the harbour.[3] The Saracens, taking advantage of these circumstances, advanced against the town, which surrendered on 13 April. It was a further blow to the Hospitallers, who had always had important interests in La Liche.[4]

The death of Bohemond VII Count of Tripolis and titular Prince of Antioch on 19 October 1287 was the beginning of the final act of

[1] See Lane-Poole's *Egypt in the Middle Ages*, p. 281.
[2] See Stevenson, *The Crusaders in the East*, p. 350, note 1.
[3] See Rey, *L'Architecture Militaire des Croisés en Syrie*, p. 177.
[4] See *Les Hospitaliers en Terre Sainte*, p. 214.

the long-drawn-out tragedy of the end of the Latin kingdom. He died childless, as usual there was no heir at the very moment when a vigorous and masterful leader was most needed, and his legitimate successor was his sister Lucia, wife of Narjot de Toucy, admiral of the kingdom of Naples. But the Dowager Countess, Sibyl of Armenia, relying upon her popularity with the people, endeavoured to seize the power. Eventually the claims of the Countess Lucia prevailed, but the people declined to receive her representative Bertrand de Lembriac, Lord of Gibelet. A period of anarchy and chaos followed. Then the popular leaders supported by the Genoese set up a Commune, and entered into a treasonable correspondence with the Sultan Kalawun.[1] The situation was too tempting to be resisted, and the Sultan prevented from taking action in 1288, owing to the death of his favourite son, moved against Tripolis in the early spring of the following year.

As soon as the imminence of the danger was known, the Countess Lucia hastened from Naples to Acre, and brought reinforcements in person to her city of Tripolis. The commune thereupon abdicated, and the people recognized the authority of their countess. Now that it was too late, every effort was made to save the doomed city. Amaury de Lusignan, Constable of the kingdom of Jerusalem, and now Lord of Tyre, took charge of the defence. The knights maintained in Palestine by the King of France arrived under John de Grailly, there was a strong force of Hospitallers under Matthew de Clermont the Marshal of the Order, one of its greatest heroes, and a powerful contingent of Templars, and the galleys of the republics of Venice, Genoa and Pisa co-operated.

The Sultan marched on Tripolis at the head of 10,000 horse and 33,000 foot, and the siege began on 17 March 1289.[2] Nineteen heavy siege-engines were employed in battering the towers and walls, while 1,500 men were continually engaged in mining underneath them. At length the ancient Bishop's Tower and the new Hospitallers' Tower fell with a crash, together with the curtain wall between them. The Saracens at once dashed to the assault, after heavy fighting the breach was successfully carried, their troops swarmed into the city, and on 26 April Tripolis fell after a siege of thirty-nine days. In the massacre that followed the fall of the city, 7,000 people perished, but a great number escaped on board the galleys and ships in the harbour and were carried in safety to Cyprus. Many unhappy people took refuge in the island of St. Nicholas off the harbour, where they all died of starvation. The Hospitallers had 40 knights killed,[3] and a few taken prisoners. Matthew de Clermont the Marshal escaped by sea, together

[1] See Stevenson, *The Crusaders in the East*, p. 349.

[2] See *Les Hospitaliers en Terre Sainte*, p. 241.

[3] See a letter of the Master John de Villiers printed in the *Cartulaire-Général*, Vol. III, No. 4,050.

with Amaury de Lusignan and John de Grailly. The great city of Tripolis met with the same fate as Antioch, it was deliberately burnt to the ground and utterly destroyed. To replace it a new Moslem town was built on Mont Pelerin, a mile inland.

The Sultan did not immediately press his victory, but a few days later he took the castle of Néphin, to the south of Tripolis, which belonged to the Hospitallers,[1] and then the castle of Botron. He permitted Bertrand de Lembriac, however, to remain in possession of Gibelet on condition that he paid him tribute, and he renewed his former treaties with the other Christian states. But it was now quite evident that without European intervention on a big scale the end could not be long delayed. The Pope appealed to the powers in vain, Philip IV of France showed no interest, and the Kings of Aragon and Sicily, determined to be on the winning side, actually went so far as to make a treaty with the Sultan, undertaking to assist him against any fresh crusade.[2] Only King Edward of England sincerely desired to go to the assistance of the Holy Land, and his own affairs rendered it impossible for him to do so. In the summer of 1290 the Pope sent out a body of armed pilgrims to Acre about 1,700 strong in 21 galleys, and their undesirable presence brought the impending catastrophe to a head. These men, recruited from the slums of the great cities of southern Europe, were worthless as soldiers and a far greater danger to their own side than to the enemy. Unpaid and idle, undisciplined and filled with fanaticism, they were ripe for any mischief. At last in August they broke away from all control, and made a raid into peaceful Saracen territory, plundering the villages and killing a great number of perfectly harmless Moslems. The Sultan, justly indignant at this outrage, at once demanded their surrender to him for punishment as having broken the treaty. Deep regret was expressed for the incident, but his demand was refused, although the Templars had advised that the criminals should be given up, and the Sultan, his patience exhausted, denounced the treaty, and began preparations for a campaign that should end the Christian occupation for ever.

The city of Acre, which as the centre of Christian power in the Holy Land, was certain to be the Sultan's main objective in the forthcoming campaign, had greatly increased in size and importance since the days of the Third Crusade. It was now the chief commercial city in the Levant, its population was between 30,000 and 40,000,[3] and it had expanded far beyond its original walls, over the area to the north-west known as Mont Musard. The city was powerfully fortified with a double line of walls and towers thoroughly up to date, covered

[1] See *Les Hospitaliers en Terre Sainte*, p. 241.

[2] See Stevenson, *The Crusaders in the East*, p. 351.

[3] Ibid., p. 352, note 6.

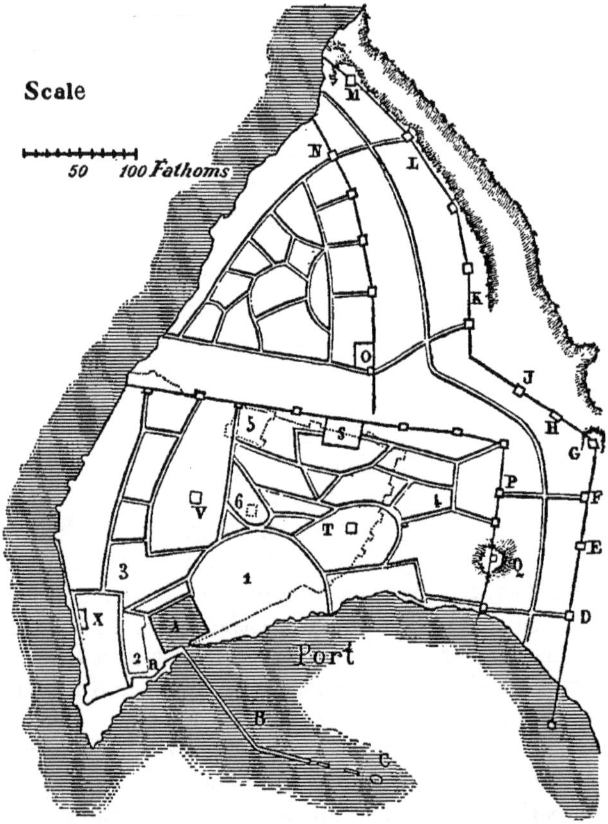

MARINO SANUDO'S PLAN OF ACRE IN THE TIME OF THE CRUSADES

A Inner harbour
B Mole covering the harbour
C Tower of Flies
D Tower of the Patriarch
E Tower of the Bridge
F Tower of St. Nicholas
G Maledictum
H King Hugh's Gate
J Sector of the Venetians
K Sector of the Hospitallers
L Sector of the Templars
M Tower of the Devil
N St. Lazarus' Gate
O St. Anthony's Gate
P Tower of the Pilgrims
Q Tower of the Germans
R The Iron Gate
S The Castle
T Palace of the Patriarch
V The Hospital
X The Temple

1 Venetian Quarter
2 Pisan Quarter
3 Genoese Quarter
4 German Quarter
5 Pacha's Palace
6 Mosque of Djezzar

Modern Ramparts

by a wide and deep ditch, and between the walls lay a broad open space providing room for cattle and refugees. The original wall and towers dividing Mont Musard from the old city still remained, with the castle in its midst. There were four main entrance gates on the land side, two leading into Mont Musard, St. Lazarus's Gate on the north, and St. Anthony's Gate at the re-entrant, where the wall of Mont Musard joined the north wall of the city. In the eastern wall were St. Nicholas's Gate and the Patriarch's Gate. The harbour was covered by two massive moles between which lay a double entrance, defended by a strong tower known as the Tower of Flies.[1] The weakest point in the defences of Acre was the sharp salient at the north-east corner of the old city, which was protected by a massive tower known as Maledictum.[2]

Within the fortifications were the palaces of the Kings of Jerusalem, the Papal Legates, the Princes of Antioch and of all the great semi-Oriental nobles of the Latin kingdom, together with the residences of the wealthy merchants of the chief Italian trading cities. There were the Convents of the five military religious Orders, Hospitallers, Templars, Teutonic Knights, St. Lazarus and St. Thomas, and the houses of the other more peaceful Orders. And all these residences were more or less strongly fortified, as were even the very churches, for Acre was a turbulent city, ever ready for rioting and civil strife, rarely completely tranquil and at peace. Its population was curiously mixed, representative of nearly every race in Europe, but with a strong preponderance of Italians and Levantines, the scum of the seaports of southern Europe and the East. Contemporary writers describe Acre as a very sink of iniquity, in which every form of vice and crime and abomination flourished triumphant and unchecked. Law and order and justice were non-existent, for there was no administration common to the whole city. Every nation claimed the right to administer its own affairs in its own way, and so did every great noble powerful enough to make good his claim. The city was always seething with hatreds and jealousies and bitter feuds. A man might commit any crime however abominable in one street, and by escaping into another was free from arrest or from any process of law. For all practical purposes within the confined space of the fortifications there were no less than seventeen different municipalities,[3] each claiming almost sovereign powers, and at times even going so far as to wage open war upon each other. Such was Acre when its doom came upon it, and yet withal it was a beautiful city filled with glorious buildings, and men

[1] For the harbour, see Rey, *L'Architecture Militaire des Croisés en Syrie*, pp. 171, 172.

[2] A good description of Acre is given in Conder's *Latin Kingdom of Jerusalem*, pp. 407–10.

[3] See Archer and Kingsford, *The Crusades*, p. 415.

loved it and were proud of it and ready to die for it, but rarely has any great city been so utterly divided against itself.

The Sultan Kalawun never lived to complete the work of Beybars and Saladin, and to drive the Christians out of Syria. In the midst of his preparations for the siege of Acre he died suddenly on 10 November 1290, being then 70 years of age. His last thoughts were of the approaching campaign, and he forbade his body to be buried until Acre should be taken. He was succeeded by his worthless son Khalil, a cruel and capricious tyrant, whom he had never intended should succeed him. But this did not delay in any way the fate of the Latin kingdom, for Khalil was eager to extirpate the infidel. The preparations of the old Sultan had been made on a great scale, for he was determined to risk no possibilities of failure. The army was even larger [1] than that assembled for the siege of Tripolis two years earlier, and in view of the well-known strength of the fortifications of Acre, a siege train had been collected of such a formidable nature as had never been seen before. No fewer than ninety-two battering-engines of the greatest power had been specially constructed for this siege. The Saracen army began to concentrate before Acre towards the end of March 1291, the Sultan arrived on 5 April, and from that date the siege may be said to have begun.

The control of the defence of the city was assumed by William de Beaujeu, Master of the Temple. He had now held office for nineteen years, and was by far the most experienced and respected soldier in Acre. Estimates of the strength of the garrison vary considerably, but it is safest to take the lowest figure of 700 knights and 14,000 infantry, but the fighting value of the latter was probably a somewhat uncertain quantity. More than half the knights were furnished by the military religious Orders. There were about 240 Templars, and 140 Hospitallers under their Master John de Villiers.[2] All available knights appear to have been called up from Europe, as we should expect, and amongst the Hospitallers to arrive in the previous autumn passage had been William de Henley, Prior of England.[3] Both Orders had been greatly weakened financially by the loss of their rich possessions in the East, and were no longer able to maintain the large forces of earlier and more prosperous days. The three remaining Orders could only provide about 50 knights between them. The Teutonic Knights had long transferred their principal activities to the crusade

[1] The most exaggerated and ridiculous estimates are given of its strength, some speaking of 60,000 horse and 140,000 foot. Armies at this period did not often exceed 30,000 men, perhaps 50,000 or a little more may have been collected for the siege of Acre. But roads and transport and military stores were as important then as they are now, and were equally ruling factors.

[2] See Taaffe's *History of the Order of St. John*, Vol. II, pp. 210, 211.

[3] See *Cartulaire-Général*, Vol. III, Nos. 4,104, 4,110.

in northern Germany against the heathen Prussians and Lithuanians, and provided only 15 knights under their Lieutenant-Master, whilst the Orders of St. Lazarus and St. Thomas, always very weak, may have furnished 25 and 10 knights respectively, but certainly not more. The city appears to have been governed by a permanent Council of War, composed of the eight senior officers, and the garrison was organized in four brigades, one for each of the four sectors into which the defences were divided. The first sector, the eastern wall from Maledictum exclusive to the sea was entrusted to a Burgundian knight Otho de Grandison, representing the King of England, who had under him the Englishmen and Picards present, and to John de Grailly, commanding the knights maintained by the King of France. The second sector, the northern wall including the important defensive work at the north-east angle known as Maledictum, as far as but exclusive of St. Anthony's Gate, was held by the King of Jerusalem's lieutenant, Amaury de Lusignan, and by the Teutonic Knights. The third sector, the right half of the wall covering Mont Musard was held by the Knights of the Hospital and St. Thomas, who had their principal force at St. Anthony's Gate held by Matthew de Clermont, the Marshal of the Hospital. The fourth sector, extending from the Hospitallers to the sea, was held by the Knights of the Temple and St. Lazarus. There was a fleet of galleys and other vessels in the harbour, and the command of the sea as usual was with the Christians.

It is not easy to reconstruct the siege of Acre from the somewhat confused accounts that have come down to us.[1] For the first month of the siege the progress made by the Saracens was very slow, their battering-engines had begun to arrive on 7 April and to get into position by the 11th, but it was another three weeks before they began to press the attack seriously.[2] The city was however closely invested, and there were constant sorties by the garrison. During this period all who could afford to do so sent away their women and children to Cyprus, and many of the more well-to-do civilians left the city. No doubt at such a time the Master of the Temple was thankful to see the departure of all useless mouths. But the venerable Patriarch of Jerusalem, Nicholas de Hanapes, insisted upon remaining behind, that he might encourage his flock to the last in the hour of their tribulation.

The crisis of the siege began on Friday, 4 May. The Saracens had selected for their main attack, the weak spot in the defensive system of the city, the sharp salient at the north-east corner, covered

[1] The principal authorities for the Siege of Acre are 'Excidium urbis Acconis', the 'Gestes des Chiprois', and the letter of John de Villiers, printed at the end of this chapter. Addison, in his *Knights Templars*, pp. 224–30, gives a very good description of the siege.

[2] See Stevenson's *Crusaders in the East*, p. 353.

by that famous work Maledictum, and the wall and towers between it and St. Anthony's Gate. On 4 May Maledictum, which had been steadily bombarded for many days, at last fell in ruins,[1] and then began that systematic and continuous bombardment of the doomed city, from the ninety-two battering-engines of the Saracens, which lasted day and night until the final assaults were delivered. But on this fatal day the garrison was greatly encouraged, in spite of the disaster, by the arrival of King Henry of Jerusalem from Cyprus, with a reinforcement of 200 knights and 500 infantry, and his ships were available for removing any further civilians, who desired to leave. Many knights and soldiers who were not legally bound to remain, appear to have taken this opportunity to abandon the city.[2] The King of Jerusalem at once assumed command of the point of danger, previously held by his brother Amaury de Lusignan, as it was fitting that he should do, but the general direction of the defence of Acre remained in the hands of that experienced soldier the Master of the Temple, as before.

After ten days' incessant bombardment, supplemented by mining operations which never ceased, the wall between Maledictum and St. Anthony's Gate began to present breaches practicable to the enemy. On Tuesday, 15 May, the Saracens set fire to one of their mines, which brought down a fresh section of the wall, and then delivered their first general assault, or rather a series of assaults lasting from sunrise to sunset, upon the positions held by the troops of King Henry and the Teutonic Knights. The continuous attacks were repulsed with terrific losses to the enemy, who were successfully prevented from breaking through, but only with the utmost difficulty.

Next day Wednesday, the 16th, at daybreak, the Saracens again advanced to the assault, and after a series of desperate attacks, during which eye-witnesses state that they saw a band of fanatical Hadjis throw themselves into the ditch, in order that their troops might mount to the assault over their bodies, the defenders worn out by their exertions and overwhelmed by superior numbers, were forced to fall back upon the inner line of defences. The exulting Moslems swarmed through the abandoned breaches by thousands, and it seemed as if Acre was lost. At this critical moment Matthew de Clermont, Marshal of the Hospital, stationed at St. Anthony's Gate, collecting together all the available knights of the Hospital and Temple, threw himself upon the right flank of the enemy as they pressed forward against the inner wall in all the disorder of success. The heavy cavalry rode through and through the Saracen ranks, cutting them down by hundreds, until at last they drove them back in panic through the breaches they had so recently stormed. Not content with this success Matthew

[1] See Addison, *The Knights Templars*, p. 226.
[2] See Stevenson's *Crusaders in the East*, p. 353.

de Clermont followed them up beyond the shattered ramparts, and in a brilliant charge flung them back upon their own lines; as an eye-witness tells us 'they fled away at his approach like sheep before a wolf'.[1] It was a fine example of what the mediaeval knight could do under favourable circumstances and on suitable terrain. The Saracen trumpets now sounded the retreat, and the troops of King Henry and the Teutonic Knights reoccupied their lost positions, which were consolidated during the night, a temporary wall being built across the opening made by the enemy, and all breaches being filled up with obstacles. But success had been purchased at a heavy price, 2,000 Christian warriors had been slain, and there remained but 7,000, many of them badly wounded, to hold the long line of ramparts.

Early the next morning before daybreak a last council of war was held in the Convent of the Hospitallers. There can have been little hope of repulsing another assault, the desperate nature of the situation was only too evident, and the possibility of relief no longer existed. They doubtless discussed the question of attempting to open negotiations with the enemy, for that was certainly done later in the day. Arrangements were also made for embarking the remaining women and children, but they failed owing to the stormy weather. Then they all confessed their sins, the venerable Patriarch in a few solemn words gave them his blessing, and commended them to the mercy of God, and after embracing each other they went down to the ramparts to meet their end.

But on that day, the 17th, there was no serious fighting, and the Saracens appear to have remained quietly in their lines, reorganizing and completing their preparations for the final assault on the following day.[2] The Master of the Temple used the respite to get into touch with the enemy in a last hopeless effort to obtain some sort of terms.[3] That evening the King of Jerusalem and his men withdrew from the ramparts, on the grounds that they had had no sleep for three nights, handing over charge of the sector to the Teutonic Knights, but undertaking to return before daybreak. They never did return, but when the Saracens resumed the attack the following morning, guessing that all was lost, they embarked upon their ships and sailed for Cyprus.[4] And so Henry de Lusignan, the last King of Jerusalem who ever reigned in the Holy Land, the unworthy descendant of generations of hard-fighting ancestors, forgetting his duty and his knightly honour, abandoned his post in the moment of danger, left the last of his subjects to their fate, and sought safety in ignominious flight. Well may the eye-witness of the siege, who has left us a record of this shameful

[1] See Michaud's *History of the Crusades*, Vol. III, p. 80.
[2] See Stevenson's *Crusaders in the East*, p. 354.
[3] See Taaffe's *History of the Order of St. John*, Vol. II, p. 229.
[4] For the exact day of the king's flight, see Stevenson, p. 353, note 4.

incident, exclaim in the heat of his indignation: 'Would to God that a whirlwind had arisen, and had submerged these base fugitives, and that they had sunk like lead to the bottom of the sea'.[1]

Early in the morning on Friday, 18 May, before sunrise, while the city was still shrouded in mist, the Saracen columns advanced once more to the assault upon the shattered ramparts. In the absence of King Henry the line was too weakly held to check the enemy for long. The gallant Teutonic Knights fell to a man, fighting to the last, but nothing could save the situation, the Saracens eventually broke through by King Hugh's Gate, also known as the English Tower, midway between Maledictum and St. Anthony's Gate, and then swarmed into the city through every breach and opening in irresistible force. With their left flank thus uncovered, John de Grailly and Otho de Grandison appear to have fallen back from the eastern wall upon the inner line of defences. A strong force of Saracens wheeling to the right flung themselves upon the Hospitallers holding St. Anthony's Gate. Here Matthew de Clermont the Marshal stood firmly to his ground, and three times the Hospitallers drove the enemy back to 'a place commonly known as Maldis (i.e. Maledictum)', as John de Villiers tells us in his letter. But the situation was desperate, and nothing but desperate remedies could be of any avail. There still stood in reserve not far distant a force of 500 cavalry, doubtless knights and Turcopoles of the Hospital and Temple. The Master of the Temple requested the Master of the Hospital to make a sortie with them and to deliver a counter-attack upon the Saracen reinforcements hastening forward in support of the assaulting troops. At that moment William de Beaujeu fell dead, shot down by a Saracen crossbowman, or pierced by a lance, for accounts differ. He was as gallant a Master as ever ruled over the Temple, his end was glorious, and he was at least spared the sorrow of witnessing the final ruin of the cause to which he had devoted his life.

John de Villiers led the reserve cavalry out through St. Lazarus's Gate and forming up on the plain beyond, charged through the Saracen reinforcements, some said up to their very camp. But the force was too small for such a task to be effective, casualties had been very heavy, the remainder, wheeling about, hacked their way back through the ranks of the enemy, and John de Villiers was amongst those who reached Acre in safety. All however was now lost, the garrison had been unable to hold the enemy on the inner line of defence, and the Saracens were pouring into the city on every side. What Templars still survived fought their way back in a compact body to their Convent near the seashore. Most of the Hospitallers had perished at St. Anthony's Gate. John de Villiers with a little group of his brethren fought his way back into the city, and made his last stand in one of the

[1] See Michaud's *History of the Crusades*, Vol. III, p. 79.

streets near the harbour, until all had fallen dead or badly wounded. Matthew de Clermont the Marshal was seen in one of the streets of Acre, vainly spurring his exhausted charger for a last dash upon a group of infidels. His horse fell beneath him, there was a rush of Saracens, and when they had passed, his lifeless body lay bleeding on the ground. So died one of the noblest heroes who ever made his profession in the Order of St. John.

Except in the Convent of the Templars there was no further organized resistance. The surviving troops threw away their arms and armour, and made a rush for the boats in the harbour. Here horrible scenes were witnessed, made still more dreadful by the storm of hail and rain that had burst upon the city at the moment of the assault. The seashore was a mass of screaming women and children, and panic-stricken soldiers, struggling to get into the boats, with the sailors haggling over the price of safety and trying to pick out those who could pay the most. Into this mob of helpless fugitives, mad with fear, rode the merciless Saracen horse, killing all whom they could reach and pursuing them into the very waves of the sea. The venerable Patriarch of Jerusalem, who had been inspired throughout the siege by the most devoted sense of duty, was forced into one of the boats. But the kindly old man insisted upon holding back in order to rescue as many people as possible, with the result that his overloaded boat sank beneath the waves. The Master of the Hospital was saved only owing to the devotion of his body-servant, who at imminent risk of death returned with a serjeant to seek him.[1] Together they carried him off to one of the boats, and returning succeeded in getting away six other knights, some of them mortally wounded, and these seven were the only Knights Hospitallers who survived the fall of Acre.[2] No English knight is known to have been amongst these survivors, all are believed to have perished; the most distinguished of them was William de Henley, Prior of England for over ten years, whose memory was long preserved by the cloisters, which he built on the south side of the Priory Church at Clerkenwell.[3]

Concerning the horrors of the sack of Acre, it is scarcely necessary to speak, there was never any mercy shown in a city taken by storm. Many took refuge in the churches, but the pitiless enemy set fire to the buildings, others for a time held out in the numerous fortified houses, only retarding a little their inevitable doom. The nuns of the various religious Orders had been sent away early in the siege, only the devoted sisters of St. Clare had remained behind to nurse the sick and wounded. When the end came they followed the example

[1] For this incident, see the letter of John de Villiers.

[2] See *Les Hospitaliers en Terre Sainte*, p. 244.

[3] That he built the cloisters, see Porter's *Knights of Malta*, Vol. II, p. 282, but he makes a curious blunder as regards the date of his death.

of the sisters of the Hospital at the sack of Antioch, and by mutilating and disfiguring their countenances,[1] provoked the indignant Moslem soldiery to slay them forthwith, and their dead bodies were seen flung into a heap in one of the streets. About 10,000 survivors were made prisoners, of these the men were all slain by the express orders of the Sultan, and the fate of the women and children was lifelong slavery.

A number of people fled for safety to the Convent of the Templars, where the surviving knights of that Order had retired. The first action of the Templars was to assemble in Chapter for the purpose of electing one of their number a certain Gaudini to be Master in the place of William de Beaujeu. Next day, the 19th, the Sultan sent in a flag of truce, and they agreed to surrender, the Sultan undertaking to send them in safety to Cyprus, with such of their belongings as they could carry with them, and all the refugees in their convent. A guard of 300 Moslems was sent down to see that the treaty was observed. But the guard began to outrage the Christian women, the Templars blind with fury cast all prudence to the winds, and bolting and barring the gates, killed every Saracen soldier in the place.[2] The troops outside at once resumed the attack, and the siege of the Convent began. The following morning, the 20th, the Master Gaudini sent the Marshal of the Temple with a flag of truce to the Sultan, to attempt to explain the slaughter of his guard, but the angry Sultan ordered him and his followers to be instantly beheaded. But one last forlorn hope remained to the desperate Templars. They knew of a boat hidden on the seashore close to their convent, and it was decided that the Master Gaudini himself should endeavour to get through the enemy's lines, and try to arrange for their rescue from the sea. That night he slipped out through a secret postern gate with a few companions, taking with them the treasures and relics of their church, and marvellous to relate they got safely away. But nothing could be done in the short time that was left. The remaining Templars, determined to sell their lives as dearly as possible, barricaded themselves in the strongest part of the Convent, known as the Tower of the Master. There they held out for a week longer, until the tower, undermined by the Saracens, fell crashing to the ground, and any who were still left died sword in hand amongst its ruins. With all resistance at an end, the fortifications and strongholds of the city were systematically destroyed and then the Sultan ordered it to be set on fire at four different points. When the Saracens had finished their work, of the once mighty and opulent city of Acre, there remained nothing but a heap of smouldering ruins.

The dramatic fall of Acre was the end of the Latin kingdom of Jerusalem, and the remaining Christian towns were abandoned without

[1] See Michaud's *History of the Crusades*, Vol. III, p. 86, footnote.
[2] See Addison, *The Knights Templars*, pp. 229, 230.

VIEW OF ACRE IN 1686

From an Engraving in the Bibliothèque Nationale

further fighting. Tyre was strongly fortified, a virgin city that had successfully defied the mighty Saladin at the height of his power, but there was no possibility of a fresh crusade for her relief as there had been a hundred years earlier. Amaury de Lusignan, its lord, whilst fighting in the defence of Acre, ordered preparations to be made for its evacuation, and on the evening that Acre fell the leading inhabitants left the city, which was occupied by Moslem troops the following day. The great Templar fortress of Château Pelerin (Athlit) was evacuated a few days later,[1] no doubt by the orders of the Master Gaudini, who must have gone there on his escape from Acre. The castle was destroyed by the Saracens the following August. Sidon, which had been refortified by St. Louis only forty years before, was abandoned by the Templars on 14 July. A week later on the 21st, Beyrout, the city of King Henry's brother Guy de Lusignan, by virtue of his marriage with its heiress, Eschiva d'Ibelin, surrendered as soon as a Saracen army appeared. Not long after Bertrand of Gibelet (Jubail) reluctantly withdrew from the town,[2] which eight generations of his ancestors had held, ever since Count Bertrand of Tripolis bestowed it upon the first Hugh de Lembriac. When the Templars finally decided to abandon Tortosa on 3 August 1291, the Latin kingdom of Jerusalem was ended for ever.

There is no more romantic or dramatic period in history than the crusades, and the long-drawn-out struggle between Cross and Crescent for the possession of the Holy Land. From the days when the first Crusaders had burst into Syria and laid siege to Antioch down to the last desperate fight at Acre the struggle had endured for nearly 200 years, and now the inevitable end had at last come in utter failure and disaster. In the words of one of the greatest of historians, 'a mournful and solitary silence prevailed along the coast which had so long resounded with the world's debate'.[3] The reasons for the failure are not difficult to see, and as we look back over its history, the Latin kingdom of Jerusalem seems doomed to destruction from the very days of its foundation. In the first place the conquest of Syria had never been completed by the Crusaders, but they had left all the interior, the long line of important cities, Aleppo, Hama, Homs, Baalbek and Damascus in Moslem hands, a strong base for the reaction that was certain to follow. Secondly colonization from Europe was never on a sufficient scale to occupy effectively the conquered territory, and the colonists themselves speedily became degenerate through intermarriage with the native population and for climatic and other reasons, so that they were regarded with utter contempt by the later Crusaders, who always speak of them as a treacherous, cowardly and

[1] See Stevenson, *The Crusaders in the East*, p. 355.

[2] Ibid., p. 355, note 2.

[3] Gibbon, *The Decline and Fall of the Roman Empire*, Chapter 59.

worthless race. Thirdly the feudal baronage of the East was as independent, as egotistical and as uncontrollable as the feudal baronage of Europe, with far more disastrous results, and this was complicated still further by the fierce rivalry of the Italian mercantile communities so powerful in the coast towns. Under such circumstances it was almost an impossibility to build up the one thing essential to stability, a strong central government, and that curious fatality which caused the very capable reigning house to produce daughters instead of sons, effectually destroyed whatever chance had ever existed.

Long before the disastrous Battle of Hattin the Latin kingdom was already showing signs of incipient degeneracy, and was beginning to lean more and more upon the military religious Orders, who were gradually taking over complete charge of the more exposed frontiers. Continually reinforced from Europe by a regular flow of recruits of the very best military type, their efficiency was unimpaired by the adverse Oriental environment, and they remained the only really stable and wholesome elements in the state. After the failure of the Third Crusade to restore the kingdom to its former frontiers, the position of the Hospitallers and Templars was one of such overwhelming preponderance, as to leave them all-powerful in the now shrunken realm. The responsibility for the defence of the country rested almost entirely upon their shoulders, more especially during the last forty years, and although unfortunately often hampered by the intensity of the rivalry between their respective Orders, yet none the less there can be no two opinions as to the entirely devoted and self-sacrificing manner in which they carried out their arduous duties. No troops in all history have ever shown a higher standard of duty or a finer fighting spirit than the knights of the Hospital and the Temple. The hopeless nature of their task was quite obvious after the Moslem counter-attack had begun under Beybars, but never for one moment did they waver in their devotion and zeal for the cause to which they had pledged their lives. In the last great fight for the Holy Land, the Hospitallers and Templars present perished almost to a man, and most worthily upheld the glorious military record of the two Orders to which they belonged. The subsequent history of the Hospital and the Temple were to be very different. Twenty years later the Templars, the victims of a dark and shameless intrigue between King Philip le Bel of France and Pope Clement V, were disbanded and their Order dissolved, with their honour and reputation blasted for ever by a series of monstrous charges, which they had no opportunity of refuting. For the Hospitallers a happier fate was reserved, and they were destined to carry on their historic rôle as the chief defenders of the Christian faith in the Levant, for centuries to come, first as the Knights of Rhodes and afterwards as the Knights of Malta. Two glorious and noble stories that have yet to be told.

APPENDIX

LETTER OF JOHN DE VILLIERS, MASTER OF THE HOSPITAL, DESCRIBING THE FALL OF ACRE

Brother John de Villiers, by the Grace of God humble Master of the Holy House of the Hospital of St. John of Jerusalem, and guardian of the poor of Jesus Christ, to his very dear Lord Brother William de Villaret, brother of the said House and Prior of St. Gilles in Provence, greeting in (the name of) Him who faileth not those who put their trust in Him, who after tribulation and sorrow and anguish sendeth them comfort from the heights of heaven.

Brother, because we know that in your kindly friendship you have always been glad to be informed of what happens to us, rejoicing in our prosperity and mourning in our adversity, we by these present letters in tears and sighs and in very great sadness announce to you the disastrous fall of Acre, the goodly city. Alas, the bitter sorrow of it! Briefly and in few words we declare it, because we know well that there are several persons, who are come from your parts, and who were present with us, from whom you can ask on their return all the details.

Know then, dear friend, that we give you the news that the first day of the month of April newly passed, the Sultan of Babylon invested the city of Acre on all sides from one sea as far as the other, between sunrise and tierce,[1] with all his forces both horse and foot, and on the other side eastwards as far as the River Euphrates,[2] with all his battering-engines, and so with numerous engines and a great host he sat down before the city. And from the day that they came until the Monday after [3] they ceased not to take up ground, some for their engines, some for their defences, some for trenches, some for stockades and to make their other works, and they brought up all their engines and defences round about the walls, and set them up against ours. And we and all the good Christian people of the city made preparations against them, and we armed ourselves completely, and we put in readiness all the instruments and engines which are intended to protect and defend the city and the bodies of men.

At last after many assaults and many defences and many sorties, that we made against them and they against us, after great shedding of blood on one side and the other, when our people had suffered grievously by wounds and injuries, they entered the city by the gate called King Hugh's Gate, on the 18th day of May recently passed. They had pierced and broken and thrown down the walls in several places with their engines, which they call 'corobonares'. They entered the city on all sides early in the morning and in very great force. We and our Convent resisted

[1] The Hour of Tierce was usually said after the morning Mass, which was about 8.30, that is Tierce was about nine o'clock in the morning. See Gasquet, *English Monastic Life*, p. 121.

[2] Evidently this Euphrates is some stream near Acre.

[3] Since 1 April 1291 was a Sunday, by the Monday after he must here mean 9 April.

them at St. Anthony's Gate, where there were so many Saracens that one could not count them. Nevertheless we drove them back three times as far as the place, which is commonly called Maldis.[1] And in that action and others, where the brethren of our Convent fought in defence of the city and their lives and country, we lost little by little all the Convent of our Religion, which then came to an end, and belongs to Holy Church. Among whom our dear friend Brother Matthew de Clermont our Marshal lay dead. He was noble and valiant and skilful in arms. May God be gracious unto him! On that same day the Master of the Temple also died of a mortal wound from a lance. May God have mercy on his soul!

We ourselves on that same day were stricken nigh to death by a lance between the shelters (*garites*), a wound that has made the writing of this letter a very hard task. Meanwhile a great multitude of Saracens entered the city, on all sides, by land and by sea, moving along the walls, which were all pierced and broken, and running through the streets of the city until they came to our shelters (*garites*). Our serjeants, our yeomen (*garçons*) and our hired soldiers and crusaders and others began utterly to despair, and to fly towards the ships, throwing down their arms and armour. We and our brethren, of whom the greater number were sore stricken and wounded to death, resisted them as long as we could. God knows it. And as some of us were lying thus half-dead and helpless before our enemies, our serjeant and our body-servant (*garçon familier*) came, and carried off ourselves, wounded almost to death, and our other brethren, at great risk of life and limb. And so we and a part of our brethren escaped, since it pleased God that it should be so, of whom the greater number were sore wounded without hope of recovery, and we had ourselves taken to the island of Cyprus. There we have remained until the date this letter was written in great sadness of heart, overwhelmed with very great sorrow.

[1] Maldis is of course Maledictum.

APPENDICES

APPENDIX A

THE MILITARY RELIGIOUS ORDERS

THE Military Religious Orders of the Middle Ages, being the outcome of the ceaseless warfare between Christendom and Islam, naturally fall into two distinct groups, their organization being modelled in all cases on that of the Hospitallers and Templars.

I. Those established in Syria, namely, Hospitallers, Templars, St. Lazarus, Teutonic Knights, and St. Thomas of Acre, but the Order of the Holy Sepulchre, which became military only in the fifteenth century, must not be confused with them.

II. Those established in the Spanish Peninsula, namely, Aviz, Calatrava, St. James of Compostella, Alcantara, and the Orders of Christ, and Our Lady of Monteza, both the latter derived from the Templars.[1]

Besides these two great groups, there were two other Orders established on the shores of the Baltic for the purpose of waging war against the Slavonic heathen of north-eastern Europe. Firstly, the Knights of the Sword in Livonia founded in 1201 by Albert Bishop of Riga, and absorbed by the Teutonic Knights in 1237. They wore a white mantle bearing on it a red sword and star. Secondly, the Order of Dobrzin on the Vistula, founded by Christian Bishop of Prussia shortly after the other, and absorbed by the Teutonic Knights in 1235.

I. The Syrian Group

1. *The Hospitallers.*—
2. *The Templars.*— } The history of these two Orders is so closely associated from the very foundation of the Templars in 1118 down to their suppression in 1312, as to be inseparable, and no history of the Hospitallers can be written that does not include within it a sufficiently adequate summary of the history of their colleagues and rivals of the Temple. Nothing further therefore need be said in this Appendix concerning either Order.

3. *The Order of St. Lazarus.*[2]—The Order of St. Lazarus has its origin in a hospital in Jerusalem for lepers, of great antiquity, and after the

[1] There were two other Spanish Orders of comparatively minor importance, which became absorbed in the greater Orders. The Order of Sainte Marie de Montjoye, founded in 1180, and after 1198 known as the Order of Montfrac, which was united to the Order of Calatrava in 1221, and the Aragonese Order of St. George of Alfama founded in 1201, and united to the Order of Monteza in 1399.

[2] See Steenacker's *Histoire des Ordres de Chevalerie,* Paris, 1867.

Latin conquest, like the Hospital of St. John, became a regular religious Order, having for its object the care of lepers, and adding to its establishment a class of military brethren. Louis VII introduced the Order into France in 1154, conferring upon it the castle of Boigny near Orleans, and in 1253 the Master [1] transferred the headquarters of the Order from Acre to France with the consent of St. Louis IX, who entrusted the port of Aigues-Mortes to its protection, and presented it with a house in Paris. Until then the Order had followed the rule of St. Basil, but it now adopted the Augustinian rule, and with its transfer to France spread rapidly throughout Europe, possessing by the middle of the fourteenth century over three hundred establishments. In 1490 Pope Innocent VIII suppressed the Order, and transferred its possessions to the Order of St. John, but the bull was not received in France and had no effect in that country. In 1565 Pope Pius IV re-established the Order and confirmed its ancient privileges, and in 1608 Henry IV of France united it in that country to his new Order of Our Lady of Mount Carmel. The combined Order was suppressed in France at the Revolution, and at that time possessed five Grand Priories and one hundred and forty Commanderies. The badge of St. Lazarus was an eight-pointed cross of green enamel having depicted on it the resurrection of Lazarus, and suspended from a green ribbon; that of Our Lady of Mount Carmel was of purple enamel with an image of Our Lady, suspended from a purple ribbon, and the united Order combined the two badges and colours.

In Italy [2] the history of the Order of St. Lazarus was entirely distinct from that of the Order in France. The remnants of the Order left in the Holy Land finally settled in Naples in 1311, and this branch alone was afterwards regarded as the legitimate descendant of the original Order. Its internal dissensions and vicissitudes during the fifteenth and sixteenth centuries, with its suppression and re-establishment, had reduced it to a very low ebb, and in 1573 it was united to the Savoyard Order of St. Maurice,[3] established the previous year for protection against the Calvinists of Geneva, with the Duke of Savoy and his successors as its Grand Masters. The united Order had for its objects the care of lepers as before, and warfare against the infidels, its galleys taking part in several expeditions against the Turks and the Barbary Corsairs. By the end of the eighteenth century the Order had lost its military character, and is now conferred by the King of Italy for distinguished services, especially those of a charitable nature, and the income of the Order is devoted

[1] It is often alleged that only a leper could be Master, until Pope Innocent IV abolished the statute concerned. But the bull quoted on the subject is said to be false, moreover only two very late writers have suggested so improbable a rule, and Article V of the ancient statutes of the Order lays down, 'The chief of the Order shall be taken from this side the sea; he shall be a healthy knight'. See Gautier de Sibert, *Histoire des Ordres de Notre Dame du Mont Carmel et de St. Lazare de Jérusalem*, 1772, Preface, pp. xvii–xxi.

[2] See Weatherly, 'Orders of Knighthood', *Encyclopaedia Britannica*, 11th Edition.

[3] The original Order of St. Maurice was founded in 1434 by Amadeus VIII, Duke of Savoy; it was not a military Order and practically ceased to exist when he became Pope Felix V in 1439.

entirely to charity. The badge is the white cross of St. Maurice resting on the green cross of St. Lazarus, suspended from a dark green ribbon.

4. *The Teutonic Knights.*[1]—The origin of the Teutonic Knights is to be found in the Hospital of St. Mary of the Germans established in Jerusalem by a German pilgrim in 1127 for the benefit of his fellow countrymen. During the siege of Acre in 1190 some merchants from Bremen and Lubeck established a field-hospital for the use of the German Crusaders, to which the brethren now expelled from Jerusalem attached themselves, and in March 1198 these German Hospitallers were transformed into a military Order, intended to be a German counterpart to the Hospitallers and Templars, which were so predominantly Latin. They wore the white mantle with a black cross, and followed the Augustinian rule. The full title of the new Order was the Teutonic Knights of the Hospital of St. Mary of Jerusalem, and only Germans were eligible for membership. They established themselves in Acre, and in 1227 built their great castle of Starkenburg or Montfort (Kurain) on the western borders of Galilee, a fortress captured by Sultan Beybars in 1271. In 1226 the Emperor Frederick II created the Master of the Teutonic Knights a Prince of the Empire, and granted the Order the privilege of bearing the imperial eagle upon its arms. He also presented the Master with a very precious ring, which is used to the present day at the installation of a new Grand Master.

In 1211 King Andrew II of Hungary invited the Teutonic Knights to assist him against his heathen neighbours, the Comans, and then in 1228 the Bishop of Prussia invoked their assistance in his wars against paganism, which resulted in their absorption of the existing Order of Dobrzin. Their power on the Baltic increased so rapidly that in 1260 they were ruling over the whole of what was known later as the provinces of East and West Prussia, as well as Livonia gained in 1237, by their union with the Knights of the Sword. Long before the loss of the Holy Land the interests of the Teutonic Knights on the Baltic were taking precedence of their original work in Syria. When Acre fell the Convent was transferred for a few years to Venice, and then in 1309 established itself at Marienburg on the Vistula, where the Grand Master ruled as a powerful territorial sovereign, with his two subordinate Masters in Livonia and Germany, the latter having his seat at Mergentheim in Swabia.

The conversion of Lithuania to Christianity in the fourteenth century terminated the religious wars against the heathen, and the real object of the Teutonic Knights was at an end. A great Slavonic revival followed. The disastrous Battle of Tannenberg in 1410 ruined the prestige of the Knights, and in 1466 West Prussia was conquered by the Poles, and Marienburg lost. The Grand Master however continued to rule over East Prussia as a vassal of the King of Poland, with his capital at Konigsberg. In 1526 the reigning Grand Master Albert of Brandenburg, one of the Hohenzollern family, became a convert to Protestantism. He secularized his territories, converting them into an hereditary duchy, and the Order ceased to exist in East Prussia. In 1561 the Master in Livonia, Gotthard

[1] See Ernest Barker, 'The Teutonic Order', *Encyclopaedia Britannica*, 11th Edition, and Woodhouse, *The Military Religious Orders of the Middle Ages.*

Kettler, followed the example of Albert of Brandenburg, became a Protestant, and hereditary Duke of Courland.

Meanwhile the Master in Germany had broken away from the Grand Master, when he became a Polish vassal, and had taken his place as a Prince of the Empire. When Albert of Brandenburg became a Protestant, the Master in Germany, Walter von Kronberg, was elected Grand Master of the Order, and Mergentheim became its headquarters. The French Revolution dealt the Teutonic Knights a deadly blow, depriving them of their estates west of the Rhine, and in 1809 the Order was suppressed. It was restored by the Emperor of Austria in 1840, and down to the outbreak of the Great War continued to exist as a semi-religious knighthood, closely connected with the Hapsburg family. The Archduke William was Grand Master until 1894, when he was succeeded by the Archduke Eugene his coadjutor. On 4 January 1926 Monseigneur Norbert Klein, Titular Bishop of Syene and former Bishop of Brunn, was elected Grand Master in the place of the Archduke Eugene, who had abdicated. The Teutonic Knights, remembering the original object of their Order, now devote themselves entirely to charitable duties in connexion with hospitals and especially to ambulance work in time of war.

5. *The Order of St. Thomas of Acre.*[1]—The Order of St. Thomas Acon, as it is more frequently called, originated at Acre during the Third Crusade, and was a purely English Order, just as the Teutonic Knights were a German Order. In 1191 a certain English priest by name William, chaplain to Ralph de Diceto, Dean of St. Paul's, in fulfilment of a vow, built a chapel and cemetery at Acre for the English Crusaders who fell in the siege, and dedicated it to St. Thomas of Canterbury. A little body of Englishmen associated themselves with him, and formed themselves into a religious community with William as their first Prior. Their objects were to ensure Christian burial to the dead Crusaders, and the defence of the Christian faith. The foundation of the new Order met with the warm approval of the family of St. Thomas à Becket, his sister and brother-in-law became founders and benefactors, and the Hospital of St. Thomas Acon, the head house of the Order in England, was built in London on the site of the house in Ironmonger Lane where the martyred Archbishop was born. The Order was always very small, the knights were never numerous, and almost certainly poor. They possessed estates in Yorkshire, Middlesex, Surrey and Ireland, and in certain foreign countries, as we know from their Master being described as 'Master of the whole Order of the Knighthood of St. Thomas the Martyr in the kingdom of Cyprus, Apulia, Sicily, Calabria, Brundusium, England, Flanders, Brabant, Scotland, Wales, Ireland and Cornwall'. In 1231 Peter des Roches, Bishop of Winchester, then in Palestine, built a new church for the Order, and placed it under the Templars, and he also left it a legacy of 500 marks in his will. The Knights of St. Thomas played an honourable part in the defence of Acre, and on the loss of the Holy Land established themselves at Nicosia in Cyprus, where their church was known as St. Nicholas

[1] See Bishop Stubbs, 'The Mediaeval Kingdoms of Cyprus and Armenia', in his *Lectures on Mediaeval and Modern History.*

of the English.[1] It is still standing, and is now used as a grain-store. The suppression of the Templars, with whom the Knights of St. Thomas were always closely associated, must have been a very severe blow to the Order. From this time their house in London, the Hospital of St. Thomas Acon, seems to have become an ordinary Augustinian hospital, and at the Reformation passed into the hands of the Mercers Company. As late as 1357 we hear of a certain Richard of Tickhill being received into the Order in the church of St. Nicholas of the English, but before many years it must have ceased to exist. The Knights of St. Thomas followed the Augustinian rule, and wore a white mantle with a red cross, charged with a silver escallop, to distinguish it from the mantle of the Templars.

6. *The Order of the Holy Sepulchre.*[2]—This Order did not become a military Order until long after the loss of the Holy Land, neither did it ever include military brethren like the Hospitallers and Templars. The Canons of the Holy Sepulchre were a fraternity following the Augustinian rule, and founded by Godfrey de Bouillon. Their superior was the Patriarch of Jerusalem, with whom they shared the possession of the Holy Sepulchre. They speedily became immensely popular, receiving important donations of lands and houses in every country in Europe, and even sharing with the Hospitallers and Templars the famous legacy of Alfonso of Aragon. In 1459 Pope Pius II united it with his new military Order of Our Lady of Bethlehem, which had but a short existence, and in 1489 Pope Innocent VIII united it with the Order of St. John, whose Grand Masters to the present day bear the subsidiary title of 'Master of the Military Order of the Holy Sepulchre of the Lord'.[3] But none the less in 1496 Pope Alexander VI, without revoking the previous amalgamation, in order to encourage the pilgrimages to the Holy Land, organized the Canons of the Holy Sepulchre into a military Order, reserving for himself and his successors the office of Grand Master.[4] Whilst retaining the title, the popes always delegated the right of conferring the Order to the Franciscan Padre Custode of the Terra Santa,[5] a right which was transferred to the Latin Patriarch, when Pope Pius IX in 1847 re-established the Patriarchate of Jerusalem. The Knightly Order of the Holy Sepulchre was formally recognized by Pope Pius IX on 24 January 1868, and by Pope Pius X on 3 May 1907, with the Pope as Grand Master and the Latin Patriarch as Lieutenant of the Grand Magistracy for the

[1] The Hospital of St. Thomas Acon in London included a Chapel of St. Stephen and St. Nicholas.

[2] See Steenackers, *Histoire des Ordres de Chevalerie*, Paris, 1867, and Jeffrey, *The Holy Sepulchre*, pp. 25, 29.

[3] See Montagnac, *L'Ordonnance des Chevaliers Hospitaliers*, p. 25, and Boisgelin, *Ancient and Modern Malta*, 1805, Vol. I, p. 285.

[4] The Knights of the Holy Sepulchre to enhance the dignity of their Order declared Philip II of Spain their Grand Master in 1588, and the Duke of Nevers in 1615, but their schemes fell to the ground owing to the protests of the Grand Master of the Order of St. John.

[5] The reputed sword of Godfrey de Bouillon was being used at the beginning of the sixteenth century to give the accolade, see Jeffrey, *The Holy Sepulchre*, p. 109.

Holy Land.[1] The badge is a red Jerusalem cross with red Latin crosses cantoned in the angles, suspended from a black ribbon.

The Order must not be confused with the French Archiconfrèrie of the Holy Sepulchre founded by Louis VII in 1149, and consisting of twenty brethren. They were placed in charge of the Sainte Chapelle and its relics by St. Louis IX in 1254, and were abolished at the French Revolution. Louis XVIII restored the Order of the Holy Sepulchre in France and the Archiconfrèrie, combining the two in what was practically a new Order. Owing to the vigorous protests of the Franciscan Padre Custode, both were suppressed in 1823.

II. The Iberian Group [2]

1. *The Knights of Aviz.*—The Portuguese Order of St. Benedict of Aviz originated in a band of warriors, who pledged themselves in 1147 to follow King Alfonso I in his Moorish wars, but without taking any religious vows. In 1162 they were fully constituted into a religious Order, following the Cistercian rule, and were known at first as the Knights of Evora, but afterwards as the Knights of Aviz, from their fortress on the Moorish frontier, the headquarters of their Order. The Knights of Calatrava in 1212 transferred their estates in Portugal to the Knights of Aviz on condition that their Master should be the Visitor of the latter Order. But the Knights of Aviz declined to observe the condition, which resulted in a long and acrimonious dispute between the two Orders, only settled in the fifteenth century, when the Council of Basle laid down that the Knights of Aviz must abide by their agreement. Eventually the popes assumed the right of nominating the Grand Masters of the Order until 1540, when Pope Paul III united the mastership with the Crown of Portugal. The Order was secularized in 1789 as an Order of military merit, and was organized in four classes. The badge is a green cross fleury, suspended from a green ribbon.

2. *The Knights of Calatrava.*—In 1158 King Sancho III of Castile presented the frontier town of Calatrava, south of Toledo, to the Cistercian abbey of Fitero in Navarre, at the suggestion of one of its monks, Diego Velasquez, on condition that they should undertake its protection. The Abbot Raymond raised a body of knights for its defence, and on his death they petitioned the Pope for recognition as a military religious Order, a request which was granted by Pope Alexander III in 1164. The Knights of Calatrava followed the Cistercian rule, and wore the white mantle with a red cross. Owing to their origin, when visiting Citeaux, they were not treated like other strangers, but were admitted within the cloister as brethren of the Cistercian Order. The Knights of Calatrava

[1] In France the Order of the Holy Sepulchre is governed by the Chapter of France, with the Grand Bailli as President assisted by a Council of Seven, and with the Cardinal Archbishop of Paris as Grand Almoner. Its publication is the *Bulletin du Chapitre de France,* 8 Rue de Liège, Paris. A council on similar lines has recently been constituted for the Order of the Holy Sepulchre in the United States.

[2] For a short account of the Spanish and Portuguese Orders, see Weatherly, *Orders of Knighthood,* and Woodhouse, *The Military Religious Orders of the Middle Ages.*

suffered very heavily in the great Moorish victory of Alarcon in 1195, and two years later Calatrava was captured by the Moors, who massacred the whole of the members of the Order found there. For a time the castle of Salvatierra became the headquarters of the Order, until Calatrava was recaptured from the Moors in 1212.

In 1221 the little Order of Montfrac, all that remained of the military religious Order of Sainte Marie de Montjoye, was united to the Order of Calatrava by St. Ferdinand King of Castile. The original Order [1] had been founded under a bull of Pope Alexander III of 15 May 1180, and its badge was a parti-coloured cross of red and white, its first Master was a certain Count Rodriguez, a former Knight of Santiago, and it followed the Cistercian rule. The Order had a house with a church in Jerusalem, and was entrusted with the defence of the Tower of Maidens and three other towers at Ascalon, and was endowed with considerable property in Spain, where its headquarters were at Alfambra. In 1198 the lands of the Order in Aragon were surrendered to the Templars, a surrender confirmed by a bull of Pope Innocent III of 24 October 1198, and after that date the knights of the Order in Castile became known as the Order of Montfrac.

During the fourteenth century the Knights of Calatrava became involved in the civil wars of their country, and there were disputes over the elections of Masters, very detrimental to the good name of their Order. But during the Moorish wars of the fifteenth century they again greatly distinguished themselves. To avoid the scandal of disputed elections the Pope assumed the right to nominate the Grand Masters, and in 1489 King Ferdinand the Catholic seized the Mastership which was finally vested in the Crown of Spain in 1523. The knights were given the right to marry in 1540. In 1808 the Order became a military Order of merit, and was reorganized in 1874; it has only one class. The badge is a green cross fleury, suspended from a green ribbon.

3. *The Knights of St. James of Compostella.*—One of the most important places of pilgrimage in the Middle Ages was the shrine of St. James of Compostella in Galicia, where the body of the apostle St. James the son of Zebedee was supposed to lie buried. So important and popular was this pilgrimage that it took precedence over all others except those to Rome and Jerusalem, and it was always especially favoured by the English. In early times the pilgrim routes were infested by brigands, and liable to be raided by the Moors. Consequently a body of thirty knights, no doubt inspired by the example of the Templars in the Holy Land, resolved to devote themselves to the sacred duty of protecting the pilgrims on the roads to Compostella. Eventually they formed themselves into a regular religious Order, and in 1175 [2] received a rule and constitution from Pope Alexander III, being known as the Knights of St. James of Compostella or the Knights of St. James of the Sword, but more generally known under the Spanish form of their title as the Knights of Santiago. The Order gained a great reputation in the Moorish wars, and became extremely wealthy. But gradually the ancient constitution was

[1] See Delaville Le Roulx, *Revue de l'Orient Latin*, 1894, pp. 42–57.

[2] According to tradition the Order of St. James of Compostella was founded by King Ramiro II of Leon in the tenth century to commemorate a victory over the Moors.

changed to meet the altered requirements of the day, in 1396 the knights received permission to marry, in 1493 the mastership was seized by King Ferdinand the Catholic, and in 1522 it was vested permanently in the Crown of Spain by Pope Adrian VI. The Order is now an Order of merit in three classes. Its badge is the red lily-hilted sword of St. James, suspended from a red ribbon.

A branch of the Order was established in Portugal at a very early date, and is generally spoken of as the Order of St. James of the Sword, rather than Compostella. These Portuguese Knights were released from the control of the Spanish Master at Compostella by Pope Nicholas IV at the end of the thirteenth century, and placed on an independent footing. The Order was secularized in 1789, and in 1862 was constituted an Order of merit for science, literature and art in five classes. Its badge is the lily-hilted sword of St. James, enamelled red with gold borders, and suspended from a violet ribbon.[1]

4. *The Knights of Alcantara.*—In 1156 two brothers, Don Suarez and Don Gomez de Barrientos, built the castle of St. Julian del Pereyro on the frontiers of Leon, to protect the countryside from Moorish raids and organized a body of knights for its defence, to whom a rule was given by the Archbishop of Salamanca. In 1177 the formation of the Order was confirmed by a bull of Pope Alexander III, who placed it under the Benedictine rule, and granted it exemption from the authority of the bishops. The knights wore a white mantle with a green cross. In 1200 King Alfonso IX of Leon, known by the unpleasant nickname of the Slobberer, captured the city of Alcantara on the Tagus from the Moors, and conferred it upon the Knights of Calatrava, on condition that they should make it the head house of their Order in Leon. But the Knights of Calatrava finding it too distant from their Convent, relinquished it in 1213 to the Knights of St. Julian del Pereyro on condition that the two Orders should be united. The union was never actually effected, but from this date the Knights of St. Julian del Pereyro are known as the Knights of Alcantara. For a time they remained in a certain degree of subjection to the Knights of Calatrava, but eventually asserted their independence, and elected a Master of their own. The Knights of Alcantara did their duty nobly against the Moors, and their wealth and influence increased to such an extent that they became scarcely less powerful than the king himself. But during the fourteenth century their Order entered upon a period of decline. The knights took part in the civil wars of the day, there were continual disputes over the mastership, frequently resulting in the scandal of rival Masters, and the records of the Order tell of little but quarrelling and bloodshed. In 1495 the office of Grand Master was vested in the crown by King Ferdinand the Catholic, an arrangement confirmed by Pope Alexander VI, and declared permanent in 1523 by Pope Adrian VI. In 1540 Pope Paul III gave permission to the knights to marry, though forbidding second marriages, and the three solemn

[1] The three Portuguese Orders of the Tower and the Sword, St. Benedict of Aviz, and St. James of the Sword, were granted a common badge in 1789 uniting the three separate crosses in a gold medallion; the joint ribbon is red, green and violet, and to the separate crosses was added a red sacred heart and small white cross.

vows of chastity, obedience and poverty were changed to *obedientia, castitas conjugalis* and *conversio morum*. When Joseph Bonaparte became King of Spain in 1808 he deprived the Order of its revenues, and only a part of them were able to be recovered when Ferdinand VII was restored to his throne in 1814. The Order ceased to exist as a spiritual body in 1835, and is now an Order of military merit in one class. Its badge is the red cross fleury, suspended from a red ribbon.

5. *The Order of Christ.*—The Order of Christ is directly descended from the Templars, and might almost be said to be the Order of the Temple under another name. When the Templars were suppressed in 1312, King Denis of Portugal flatly declined to give credence to the abominations with which they were charged, or to join in their persecution, and took them under his royal protection. But it was impossible for the papacy to permit its authority to be thus openly flouted and so to meet this difficulty King Denis compromised in 1318 by founding a new military religious Order, which he called the Order of Christ, and to which he transferred the Templars and their estates. Pope John XXII confirmed the foundation of this new Order, reserving to himself the right to nominate to it, and he transferred to it those Templars in his own dominions, who were of good character and repute. The Order of Christ remains to the present day the supreme papal Order. It consists of one class only, and its badge is a long red cross with expanded flat ends bearing a small cross in white, and suspended from a red ribbon.

In Portugal the Order of Christ became a separate national Order in 1522, quite distinct from the papal Order, and in 1540 the Grand Mastership became vested in the Portuguese Crown. In 1789 it ceased to be a spiritual body, and became entirely secularized, with the one exception that its members must belong to the Roman Catholic faith. It is organized in three classes, and now has a different badge to the papal Order, namely a blue enamelled cross resting on a green laurel wreath, the central medallion in white, containing the old red and white cross. But the older papal form is worn with the collar by the Grand Crosses of the Order.

6. *The Order of Our Lady of Monteza.*—The Order of Monteza is directly descended from the Templars, in the same manner as the Order of Christ. Following the example of King Denis of Portugal, King James II of Aragon on 22 July 1319 founded a new military religious Order, which he called the Order of Our Lady of Monteza, and to which he transferred the Templars and their estates in Valencia.[1] The new Order had its headquarters at Monteza, like the Templars it followed the Benedictine rule, and it adopted the white mantle and plain red cross of its predecessors. In 1399 it absorbed the older military religious Order of St. George of Alfama, founded in 1201 by King Peter II of Aragon. The Knights of Monteza were the last of the Spanish military Orders to lose their independence, they were given permission to marry in 1572, and in 1587 the Mastership became vested in the Crown of Spain. The ribbon of the Order is poppy-red.

[1] The Templar estates in Aragon and Catalonia were transferred to the Order of St. John. See Vertot, *Histoire des Chevaliers de Malthe*, Book IV.

APPENDIX B

THE CHRONICLE OF THE DECEASED MASTERS

(NOTE.—This Chronicle is an official eulogy of the Masters of the Hospital, appearing at the head of most of the old manuscripts of the Statutes of the Hospital. It was probably compiled between 1353 and 1355, since it closes with the words 'Postea fuit magister Petrus Cornelian', and gives no details concerning him. The great value of this record, which represents the most ancient tradition of the Hospital, is sometimes overlooked because of the errors of the transcriber, who has muddled the order of the names, so attributing to some Masters descriptions which clearly belong to others, but the errors are for the most part fairly obvious, enabling the necessary corrections to be easily made. The Chronicle has been published in Latin in Dugdale's *Monasticon*, Vol. VI, Part 2, pp. 796, 797.)

1. The first Master was Gerard, who was Warden of the Hospital of the poor in Jerusalem. He was found there, when Godfrey de Bouillon and the Christian pilgrims captured the city.

2. Afterwards was Raymond du Puy, who was the first brother of the Hospital. He ordained and established the Rule and Statutes, and had them confirmed by the Lord Pope Eugenius [1]: they were lost in Jerusalem.

3. After him Auger de Ballen was Master. He was a man overflowing with piety, and strictly upright.

4. After him Arnold de Comps was Master. He was a man of high purpose, under whom the Religion increased both in the number of the brethren and in the quantity of its possessions, and he made good ordinances, etc.

5. After him Gilbert Assailli was Master. He was very aged, and during the short time that he lived he procured many advantages for the Religion, and served our lords the sick with great kindness.[2]

6. After him Caste was Master. He was a man overflowing with the virtues of deep humility and great benevolence and kindness of heart; and owing to his upright dealings and good repute, many great benefactions were made to our Religion throughout the entire world.

[1] Pope Eugenius III, 1145–53.

[2] The description given to Gilbert d'Assailly clearly belongs to his predecessor Arnold de Comps, since it mentions his great age, and short reign, and the description given to Arnold de Comps therefore belongs to Gilbert d'Assailly, to whom it fully applies.

7. After him Jobert was Master. He established good Statutes for the service of God and the Church, and for the benefit of our lords the sick.

8. After him Geoffrey de Dinson [1] was Master, who captured Le Crac and Margat. He was a man of great wisdom, and vigorous in battle; a good man and pious and very high-minded, and he loved much his brethren and our lords the sick.

9. After him Armengaud Daps was Master. He was much persecuted by the enemies of the faith,[2] and in his time the Christians lost Jerusalem, but he lived only a short time afterwards.

10. After him Roger de Molins was Master, who procured a confirmation of the Rule by Pope Lucius, and laid down good Statutes.

11. After him Garnier de Nablus was Master. He showed great courage in deeds of arms against the enemies of the faith.[3] He protected vigorously the endowments of the House, and also ruled over his brethren with dignity.

12. After him Alfonso of Portugal was Master, in whose time the good customs laid down by the Master Roger were confirmed at Margat. He made good Statutes, and it so happened that he issued a certain order to his Convent, and because the Convent did not obey him, he resigned his office as Master, and flung down the seal, which was taken up by the Bailiffs, and they chose another Master. Then he set out for Portugal, but was poisoned on the journey by those of his own race, and died, etc.

13. After him Geoffrey Rat was Master. He was a very upright man, and was deeply distressed at the resignation of the Master Alfonso, for he had a great affection for him on account of his honourable character. In his time many gifts were made to our House in the kingdom of France.

14. After him Garin de Montagu was Master. In person he was strong and vigorous, and a vigilant protector of the possessions of the Religion, and he lived only a short time.[4]

15. After him Bertrand de Gexi [5] was Master. He found a reputation very upright and pious and virtuous, and greatly increased it. In Syria he endowed the House with much property, and was very zealous in the duties owing to our lords the sick.

16. After him Guérin was Master. He was very thrifty, and abjured

[1] The name should read Roger de Molins, to whom the description applies, he obtained Margat in 1186 though not by force, but Le Crac was obtained long before this time. Para. 10, following the description of Armengaud Daps, is obviously a part of Para. 8, which has somehow got out of its proper place, since Pope Lucius III was reigning from 1181 to 1185.

[2] Presumably this means that at one time he had been a prisoner-of-war amongst the Saracens, unless it refers to his having been forced to resign his office as Master.

[3] Probably at this point we ought to insert the words from Para. 8: 'After him Geoffrey de Dinson was Master', and the following sentence would then relate to him. It can scarcely relate to Garnier de Nablus, whose career as Master was confined entirely to the military operations of the Third Crusade.

[4] The description given to Garin de Montaigu clearly belongs to his predecessor Geoffrey Rat, since it mentions his short reign, and the description given to Geoffrey Rat would therefore belong to Garin de Montaigu, to whom it is fully appropriate.

[5] Should read Texi, not Gexi.

all empty pomp and glory, and he amassed a great treasure, because he maintained peace with his enemies.

17. After him Bertrand de Cons was Master. By his upright and wise handling of affairs, he restored to the sway of the Religion much Saracen territory, and through his great treasure he resumed for the Hospital many increased privileges, and he made concessions to the knightly brethren, and he exalted them in the Religion with many honours, and increased their superiority over the other brethren more than any other Master.

18. After him Peter de Villa Brida was Master. He exercised great influence by his upright and straightforward character, and maintained strict discipline. As the result of his labours three houses were established and many other properties were obtained.

19. After him William de Castello Novo was Master. He was an example of upright conduct and of many and courageous activities. In his time the Hospital resumed the balance of the rights of the Temple, which he afterwards purchased from the Master of the Temple, who was his brother, for the price of a horse, etc.[1]

20. After him Hugh Ryvell was Master. He was a man remarkable for the soundness of his judgement and his capacity, and he placed the affairs of the House on a sound basis. For the other Masters, his predecessors, had made no reforms, but had merely maintained the good customs of the House. But he laid down everything afresh, not only by codifying the Statutes of others, but by ordaining new and useful Statutes of his own.

21. After him Nicholas de Lorgne was Master. In his time red shields with a white cross were introduced, and it was laid down that the brethren should wear black mantles, also the Conventual Seal was instituted, and many other good Statutes of the House besides.[2]

22. After him Odo was Master, &c., &c.

[1] This last incident obviously belongs to the reign of Garin de Montaigu whose younger brother Peter de Montaigu was Master of the Temple from 1218 to 1233. For the price of a horse in the Holy Land at this period, see p. 204 of this work.

[2] The name of John de Villiers, in whose time Acre was lost, should follow, but is omitted altogether.

APPENDIX C

ON THE SEALS OF THE MASTER AND BAILIFFS[1]

DURING the two centuries that the Knights Hospitallers resided in the Holy Land, three seals were in use by the Masters of the Hospital:

1. The Master's Great Seal, or leaden bulla.
2. The Master's Privy Seal, or seal in wax.
3. The Conventual Great Seal, or leaden bulla.

In his use of a bulla, or seal in metal, the Master of the Hospital was following the example of the Popes, the Emperors of the East, and certain of the Eastern Patriarchs, and the term bulla is applied not only to the matrix and its impression, but also to the document to which it is affixed.[2]

1. The Master's Great Seal

This seal is of lead, with a diameter of 1½ inches, it has two faces, and is attached to documents by a tape or string passing through it. It must have been in use from the first foundations of the Order. The oldest seal known to exist is that of the Master Caste de Murols (1170–2), and is of the following design:

Obverse: The Master of the Hospital facing right, his hands joined in prayer, kneeling before a patriarchal cross, having on each side of the shaft the letters AW, the whole surrounded by two beaded circles, between which is the inscription:

+ CASTVS : CVSTOS

Reverse: Before a tabernacle, a corpse lying on a bier, head to the right, having a cross at its head and feet, above, a domed canopy with three cupolas, having a lamp suspended from the dome, the whole surrounded by two beaded circles, between which is the inscription:

+ HOSPITALIS . HIERVSALEM

The design of this seal remained practically unaltered until after the death of the Master Garin de Montaigu (1207–28). But one of his successors modified the design of the Obverse by representing the Master of the Hospital facing left instead of right, adding to the inscription the

[1] For a detailed study of the Seals of the Order, see Delaville Le Roulx, 'Note sur les sceaux de l'Ordre de St. Jean de Jérusalem', 1881, printed in his *Mélanges sur l'Ordre, etc.*, 1910.

[2] See J. H. Bloom, *English Seals*, p. 259.

word FRATER, and placing the skull of Adam under the patriarchal cross. Such is the design of the Seal of the Master Nicholas le Lorgne (1277–85), but whether he made the change or some earlier Master is quite uncertain, since too many seals are missing.[1]

The subsequent modifications in the designs of these seals belong to a later period, when the Knights Hospitallers had become the Knights of Rhodes.

2. The Master's Privy Seal

The existence of this Seal, generally called the Seal in Wax, is first mentioned in the Statutes of the Master Alfonso of Portugal (1203–6), but the only specimens known to exist are those of the Masters Garin de Montaigu and Hugh Revel (1258–77). The seal is of black wax, with a diameter of 1¼ inches, and since it is affixed to documents in the ordinary manner has only one face. Ultimately at a much later date it developed into the paper seal.[2] The design of the earlier of the known seals, that of Garin de Montaigu, is as follows:

A bust of the Master of the Hospital, full-face, having a cross on the left side of his robe, the whole surrounded by two beaded circles, between which is the inscription:

+ GVARINVS CVSTOS

The similar seal of Hugh Revel has the inscription + FRATER : HVGO : CVSTOS, and there are variations in the representation of the Master.[3]

According to the Statutes of Alfonso of Portugal, the Grand Commander might use the Master's seal in wax in any place, where the Master might not happen to be, that is to say when acting as his Lieutenant, whilst the Treasurer might seal documents in the Master's name with his seal in wax.

No doubt after this less important seal had been adopted, the use of the Master's Great Seal was restricted to transfers of property, legal instruments, and important state documents, the Privy Seal being used for correspondence, and the ordinary affairs of daily administration.

3. The Conventual Great Seal

The Conventual Great Seal, generally spoken of as the Seal of the Master and Convent, which means the Master in Council, was instituted by the Master Nicholas le Lorgne in 1278. It is of lead like the Master's Great Seal, of the same size, having two faces, and affixed to documents in the same manner. Since this seal does not mention the Master's name, it was not necessary to change it at his death. The earliest designs are as follows:

Obverse: The Master and the six Conventual Bailiffs, facing left, their hands joined in prayer, kneeling before a patriarchal cross, having

[1] There are illustrations of the Great Seals of Caste de Murols, Garin de Montaigu and Nicholas le Lorgne to face pages 102, 181 and 280.

[2] See 'Note sur les sceaux de l'Ordre, etc.', p. 22.

[3] There is an illustration of these two seals facing page 254.

on each side of the shaft the letters AW, below it the skull of Adam, the whole surrounded by two beaded circles, between which is the inscription:

+ . BVLLA MAGISTRI ET CONVENTVS

Reverse: The design and the inscription are identical with those on the Reverse of the Master's Great Seal.[1]

The six Conventual Bailiffs represented on this seal are the Prior, Grand Commander, Marshal, Hospitaller, Drapier and Treasurer. Delaville Le Roulx states that in later times the number of figures shown on the obverse was increased as the number of Conventual Bailiffs was increased.[2] The design of this seal, but little changed, has continued in use to the present day.

The Statute of Nicholas le Lorgne instituting the Conventual Great Seal lays down that it was to be used on all charters relating to donations, sales and transfers of property, which could only be effective with the consent of the Master and Convent, and to all those obligations, compositions and procurations, which required the same authority. But in all other matters the seals of the Master were to be sufficient, whether in lead or in wax.[3]

The seals of the Bailiffs of the Hospital are given in the following document, which was probably drawn up in the middle of the thirteenth century,[4] since it includes the Castellans of Margat and Le Crac, and does not mention the Conventual Bulla. The inclusion of the Priors of Catalonia, who are generally regarded as having been instituted about 1319, must be a later addition.

CONCERNING THE SEALS USED BY THE MASTER AND THE OTHER BAILIFFS OF THE HOSPITAL

In the first place the Master seals with two seals, one of lead, and the other of wax. And that of lead has on one side the Master kneeling before the Cross, and on the other side the body of a dead man before a tabernacle. And that of black wax has a demi-man.

2. Then the Grand Commander General beyond the Seas seals with a seal like the Master in wax.

3. The Grand Commander on this side the sea with a seal of green wax with a bird-griffin.

4. The Marshal of green wax with a knight fully armed with a banner in his hand.

5. The Hospitaller with a seal of black wax with a bed having on it a sick man, with a brother who gives him to eat.

[1] There is an illustration of this seal facing page 280.

[2] See 'Note sur les sceaux de l'Ordre, etc.', p. 24.

[3] See *Cartulaire-Général*, Vol. III, No. 3,670.

[4] Printed in mediaeval French in Delaville Le Roulx, 'Note sur les sceaux de l'Ordre, etc.', pp. 3, 4.

6. The Commander of Cyprus seals with a seal having on it a vessel without mast and without sails.

7. The Commander of Armenia seals with a demi-lion.

8. The Castellan of Margat seals with an oriflamme.

9. The Castellan of Le Crac with a castle.

10. The Drapier and the Treasurer seal each with their seals.

11. The Prior of St. Gilles with one of black wax with the Lamb of God.

12. The Prior of France with a seal of green wax with an eagle between two fleur-de-lys.

13. The Grand Commander of Germany seals with a seal of red wax whereon is St. John Baptist.

14. The Commander of Spain seals with a seal with an eagle, of green wax.

15. The Castellan of Amposta with a seal of green wax with a castle.

16. The Prior of Navarre seals with his seal.

17. The Prior of Castile with a castle of black wax.

18. The Prior of Catulia (i.e. Catalonia) [1] with a seal of green wax, half the seal of the King of Aragon, the other half a cross.

[1] According to Delaville Le Roulx the Priory of Catalonia was not founded until 1319, see *Les Hospitaliers en Terre Sainte*, pp. 379, 381.

APPENDIX D

ON THE HERALDRY OF THE MASTERS [1]

ARMORIAL Bearings began to come into general use in Western Europe during the latter half of the twelfth century. Whilst custom on the subject was still fluctuating, the assembly of knights of almost every nation under the banners of the Third Crusade, caused it suddenly to crystallize in a form common to almost the entire military aristocracy of Europe. By the year 1200 the science of Heraldry was beginning to be firmly established everywhere, and a century later its complicated rules and distinctive phraseology had come into general use, and the customs of quartering and impaling (originally dimidiation), and the systems of differencing and marshalling were beginning to emerge. From that time down to the present day the rules of Heraldry have remained practically unchanged.

The first definite indication that we have concerning the armorial bearings of the Knights Hospitallers is contained in the bull of Pope Alexander IV of 1259,[2] where it is stated that the Standard of the Order was at that time, as it is at the present day, 'Gules, a cross argent'. There is nothing to show at what date this Standard was adopted, but it must almost certainly have been used by the Hospitallers during the Third Crusade, and possibly even earlier. Under the bull of 1259 the knights are authorized to wear surcoats of these arms, and during the rule of the Master Nicholas le Lorgne (1277–85) the custom of painting the arms on the shields of the knights was adopted,[3] a custom that remained in use until shields were abandoned.

About the same time as the bull of Pope Alexander IV, the famous statute of the Master Hugh Revel came into force requiring the Knights Hospitallers to give authentic evidence of their right to bear arms. From this time onwards, therefore, some sort of record must have existed in the Convent of the armorial bearings of the knights. Now we possess a list of the arms borne by the whole of the Masters of the Hospital, from those of the founder the Blessed Gerard inclusive. This list may have been originally compiled whilst the Convent was still at Acre, in fact it is only reasonable to suppose that when the Order began to take serious cognizance of the arms of its military brethren, an attempt would natur-

[1] For the arms of the Masters of the Hospital see Eugene Harot, *Essai d'Armorial des Grands Maîtres de l'Ordre de St. Jean de Jérusalem*, Rome, 1911.

[2] See page 279.

[3] See the 'Chronicle of the deceased Masters' in Appendix B of this work.

ARMORIAL BEARINGS OF THE MASTERS OF THE HOSPITAL

ally be made to compile some record of those of its Masters. And since armorial bearings had then only been in general use about half a century, there should have been no serious difficulty in compiling a genuine and reliable list, which would have been the foundation of all subsequent lists. We are justified therefore in assuming that the arms of the Masters from the days of Garin de Montaigu, or even possibly as far back as Garnier de Nablus, were probably actually borne by them. But the arms attributed to the earlier Masters were of course never so borne, for the simple reason that armorial bearings had not come into use at that early date. These early arms are therefore only of interest, as being the arms of the families to which the compilers believed the Masters concerned to have belonged, and to that extent they have obviously a certain value, which must not be overlooked, but some of them seem to be purely arbitrary, invented later for the purpose of filling gaps in the list or even for the glorification of particular families, as when the arms of St. Didier were attributed to the Blessed Gerard, or those of De Sully to Gilbert d'Assailly.

Long after the loss of the Holy Land, certain heraldic customs grew up amongst the Knights Hospitallers, which are familiar to those with a knowledge of heraldry, because they have remained in use to the present day. It became the custom for the Masters of the Hospital to quarter their personal arms, with those of the Order, and for the Bailiffs or Grand Crosses, to bear above their personal arms a chief of the arms of the Order. The former custom probably came into use during the second half of the fourteenth century, and the latter custom early in the fifteenth century. Later still, after the loss of Rhodes, it became customary for the knights to display their arms over the eight-pointed cross of their Order.

The arms of the Masters of the Hospital in the Holy Land were as follows:

Blessed Gerard.—'Azure, a lion rampant, argent.' These arms belonged to the family of St. Didier of Languedoc with which family some claimed that Gerard was connected. This family afterwards bore these arms within a 'bordure gules besantée'.[1]

Blessed Raymond du Puy.—'Or, a lion rampant gules, armed and langued azure.' These are the arms of the family of Du Puy-Montbrun of Dauphiné, to which family Raymond du Puy is usually supposed to have belonged.

Auger de Balben.—'Sable, on a bend between two cotises wavy argent, three martlets gules.' These arms belong to the family of De Balbins of Dauphiné.[2]

Arnold de Comps.—'Gules, an eagle displayed, checky, argent and sable.' These are doubtless the arms of the family of De Comps of Dauphiné and Provence, but see Bertrand de Comps.

Gilbert d'Assailly.—'Azure, semée of estoiles, argent, over all a lion rampant, or.' These arms are almost identical with those of the family of De Sully, except that the 'estoiles' are 'mullets'.

[1] See Viscount Oscar de Poli, *Les Onze Premiers Grand-Maîtres, etc.*, p. 59.
[2] Ibid., pp. 67, 68.

Caste de Murols.—'Gules, a cross pointed, vair.' From his name it is evident that his family came originally from Auvergne.

Jobert.—'Or, on a cross sable, five escallops, argent.' These are the arms of the Seigneurs de Barrault, a branch of the family of De Jaubert.[1]

Roger des Moulins.—'Argent, on a cross recercelée sable, an escallop or.' Except for the escallop, these are the arms of the family of De Moulines in Lower Normandy, which became extinct towards the end of the thirteenth century.[2]

Armengaud d'Aspe.—'Argent, a tower azure, masoned sable.' He belonged to the family of D'Aspe of Béarn.

Garnier de Nablus.—'Sable, a cross potent, argent.' The Syrian branch of the Flemish family of De Milly took the name of De Nablus, and it is interesting to note that the arms of De Milly have the same tinctures as those of De Nablus, namely 'Sable, a chief argent'.[3]

Geoffrey de Donjon.—'Gules, a bend argent', but some give 'Azure, a bend ermine'. It seems probable that he actually bore these arms, otherwise when an attempt was made to glorify the family of De Duisson, by giving him that name, their arms which are totally different would undoubtedly have been attributed to him.[4]

Alfonso of Portugal.—'Argent, five inescutcheons cross-wise azure, each charged with five besants in saltire having their centres sable, the whole within a bordure gules charged with seven castles, or.' Obviously these arms can never have been borne by him, since they are the arms of Portugal at a much later date, possibly he might have borne them without the bordure of Castile.

Geoffrey Le Rat.—'Azure, a unicorn rampant, argent.' Presumably these are the arms of the ancient family of Le Rat of Touraine.

Garin de Montaigu.—'Gules, a triple-storied tower argent, masoned sable.' These are the arms of the family of De Montaigu-Champeix, which vary considerably in the different branches of that family.[5]

Bertrand de Thessy.—'Or, a fesse, gules.' These arms by their very simplicity give the impression of being genuine.

Guérin.—'Argent, a double-headed eagle displayed, sable.' We know nothing of his family, and do not even know his surname.

Bertrand de Comps.—'Gules, an eagle displayed checky, argent and sable.' These are doubtless the ancient arms of the family of De Comps of Dauphiné and Provence, although La Chenaye-Desbois gives the eagle as 'checky or and sable', and other writers give different arms.[6]

Peter de Villebride.—'Checky, argent and gules, a chief ermine.' There are no reasons for supposing that these arms are not perfectly genuine, the family originated in Auvergne.

William de Chateauneuf.—'Gules, three triple-storied towers or, masoned sable.' There can be no reason for doubting these arms. He

[1] See Viscount Oscar de Poli, *Les Onze Premiers Grand-Maîtres, etc.*, p. 72.

[2] Ibid., pp. 74, 75. [3] Ibid., p. 78.

[4] For the attempt to include this Master in the family of De Duisson, and for the arms of that family, see *Les Onze Premier Grand-Maître, etc.*, pp. 79–82.

[5] See Delaville Le Roulx, *Les Hospitaliers en Terre Sainte*, p. 137, note 3.

[6] See *Les Hospitaliers en Terre Sainte*, p. 179, note 2.

probably belonged to some family in northern France of the not uncommon name of Chateauneuf.

Hugh Revel.—'Or, a demi-vol, azure.' These are the arms of the family of Revel of Dauphiné, to which he undoubtedly belonged.

Nicholas le Lorgne.—'Argent, a fesse gules.' He probably belonged to a Provençal family of that name.

John de Villiers.—'Or, three chevronels, azure.' He belonged to the family of De Villiers in the Beauvaisis.[1]

[1] See Harot, *Essai d'Armorial des Grands Maîtres*, p. 15.

APPENDIX E

THE RULE OF RAYMOND DU PUY [1]

THIS IS THE CONSTITUTION ORDAINED BY BROTHER RAYMOND.—In the name of God I Raymond Servant of Christ's poor and Warden of the Hospital of Jerusalem with the advice of all the Chapter, both clerical and lay brethren, have established these rules and statutes in the house of the Hospital of Jerusalem.

1. *How the Brethren should make their Profession.*—Firstly I ordain that all the brethren engaging in the service of the poor shall keep with God's help the three promises that they have made to God, that is to say, chastity, obedience which is anything that is commanded them by their masters, and to live without any property of their own, because God will require of them at the Last Judgement the fulfilment of these three promises.

2. *What the Brethren should claim as their Due.*—And let them not claim as their due more than bread and water and raiment which things are promised to them. And let their raiment be humble because Our Lord's poor whose servants we profess ourselves to be go naked and miserably clad. And it is wrong for the servant to be proud and his Lord humble.

3. *Concerning the Conduct of the Brethren and the Service of the Churches and the Reception of the Sick.*—Moreover it is laid down that their conduct in church shall be decorous and their conversation appropriate, that is to say that the clerics shall serve the priest at the Altar in white raiment, that a deacon or subdeacon, and should the necessity arise some other cleric, shall exercise this office, and let there be a light always burning in the church by day and by night, and the priest shall go to visit the sick in white raiment bearing reverently the Body of Our Lord, and the deacon or the subdeacon or at least an acolyte shall precede him, bearing the lantern with a candle burning and the sponge with the holy water.

4. *How the Brethren should go Abroad and Conduct Themselves.*—Furthermore when the brethren shall enter into cities and castles let them not go alone but in twos and threes, and not with those whom they will, but with those whom the master shall have ordained, and when they shall have come where they will, let them remain together; in their dress and in all their movements let nothing be done which might offend the eyes of anyone, but only that which is in keeping with their sacred

[1] The Rule is published in Latin and in old French in the *Cartulaire-Général*, Vol. I, No. 70.

calling. Moreover whenever they shall be in a house or a church or anywhere where women shall be present, let them keep guard over their modesty and let no woman wash their heads or their feet nor make their bed. So may God who dwelleth on high keep guard over them in this matter. Amen.

5. *By Whom and in What Manner Alms should be Sought.*—Also let religious persons both clerical and lay brethren go forth to seek alms for the holy poor, and when they shall have need of hospitality let them go to the church or to some proper person, and let them ask food of them for charity's sake and let them buy nothing else. If in truth they shall not have found any who will help them, let them purchase by measure one meal only wherewith to support life.

6. *Concerning the Alms obtained and their Use in the Houses.*—Also let them take neither land nor security from the alms collected, but let them deliver them up to the master with an account in writing, and also let the master transmit them to the Hospital under his own hand for the use of the poor, and of all the donations let the master receive a third part of the bread and wine and of all food, and if anything shall have remained over let him add this to the alms and let him send it to Jerusalem under his own hand for the use of the poor.

7. *Who and in What Manner they should go Abroad to Preach.*—And let not any of the brethren, of whatsoever obedience they may be, go forth to preach or to make collections, except only those whom the chapter and master of the church shall send. And let those selected brethren, who shall have gone forth to make collections, be received into whatsoever obedience they shall come, and let them accept the same food as the brethren shall have distributed among themselves, and let them not cause any trouble there. Let them carry a light with them, and in whatsoever house they shall have been received by night with hospitality, let them cause the light to burn before them.

8. *Concerning the Clothing and Food of the Brethren.*—Furthermore we forbid the brethren at any time to wear brightly coloured cloth and velvet and never under any circumstances the furs of animals. And let them eat no more than twice in the day, and on the fourth day of the week and on the Sabbath day (i.e. Saturday) and from Septuagesima until Easter let them eat no meat, except those who are infirm and feeble, and let them never lie down naked but clothed in shirts of wool or linen or other similar garments.

9. *Concerning the Brethren Guilty of Fornication.*—And if any brother, would that such a thing may never happen, shall have fallen into fornication by the force of evil passions, if he shall have sinned in secret let him repent in secret and let him impose upon himself a suitable penance; but if it shall be well known and proved beyond question, then in the same town in which he shall have committed the sin, on the Lord's Day after Mass when the people shall have left the church, let him be stripped in the sight of all and let him be beaten by his clerical master, if he shall be a cleric who shall have sinned, but if he shall be a layman let him be flogged and beaten very severely with whips or rods by a cleric or by him whom the cleric shall enjoin, and let him be completely expelled

from our society; afterwards however if God shall have enlightened his heart, and he shall return to the house of the poor, and shall confess himself to have been a guilty sinner and a transgressor against the law of God, and shall promise amendment, let him be received and let a suitable penance be imposed upon him, and for an entire year let him be treated as a stranger, and during this time let the brethren watch whether his conduct is satisfactory, and afterwards let them do what seems best to them.

10. *Concerning the Brethren Quarrelling and Striking One Another.*—And if a brother shall have had a dispute with another brother, and the procurator of the house shall have noticed the disturbance, let this be his penance: let him fast for seven days, on the fourth and sixth days on bread and water, eating upon the ground without table or napkin. And if he shall have struck a blow, let him fast for forty days. And if he shall have absented himself from the house or from the master to whom he shall have been committed, wilfully without his authority, and afterwards shall have returned, let him eat his meals for forty days on the ground, fasting on the fourth and sixth days on bread and water, and for as long a time as he was absent let him be treated as a stranger, unless the time shall have been so prolonged that it shall seem proper to the chapter to modify its duration.

11. *Concerning the Silence of the Brethren.*—Moreover at table as the apostle says,[1] let each one eat his bread in silence, and after Compline [2] let him drink nothing except pure water. And in bed let the brethren keep silence.

12. *Concerning the Unsatisfactory Conduct of the Brethren.*—And if the conduct of any brother is unsatisfactory, and he shall have been corrected and admonished three times by his master or by the other brethren, and at the instigation of the Devil he shall have refused to amend his ways, let him be sent to us on foot with a report in writing on his offence; nevertheless let a slender maintenance be given to him that he may be able to come to us, and we will correct him; and let no one strike the servants committed to him, but let the master of the house and the brethren exact vengeance in the presence of all; nevertheless let the justice of the house be maintained always.

13. *Concerning the Brethren found with Private Property.*—And if any of the brethren shall have made a disposition of his private property at his death, and whilst still living shall not reveal it to his master, let no divine office be celebrated for him, but let him be buried as one excommunicated; and if whilst still living he should have private property

[1] See St. Paul, 2 Thessalonians iii. 12.

[2] 'At seven o'clock in the winter, and eight in the summer, the tolling of the bell called the community to Compline—the last conventual act of the monastic day. This hour was not necessarily said in the choir of the church. Immediately the prayers were finished, the superior gave a signal, and the community rose and passed to the door of the church. Here either the superior or the junior priest who had said the prayers at Compline was ready to sprinkle each with holy water as he passed in solemn silence to the dormitory. Before half-past seven, in winter, and an hour later than this in the summer, all would have been in bed.'—Gasquet, *English Monastic Life*, p. 153.

and shall have concealed it from his master, and it shall afterwards have been found upon him, let that money be tied round his neck and let him be led naked through the Hospital of Jerusalem or through the other houses where he dwells and let him be beaten by a cleric if he is a cleric, but if a layman let him be beaten by another brother, and let him fast for forty days, on the fourth and sixth days on bread and water.

14. *What Office should be Celebrated for the Deceased Brethren.*—Moreover since it is necessary for us to lay down a statute for you all, we ordain and in ordaining command that for all who shall enter upon the universal way of the flesh, in whatsoever obediences they may die, for thirty days a Mass shall be sung for the good of his soul; at the first Mass let each one of the brethren present offer a candle with a piece of money. And let that money be given to the poor, however much it may be, and the priest who shall have sung the Masses, if he does not belong to the house, shall have his maintenance on those days, and when he shall have completed his office, the master himself shall entertain him, and let all the clothing of the deceased brother be given to the poor; but the brethren who are priests, when they shall have sung the Masses for the good of his soul, let them pour forth prayers to the Lord Jesus Christ, and let each of the clerics sing one psalm, but each of the laymen one hundred and fifty paternosters. And concerning all other sins and business and complaints let them judge in chapter and let them pronounce a just sentence.

15. *How the Rules here laid down are Ordered to be Firmly Kept.*—And all these things just as we have written them above, in the name of God Almighty and the Blessed Mary and the Blessed John and of the poor, we ordain shall be held with the utmost zeal in every respect.

16. *How our Lords the Sick should be Received and Served.*—And in that obedience where the master of the Hospital shall have permitted, when a sick person shall have come there, let him be received thus: firstly having confessed his sins to a priest of the Religion (i.e. the Order), let him partake of holy communion, and afterwards let him be carried to bed, and there just as if he were the Lord let them be charitably entertained every day of the best the house can provide, before the brethren shall break their fast, and on every Lord's Day let the epistle and gospel be sung in that house, and in the procession let it be sprinkled with holy water. Furthermore if any of the brethren, who hold obediences in different lands, shall have given to any secular person the moneys of the poor, in order that he may by his power cause him to have the authority against his master and brethren, let him be cast out from the general society of the brethren.

17. *In what manner Brethren may Correct Brethren.*—And if two or more brethren shall live together, and one of them shall have conducted himself outrageously by evil living, the other brother should not defame him neither to the people nor to the prior, but first should chastise him by himself, and if he will not allow him to chastise him, let him summon two or three others with himself for the purpose of chastising him. And if he shall have amended his ways he should rejoice thereat; but if he shall have been unwilling to amend his ways, then let him put his sins

into writing, and let him send it secretly to the master, and let it be done unto him according as the master shall have ordered.

18. *How Brother should Accuse Brother.*—And let not any of the brethren accuse another brother unless he be well able to prove it; and if he shall have done so (i.e. without proof), he is no true brother, and let him undergo the same punishment as the accused would have undergone, if he were able to prove it.

19. *That the Brethren bear on their Breasts the Sign of the Cross.*—Furthermore let all the brethren of all the obediences, who now or formerly have offered themselves to God and to the holy Hospital of Jerusalem, bear crosses to the honour of God and the Holy Cross, on the breast of each one on robes and mantles likewise, in order that God may protect us through that outward sign and through faith and works and obedience, and may protect us from the power of the Devil in this world and in the world to come, in soul and in body, together with all our Christian benefactors. Amen.

INDEX

Lightning Source UK Ltd.
Milton Keynes UK
UKHW011937061218
333598UK00010B/548/P

9 780282 654528